Turbo Assembler®

User's Guide

Version 1.0

Borland International
1800 Green Hills Road
P.O. Box 660001
Scotts Valley, CA 95066-0001

This manual was produced with
Sprint® The Professional Word Processor

R3

Table of Contents

List of Figures

List of Tables

Welcome to Borland's Turbo Assembler, a one-pass assembler with forward-reference resolution, assembly speeds of up to 48,000 lines per minute (on an IBM PS/2 model 60), MASM compatibility, and an optional Ideal mode extended syntax. Whether you're a novice or an experienced programmer, you'll appreciate these features along with a number of others we've provided to make programming in assembly language easier. We'll mention just a few of the highlights here and describe them in detail later in the book:

- full 80386 support
- improved syntax type-checking
- simplified segmentation directives
- improved listing controls
- local labels
- local stack symbols and calling arguments in procedures
- structures and unions
- nested directives
- *Quirks mode* to emulate MASM
- full source debugging output for Turbo Debugger
- built-in cross-reference utility (TCREF)
- configuration and command files

Turbo Assembler is a powerful command-line assembler that takes your source (.ASM) files and produces object (.OBJ) modules. You then use TLINK.EXE, Borland's high-speed linker program, to link your object modules and create executable (.EXE) files.

Turbo Assembler is set up to work with the 80x86 and 80x87 processor families. (For more information about the instruction sets of the 80x86/80x87 families, consult the data books provided by Intel.)

Hardware and Software Requirements

Turbo Assembler runs on the IBM PC family of computers, including the XT, AT, and PS/2, along with all true compatibles. Turbo Assembler requires MS-DOS 2.0 or later, and at least 256K of memory.

Turbo Assembler generates instructions for the 8086, 80186, 80286, and 80386 processors. It also generates floating-point instructions for the 8087, 80287, and 80387 numeric coprocessors.

About The Manuals

Turbo Assembler comes with two books: *Turbo Assembler User's Guide* (this book) and *Turbo Assembler Reference Guide*. The *User's Guide* provides basic instructions for using Turbo Assembler and a thorough examination of assembler programming. The *Reference Guide* describes the operators, predefined symbols, and directives Turbo Assembler uses.

Here's a more detailed look at what the *User's Guide* contains.

The User's Guide

Chapter 1: Getting Started tells you about the files on your distribution disks and what you need to do to install Turbo Assembler on your system.

Chapter 2: Programming in Turbo Assembler provides you with an introduction to programming in assembly language, and a few sample programs to make you comfortable using the command-line switches. There's also a discussion of computers in general and the 8088 processor in particular.

Chapter 3: Command-Line Reference details all the command-line options, plus tells you about using the configuration file and command files.

Chapter 4: The Basic Elements of an Assembler Program describes the basic components of assembler, with some good solid information about directives, instructions, accessing memory, segments, and more.

Chapter 5: More About Programming in Turbo Assembler goes one step further than Chapter 4, discussing some advanced aspects of Turbo Assembler—more about directives, string instructions, and so on. This chapter also covers some common pitfalls you may encounter as an assembly programmer.

Chapter 6: Interfacing Turbo Assembler with Turbo C describes how to use Turbo C, a high-level language, with assembly language. We detail how to link assembler modules to Turbo C and how to call Turbo Assembler functions from Turbo C.

Chapter 7: Interfacing Turbo Assembler with Turbo Pascal tells you how to interface your assembler code with your Turbo Pascal code; sample programs are also provided.

Chapter 8: Interfacing Turbo Assembler with Turbo Basic illustrates how to use Turbo Assembler with Turbo Basic, replete with example programs.

Chapter 9: Interfacing Turbo Assembler with Turbo Prolog describes how to use Turbo Prolog with Turbo Assembler and provides sample programs.

Chapter 10: Advanced Programming in Turbo Assembler provides you with more details about everything we've touched on in earlier chapters, such as segment override prefixes, macros, segment directives, and so on.

Chapter 11: The 80386 and Other Processors covers programming with the 80386.

Chapter 12: Turbo Assembler Ideal Mode tells you all about Ideal mode and why you'll want to use it.

References lists several useful books about assembly programming.

Notational Conventions

When we talk about IBM PCs or compatibles, we're referring to any computer that uses the 8088, 8086, 80186, 80286, and 80386 chips (all of these chips are commonly referred to as 80x86). When discussing PC-DOS, DOS, or MS-DOS, we're referring to version 2.0 or greater of the operating system.

All typefaces were produced by Borland's Sprint: The Professional Word Processor, output on a PostScript printer. The different typefaces displayed are used for the following purposes:

Italics   In text, italics represent labels, placeholders, variables, and arrays. In syntax expressions, placeholders are set in italics to indicate that they are user-defined.

Boldface   Boldface is used in text for directives, instructions, symbols, and operators, as well as for command-line options.

CAPITALS   In text, capital letters are used to represent instructions, directives, registers, and operators.

Monospace	Monospace type is used to display any sample code, text or code that appears on your screen, and any text that you must actually type to assemble, link, and run a program.
Keycaps	In text, keycaps are used to indicate a key on your keyboard. It is often used when describing a key you must press to perform a particular function; for example, "Press *Enter* after typing your program name at the prompt."

How to Contact Borland

If, after reading this manual and using Turbo Assembler, you would like to contact Borland with comments, questions, or suggestions, we suggest the following procedures:

- The best way is to log on to Borland's forum on CompuServe: Type `GO BPROGB` at the main CompuServe menu and follow the menus to Turbo Assembler. Leave your questions or comments here for the support staff to process.

- If you prefer, write a letter detailing your problem and send it to

> Technical Support Department
> Borland International
> P.O. Box 660001
> 1800 Green Hills Drive
> Scotts Valley, CA 95066 U.S.A.

- You can also telephone our Technical Support department at (408) 438-5300. To help us handle your problem as quickly as possible, have these items handy before you call:

  - product name and version number
  - product serial number
  - computer make and model number
  - operating system and version number

If you're not familiar with Borland's No-Nonsense License statement, now's the time to read the agreement at the front of this manual and mail in your completed product registration card.

1

Getting Started

Before we get you up to speed on programming in assembler, you'll need to get one thing out of the way. Take the Turbo Assembler disks and make copies (via DOS) of each one to create your "working" copies. Once you've done that, put the original disks away. (There's a fee to replace disks that you damage, so only use the originals to make backups and work copies.)

If you are going to use Turbo Assembler as a replacement for MASM, read Appendix B to see in which areas Turbo Assembler behaves differently from MASM.

Note: Be sure to read the README file before working with Turbo Assembler. This file contains the latest information about the program, as well as corrections and/or additions to the manuals.

Files on Disk

- TASM.EXE: Turbo Assembler
- TLINK.EXE: Turbo Linker
- MAKE.EXE: Command-line MAKE utility
- TLIB.EXE: Turbo Librarian
- README.COM: Program to display README file
- README: Any last minute information about the software and documentation
- TCREF.EXE: A source file cross-reference utility
- OBJXREF.COM: Object file cross-reference utility

- GREP.COM: Grep utility
- TOUCH.COM: A file-update utility
- INSTALL.EXE: Installation program
- MMACROS.ARC: An archived file of MASM mode macros

Installing Turbo Assembler

The INSTALL disk contains a program called INSTALL.EXE that will assist you with the installation of Turbo Assembler 1.0. There are two options for installation:

1. **Hard Disk Users:** This option allows you to pick the subdirectories where the files will be loaded.
2. **Floppy Disk Users:** This option will install the files necessary to use Turbo Assembler on a two-drive system. Be sure to have four formatted disks ready before you start.

To start the installation, change your current drive to the one that has the INSTALL program on it and type INSTALL. You will be given instructions for each prompt in a box at the bottom of the screen. For example, if you will be installing from Drive A, type

```
INSTALL
```

Before you install Turbo Assembler, be sure to read the README file to get further information about this release.

Note: If you will be running INSTALL on a laptop or any other system that uses an LCD display, you should set your system to black and white mode before running INSTALL. You can do this from DOS with the following command line:

```
mode bw80
```

You can also force INSTALL to come up in black and white mode by using the **/b** switch:

```
INSTALL /b
```

2

Programming in Turbo Assembler

If you've never programmed in assembly language before, this is the place to begin. You might have heard that assembly language programming is a black art suited only to hackers and wizards. Don't believe it! Assembly language is nothing more than a human form of the language of the computer itself and, as you'd expect, the computer's own language is highly logical. As you might also expect, assembly language is very powerful—in fact, assembly language is the only way to tap the full power of the Intel 80x86 family, the processors at the heart of the IBM PC family and compatibles.

You can write whole programs in nothing but assembly language or you can, if you want, mix assembly language into programs written in Turbo C, Turbo Pascal, Turbo Prolog, Turbo Basic, and other languages. Either way, with assembly language, you can write small and blindingly fast programs. As important as speed is the assembly language code's ability to control every aspect of your computer's operation, down to the last tick of the system clock.

In this chapter, we'll introduce you to assembly language and explore the unique qualities of assembly language programming. First, you'll enter and run several working assembly language programs, both to get a feel for the language and to get used to working with the assembler. Next, we'll cover the nature of computers in general, and the 8086 processor in particular, to give you an understanding of the special strengths of assembly language programming on the 8086. We'll also discuss issues of assembly language programming specifically related to the IBM PC.

Chapter 4, "The Basic Elements of an Assembler Program," picks up where this chapter leaves off, covering the structure of an assembly language program and fundamental program elements and summing up everything you've learned in the two chapters with a full-fledged example program.

Chapter 5, "More About Programming in Turbo Assembler," continues to explore assembly language programming, and Chapter 10, "Advanced Programming in Turbo Assembler," progresses to memory models, macros, and other advanced topics.

Naturally, we can't make you expert assembly language programmers in the course of a few chapters; we're simply introducing you to assembly language and getting you started on the road to writing your own programs. We strongly suggest that you get one of the many excellent books devoted entirely to assembly language programming and PC architecture (see the references at the end of this book). In addition, you may find IBM's *DOS Technical Reference, BIOS Interface Technical Reference*, and *Personal Computer XT Technical Reference* manuals to be useful reference material; these manuals document the assembly language programming interface to the systems software and hardware of IBM's personal computers.

Before you read further, you might want to read Chapter 3, "Command-Line Reference," to familiarize yourself with the command-line options. You should also install Turbo Assembler (make working copies of your Turbo Assembler disks or copy the files from your Turbo Assembler disks onto your hard disk) as described in Chapter 1, "Getting Started," if you haven't already done so.

One final point: Assembly language is a complex topic, and there are many things you will need to know in order to write even a relatively simple assembly language program. Sometimes we'll have to use features in our examples that we haven't discussed yet, simply because we have to start *somewhere*. Bear with us; we'll explain everything in due course. If, at any time, you're curious about a specific feature, just look it up in Chapter 3, "Directives," in the *Reference Guide*.

With that out of the way, and with Chapter 3 of the second volume close at hand, it's time to create your first assembly language program.

Writing Your First Turbo Assembler Program

In the world of programming, the first program is traditionally a program that displays the message, "Hello, world" and that's as good a place as any for us to start.

Get into your text editor of choice (one that outputs ASCII files), and type in the following lines that make up the program HELLO.ASM:

```
        .MODEL small
        .STACK 100h
        .DATA
HelloMessage DB 'Hello, world',13,10,'$'
        .CODE
    mov  ax,@data
    mov  ds,ax                      ;set DS to point to the data segment
    mov  ah,9                       ;DOS print string function
    mov  dx,OFFSET HelloMessage     ;point to "Hello, world"
    int  21h                        ;display "Hello, world"
    mov  ah,4ch                     ;DOS terminate program function
    int  21h                        ;terminate the program
    END
```

As soon as you've entered HELLO.ASM, save it to disk.

If you're familiar with C or Pascal, you might be thinking that the assembler version of "Hello, world" seems a bit long. Well, yes, assembler programs do tend to be long because each assembler instruction by itself does less than a C or Pascal instruction. On the other hand, you've got complete freedom in combining those assembler instructions in any way you want. That means that, unlike C and Pascal, assembler lets you program the computer to do *anything* it's capable of—and that's often worth typing a few extra lines.

Assembling Your First Program

Now that you've saved HELLO.ASM, you'll want to run it. Before you can run the program, though, you'll have to convert it into an executable (able to be run or executed) form. This requires two additional steps, assembling and linking, as shown in Figure 2.1, which depicts the complete edit, assemble, link, and run program development cycle.

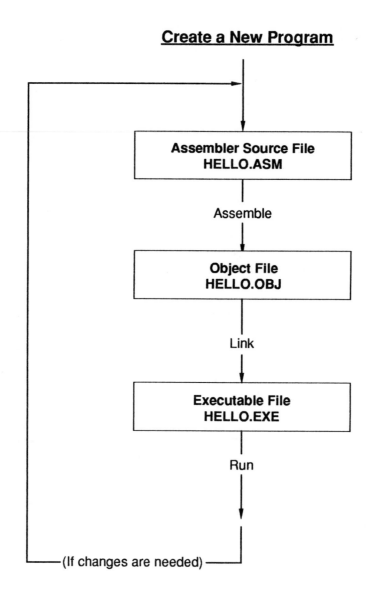

Create a New Program

Figure 2.1: The Edit, Assemble, Link, and Run Cycle

The assembly step turns your source code into an intermediate form called an *object module,* and the linking step combines one or more object modules into an executable program. You can do your assembling and linking from the command line.

To assemble HELLO.ASM, type

```
TASM hello
```

Unless you specify another file name, HELLO.ASM will be assembled to HELLO.OBJ. (Note that you don't need to type in the file extension name; Turbo Assembler assumes .ASM in this case.) This is what you'll see onscreen:

```
Turbo Assembler Version 1.0 Copyright (C) 1988 by Borland International, Inc.

Assembling file: HELLO.ASM
Error messages: None
Warning messages: None
Remaining memory: 266K
```

You won't receive any warnings or errors if you typed HELLO.ASM exactly as shown. If you get warnings or errors, they'll appear onscreen, along with the line numbers to indicate where they occurred. If you get errors, check your code and make sure it's precisely the same as the code we've shown you, then assemble the program again.

Linking Your First Program

After you've successfully assembled HELLO.ASM, you're only one step away from running your first assembler program. Once you've linked the just-assembled object code into an executable form, you can run the program.

To link the program, you'll use TLINK, the linker accompanying Turbo Assembler. At the command line, type

```
TLINK hello
```

Again, there's no need to enter the extension name; TLINK assumes it's .OBJ. When linking completes (again, after a few seconds at most), the linker automatically gives the .EXE file the same name as your object file, unless you've specified otherwise. When linking is successful, this message appears onscreen:

```
Turbo Linker Version 2.0 Copyright (c) 1987, 1988 by Borland International, Inc.
```

Errors can occur during the linking process, although that's unlikely with this example program. If you do receive any link errors (they'll appear onscreen), modify your code to exactly match the code shown here, then assemble and link again.

Running Your First Program

Now you're ready to run your program. Type `hello` at the DOS prompt. The message

```
Hello, world
```

will be displayed onscreen. And that's all there is to it—you've just created and run your first Turbo Assembler program!

What Happened?

Now that you've gotten HELLO.ASM up and running, let's go back and figure out exactly what happened along the path from entering text to running the program.

When you first entered the assembler source code, the text was stored by your text editor in memory. If the computer had been turned off at this point, for whatever reason, the source code would have been lost; consequently, we suggest you save your source code early and often in order to avert possible tragedy. When you saved the source code to disk, a permanent copy of the text was stored in the file HELLO.ASM, where it would survive even if you shut off your computer. (HELLO.ASM might not survive a disk crash, however, so we also suggest that you back up your disks regularly.) HELLO.ASM is a standard ASCII text file; you can display it at the DOS prompt by typing

```
type hello.asm
```

and you can edit it with any text editor.

When you assembled HELLO.ASM, Turbo Assembler turned the text instructions in HELLO.ASM into their binary equivalents in the object file HELLO.OBJ. HELLO.OBJ is an intermediate file, partway between source code and an executable file. HELLO.OBJ contains all the information needed to make executable code out of the instructions that started out in HELLO.ASM, but it's in a form that can readily be combined with other object files into a single program. In Chapter 5, "More About Programming in Turbo Assembler," you'll see how useful this can be when you're developing large programs.

Next, when you linked HELLO.OBJ, TLINK converted it into the executable file HELLO.EXE. Finally, you ran HELLO.EXE when you typed `hello` at the prompt.

Now type

```
dir hello.*
```

to list the various HELLO files on your disk. You'll find HELLO.ASM, HELLO.OBJ, HELLO.EXE, and HELLO.MAP.

Modifying Your First Turbo Assembler Program

Now go back to your editor and modify your program to accept a bit of input from the outside world. (The outside world is you, typing at your keyboard.) Change the code to the following:

```
    .MODEL  small
    .STACK  100h
    .DATA
TimePrompt DB 'Is it after 12 noon (Y/N)?$'
GoodMorningMessage  LABEL  BYTE
    DB  13,10,'Good morning, world!',13,10,'$'
GoodAfternoonMessage  LABEL  BYTE
    DB  13,10,'Good afternoon, world!',13,10,'$'
    .CODE
    mov  ax,@data
    mov  ds,ax                       ;set DS to point to data segment
    mov  dx,OFFSET TimePrompt        ;point to the time prompt
    mov  ah,9                        ;DOS print string function #
    int  21h                         ;display the time prompt
    mov  ah,1                        ;DOS get character function #
    int  21h                         ;get a single-character response
    cmp  al,'y'                      ;typed lowercase y for after noon?
    jz   IsAfternoon                 ;yes, it's after noon
    cmp  al,'Y'                      ;typed uppercase Y for after noon?
    jnz  IsMorning                   ;no, it's before noon
IsAfternoon:
    mov  dx,OFFSET GoodAfternoonMessage   ;point to the afternoon greeting
    jmp  DisplayGreeting
IsMorning:
    mov  dx,OFFSET GoodMorningMessage     ;point to the before noon greeting
DisplayGreeting:
    mov  ah,9                        ;DOS print string function #
    int  21h                         ;display the appropriate greeting
    mov  ah,4ch                      ;DOS terminate program function #
    int  21h                         ;terminate the program
    END
```

You've added two important new capabilities to your program: input and decision-making. This program asks you whether it's *after* noon, then accepts a single-character response from the keyboard. If the character typed is an uppercase or lowercase *Y*, the program displays a greeting appropriate for the afternoon; otherwise, it gives a morning greeting. All the essential elements of a useful program—input from the outside world, data processing and decision-making, and output to the outside world—are present in this code.

Save the modified program to disk. (This replaces your original version of HELLO.ASM with the modified code, so the original version will be lost.) Then reassemble and relink the program just as you did in the previous examples. Run the program again by typing `hello` at the DOS prompt. The message

```
Is it after 12 noon (Y/N)?
```

is displayed, with the cursor blinking after the question mark, waiting for your response. Press Y. The program responds

```
Good afternoon, world!
```

HELLO.ASM is now an interactive, decision-making program.

In the course of your assembler programming, you will surely make a wide variety of mistakes in typing and in program syntax. Turbo Assembler catches many mistakes for you as it assembles your code, reporting all such errors. The mistakes reported fall into two categories: warnings and errors. Turbo Assembler displays a *warning* message if it detects something suspicious, but not necessarily wrong, in your code; sometimes warnings can be ignored, but it's always best to check them out and make sure you understand the problem. Turbo Assembler displays an *error* message if it encounters something clearly wrong in your code that makes it impossible to complete assembly and generate an object file.

In other words, warnings are cautionary or nonfatal, while errors *must* be fixed before you can run a program. The many error and warning messages Turbo Assembler can generate are covered in Appendix E in the *Reference Guide*.

As with any programming language, Turbo Assembler can't catch logic errors for you. Turbo Assembler can tell you whether your code can be assembled, but it can't tell you whether the assembled code will perform as you intended it to—only you can be the judge of that.

Don't worry if the example code doesn't make much sense to you right now. Even programmers experienced in other languages take some time to become fluent in 8086 assembly language; there's really nothing quite like it under the sun. At this point, you're just getting a feel for what assembler programs look like. Later in this chapter, and in Chapter 4, "The Basic Elements of an Assembler Program," we'll cover each of the elements of the programs presented.

To list or send your program to a printer, consult your specific text editor's manual. Turbo Assembler source files are normal ASCII text files, so you can also print any assembler source file from the DOS prompt with the PRINT command.

Sending Output to a Printer

The printer is a handy output device; not only will you sometimes want to send your program files to the printer, but you'll also want your programs to send output to the printer on occasion. The following is a version of the "Hello, world" program that displays its output on the printer rather than on the screen:

```
    .MODEL small
    .STACK 100h
    .DATA
HelloMessage DB 'Hello, world',13,10,12
HELLO_MESSAGE_LENGTH EQU $ - HelloMessage
    .CODE
    mov  ax,@data
    mov  ds,ax                  ;set DS to point to the data segment
    mov  ah,40h                 ;DOS write to device function #
    mov  bx,4                   ;printer handle
    mov  cx,HELLO_MESSAGE_LENGTH ;number of characters to print
    mov  dx,OFFSET HelloMessage  ;string to print
    int  21h                    ;print "Hello, world"
    mov  ah,4ch                 ;DOS terminate program function #
    int  21h                    ;terminate the program
    END
```

In this version of the "Hello, world" program, you've replaced the DOS function to print a string on the screen with a DOS function that sends a string to a selected device or file—in this case, the printer. Enter and run the program, and see that a sheet containing the familiar "Hello, world" message is printed. (Don't forget to save the program before running it. Again, this saves the modified code in HELLO.ASM, and the previous version of the program will be lost.)

You can modify this program to send output to the screen rather than to the printer, displaying "Hello, world" onscreen again, simply by changing

```
    mov  bx,4   ;printer handle
```

to

```
mov  bx,1    ;standard output handle
```

Make this change, then reassemble and relink before running the program again. You'll note that when the output is displayed on the screen, the final character shown is the universal symbol for "female" (♀). This is actually a *formfeed character*, which the program sent to the printer to force it to eject the sheet on which you'd printed "Hello, world." Since the screen doesn't have sheets, it doesn't know about formfeeds, so it simply displays the corresponding member of the PC's character set when told to print a formfeed character.

Writing Your Second Turbo Assembler Program

Now you're ready to enter and run a program that actually *does* something, REVERSE.ASM. Go back into your text editor and enter the following:

```
    .MODEL small
    .STACK 100h
    .DATA
MAXIMUM_STRING_LENGTH   EQU  1000
StringToReverse  DB  MAXIMUM_STRING_LENGTH DUP(?)
ReverseString    DB  MAXIMUM_STRING_LENGTH DUP(?)
    .CODE
    mov  ax,@data
    mov  ds,ax                 ;set DS to point to the data segment
    mov  ah,3fh                ;DOS read from handle function #
    mov  bx,0                  ;standard input handle
    mov  cx,MAXIMUM_STRING_LENGTH ;read up to maximum number of characters
    mov  dx,OFFSET StringToReverse ;store the string here
    int  21h                   ;get the string
    and  ax,ax                 ;were any characters read?
    jz   Done                  ;no, so you're done
    mov  cx,ax                 ;put string length in CX, where
                               ; you can use it as a counter
    push cx                    ;save the string length
    mov  bx,OFFSET StringToReverse
    mov  si,OFFSET ReverseString
    add  si,cx
    dec  si                    ;point to the end of the
                               ; reverse string buffer
ReverseLoop:
    mov  al,[bx]               ;get the next character
    mov  [si],al               ;store the characters in reverse order
    inc  bx                    ;point to next character
```

```
        dec  si                          ;point to previous location
                                         ; in reverse buffer
        loop ReverseLoop                 ;move next character, if any
        pop  cx                          ;get back the string length
        mov  ah,40h                      ;DOS write from handle function #
        mov  bx,1                        ;standard output handle
        mov  dx,OFFSET ReverseString     ;print this string
        int  21h                         ;print the reversed string
Done:
        mov  ah,4ch                      ;DOS terminate program function #
        int  21h                         ;terminate the program
        END
```

You'll see what the program actually does in a moment; first, as always, you should save your work.

Running REVERSE.ASM

To run REVERSE.ASM, you must first assemble it; type

```
TASM reverse
```

then type

```
TLINK reverse
```

to create the executable file.

Type reverse at the prompt to run your program. If Turbo Assembler reports any errors or warnings, carefully check your code to see that it matches the code shown previously, then try running the program again.

After you run your program, the cursor will sit blinking onscreen. Apparently, the program is waiting for you to type something. Try typing

```
ABCDEFG
```

then press *Enter*. The program displays

```
GFEDCBA
```

and ends. Type reverse again at the command line. This time, type

```
0123456789
```

and press *Enter*. The program displays

```
9876543210
```

Now it's clear what REVERSE.ASM does: It reverses whatever string of characters you type in. Speedy manipulation of characters and strings is one of the areas in which assembly language excels, as you'll see in the next few chapters.

Congratulations! You've entered, assembled, linked, and run several assembler programs, and you've seen the fundamentals of assembler programming—input, processing, and output—in action.

If you don't want an object file but you do want a listing file, or if you want a cross-reference file but don't want a listing file or object file, you can specify the null device (NUL) as the file name. For example,

```
TASM FILE1,,NUL,
```

assembles file FILE1.ASM to object file FILE1.OBJ, doesn't produce a listing file, and creates a cross-reference file FILE1.XRF.

Now you're ready to learn the basic elements of assembler programming. We'll start by teaching you just what it is that makes assembly language unique among the many languages of the computer world.

The Architecture of a Computer

Earlier, we said that assembly language is the computer's own language. In order to understand what that means, you first need to learn exactly what a computer is.

Deep down, a computer is nothing more than a device that moves data from one place to another, sometimes transforming the data in various logical and arithmetical ways. For our purposes, however, it's more useful to view a computer as a system consisting of five functional sub-systems—input, control, arithmetic and logical processing, memory, and output—as shown in Figure 2.2.

(For the moment, we're talking about computers in general; we'll get to the 8088 shortly.)

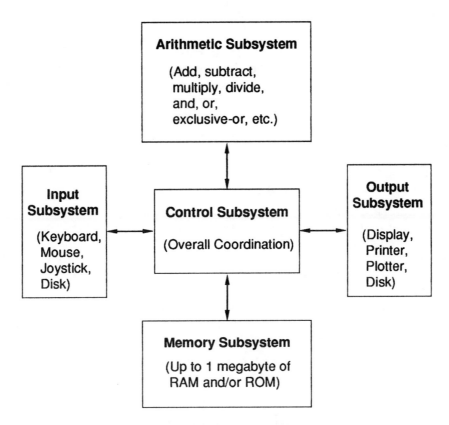

Figure 2.2: Five Subsystems

The arithmetic subsystem of the computer is the aspect most people think of when they think of a computer. After all, what is a computer if not a number-cruncher? As it turns out, though, most computers spend very little time crunching numbers, and a great deal of time working with character strings and performing input and output; what need does a word processor have for arithmetic? Nonetheless, the arithmetic subsystem is important, for it is there that not only addition, subtraction, multiplication, and division are performed, but logical operations (such as *and*, *or*, and *exclusive-or*) as well.

It's all very well to perform arithmetic, but where do the source values for, say, addition come from, and where does the result of each operation go? The computer's memory subsystem comes into play here, providing instantly accessible storage for many thousands of characters or numbers. Computers also have floppy and hard disk drives, which provide permanent (but relatively slow) storage for enormous amounts of data, but these are actually input/output (I/O) devices, not part of the memory subsystem.

The input subsystem allows programs to manipulate data from the outside world, ranging from single keystrokes to mouse motions to whole databases stored in disk files. The output subsystem lets programs display prompts and results on screens and printers, and send data to disk files and tapes. Programs without input and output tend to be rare, since they can't accept new data from the outside world and can't do anything with whatever results they do generate.

Finally, the control subsystem ties together the operation of the other four subsystems and controls data movement.

The control and arithmetic subsystems together form what is known as the processing unit, or *processor*. A processor forms the core of any computer, providing data processing and controlling the memory, input, and output subsystems. The processor sets the tone for any computer, since it is the processor that controls the operation of each of the subsystems and coordinates them into a smoothly functioning unit. Nowadays, an entire processor is frequently built on a single chip. For instance, the 8088 is a processor on a chip, complete with arithmetic processing, control, and interfaces to input, output, and memory.

It's with the processor that we make the connection between the architecture of the computer and the unique nature of assembly language.

The Nature of Assembly Language

We've said that the processor orchestrates the activities of the five subsystems of a computer—adding values, moving them about from memory to output, and so on—but that begs a fundamental question: How does the processor know *which* operations to perform? So far, the computer has all the capabilities we need, but no script to follow.

The answer is surprisingly simple: The processor fetches data from memory, and that data tells it what to do next. Data that tells a processor what to do is usually called instructions, but instructions are simply values stored in memory, just like any other data. The set of instructions that a processor can execute (the *instruction set*) corresponds exactly to the actions that that processor's hardware can perform. Put another way, a processor's instructions comprise all the operations that any software can ever ask the processor to do.

For example, if a processor lacks a multiplication instruction, then there is no way the hardware of that computer can perform a multiplication. Multiplication can instead be performed in software by performing adds and shifts, but this tends to be much slower. The key point here is that a processor's instruction set reflects the actions that the computer's hardware is inherently capable of performing. By the same token, each processor's assembly language is unique to that processor because each processor has unique capabilities and, therefore, a unique instruction set.

Each instruction value has a specific, well-defined meaning to a given processor. For example, the instruction value 4 tells the 8088 to add the value stored at the next memory address to the AL register. (Don't worry about what the AL register is right now—we'll get to that soon.) Consequently, a processor can be put through a desired sequence of actions by an appropriate series of instruction values; indeed, a program is nothing more than a sequence of instruction values.

How does a processor know which instruction to execute next? By maintaining an internal pointer that points to the place in memory where the value of the next instruction to be performed is stored. When that next instruction is read from memory and executed, the pointer is advanced to the following instruction. Some instructions can set the instruction pointer to a new value; this gives a processor the ability to execute nonsequential series of instructions, and even the ability to perform different series of instructions depending on certain conditions.

Great, but what does that have to do with assembly language? Just this: A processor's instruction set *is* that processor's assembly language. Or, rather, assembly language is a human-oriented form of a processor's instruction set (known as the processor's *machine language*), which an assembler such as Turbo Assembler then converts to machine language. While assembly language and machine language are functionally equivalent, assembly language is much easier for people to program in. After all, surely you'd rather program with instructions like

```
add  al,1
```

than with

```
4
1
```

wouldn't you? Both forms work equally well, but assembly language lets you work with mnemonic names for machine-language instructions, with the assembler translating from mnemonic instructions to their machine-language equivalents. This is, of course, a tremendous advantage, since humans simply don't think very well in purely numeric languages.

Basically, assembly language is a direct analog to machine language, but implemented in a form with which humans can work efficiently.

The good news about assembly language is that it lets you control the processor's actions one by one, for maximum efficiency. The bad news is that each of the processor's actions, taken individually, tend to do relatively little, reflecting the limited repertoire of which the processor is actually capable. For example, the process of adding two long integers and storing the result in a third long integer takes only one line in C:

```
i = j + k;
```

but requires six lines in 8088 assembler:

```
mov   ax,[j]
mov   dx,[j+2]
add   ax,[k]
adc   dx,[k+2]
mov   [i],ax
mov   [i+2],dx
```

Of course, the C code compiles to no less (and possibly more) than the same six machine language instructions required by the assembler code, but it is easier to write the one line of C code than the six lines of assembler. (Remember, assembler instructions reflect the basic ability of the computer, and programs written in all languages must eventually be translated to machine language before they can be run.)

Why use assembler at all if it's harder to program in than other languages? For one thing, assembler lets you reach any part of memory and control any input or output device directly, since assembly language programs can do anything the processor is capable of. For another, because assembler is the native language of the computer, it stands to reason that well-written assembler code must be the fastest code possible. The quality of the code produced by any other language suffers from the need to translate from that language to machine language, but assembler code maps directly to machine language, with not one whit of efficiency lost. In assembly language, you tell the computer what to do, and it does it—no more and no less.

Of course, if you write an inefficient assembler program, it won't run very rapidly, since the processor does *exactly* what assembly language programs specify. Similarly, assembly language has relatively little built-in support for data-type conversion, or for guarding against mistakes, such as accidentally overwriting a variable or running off the end of an array. What all this means is that assembly language gives you the ability to write wonderfully fast and clever programs, but those programs demand more care and skill from you as a programmer than do programs written in other languages.

Now that you understand how a processor and its assembly language relate to one another, let's look specifically at assembly language for the 8088.

The 8088 and 8086 Processors

The 8088 is the processor used in the IBM PC and XT computers, which form perhaps one of the most successful line of computers. However, the 8088 is actually only one of a family of processors known as the iAPx86 family. Other members of this family include the 8086 processor used in the IBM Models 25 and 30; the 80286 processor used in the IBM AT, and the IBM PS/2 Models 50 and 60; and the 80386 processor used in the IBM PS/2 Model 80. Each of these processors is, in some way, different from the 8088. Chapter 11, "The 80386 and Other Processors," provides a detailed discussion of the various members of the iAPx86 family. The one thing all iAPx86 family processors share is the ability to run code written for the 8086 and 8088 processors.

The 8086 is actually the root of the iAPx86 family tree. The 8088 is just an 8086 with a scaled-down external data bus; while the 8086 can transfer data to and from memory 16 bits at a time, the 8088 can transfer data only 8 bits at a time. The two processors have exactly the same instruction sets. Consequently, the assembly language used to program the IBM PC and its successors is properly known as 8086 assembly language, not 8088 assembly language. For the remainder of this chapter, understand that 8086 assembly language includes the 8088 as well.

The Capabilities of the 8086

By today's standards, the 8086 is a processor of modest capabilities. After all, the 8086 was designed ten years ago, and ten years of technological evolution have brought major innovations to the chip-design field. Nonetheless, the 8086 remains an important processor. One reason for this is the sheer number of IBM PCs and compatibles; no one can afford to ignore ten-million-plus computers. Another reason, however, is that the 8086 meets the needs, even today, of advanced software.

The 8086 can address a large amount of memory (over one million characters or other byte-sized—8-bit—values), has a powerful instruction set, and properly programmed can support high-performance programs.

But the 8086 is not a super-fast processor, not every language is capable of providing decent performance on the 8086, and no other language can match assembly language when it comes to writing excellent 8086 programs. (The 8086 runs at 4.77 or 8 MHz speeds; the 80286 can run at 6, 8, 10, 12, and even 16 MHz; the 80386 can run at 16, 20, and 25 MHz.)

The resources the 8086 provides to the assembly language programmer are memory, input and output (I/O) interfacing, registers, and, of course, instructions. We'll explore those resources next.

Memory

The 8086 is capable of addressing 1 Mb (1 megabyte, which is 2 to the 20th power or 1,048,576 storage locations, each of which is 8 bits long) of memory at any one time. The first byte of memory is at address 0, and the last byte of memory is at address 0FFFFFh as shown in Figure 2.3 on page 25.

(The last address, 0FFFFFh, was given in hexadecimal, or base 16, notation as denoted by the *h* suffix; it is equivalent to 1,048,575 in the familiar decimal, or base 10, notation.) Fluency in hexadecimal notation is essential in assembly language programming. We'll touch on hexadecimal notation in Chapter 4, "The Basic Elements of an Assembler Program."

Hexadecimal Address		Decimal Address
00000		0
00001		1
00002		2
00003		3
00004		4
00005		5
00006		6
00007		7
00008		8
00009		9
0000A		10
0000B		11
0000C		12
0000D		13
0000E		14
0000F		15
00010		16
FFFEF		1048559
FFFF0		1048560
FFFF1		1048561
FFFF2		1048562
FFFF3		1048563
FFFF4		1048564
FFFF5		1048565
FFFF6		1048566
FFFF7		1048567
FFFF8		1048568
FFFF9		1048569
FFFFA		1048570
FFFFB		1048571
FFFFC		1048572
FFFFD		1048573
FFFFE		1048574
FFFFF		1048575

Figure 2.3: Memory Address Space of the 8086

One byte, 8 bits long, can hold one character, or one integer value in the range 0 to 255. That doesn't mean that the 8086 can't handle larger values. Two bytes taken together (known as a *word*) can hold one integer value in the range 0 to 65,535; the 8086 can manipulate word values as readily as byte values.

Four bytes taken together (known as a *doubleword*, or *dword*) can hold one integer value in the range 0 to 4,294,967,295, or can hold one single-precision floating-point value. Eight bytes together (known as a *quadword*, or *qword*) can hold one double-precision floating-point value. The 8086 doesn't handle these two data types directly; however, the 8087 numeric coprocessor can work directly with floating-point values and extended precision integer values, and given the proper software, the 8086 can be made to handle virtually any data type, albeit fairly slowly.

At any time, an 8086 program can read or change the contents of any of the more than 1,000,000 bytes of memory. For example, the code fragment

```
    .
    .
    .
mov  ax,0
mov  ds,ax
mov  bx,0
mov  al,[bx]
    .
    .
    .
```

loads the contents of the byte at address 0 into the AL register. Don't worry about the details here; the point is that the 8086's memory address space provides for storage of slightly more than 1,000,000 working values that the 8086 can access quickly and flexibly.

One megabyte (1 Mb) is a considerable amount of memory, far more than the 64 Kb (2 to the 16th power, or 65,536 bytes) addressable by the processors that preceded the 8086. On the other hand, the 8086's latest descendent, the 80386, can address about 4,000 times as much memory as the 8086, so you can see that the 8086 is, in fact, a little squeezed for memory space. Also, in the IBM PC, only 640 Kb of the 1 Mb address space is actually available for use as general-purpose memory; the rest of the address space is dedicated to use by system software and the memory used for the display. Then, too, don't forget that instructions, as well as data, are stored in memory, so both program code and data must fit into no more than 640 Kb of memory on the PC.

While the 8086 is capable of addressing 1 Mb of memory, it does not make it particularly *easy* to access more than 64 Kb at any one time, due to a rather peculiar feature known as *segmentation*. We'll look at segmentation in a later section, "The Segment Registers," on page 40.

Input and Output

The 8086 supports input and output devices in two ways: through input/output (I/O) instructions and through memory addresses. Some input and output devices are controlled through *ports*, which are special I/O addresses in a 64K address space that's separate from the 1 Mb memory address space, as shown in Figure 2.4.

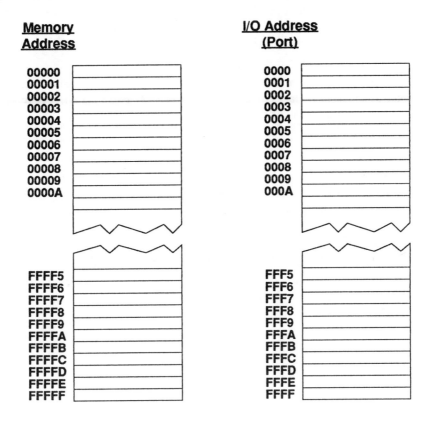

Figure 2.4: Separate Memory and I/O Address of 8086

There are far fewer I/O addresses on the 8086 than there are memory addresses; while there are technically 64K I/O addresses on the PC, practically speaking, only 4K I/O addresses are available. Consequently, I/O addresses are not used for storing values, but rather for providing control and data channels to input and output devices. For example, serial devices such as modems are controlled entirely through a few I/O addresses.

I/O addresses can be accessed only with two special instructions, IN and OUT, which are used for nothing else. For example,

```
out  dx,al
```

sends the contents of the AL register to the I/O port selected by the DX register. We'll return to IN and OUT, and to I/O in general, in Chapter 4, "The Basic Elements of an Assembler Program."

Some output devices are *memory-mapped*, meaning they are controlled through normal memory addresses rather than I/O. This is particularly true of display adapters, which can take up 16K, 32K, or even 256K of the 8086's memory address space with their *bit maps* (the arrays of bytes describing the dots that the adapters display on the screen).

A given device can be controlled through both I/O ports and memory-mapped addresses. In fact, most display adapters respond to I/O instructions for some functions and to memory addresses for others.

Registers

The 8086 offers a few fast, on-chip storage elements known as *registers*. You might think of registers as memory locations that the 8086 can access faster than it can access regular memory, but that's only part of what makes registers special. Each of the registers has a unique nature, and provides certain capabilities that no other register or memory location supports.

The registers fall into four categories: the flags register, the general-purpose registers, the instruction pointer, and the segment registers, as shown in Figure 2.5. Let's look at each in turn.

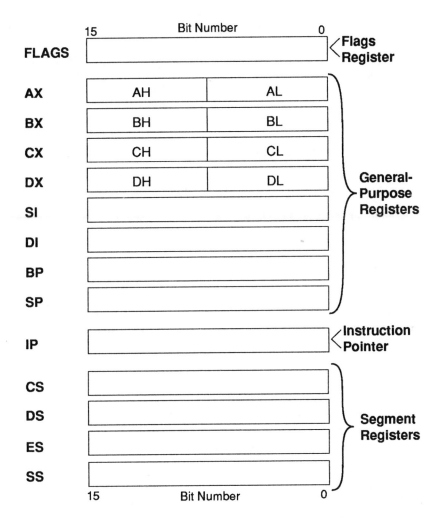

Figure 2.5: Registers of the 8086

The Flags Register

The 16-bit flags register contains all pertinent information about the state of the 8086 and the results of recent instructions, as shown in Figure 2.6.

Bit Number

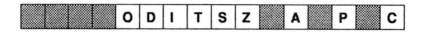

Flag Bits

O = Overflow Flag	**T** = Trap Flag	**A** = Auxiliary Carry Flag
D = Direction Flag	**S** = Sign Flag	**P** = Parity Flag
I = Interrupt Flag	**Z** = Zero Flag	**C** = Carry Flag

Figure 2.6: Flags Register of the 8086

For example, if you wanted to know whether a subtraction produced a zero result, you would check the *zero flag* (the Z bit in the flags register) immediately after the instruction; if it were set, you would know the result was zero. Other flags, such as the *carry* and *overflow flags*, similarly report the results of arithmetic and logical operations.

Other flags control modes of operation of the 8086. The *direction flag* controls the direction in which the string instructions move, and the *interrupt flag* controls whether external hardware, such as a keyboard or modem, is allowed to halt the current code temporarily so that urgent needs can be serviced. The *trap flag* is used only by software that debugs other software.

The flags register isn't modified or read directly. Instead, the flags register is generally controlled through special instructions (such as **CLD**, **STI**, and **CMC**) and through arithmetic and logical instructions that modify certain flags. Likewise, the contents of certain bits of the flags register affect the operation of instructions such as **JZ**, **RCR**, and **MOVSB**. The flags register is not really used as a storage location, but is rather the status and control network of the 8086.

To put it another way: Other registers and memory contain data; the flags register contains information about relationships between data, about the results of operations, and about the state of the 8086 itself.

The General-Purpose Registers

The 8 general-purpose registers of the 8086 (each 16 bits long) are involved in the operation of most instructions, as source and destination for calculations and data moves, as pointers to memory, and as counters. Each of the general-purpose registers can store any 16-bit value, can be loaded from and written to memory, and can be used in arithmetic and logical operations. For example, this code fragment

```
.
.
.
mov   ax,5
mov   dx,9
add   ax,dx
.
.
.
```

loads the value 5 in AX, loads the value 9 in DX, and adds the two values together, storing the result, 14, back into the AX register. CX, SI, or any of the other general-purpose registers could have been substituted for AX or DX in this example, with equal success.

Beyond the common ability to store values and serve as source and destination for data manipulation instructions, however, each of the general-purpose registers has its own personality. Let's look at each of the general-purpose registers separately.

The AX Register

The AX register is also known as the *accumulator*. The AX register is always involved when you perform multiplication and division, and is also the most efficient register to use for some arithmetic, logical, and data-movement operations.

The lower 8 bits of the AX register are also known as the AL register (for *A*-Low), and the upper 8 bits of the AX register are also known as the AH register (for *A*-High). This can be convenient for handling byte-sized data, since it allows AX to serve as two separate registers. The following code sets AH to 0, copies the value to AL, then adds 1 to AL:

```
.
.
.
mov   ah,0
mov   al,ah
```

```
inc  al
   .
   .
   .
```

The end result is that AX is set to 1. The BX, CX, and DX registers can similarly serve as either one 16-bit register or two 8-bit registers.

The BX Register

The BX register can point to memory locations. We'll cover this in more detail in Chapter 4, "The Basic Elements of an Assembler Program," but, briefly, a 16-bit value stored in BX can be used as a part of the address of a memory location to be accessed. For instance, the following code loads AL with the contents of memory address 9:

```
   .
   .
   .
mov  ax,0
mov  ds,ax
mov  bx,9
mov  al,[bx]
   .
   .
   .
```

You'll notice that we loaded the DS register with 0 (by way of AX), before accessing the memory location pointed to by BX. This is a result of the segmented nature of 8086 memory that we referred to previously—a topic we'll return to in the section "The Segment Registers" (page 40). By default, when BX is used as a memory pointer, it points relative to the DS segment register.

Like AX, CX, and DX, the BX register can be treated as two 8-bit registers, BH and BL.

The CX Register

The CX register's specialty is counting. Suppose you wanted to repeat a block of instructions 10 times. You could do that with

```
        .
        .
        .
    mov  cx,10
BeginningOfLoop:
        .
        .
        .
    <instructions to be repeated>
        .
        .
        .
    sub  cx,1
    jnz  BeginningOfLoop
        .
        .
        .
```

Don't worry about unfamiliar elements of this program; the important point is that the instructions between the label *BeginningOfLoop* and the **JNZ** instruction are executed repeatedly until CX becomes 0. Notice that two instructions—**SUB CX,1** and **JNZ** *BeginningOfLoop*—are required in order to count down CX and jump back to *BeginningOfLoop* if CX is not yet 0.

Counting down and looping is a frequently used program element, so the 8086 provides a special instruction to make loops faster and more compact. Not surprisingly, that instruction is called **LOOP**. The **LOOP** instruction subtracts 1 from CX and jumps if CX isn't 0, all in one instruction. The following is equivalent to the last example:

```
        .
        .
        .
    mov  cx,10
BeginningOfLoop:
        .
        .
        .
    <instructions to be repeated>
        .
        .
        .
    loop BeginningOfLoop
        .
        .
        .
```

We'll cover looping again in Chapter 4, "The Basic Elements of an Assembler Program." For now, just remember that the CX register is especially useful for counting and looping.

Like AX, BX, and DX, the CX register can be treated as two 8-bit registers, CH and CL.

The DX Register

The DX register is the only register that can be used as an I/O address pointer with the **IN** and **OUT** instructions. In fact, there is no way to address I/O ports 256 through 65,535 without using DX. For example, the following code writes the value 62 to I/O port 1000:

```
        .
        .
        .
mov   al,62
mov   dx,1000
out   dx,al
        .
        .
        .
```

The other unique properties of DX relate to division and multiplication. When you divide a 32-bit dividend by a 16-bit divisor, the upper 16 bits of the dividend must be placed in DX; after the division, the remainder of the division is stored in DX. (The lower 16 bits of the dividend must be placed in AX, and the quotient is stored in AX.) Similarly, when you multiply two 16-bit factors, the upper 16 bits of the product are stored in DX (the lower 16 bits of the product are stored in AX).

Like AX, BX, and CX, the DX register can be treated as two 8-bit registers, DH and DL.

The SI Register

Like the BX register, the SI register can be used as a memory pointer. For example,

```
        .
        .
        .
mov  ax,0
```

```
mov  ds,ax
mov  si,20
mov  al,[si]
  .
  .
  .
```

loads the 8-bit value stored at address 20 into AL. SI becomes an unusually powerful memory pointer when used with the 8086's string instructions. For example,

```
  .
  .
  .
cld
mov  ax,0
mov  ds,ax
mov  si,20
lodsb
  .
  .
  .
```

not only loads AX with the value at the memory address pointed to by SI, but also adds 1 to SI. This can be very effective when accessing a sequential series of memory locations, such as a text string. Better still, the string instructions can be made to automatically repeat their actions any number of times, so a single instruction can perform hundreds or even thousands of actions. We'll discuss the string instructions in detail in Chapter 5, "More About Programming in Turbo Assembler."

The DI Register

The DI register is much like the SI register in that it can be used as a memory pointer and has special properties when used with the powerful string instructions. For example,

```
  .
  .
  .
mov  ax,0
mov  ds,ax
mov  di,1024
add  bl,[di]
  .
  .
  .
```

adds the 8-bit value stored at address 1024 to BL. The DI register is a little different from SI when it comes to string instructions; where SI always serves as a source memory pointer for string instructions, DI always serves as a destination memory pointer. Moreover, with the string instructions, SI normally addresses memory relative to the DS segment register, while DI always addresses memory relative to the ES segment register. (When SI and DI are used as memory pointers with nonstring instructions, they always point relative to DS.) For example,

```
        .
        .
        .
cld
mov  dx,0
mov  es,dx
mov  di,2048
stosb
        .
        .
        .
```

uses the **STOSB** string instruction to both store the value in AL at the memory address pointed to by DI and add 1 to DI. But we're getting ahead of ourselves here; you need to learn about segments and segment registers before you can study the string instructions. Again, we'll look at the string instructions in Chapter 5, "More About Programming in Turbo Assembler."

The BP Register

Like BX, SI, and DI, the BP register can be used as a memory pointer, but with a difference. While the BX, SI, and DI registers normally act as memory pointers relative to the DS segment register (or, in the case of DI used with the string instructions, the ES segment register), BP points relative to SS, the *stack segment register*.

Once again, we're getting ahead of ourselves, since we haven't covered segments yet, but the principle is as follows. One useful way to pass parameters to a subroutine is by pushing the parameters onto the stack. C and Pascal do this; see Chapter 6, "Interfacing Turbo Assembler with Turbo C," for an explanation of how and why C uses the stack to pass parameters.

The stack resides in the segment pointed to by SS, or the stack segment. Data, on the other hand, normally resides in the segment pointed to by DS, or the data segment. Since BX, SI, and DI normally point to the data segment, there's no efficient way to use BX, SI, or DI to point to parameters passed on the stack because the stack is usually in a different segment altogether.

BP solves this problem by providing addressing into the stack segment. For example,

```
      .
      .
      .
push bp
mov  bp,sp
mov  ax,[bp+4]
      .
      .
      .
```

accesses the stack segment to load AX with the first parameter passed by a Turbo C call to an assembler subroutine.

In short, BP is designed to provide support for parameters, local variables, and other stack-based memory-addressing needs.

The SP Register

The SP register, also known as the *stack pointer*, is the least general of the general-purpose registers, for it is almost always dedicated to a specific purpose: maintaining the stack. The stack is an area of memory into which values can be stored and from which they can be retrieved on a last-in, first-out basis; that is, the last value stored onto the stack is the first value you'll get when you read a value from the stack. The classic analogy for the stack is that of a stack of dishes. Since you can only add plates at the top of the stack and remove them from the top of the stack, it stands to reason that the first plate you put on the stack will be the last plate you can remove.

The SP register points to the top of the stack at any given time; as with the stack of dishes, the top of the stack is the location at which the next value placed on the stack will be stored. The action of placing a value on the stack is known as *pushing* a value on the stack, and, indeed, the **PUSH** instruction is used to place values on the stack. Similarly, the action of retrieving a value from the stack is known as *popping* a value from the stack, and the **POP** instruction is used to retrieve values from the stack.

For example, Figure 2.7 illustrates how SP, AX, and BX change as the following code is executed, assuming that SP is initially set to 1,000:

```
        .
        .
        .
    mov   ax,1
    push  ax
    mov   bx,2
    push  bx
    pop   ax
    pop   bx
        .
        .
        .
```

While the 8086 allows you to store values in SP, and add to or subtract from the value stored in SP, just as with the other general-purpose registers, you should never do this unless you know exactly what you're doing. If you change SP, you're changing the location of the top of the stack, and that can quickly lead to disaster.

Why? Well, pushes and pops aren't the only way the stack is used. Whenever you call to or return from a subroutine (a procedure or function), the stack is used. Also, some system resources, such as the keyboard and the system clock, use the stack when they interrupt the 8086 in order to perform their functions. What this means is that the stack might be needed at *any* time. If you change SP, even if only for a few instructions, then the correct stack might not be available when some system resource needs it.

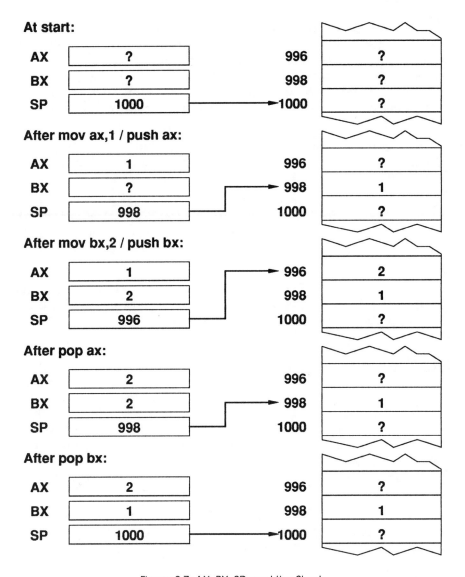

Figure 2.7: AX, BX, SP, and the Stack

In short, leave SP alone unless you know just what you're doing. Feel free to perform pushes, pops, calls, and returns, but don't change the value of SP directly. Any of the other seven general-purpose registers can be changed directly at any time.

The Instruction Pointer

The instruction pointer (IP) always contains the memory offset at which the next instruction to be executed is stored. As one instruction is executed, the instruction pointer is advanced to point to the instruction at the next memory address. Normally, the instruction at the next memory address is the next instruction executed, but some instructions, such as calls and jumps, can cause the instruction pointer to be loaded with a new value, thereby branching to other code.

The instruction pointer can't be written to or read from directly; only branching instructions such as those just described can load the instruction pointer with a new value.

The instruction pointer does not, by itself, fully specify the address at which the next instruction to be executed resides. Once again, the segmented nature of 8086 memory addressing complicates the picture. For instruction fetching, the CS segment register provides a base address, and the instruction pointer then provides an offset from that base address.

Each time we've talked about addressing memory, we've run into segments, and each time we've postponed a full explanation until the time came to talk about segments. That time has come.

The Segment Registers

Now we come to a most unusual aspect of the 8086—memory segmentation. The basic premise of segmentation is this: The 8086 is capable of addressing 1 Mb of memory. Twenty-bit memory addresses are required to address all locations in a 1 Mb memory space. However, the 8086 only uses 16-bit pointers to memory; for example, recall that the 16-bit BX register can be used to point to memory. How, then, does the 8086 reconcile 16-bit pointers with a 20-bit address space?

The answer is that the 8086 uses a two-part memory-addressing scheme. True, 16-bit memory pointers are used, but these form only part of the full memory address. Each 16-bit memory pointer, or memory *offset*, is combined with the contents of a 16-bit segment register to form a full 20-bit memory address.

Segments and offsets are combined as follows: The segment value is shifted left by 4 bits (multiplied by 16) and then added to the offset as shown in Figure 2.8.

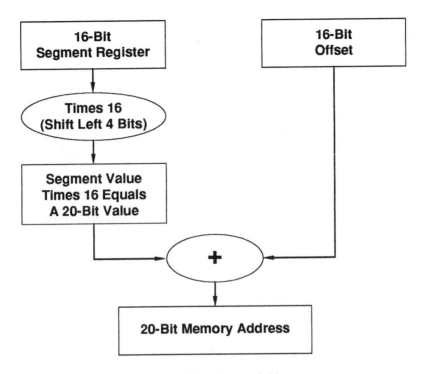

Figure 2.8: 20-Bit Memory Addresses

So, for example, consider the following code:

```
   .
   .
   .
mov   ax,1000h
mov   ds,ax
mov   si,201h
mov   dl,[si]
   .
   .
   .
```

Here the DS segment register is set to 1000h, and SI is set to 201h, which we can represent as the segment:offset pair 1000:201h. (Segment:offset calculations can only be performed efficiently in base 16—another good reason to familiarize yourself with hexadecimal notation.) The address DL is loaded from is $((DS * 16) + SI)$, or $((1000h * 16) + 201h)$:

```
  1000h
×   16
──────
10000h
+ 201h
──────
10201h
```

Figure 2.9 illustrates this example.

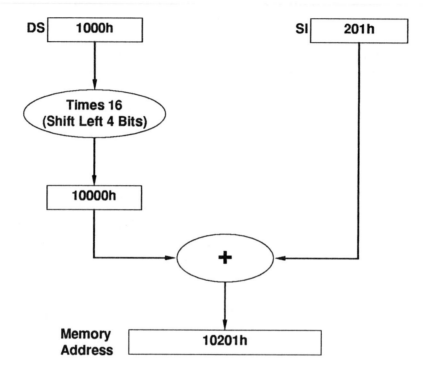

Figure 2.9: Calculation of Memory Address by mov

Another way to look at this is to simply shift the segment value left 4 bits, or one hexadecimal digit, which is the same as multiplying by 16:

```
10000
+ 201
─────
10201
```

You can now see that programs can only access the 8086's full 1 Mb memory space by using segment:offset pairs. In fact, you must *always* use segment:offset pairs to access memory; all the instructions and addressing modes of the 8086 default to operating relative to one or another of the segment registers, although some instructions can be explicitly told to use a different segment register if desired.

Rarely will you actually load a number into a segment register. Instead, you'll load segment registers with segment names, which are turned into numbers in the course of assembling, linking, and running a program. This is necessary because there's no way to tell beforehand where in memory a given segment will reside; it all depends on the version of DOS, the number and size of memory-resident programs, and the memory needs of the rest of the program. Using segment names lets Turbo Assembler and DOS deal with all those complications.

The most common segment name is **@data**, which refers to the default data segment when the simplified segment directives are used. For example,

```
    .MODEL small
    .DATA
Var1 DW 0
    .
    .
    .
    .CODE
    mov  ax,@data
    mov  ds,ax
    .
    .
    .
END
```

loads DS to point to the default data segment, in which *Var1* resides.

Once again, we're getting a bit ahead; in the next chapter, we'll discuss the simplified segment directives and the loading of segment registers.

The use of segments on the 8086 has a couple of interesting implications. For one thing, only a 64 Kb block of memory is addressable relative to a segment register at any one time because 64 Kb is the maximum amount of memory that can be addressed with a 16-bit offset. This means that it can be a real nuisance to handle large (greater than 64 Kb) blocks of data on the 8086, since both a segment register and the offset value must be changed frequently.

The addressing of large blocks of memory on the 8086 is made still more difficult because, unlike the general-purpose registers, the segment registers cannot serve as either source or destination for arithmetic and logical instructions. In fact, the *only* operations that can be performed on segment registers involve copying values between segment registers and either general-purpose registers or memory. For instance, adding 100 to the ES register requires the following:

```
    .
    .
    .
mov  ax,es
add  ax,100
mov  es,ax
    .
    .
    .
```

The upshot of all this is that the 8086 is best suited to handling memory in chunks no larger than 64 Kb.

A second implication of the use of segments is that any given memory location is addressable with many possible segment:offset combinations. For instance, the memory address 100h is addressable with segment:offset values of 0:100h, 1:F0h, 2:E0h, and so on, since all those segment:offset pairs work out to address 100h.

Like the general-purpose registers, each segment register plays a specific role. The CS register points to program code, the DS register points to data, the SS register points to the stack, and the ES segment is a wildcard ("extra") segment, free to point wherever it's needed. Let's look at the segment registers in a bit more detail.

The CS Register

The CS register points to the start of the 64 Kb memory block, or *code segment*, in which the next instruction to be executed resides. The next instruction to be executed resides at the offset specified by IP in the code segment; that is, at the segment:offset address CS:IP. The 8086 can never fetch an instruction from a segment other than that defined by CS.

The CS register can be changed by a number of instructions, including certain jumps, calls, and returns. The CS register cannot be loaded directly under any circumstances.

No memory-addressing modes or memory pointers other than IP normally operate relative to CS.

The DS Register

The DS register points to the start of the data segment, which is the 64K memory block where most memory operands reside. Normally, memory offsets involving BX, SI, or DI operate relative to DS, as do direct memory addresses. The data segment is, basically, what its name implies: the segment in which the current data set normally resides. Memory addressing is discussed further in Chapter 4, "The Basic Elements of an Assembler Program."

The ES Register

The ES register points to the start of a 64K memory block known as the *extra segment*. As the name implies, the extra segment isn't dedicated to any one purpose, but is available for whatever needs arise. Sometimes, the extra segment is used to make an additional 64K block of memory available for data storage, but accessing memory in the extra segment is normally less efficient than accessing memory in the data segment, as discussed in Chapter 10, "Advanced Programming in Turbo Assembler."

Where the extra segment really shines is when the string instructions are used. All string instructions that write to memory use ES:DI as the memory address to write to. This means that ES is extremely useful as the destination segment for block copies, string comparisons, memory scanning, and clearing blocks of memory. We'll look at the string instructions and the use of ES registers in connection with them in Chapter 5, "More About Programming in Turbo Assembler."

The SS Register

The SS register points to the start of the stack segment, which is the 64K memory block, where the stack resides. All instructions that implicitly use the SP register—including pushes, pops, calls, and returns—work in the stack segment because SP is *only* capable of addressing memory in the stack segment.

As we discussed earlier, the BP register also operates relative to the stack segment. This allows BP to be used for addressing parameters and variables that are stored on the stack. Again, we will discuss memory addressing in detail in the next chapter.

The 8086 Instruction Set

To a programmer, the key resource of the 8086 is the instruction set. As we discussed earlier, the instruction set includes all the actions that a programmer can possibly tell the 8086 to perform. The complete instruction set of Turbo Assembler is shown in Table 2.1 beginning on page 46.

Table 2.1: Turbo Assembler Instruction Set

Instruction	Processor	Instruction	Processor
ADD	All	SAL	All
OR	All	SHL	All
ADC	All	SAR	All
SBB	All	SHR	All
AND	All	RCL	All
SUB	All	RCR	All
XOR	All	AAA	All
CMP	All	AAS	All
XCHG	All	CBW	All
TEST	All	CWDE	386
MOV	All[1]	CLC	All
ESC	All	CLD	All
JMP	All	CLI	All
CALL	All	CMC	All
INT	All	CMPSB	All
INC	All	CMPSW	All
DEC	All	CMPSD	386
PUSH	All	CWD	All
POP	All	CDQ	386
AAD	All[2]	DAA	All
AAM	All[2]	DAS	All
IN	All	HLT	All
OUT	All	INTO	All
LEA	All	IRET	All
LDS	All	IRETD	386
LES	All	LAHF	All
LSS	386	LODSB	All
LFS	386	LODSW	All
LGS	386	LODSD	386
DIV	All	MOVSB	All
MUL	All	MOVSW	All
IDIV	All	MOVSD	386
IMUL	All[3]	NOP	All
NEG	All	POPF	All
NOT	All	POPFD	386
ROL	All	PUSHF	All
ROR	All	PUSHFD	386
SAHF	All	REPE	All
SCASB	All	REPZ	All

[1]Implements 386 special register moves
[2]Can be followed by any 8-bit immediate value x
[3]286 extensions

Table 2.1: Turbo Assembler Instruction Set (continued)

Instruction	Processor	Instruction	Processor
SCASW	All	REPNE	All
SCASD	386	REPNZ	All
STC	All	SEGCS	All[4]
STD	All	SEGDS	All[5]
STI	All	SEGSS	All[6]
STOSB	All	SEGES	All[7]
STOSW	All	SEGFS	386[8]
STOSD	386	SEGGS	386[9]
WAIT	All	RET	All
XLATB	All	RETN	All[10]
STOS	All	RETF	All[11]
SCAS	All	JA	All[12]
LODS	All	JNBE	All[12]
XLAT	All	JAE	All[12]
MOVS	All	JNB	All[12]
CMPS	All	JNC	All[12]
PUSHA	186-386	JB	All[12]
PUSHAD	386	JNAE	All[12]
POPA	186-386	JC	All[12]
POPAD	386	JBE	All[12]
LEAVE	186-386	JNA	All[12]
INSB	186-386	JE	All[12]
INSW	186-386	JZ	All[12]
INSD	386	JG	All[12]
OUTSB	186-386	JNLE	All[12]
OUTSW	186-386	JGE	All[12]
OUTSD	386	JNL	All[12]
INS	186-386	JL	All[12]
OUTS	186-386	JNGE	All[12]
BOUND	186-386	JLE	All[12]
ENTER	186-386	JNG	All[12]
LOCK	All	JNE	All[12]
REP	All	JNZ	All[12]
JNO	All[12]	SETA	386

[4]Generates CS override; can be followed by an instruction
[5]Generates DS override; can be followed by an instruction
[6]Generates SS override; can be followed by an instruction
[7]Generates ES override; can be followed by an instruction
[8]Generates FS override; can be followed by an instruction
[9]Generates GS override; can be followed by an instruction
[10]Explicit near return
[11]Explicit far return
[12]Accepts a near or far arg when JUMPS on

Instruction	Processor	Instruction	Processor
JNS	All[12]	SETAE	386
JNP	All[12]	SETB	386
JPO	All[12]	SETBE	386
JO	All[12]	SETC	386
JP	All[12]	SETE	386
JPE	All[12]	SETG	386
JS	All[12]	SETGE	386
LOOP	All[13]	SETL	386
LOOPE	All[14]	SETLE	386
LOOPZ	All[14]	SETNA	386
LOOPNE	All[14]	SETNAE	386
LOOPNZ	All[14]	SETNB	386
LOOPW	All[15]	SETNBE	386
LOOPWE	All[16]	SETNC	386
LOOPWZ	All[16]	SETNE	386
LOOPWNE	All[16]	SETNG	386
LOOPWNZ	All[16]	SETNGE	386
LOOPD	386[17]	SETNL	386
LOOPDE	386[17]	SETNLE	386
LOOPDZ	386[17]	SETNO	386
LOOPDNE	386[17]	SETNP	386
LOOPDNZ	386[17]	SETNS	386
JCXZ	All[18]	SETNZ	386
JECXZ	386[19]	SETO	386
BT	386	SETP	386
BTC	386	SETPE	386
BTR	386	SETS	386
BTS	386	SETZ	386
BSF	386		
BSR	386	ARPL	286p+386p
MOVSX	386	CLTS	286p+386p
MOVZX	386	LLDT	286p+386p
SHLD	386	LMSW	286p+386p
SHRD	386	LTR	286p+386p
SLDT	286p+386p	FXAM	8087-387
SMSW	286p+386p	FXTRACT	8087-387

[12] Accepts a near or far arg when JUMPS on
[13] Operand size of loop determined by segment size
[14] Similar to LOOP
[15] Operand size of loop is always a word (CX)
[16] Similar to LOOPW
[17] Operand size of loop is always a dword (ECX)
[18] Operand size of JCXZ is word (CX)
[19] Operand size of JECXZ is dword (ECX)

Instruction	Processor	Instruction	Processor
STR	286p+386p	FXAM	8087-387
VERR	286p+386p	FXTRACT	8087-387
VERW	286p+386p	FYL2X	8087-387
LGDT	286p+386p	FYL2XP1	8087-387
LIDT	286p+386p	FNCLEX	8087-387
SGDT	286p+386p	FNDISI	8087-387
SIDT	286p+386p	FNENI	8087-387
LAR	286p+386p	FNINIT	8087-387
LSL	286p+386p	FADDP	8087-387
FMULP	8087-387	FDIVP	8087-387
FADD	8087-387	FDIVRP	8087-387
FDIV	8087-387	FSUBP	8087-387
FDIVR	8087-387	FSUBRP	8087-387
FMUL	8087-387	FXCH	8087-387
FSUB	8087-387	FCOMPP	8087-387
FSUBR	8087-387	FFREE	8087-387
FCOM	8087-387	FIADD	8087-387
FCOMP	8087-387	FICOM	8087-387
FST	8087-387	FICOMP	8087-387
F2XM1	8087-387	FIDIV	8087-387
FABS	8087-387	FIDIVR	8087-387
FCHS	8087-387	FIMUL	8087-387
FCLEX	8087-387	FIST	8087-387
FDECSTP	8087-387	FISUB	8087-387
FDISI	8087-387	FISUBR	8087-387
FENI	8087-387	FLDCW	8087-387
FINCSTP	8087-387	FSTCW	8087-387
FINIT	8087-387	FSTSW	8087-387
FLD1	8087-387	FNSTCW	8087-387
FLDL2E	8087-387	FNSTSW	8087-387
FLDL2T	8087-387	FLDENV	8087-387
FLDLG2	8087-387	FRSTOR	8087-387
FLDLN2	8087-387	FSAVE	8087-387
FLDPI	8087-387	FSTENV	8087-387
FLDZ	8087-387	FNSAVE	8087-387
FNOP	8087-387	FNSTEVN	8087-387
FPATAN	8087-387	FLD	8087-387
FPREM	8087-387	FSTP	8087-387
FPTAN	8087-387	FILD	8087-387
FRNDINT	8087-387	FISTP	8087-387
FSCALE	8087-387	FBLD	8087-387
FSQRT	8087-387	FBSTP	8087-387
FIST	8087-387	FWAIT	8087-387
FSETPM	287-387	FCOS	387
FPREM1	387	FPREMI	387
FSIN	387	FSINCOS	387
FUCOM	387	FUCOMP	387
FUCOMPP	387		

As you can see, there are many instructions in the 8086 instruction set. These instructions perform a wide variety of actions, ranging from doing nothing (**NOP**) to copying as many as 65,535 bytes (**REP MOVSB**). We will spend much of the rest of this chapter, and chapters 4, 5, and 10 as well, covering the 8086's instruction set in detail.

The IBM PC and XT

We've focused on 8086 assembly language, but the truth of the matter is that the 8086 processor is just part of a computer system, and the hardware configuration and operating system of a computer greatly affect assembly language programming.

The vast majority of programs written for the 8086 processor (and perhaps the majority of programs written in the history of computers) have been written for the IBM PC and XT and compatible computers, running the MS-DOS operating system. Turbo Assembler itself runs under the MS-DOS operating system on IBM PCs, XTs, and compatibles (from now on referred to simply as the IBM PC), so it's likely that you're planning to use your copy of Turbo Assembler to develop assembler programs for the IBM PC environment.

Without knowledge of the hardware configuration and the operating system your assembler programs will run under, there's no way for you to perform input or output, or even terminate your programs. We haven't the space to cover nearly all the capabilities of the IBM PC and its system software, but we'll show you a few of the basic features of the PC. We suggest you read more on your own in the books and manuals suggested at the beginning of this chapter.

Input and Output Devices

All IBM PCs provide a keyboard, a display adapter and a monitor, and a floppy disk drive. Modems, printers, mice, and hard disks are frequently installed as well. Each of these devices is controlled with a fairly complex series of accesses to I/O ports or memory (or both). For example, selecting a new video mode on the Color Graphics Adapter (CGA) requires over 30 **OUT** instructions; keyboard, modem, and disk control sequences are more complicated still.

Does this mean that you need to master endless control sequences in order to write useful assembler programs on the IBM PC? Not at all; your PC's systems software already does most of the work for you.

Systems Software for the IBM PC Family

Systems software is software that serves as a control and interface layer between applications software, such as Turbo Assembler and Quattro, and the hardware of your computer, as shown in Figure 2.10.

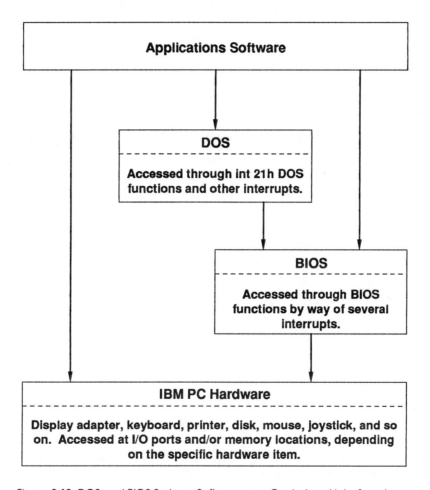

Figure 2.10: DOS and BIOS Systems Software as a Control and Interface Layer

In particular, systems software handles the complexities of interfacing to individual devices. For example, several hundred lines of assembly language code are required in order for your PC to process a single keystroke, but your assembler programs can get keystrokes by invoking just one system function. This is made possible by the two main systems software components of the PC: DOS and the BIOS (Basic Input/Output System).

As you can see in Figure 2.10 on page 51, the DOS and BIOS systems software serves as a control and interface layer between applications software and the hardware of the IBM PC. Applications software always has the option of controlling the hardware directly, but should use DOS or BIOS functions instead whenever possible.

DOS

DOS (short for Disk Operating System—also known as MS-DOS and PC-DOS) is the program that controls your computer from the moment it reads the disk at power-up until you turn the power off. DOS takes up part of your precious 640 Kb of available memory, but there's no helping that, since without DOS your PC is a very expensive paperweight. It's DOS that provides you with the A> prompt (or C>, or whatever the prompt is on your computer), and it's DOS that accepts and executes commands such as DIR.

That's just the visible part of DOS. It also provides a broad array of functions that are used heavily by just about every application. It's through DOS functions that applications read from and write to files, get keystrokes, allocate memory, run other programs, and even set and get the time of day. For example, the assembler code

```
        .
        .
        .
    mov  ah,2       ;DOS function to display a character
    mov  dl,'A'     ;A is the character to display
    int  21h        ;invoke DOS to execute the function
        .
        .
        .
```

invokes the DOS "Display Output" function in order to display the character *A* at the current cursor location on the screen.

You should use DOS functions to perform operations such as keyboard and file input, screen and file output, and printing whenever possible. Since DOS itself is actually nothing but an assembler program, it is certainly *possible* for you to do with your own code everything that DOS functions do, but that's generally not a good idea. Not all PC-compatible computers are alike, and DOS frequently masks differences between makes of computers; if you ignore the DOS functions and go straight to the hardware, your programs might not run on other computers.

Then, too, programs that go around DOS might not coexist with other programs, most notably memory-resident programs such as SideKick and SuperKey. Besides, why spend time writing extra code when DOS has already done the work for you? In short, whenever a DOS function can do what you need done, use it!

IBM's *DOS Technical Reference* manual is the primary reference for DOS functions.

In cases where DOS simply doesn't provide the functions you need, it's time to use a BIOS function. We'll cover BIOS functions shortly, but first let's take a look at some DOS functions that fulfill essential needs: input, output, and program termination.

Getting Keystrokes

Typing at the keyboard is the fundamental means of user interaction with the PC. DOS provides a number of functions by which an assembler program can obtain keystrokes; we're only going to discuss one of those functions.

Perhaps the simplest means of getting keystrokes is with the "Keyboard Input" function, DOS function number 1. DOS functions are invoked by placing the function number in AH and then executing an **INT 21h** instruction. (The actual operation of the **INT** instruction is a bit complex, but right now, all you need to know is that you must execute an **INT 21h** instruction each time you want to invoke a DOS function.) The next character typed at the keyboard is returned in AL.

For example, when this code is executed

```
    .
    .
    .
mov  ah,1
int  21h
    .
    .
    .
```

DOS places the next character typed at the keyboard into AL. Note that if there is no keystroke waiting to be read, DOS waits until a key is pressed, so this function can take an indefinitely long period of time to complete.

Displaying Characters on the Screen

If keystrokes are the means of user interaction with software, the screen is the complement. The PC is capable of all sorts of displays, ranging from color text to high-resolution graphics, but for the moment, we'll just go over displaying characters.

DOS function number 2 is a straightforward way to print a character. Simply put 2 in AH and the character in DL, then invoke DOS with **INT 21h**. The following code echoes each character typed to the screen:

```
    .
    .
    .
mov  ah,1
int  21h         ;get next key pressed
mov  ah,2
mov  dl,al       ;move character read from AL to DL
int  21h         ;display the character
    .
    .
    .
```

Several other functions are available for reading and printing characters and character strings, and you'll encounter some of them in the example programs in this manual. Since a whole book would be needed to cover all the DOS functions, we can't cover them here. We strongly recommend, however, that you do get one or more of the books and manuals listed at the end of this book and learn more about the DOS functions—they're a key resource in assembler programming.

There's one more point we'd like to make about keyboard, screen, and file input and output in assembly language. Those of you who are used to **scanf** and **printf** in C and *Readln* and *Writeln* in Pascal might be surprised to learn that DOS (and hence assembly language) provides no support whatsoever for formatted input and output; DOS only handles character and string input and output. In C, all you need to do to print an integer variable *i* is this:

```
printf("%d\n",i);
```

C automatically converts the integer value, which is stored in a 16-bit memory location, into a string of ASCII characters and prints the characters. In assembler, your code must explicitly convert variables to character strings before displaying them. Likewise, DOS only knows how to read characters and strings from the keyboard, so you'll have to write code to convert characters and strings entered by the user to other data types in your assembler programs.

At the end of the next chapter, we'll show you an example program that illustrates exactly what you have to do in an assembler program to print out the value of a variable. For now, bear in mind that DOS functions can print a character, or a string of characters—and that's it. It's up to you to convert your data to the character form that DOS can handle.

Ending a Program

Now that you know a bit about reading and writing a program, let's write a simple program that does nothing but echo one line of keystrokes to the screen. You know all the DOS functions you'll need, save one: You have no way to end the program once it's finished executing.

Again, those of you familiar with C or Pascal might think that assembler programs would simply end when they come to the end of the main program, but that's not the case. You must explicitly invoke a DOS function in order to terminate your assembler programs.

There are several DOS functions for terminating programs, but the preferred method is to execute a DOS function number 4Ch (that's 76, for those of you who prefer decimal). With that knowledge, here's the complete echo program:

```
        .STACK 100h
        .MODEL small
        .CODE
EchoLoop:
    mov  ah,1              ;DOS keyboard input function #
    int  21h               ;get the next key
    cmp  al,13             ;was the key the Enter key?
    jz   EchoDone          ;yes, so we're done echoing
    mov  dl,al             ;put the character into DL
    mov  ah,2              ;DOS display output function
    int  21h               ;display the character
    jmp  EchoLoop          ;echo the next character
EchoDone:
    mov  ah,4ch            ;DOS terminate program function #
    int  21h               ;terminate the program
    END
```

Enter the program exactly as shown and run it. You'll see that each character you type appears twice; once when it is echoed by DOS as it's typed, and once as your program echoes it. The important point about this program is that it reads keystrokes, writes characters to the display, and terminates, all by way of DOS functions.

The BIOS

Sometimes DOS functions just don't meet your needs; then it's time to turn to the PC's Basic Input/Output System, or BIOS. Unlike DOS and applications software, the BIOS is not loaded from disk and does not take up any of your 640 Kb of available memory; instead, the BIOS is stored in Read-Only Memory (ROM) in the portion of the 8086's address space reserved for system functions.

The BIOS is the lowest-level software in the PC; even DOS uses BIOS functions to control the hardware. It's better to use BIOS functions than to control hardware directly, since, like DOS, the BIOS can mask differences between various computers and devices. On the other hand, you should use DOS functions rather than BIOS functions whenever you can, since programs that use the BIOS can conflict with other programs, and tend to be less portable across a variety of computer models.

Selecting Display Modes

The most pressing reason to use the BIOS is for controlling the display, since DOS provides virtually no support for the rich display capabilities of the PC. Only by invoking BIOS functions can you set the screen mode, control colors, get display adapter information, and so on. For example, the following code invokes the BIOS to set the screen to four-color graphics mode on a CGA:

```
        .
        .
        .
    mov  ah,0      ;BIOS set mode function #
    mov  al,4      ;mode number for 320x200 4-color graphics
    int  10h       ;execute BIOS video interrupt to set mode
        .
        .
        .
```

If you recall that we said that over 30 **OUT** instructions are required to set a video mode, you'll realize that the BIOS "Set Mode" function saves you a great deal of work.

The BIOS provides a variety of functions other than those related to display control, including keystroke-handling and disk control. In general, however, you're better off performing these tasks through DOS functions.

IBM's *BIOS Interface Technical Reference* manual is the primary reference for BIOS functions.

Sometimes You Absolutely Need to Go to the Hardware

Now that you've heard all the reasons to use DOS functions (or, if absolutely necessary, BIOS functions), it's time to admit that sometimes you just flat-out have to access the hardware directly. For instance, communications software has to control the PC's serial port directly with **IN** and **OUT** instructions, since neither DOS nor the BIOS provides adequate support for serial communications. Similarly, high-performance graphics must be performed by accessing display memory directly, since DOS doesn't support graphics, and the BIOS does so only in a painfully slow manner.

The basic rule about going to the hardware is to make sure you have no alternative. If there's a DOS or BIOS function you can use, use it; if not, access the hardware directly. After all, the object of programming is to produce useful programs, not to follow rules. On the other hand, the fewer rules you break, the fewer problems you'll generally have.

Other Resources

The PC provides a number of other hardware and software resources for the assembly language programmer. We can't go into those resources here, but we can list a few; for more information, refer to the materials mentioned at the start of this chapter.

- The ANSI.SYS driver provides enhanced display control without the need for BIOS functions.
- The system timers support a time-of-day clock; they also support sound-generation via the PC's speaker and precision timing.
- The optional 8087 numeric coprocessor speeds up floating-point calculations by orders of magnitude.

3

Command-Line Reference

This chapter is dedicated to familiarizing you with Turbo Assembler's command-line options. We'll describe each of the command-line options you can use to alter the assembler's behavior, then show how and when to use command files. Finally, we describe the configuration file.

Starting Turbo Assembler from DOS

Turbo Assembler has a very powerful and flexible command-line syntax. If you start Turbo Assembler without giving it any arguments, like this,

```
TASM
```

you'll get a screenful of help describing many of the command-line options and the syntax for specifying the files you want to assemble. Figure 3.1 shows you how this looks.

```
Turbo Assembler Version 1.0  Copyright (C) 1988 by Borland International, Inc.

Usage:  TASM [options] source [,object] [,listing] [,xref]
/a,/s          Alphabetic or Source-code segment ordering
/c             Generate cross-reference in listing
/dSYM[=VAL]    Define symbol SYM = 0, or = value VAL
/e,/r          Emulated or Real floating-point instructions
/h,/?          Print this help screen
/iPATH         Search PATH for include files
/jCMD          Jam in a assembler directive CMD (eg. /jIDEAL)
/kh#,/ks#      Hash table capacity #, String space capacity #
/l,/la         Generate listing: l=normal listing, la=expanded listing
/ml,/mx,/mu    Case sensitivity on symbols: ml=all, mx=globals, mu=none
/n             Suppress symbol tables in listing
/p             Check for code segment overrides in protected mode
/t             Suppress messages if successful assembly
/w0,/w1,/w2    Set warning level: w0=none, w1=w2=warnings on
/w-xxx,/w+xxx  Disable (-) or enable (+) warning xxx
/x             Include false conditionals in listing
/z             Display source line with error message
/zi,/zd        Symbolic debug info: zi=full, zd=line numbers only
```

Figure 3.1: Turbo Assembler Command Line

With the command-line options, you can specify the name of one or more files that you want to assemble, as well as any options that control how the files get assembled.

The general form of the command line looks like this:

```
TASM fileset [; fileset]...
```

The semicolon (;) after the left bracket ([) allows you to assemble multiple groups of files on one command line by separating the file groups. If you prefer, you can set different options for each set of files; for example,

```
TASM /e FILE1; /a FILE2
```

assembles FILE1.ASM with the */e* command-line option and assembles file FILE2.ASM with the */a* command-line option.

In the general form of the command line, *fileset* can be

```
[option]... sourcefile [[+] sourcefile]...
          [,[objfile] [, [listfile], [, [xreffile]]]]
```

This syntax shows that a group of files can start off with any options you want to apply to those files, followed by the files you want to assemble. A file name can be a single file name, or it can use the normal DOS wildcard characters * and ? to specify multiple files to assemble. If your file name does not have an extension, Turbo Assembler adds the .ASM extension. For example, to assemble all the .ASM files in the current directory, you would type

    TASM *

If you want to assemble multiple files, you can separate their names with the plus sign (+):

    TASM MYFILE1 + MYFILE2

You can follow the file name you want to assemble by an optional object file name, listing file name, and a cross-reference file name. If you do not specify an object file or listing file, Turbo Assembler creates an object file with the same name as the source file and an extension of .OBJ.

A listing file is not generated unless you explicitly request one. To request one, place a comma after the object file name, followed by a listing file name. If you don't explicitly provide a listing file name, Turbo Assembler creates a listing file with the same name as the source file and the extension .LST. If you supply a listing file name without an extension, .LST is appended to it.

A cross-reference file is not generated unless you explicitly request one. To request one, place a comma after the listing file name, followed by a cross-reference file name. If you don't explicitly provide a cross-reference file name, Turbo Assembler creates a cross-reference file with the same name as the source file and the extension .XRF. If you supply a cross-reference file name without an extension, .XRF is appended to it. See Appendix D in the *Reference Guide* for a discussion of how to process cross-reference files with the global cross-reference utility (TCREF).

If you want to accept the default object file name and also request a listing file, you must supply the comma that separates the object file name from the listing file name:

    TASM FILE1,,TEST

This assembles FILE1.ASM to FILE1.OBJ and creates a listing file named TEST.LST.

If you want to accept the default object and listing file names and also request a cross-reference file, you must supply the commas that separate the file names:

    TASM MYFILE,,,MYXREF

This assembles file MYFILE.ASM to MYFILE.OBJ, with a listing in file MYFILE.LST and a cross-reference in MYXREF.XRF.

If you use wildcards to specify the source files to assemble, you can also use wildcards to indicate the object and listing file names. For example, if your current directory contains XX1.ASM and XX2.ASM, the command line

```
TASM XX*,YY*
```

assembles all the files that start with *XX*, generates object files that start with *YY*, and derives the remainder of the name from the source file name. The resulting object files are therefore called YY1.OBJ and YY2.OBJ.

If you don't want an object file but you do want a listing file, or if you want a cross-reference file but don't want a listing file or object file, you can specify the null device (NUL) as the file name. For example,

```
TASM FILE1,,NUL,
```

assembles file FILE1.ASM to object file FILE1.OBJ, doesn't produce a listing file, and creates a cross-reference file FILE1.XRF.

Command-Line Options

The command-line options let you control the behavior of the assembler, and how it outputs information to the screen, listing, and object file. Turbo Assembler provides you with some options that produce no action, but are accepted for compatibility with the current and previous versions of MASM:

/b   Sets buffer size
/v   Displays extra statistics

You can enter options using any combination of uppercase and lowercase letters. You can also enter your options in any order except where you have multiple **/i** or **/j** options; these are processed in sequence. When using the **/d** option, you must also be careful to define symbols before using them in subsequent **/d** options.

Note: You can override command-line options by using conflicting directives in your source code.

Figure 3.1 on page 60 summarizes the Turbo Assembler command-line options; here's a detailed description of each option.

/a

Function	Specifies alphabetical segment-ordering
Syntax	/a
Remarks	The **/a** option tells Turbo Assembler to place segments in the object file in alphabetical order. This is the same as using the **.ALPHA** directive in your source file.

You usually only have to use this option if you want to assemble a source file that was written for very early versions of the IBM or Microsoft assemblers.

The **/s** option reverses the effect of this option by returning to the default sequential segment-ordering.

If you specify sequential segment-ordering with the **.SEQ** directive in your source file, it will override any **/a** you provide on the command line.

Example	TASM /a TEST1

This command line creates an object file, TEST1.OBJ, that has its segments in alphabetical order.

/b

Syntax	/b
Remarks	The **/b** option is included for compatibility. It does nothing and has no effect on the assembly.

/c

Function	Enables cross-reference in listing file
Syntax	/c
Remarks	The **/c** option enables cross-reference information in the listing file. Turbo Assembler adds the cross-reference information to the symbol table at the end of the listing file. This means that, in order to see the cross-reference information, you must either explicitly specify a listing

file on the command line or use the /l option to enable the listing file.

For each symbol, the cross-reference shows the line on which it is defined and all lines that refer to it.

Example   TASM /l /c TEST1

This code creates a listing file that also has cross-reference information in the symbol table.

/d

Function   Defines a symbol

Syntax   /dsymbol[=value or expression]

Remarks   The **/d** option defines a symbol for your source file, exactly as if it were defined on the first line of your file with the = directive. You can use this option as many times as you want on the command line.

You can only define a symbol as being equal to another symbol or a constant value. You can't use an expression with operators to the right of the equal sign (=). For example, /dX=9 and /dX=Y are allowed, but /dX=Y-4 is not allowed.

Example   TASM /dMAX=10 /dMIN=2 TEST1

This command line defines two symbols, **MAX** and **MIN**, that other statements in the source file TEST1.ASM can refer to.

/e

Function   Generates floating-point emulator instructions

Syntax   /e

Remarks   The **/e** option tells Turbo Assembler to generate floating-point instructions that will be executed by a software floating-point emulator. Use this option if your program contains a floating-point emulation library that mimics the functions of the 80x87 numeric coprocessor.

Normally, you would only use this option if your assembler module is part of a program written in a high-level language that uses a floating-point emulation library. (Turbo C, Turbo Pascal, Turbo Basic, and Turbo Prolog all support floating-point emulation.) You can't just link an assembler program with the emulation library, since the library expects to have been initialized by the compiler's startup code.

The **/r** option reverses the effect of this option by enabling the assembly of real floating-point instructions that can only be executed by a numeric coprocessor.

If you use the **NOEMUL** directive in your source file, it will override the **/e** option on the command line.

The **/e** command-line option has the same effect as using the **EMUL** directive at the start of your source file, and is also the same as using the **/jEMUL** command-line option.

Example

```
TASM /e SECANT
TCC -f TRIG.C SECANT.OBJ
```

The first command line assembles a module with emulated floating-point instructions. The second command line compiles a C source module with floating-point emulation and then links it with the object file from the assembler.

/h or /?

Function Displays a help screen

Syntax /h or /?

Remarks The **/h** option tells Turbo Assembler to display a help screen that describes the command-line syntax. This includes a list of the options, as well as the various file names you can supply. The **/?** option does the same thing.

Example `TASM /h`

/i

Function	Sets an Include file path
Syntax	/iPATH
Remarks	The /i option lets you tell Turbo Assembler where to look for files that are included in your source file by using the **INCLUDE** directive. You can place more than one /i option on the command line (the number is only limited by RAM).

When Turbo Assembler encounters an **INCLUDE** directive, the location where it searches for the Include file is determined by whether the file name in the **INCLUDE** directive has a directory path or is just a simple file name.

If you supply a directory path as part of the file name, that path is tried first, then Turbo Assembler searches the directories specified by /i command-line options in the order they appear on the command line. It then looks in any directories specified by /i options in a configuration file.

If you don't supply a directory path as part of the file name, Turbo Assembler searches first in the directories specified by /i command-line options, then it looks in any directories specified by /i options in a configuration file, and finally it looks in the current directory.

Example   TASM /i\INCLUDE /iD:\INCLUDE TEST1

If the source file contains the statement

    INCLUDE MYMACS.INC

Turbo Assembler will first look for \INCLUDE\ MYMACS.INC, then it will look for D:\INCLUDE\ MYMACS.INC. If it still hasn't found the file, it will look for MYMACS.INC in the current directory. If the statement in your source file had been

    INCLUDE INCS\MYMACS.INC

Turbo Assembler would first look for INCS\ MYMACS.INC and then it would look for \INCLUDE\ MYMACS.INC, and finally for D:\INCLUDE\ MYMACS.INC.

/j

Function	Defines an assembler startup directive
Syntax	`/jdirective`
Remarks	The **/j** option lets you specify a directive that will be assembled before the first line of the source file. *directive* can be any Turbo Assembler directive that does not take any arguments, such as **.286**, **IDEAL**, **%MACS**, **NOJUMPS**, and so on. See Chapter 3 in the *Reference Guide* for a complete description of all Turbo Assembler directives.
	You can put more than one **/j** option on the command line; they will be processed from left to right across the command line.
Example	`TASM /j.286 /jIDEAL TEST1`
	This code assembles the file TEST1.ASM with 80286 instructions enabled and Ideal mode expression-parsing enabled.

/kh

Function	Sets the maximum number of symbols allowed
Syntax	`/khnsymbols`
Remarks	The **/kh** option sets the maximum number of symbols that your program can contain. If you don't use this option, your program can only have up to 8,192 symbols; using this option increases the number of symbols to *nsymbols*, up to a maximum of 32,768.
	Use this option if you get the `Out of hash space` message when assembling your program.
	You can also use this option to reduce the total number of symbols below the default 8,192. This will release some memory that can be used when you are trying to assemble a program but don't have enough available memory.
Example	`TASM /kh10000 BIGFILE`

This command tells Turbo Assembler to reserve space for 10,000 symbols when assembling the file BIGFILE.

/ks

Function	Sets the maximum size of Turbo Assembler's string space
Syntax	`/kskbytes`
Remarks	Usually the string size is determined automatically and does not need to be adjusted. However, if you have a source file that results in an `Out of string space` message, you might want to increase the string space size by using this option. Try starting with a value of 100, and increase it until your program assembles without error. The maximum allowable value for *kbytes* is 255.
Example	`TASM /ks150 SFILE`

This tells Turbo Assembler to reserve 150K of string space.

/l

Function	Generates a listing file
Syntax	`/l`
Remarks	The /l option indicates that you want a listing file, even if you did not explicitly specify it on the command line. The listing file will have the same name as the source file, with an extension of .LST.
Example	`TASM /l TEST1`

This command line requests a listing file that will be named TEST1.LST.

/la

Function	Shows high-level interface code in listing file
Syntax	/la
Remarks	The **/la** option tells Turbo Assembler to show all generated code in the listing file, including the code that gets generated as a result of the high-level language interface **.MODEL** directive.
Example	TASM /la FILE1

/ml

Function	Treats symbols as case-sensitive
Syntax	/ml
Remarks	The **/ml** option tells Turbo Assembler to treat all symbol names as case-sensitive. Normally, uppercase and lowercase letters are considered equivalent so that the names *ABCxyz*, *abcxyz*, and *ABCXYZ* would all refer to the same symbol. If you specify the **/ml** option, these three symbols will be treated as distinct. Even when you specify **/ml**, you can still enter any assembler keyword in uppercase or lowercase. Keywords are the symbols built into the assembler that have special meanings, such as instruction mnemonics, directives, and operators.
Example	TASM /ml TEST1

where TEST1.ASM contains the following statements:

```
abc DW 0
ABC DW 1          ;not a duplicate symbol
    Mov Ax,[Bp]   ;mixed case OK in keywords
```

/mu

Function	Converts symbols to uppercase
Syntax	/mu
Remarks	The **/mu** option tells Turbo Assembler to ignore the case of all symbols. By default, Turbo Assembler specifies that any lowercase letters in symbols will be converted to uppercase unless you change it by using the **/ml** directive.
Example	TASM /mu TEST1

makes sure that all symbols will be converted to uppercase (which is the default):

```
EXTRN myfunc:NEAR
call myfunc         ;don't know if declared as
                    ; MYFUNC, Myfunc,...
```

/mx

Function	Makes public and external symbols case-sensitive
Syntax	/mx
Remarks	The **/mx** option tells Turbo Assembler to treat only external and public symbols as case-sensitive. All other symbols used (within the source file) will be treated as uppercase.

You should use this directive when you call routines in other modules that were compiled or assembled so that case-sensitivity is preserved; for example, modules compiled by Turbo C.

Example	TASM /mx TEST1;

where TEST1.ASM contains the following source lines:

```
EXTRN Cfunc:NEAR
myproc PROC NEAR
call  Cfunc
    .
    .
    .
```

/n

Function	Suppresses symbol table in listing file
Syntax	/n
Remarks	The **/n** option indicates that you don't want the usual symbol table at the end of the listing file. Normally, a complete symbol table listing appears at the end of the file, showing all symbols, their types, and their values.
	You must specify a listing file, either explicitly on the command line or by using the **/l** option; otherwise, **/n** will have no effect.
Example	TASM /l /n TEST1
	This code generates a listing file showing the generated code only, and not the value of your symbols.

/p

Function	Checks for impure code in protected mode
Syntax	/p
Remarks	The **/p** option specifies that you want to be warned about any instructions that generate "impure" code in protected mode. Instructions that move data into memory by using a **CS:** override in protected mode are considered impure because they might not work correctly unless you take special measures.
	You only need to use this option if you are writing a program that runs on the 80286 or 80386 in protected mode.
Example	TASM /p TEST1
	where TEST1.ASM contains the following statements:

```
      .286P
CODE SEGMENT
temp DW  ?
     mov CS:temp,0   ;impure in protected mode
```

/r

Function	Generates real floating-point instructions
Syntax	/r
Remarks	The **/r** option tells Turbo Assembler to generate real floating-point instructions (instead of generating emulated floating-point instructions). Use this option if your program is going to run on machines equipped with an 80x87 numeric coprocessor.

The **/e** option reverses the effect of this option in generating emulated floating-point instructions.

If you use the **EMUL** directive in your source file, it will override the **/r** option on the command line.

The **/r** command-line option has the same effect as using the **NOEMUL** directive at the start of your source file, and is also the same as using the **/jNOEMUL** command-line option.

Example	TASM /r SECANT TPC /$N+ /$E- TRIG.PAS

The first command line assembles a module with real floating-point instructions. The second compiles a Pascal source module with real floating-point instructions that links in the object file from the assembler.

/s

Function	Specifies sequential segment-ordering
Syntax	/s
Remarks	The **/s** option tells Turbo Assembler to place segments in the object file in the order in which Turbo Assembler encountered them in the source file. By default, Turbo Assembler uses segment-ordering, unless you change it by placing an **/a** option in the configuration file.

If you specify alphabetical segment-ordering in your source file with the **.ALPHA** directive, it will override the **/s** you put on the command line.

Example	TASM /s TEST1

This code creates an object file (TEST1.OBJ) that has its segments ordered exactly as they were specified in the source file.

/t

Function	Suppresses messages on successful assembly
Syntax	/t
Remarks	The /t option stops any display by Turbo Assembler unless warning or error messages result from the assembly.
	You can use this option when you are assembling many modules, and you only want warning or error messages to be displayed onscreen.
Example	TASM /t TEST1

/v

Syntax	/v
Remarks	The /v option is included for compatibility. It does nothing and has no effect on the assembly.

/w

Function	Controls the generation of warning messages
Syntax	/w w-[*warnclass*] w+[*warnclass*]
Remarks	The /w option controls which warning messages are emitted by Turbo Assembler.
	If you specify /w by itself, "mild" warnings are enabled. Mild warnings merely indicate that you can improve some aspect of your code's efficiency.
	If you specify /w- without *warnclass*, all warnings are disabled. If you follow /w- with *warnclass*, only that warning is disabled. Each warning message has a three-letter identifier:

ALN	Segment alignment
ASS	Assuming segment is 16-bit
BRK	Brackets needed
ICG	Inefficient code generation
LCO	Location counter overflow
OPI	Open IF conditional
OPP	Open procedure
OPS	Open segment
OVF	Arithmetic overflow
PDC	Pass-dependent construction
PQK	Assuming constant for [const] warning
PRO	Write-to memory in protected mode needs CS override
RES	Reserved word warning
TPI	Turbo Pascal illegal warning

If you specify /w+ without *warnclass*, all warnings are enabled. If you specify /w+ with *warnclass* from the preceding list, only that warning will be enabled.

By default, Turbo Assembler first starts assembling your file with all warnings enabled except the inefficient code-generation (ICG) and the write-to-memory in protected mode (PRO) warnings.

You can use the **WARN** and **NOWARN** directives within your source file to control whether a particular warning is allowed for a certain range of source lines. See Chapter 3 in the *Reference Guide* for more information on these directives.

Example

```
TASM /w TEST1
```

The following statement in TEST1.ASM will issue a warning message that would not have appeared without the /w option:

```
mov bx,ABC      ;inefficient code generation warning
ABC = 1
```

With the command line

```
TASM /w-OVF TEST2
```

no warnings will be generated if TEST2.ASM contains

```
dw   1000h * 20h
```

/x

Function	Includes false conditionals in listing
Syntax	/x
Remarks	If a conditional **IF**, **IFNDEF**, **IFDEF**, and so forth evaluates to False, the **/x** option causes the statements inside the conditional block to appear in the listing file. This option also causes the conditional directives themselves to be listed; normally they are not.
	You must specify a listing file on the command line or via the **/l** option, otherwise **/x** will have no effect.
	You can use the **.LFCOND**, **.SFCOND**, and **.TFCOND** directives to override the effects of the **/x** option.
Example	TASM /x TEST1

/z

Function	Displays source lines along with error messages
Syntax	/z
Remarks	The **/z** option tells Turbo Assembler to display the corresponding line from the source file when an error message is generated. The line that caused the error is displayed before the error message. With this option disabled, Turbo Assembler just displays a message that describes the error.
Example	TASM /z TEST1

/zd

Function	Enables line number information in object files
Syntax	/zd
Remarks	The **/zd** option causes Turbo Assembler to place line-number information in the object file. This lets Borland's stand-alone debugger, Turbo Debugger, display the current location in your source code, but does not put the information in the object file that would allow the debugger to access your data items.

If you run out of memory when trying to debug your program under Turbo Debugger, you can use **/zd** for some modules and **/zi** for others. |
| **Example** | TASM /zd TEST1 |

/zi

Function	Enables debug information in object file
Syntax	/zi
Remarks	The **/zi** option tells Turbo Assembler to output complete debugging information to the object file. This includes line number records to synchronize source code display and data type information to allow you to examine and modify your program's data.

The **/zi** option lets you use all the features of Turbo Debugger to step through your program and examine or change your data items. You can use **/zi** on all your program's modules, or just on those you're interested in debugging. Since the **/zi** switch adds information to the object and executable programs, you might not want to use it on all your modules if you run out of memory when running a program under Turbo Debugger. |
| **Example** | TASM /zi TEST1 |

Indirect Command Files

At any point when entering a command line, Turbo Assembler lets you specify an *indirect* command file by preceding its name with an "at" sign (@). For example,

```
TASM /dTESTMODE @MYPROJ.TA
```

causes the contents of the file MYPROJ.TA to become part of the command line, exactly as if you had typed in its contents directly.

This useful feature lets you put your most frequently used command lines and file lists in a separate file. And you don't have to place your entire command line in one indirect file, since you can use more than one indirect file on the command line and can also mix indirect command files with normal arguments; for example,

```
TASM @MYFILES @IOLIBS /dBUF=1024
```

This way you can keep long lists of standard files and options in files, so that you can quickly and easily alter the behavior of an individual assembly run.

You can either put all your file names and options on a single line in the command file or you can split them across as many lines as you want.

The Configuration File

Turbo Assembler also lets you put your most frequently used options into a configuration file in the current directory. If running on DOS 3.x or later, it will also look in the directory that TASM was loaded from. This way, when you run Turbo Assembler, it will look for a file called TASM.CFG in your current directory. If Turbo Assembler finds the file, it will treat the file as an indirect file and process it before anything else on the command line.

This is helpful when you have all the source files for a project in a single directory and you know that, for example, you always want to assemble with emulated floating-point instructions (the /e option). You can place that option in the TASM.CFG file, so you don't have to specify that option each time you start Turbo Assembler.

The contents of the configuration file have exactly the same format as an indirect file. The file can contain any valid command-line options, on as many lines as you want. The options are treated as if they all appeared on one line.

The contents of the configuration file are processed before any arguments on the command line. This lets you override any options set in the configuration file by simply placing an option with the opposite effect on the command line. For example, if your configuration file contains

```
/a /e
```

and if you invoke Turbo Assembler with

```
TASM /s /r MYFILE
```

where MYFILE is your program file, your file will be assembled with sequential segment-ordering (**/s**) and real floating-point instructions (**/r**), even though the configuration file contained the **/a** and **/e** options that specified alphabetical segment-ordering and emulated floating-point instructions.

The Basic Elements of an Assembler Program

Now that you understand what it is that makes assembly language unique, you're ready to tackle the nuts and bolts of assembler programming.

You'll spend this chapter learning about the fundamental components of an assembler program. First, we'll teach you about the minimum requirements of a working assembler program. Next, we'll discuss the various components of a line, and the ways in which they can be combined. Along the way, you'll learn a good bit about instructions, directives, and the ways in which assembler programs can access memory. You'll find out how segments are defined and used in Turbo Assembler, and you'll look at the allocation and initialization of memory variables. Finally, we'll look at some commonly used instructions.

That's a lot of ground to cover, but when you're done with this chapter, you'll know enough to start writing programs. You can put that knowledge to work with a word-counting program provided at the end of the chapter.

Still, this chapter only begins to explore the many aspects of assembly language, so Chapter 5, "More About Programming in Turbo Assembler," and Chapter 10, "Advanced Programming in Turbo Assembler," continue on to new assembly language topics.

The Components and Structure of an Assembler Program

Now that you've developed an understanding of what 8086 assembly language is, you're ready to start writing assembler programs. Let's start by looking at the minimum requirements of a working assembler program. Even a simple assembler program requires quite a few lines. For instance, consider the following program:

```
        .MODEL  small                       ;near code and data models
        .STACK  200h                        ;512-byte stack
        .DATA                               ;start of the data segment
DisplayString  DB   13,10                   ;carriage-return/linefeed pair
                                            ; to start a new line
ThreeChars     DB   3 DUP (?)               ;storage for three characters
                                            ; typed at the keyboard
               DB   '$'                     ;a trailing "$" to tell DOS when
                                            ; to stop printing DisplayString
                                            ; when function 9 is executed
        .CODE                               ;start of the code segment
Begin:
        mov ax,@data
        mov ds,ax                           ;point DS to the data segment
        mov bx,OFFSET ThreeChars            ;point to the storage location
                                            ; for first character
        mov ah,1                            ;DOS keyboard input function #
        int 21h                             ;get the next key pressed
        dec al                              ;subtract 1 from the character
        mov [bx],al                         ;store the modified character
        inc bx                              ;point to the storage location
                                            ; for the next character
        int 21h                             ;get the next key pressed
        dec al                              ;subtract 1 from the character
        mov [bx],al                         ;store the modified character
        inc bx                              ;point to the storage location
                                            ; for the next character
        int 21h                             ;get the next key pressed
        dec al                              ;subtract 1 from the character
        mov [bx],al                         ;store the modified character
        mov dx,OFFSET DisplayString         ;point to the string of
                                            ; modified characters
        mov ah,9                            ;DOS print string function #
        int 21h                             ;print the modified characters
        mov ah,4ch                          ;DOS end program function #
        int 21h                             ;end the program
```

```
END  Begin                    ;directive to mark the end of the source
                              ; code and to indicate where to start
                              ; execution when the program is run
```

This program contains the simplified segment directives **.MODEL**, **.STACK**, **.DATA**, and **.CODE**, as well as the **END** directive. Segment directives, either simplified or standard, are required in every assembler program in order to define and control segment usage, and the **END** directive must always terminate assembler code. We'll cover both segment directives and **END** in this chapter, and some other directives as well.

Directives only provide the framework for an assembler program, though; you also need lines in your source code that actually *do* something, lines like

```
mov  [bx],al
```

and

```
inc  dx
```

These are instruction mnemonics, corresponding to the instruction set of the 8086 that you learned about in the last chapter. Before you can use either instructions or directives, however, you must first learn about the format of a line of assembler code, which we'll get to right after a cursory look at Turbo Assembler's reserved words.

In case you were wondering what the first example program does, enter it, type in IBM, and the program will respond

```
HAL
```

The program reads three characters, subtracts the value 1 from each of them, and prints the result.

Reserved Words

Turbo Assembler reserved words, or keywords, are strictly for use by the assembler. The words listed in Table 4.1 include operators (**+**, __*__, **−**, **+**), directives (**.386, ASSUME, MASM, QUIRKS**), and predefined symbols (**??time, ??version, @WordSize**), which are like predefined equates, and aliases.

Since reserved words have a special meaning to the assembler, you can't use them for defining your own equates or labels, or procedure names; rather, you should think of reserved words as the building blocks of assembly language.

Table 4.1: TASM Reserved Words

:	DATASEG	@fardata?	MODEL	QWORD
:	@datasize	.FARDATA?	.MODEL	RADIX
=	??date	@filename	MULTERRS	.RADIX
?	DB	??filename	NAME	RECORD
[]	DD	FWORD	NE	REPT
/	%DEPTH	GE	NEAR	.SALL
()	DF	GLOBAL	%NEWPAGE	SEG
+	DISPLAY	GROUP	%NOCONDS	SEGMENT
–	DOSSEG	GT	%NOCREF	.SEQ
*	DP	HIGH	%NOCTLS	.SFCOND
	DQ	IDEAL	NOEMUL	SHL
.186	DT	IF	%NOINCL	SHORT
.286	DUP	IF1	NOJUMPS	SHR
.286C	DW	IF2	%NOLIST	SIZE
.286P	DWORD	IFB	NOLOCALS	SIZESTR
.287	ELSE	IFDEF	%NOMACS	SMALL
.386	ELSEIF	IFDIF	NOMASM51	STACK
.386C	EMUL	IFDIFI	NOMULTERRS	.STACK
.387	END	IFE	%NOSYMS	STRUC
.8086	ENDIF	IFIDN	NOT	SUBSTR
.8087	ENDM	IFIDNI	NOTHING	SUBTTL
ALIGN	ENDP	IFNB	%NOTRUNC	%SUBTTL
.ALPHA	ENDS	IFNDEF	NOWARN	%SYMS
AND	EQ	%INCL	OFFSET	SYMTYPE
ARG	EQU	INCLUDE	OR	%TABSIZE
ASSUME	ERR	INCLUDELIB	ORG	TBYTE
%BIN	.ERR	INSTR	%OUT	%TEXT
BYTE	.ERR1	IRP	P186	.TFCOND
CATSTR	.ERR2	IRPC	P286	THIS
@code	.ERRB	JUMPS	P286N	??time
CODESEG	.ERRDEF	LABEL	P287	TITLE
@CodeSize	ERRDIF	.LALL	P386	%TITLE
COMM	ERRDIFI	LARGE	P386N	%TRUNC
COMMENT	ERRE	LE	P386P	TYPE
%CONDS	ERRIDN	LENGTH	P387	.TYPE
.CONST	ERRIDNI	.LFCOND	P8086	UDATASEG
CONST	ERRIFNB	%LINUM	P8087	UFARDATA
@Cpu	ERRIFNDEF	%LIST	PAGE	UNION
%CREF	ERRNB	.LIST	%PAGESIZE	UNKNOWN
.CREF	ERRNDEF	LOCAL	%PCNT	USES
%CREFALL	ERRNZ	LOCALS	PNO87	??version
%CREFREF	EVEN	LOW	%POPLCTL	WARN
%CREFUREF	EVENDATA	LT	PROC	WIDTH
%CTLS	EXITM	MACRO	PTR	WORD
@curseg	EXTRN	%MACS	PUBLIC	@WordSize
@data	FAR	MASK	PURGE	.XALL
.DATA	FARDATA	MASM	%PUSHLCTL	.XCREF
.DATA?	@fardata	MASM51	PWORD	.XLIST
DATAPTR	.FARDATA	MOD	QUIRKS	XOR

The Format of a Line

Assembly language source code lines follow this format:

```
<label> <instruction/directive> <operands> <;comment>
```

where *<label>* is an optional symbolic name; *<instruction/directive>* is either the mnemonic for an instruction or a directive; *<operands>* contains a combination of zero, one, or two (or sometimes more) constants, memory references, register references, and text strings, as required by the particular instruction or directive; *<;comment>* is an optional comment.

Let's look more closely at each of these elements of assembly language code.

Labels

Labels are nothing more than names used for referring to numbers and character strings or memory locations within a program. Labels let you give names to memory variables, values, and the locations of particular instructions. For example, the following code, which calculates five factorial ($1 \times 2 \times 3 \times 4 \times 5 = 120$), uses several labels:

```
        .MODEL  small
        .STACK  200h
        .DATA
FactorialValue DW   ?
Factorial      DW   ?
        .CODE
FiveFactorial  PROC
        mov   ax,@data
        mov   ds,ax
        mov   [FactorialValue],1
        mov   [Factorial],2
        mov   cx,4
FiveFactorialLoop:
        mov   ax,[FactorialValue]
        mul   [Factorial]
        mov   [FactorialValue],ax
        inc   [Factorial]
        loop  FiveFactorialLoop
        ret
FiveFactorial  ENDP
        END
```

The labels *FactorialValue* and *Factorial* are equivalent to the addresses of two 16-bit variables; they're used to refer to those two variables later in the code. The label *FiveFactorial* is the name of the subroutine (or function or procedure) containing the code, allowing other parts of this program to call this code. Finally, the label *FiveFactorialLoop* is equivalent to the address of the instruction

```
    mov   ax,[FactorialValue]
```

so that the **LOOP** at the end of the code can branch back to that particular instruction.

Labels can consist of the following characters:

```
A-Z    a-z    _    @    $    ?    0-9
```

A period (.) is also allowed in MASM mode (discussed in Chapter 12), as the first character only. The digits 0-9 cannot be used as the first character of a label. A single $ or ? has a special meaning, so they may not be used as a user symbol name.

Each label must be defined only once; that is, labels must be unique. (There are exceptions to this rule; for example, special labels defined with the = directive and local labels in macros and Ideal mode subroutines.) Labels may be used as operands any number of times.

A label may appear on a line by itself, that is, on a line without an instruction or directive. In this case, the value of the label is the address of the instruction or directive on the next line in the program. For instance, in the code

```
        .
        .
        .
        jmp    DoAddition
        .
        .
        .
DoAddition:
        add    ax,dx
        .
        .
        .
```

the next instruction executed after the **JMP** instruction, which branches to the label *DoAddition*, is **ADD AX,DX**. The preceding example is exactly the same as

```
        .
        .
        .
        jmp    DoAddition
        .
        .
        .
DoAddition:    add    ax,dx
        .
        .
        .
```

There are two advantages to putting each label on its own line. First, when you put each label on its own line, it's easier to use long labels without messing up the format of your assembler source code. (Note that in the last example **ADD AX,DX** was forced to the right because of the length of *DoAddition*, making for less readable code.) Second, it's easier to add a new instruction right at a label if the label's not on the same line as an instruction. To convert the last example to

```
        .
        .
        .
        jmp    DoAddition
        .
        .
        .
DoAddition:    mov    dx,[MemVar]
        add    ax,dx
        .
        .
        .
```

you would have to split *DoAddition* from **ADD AX,DX** and then add the new text. By contrast, if *DoAddition* were on a line by itself (as in the earlier example), you could simply add a new line after *DoAddition* and be done with it.

A label cannot be the same as any of the built-in symbols used in expressions. This includes the register names (AX, BX, and so on), and the operators used in expressions (**PTR, BYTE, WORD**, and so on). You also cannot use any of the **IF**xxx directives or **.ERR**xxx directives as label names. A few other symbols reserved by Turbo Assembler can only be used in certain contexts: These include **NAME**, **INCLUDE**, and **COMMENT**, which can be used as structure member names but not as general-purpose symbols. (Refer to Chapter 10 for more about structures.)

A safe approach is to avoid using any of the built-in symbol names for your labels. As an example, the labels

```
bx    DW   0
PTR:
```

would be unacceptable, since BX is a register and **PTR** is an expression operator. However, the label

```
Old_BX  DW    0
```

would be fine. Chapter 3 in the *Reference Guide* lists all directives; instruction mnemonics are listed in Table 2.1 on page 46; the registers of the 8086 are listed in Chapter 2, "Programming in Turbo Assembler."

The following are examples of acceptable labels:

```
MainLoop
calc_long_sum
Error0
iterate
Draw$Dot
Delay_100_milliseconds
```

Both labels that appear on lines without directives or instruction mnemonics and labels that appear on lines with instructions must end with a colon. The colon merely ends the label, and is not part of the label itself. For example, in

```
        .
        .
        .
LoopTop:
        mov    al,[si]
        inc    si
        and    al,al
        jz     Done
        jmp    LoopTop
Done:   ret
        .
        .
        .
```

the labels *LoopTop* and *Done* are defined with colons, but references to those labels do not use colons.

Other labels generally should not have colons. The example code at the start of this section provides several instances of labels without colons.

Make your labels meaningful. Contrast

```
        .
        .
        .
        cmp    al,'a'
        jb     NotALowerCaseLetter
        cmp    al,'z'
        ja     NotALowerCaseLetter
        sub    al,20h                  ;convert to uppercase
NotALowerCaseLetter:
        .
        .
        .
```

and

```
            .
            .
            .
        cmp    al,'a'
        jb     P1
        cmp    al,'z'
        ja     P1
        sub    al,20h                    ;convert to uppercase
    P1:
            .
            .
            .
```

The version with descriptive labels is largely self-documenting, while the second version is cryptic, to say the least. Labels can also contain underscores; if you prefer, you can use labels like *not_a_lower_case_letter* or *Not_A_Lower_Case_Letter*. It's purely a matter of taste.

Instruction Mnemonics and Directives

The key field in a line of assembler code is the *<instruction/directive>* field. This field may contain either an instruction mnemonic or a directive, two very different beasts.

You've encountered instruction mnemonics earlier in this chapter; they're the human-readable names for the machine-language instructions the 8086 executes directly. **MOV, ADD, MUL,** and **JMP** are all instruction mnemonics, corresponding directly to the data movement, addition, multiplication, and branching instructions of the 8086.

Turbo Assembler assembles each instruction mnemonic directly to the corresponding machine-language instruction. Whenever you insert one instruction mnemonic in an assembler program, the result is one corresponding machine-language instruction in the executable code.

Directives are quite the opposite of instruction mnemonics: They generate no executable code at all, but rather control various aspects of how Turbo Assembler operates, from the type of code assembled (8086, 80286, 80386, and so on), to the segments used, to the way in which listing files are generated. Although the distinction blurs at times, you might think of instruction mnemonics as generating the actual 8086 machine-language program, while directives are responsible for providing high-level features of Turbo Assembler that make assembly language programming easier.

We will spend much of this manual teaching you about the various instruction mnemonics and directives provided by Turbo Assembler, all of which are discussed in Chapter 3 of the *Reference Guide* as well. There are a few directives that you'll need in every program you write, most notably the segment directives, which we'll cover in a section later in this chapter called "Segment Directives" on page 107. Another directive you'll always need is the **END** directive, which we'll look at next.

The END Directive

Each and every program must contain an **END** directive to mark the end of the program's source code. Any lines following an **END** directive are ignored by Turbo Assembler. If you omit the **END** directive, an error is generated; you might think that the end of the file would mark the end of the program, but not so—an **END** directive is always required.

END is typical of directives in general in that it generates no code. For example,

```
        .MODEL  small
        .STACK  200h
        .CODE
ProgramStart:
        mov   ah,4ch
        int   21h
        END   ProgramStart
```

is perhaps the simplest possible assembler program, doing nothing more than immediately returning to DOS. Note the use of the **END** directive to terminate the bit of code this program consists of.

You've no doubt noticed that *ProgramStart* appears on the same line with **END** in the example. Besides terminating programs, **END** optionally does double duty by indicating where execution should begin when the program is run. For any of a number of reasons, you may not want to start executing a program with the first instruction in the .EXE file; **END** takes care of such cases. For example, suppose you run the program assembled and linked from this code:

```
        .MODEL  small
        .STACK  200h
        .CODE
Delay:
        mov   cx,0
DelayLoop:
        loop  DelayLoop
        ret

ProgramStart:
        call  Delay        ;pause for the time required to
                           ; execute 64K loops
```

```
mov   ah,4ch
int   21h
END   ProgramStart
```

Execution does not start with the first instruction in the source code, the **MOV CX,0** at label *Delay*. Instead, execution starts with the **CALL** *Delay* instruction at label *ProgramStart*, as specified by the **END** directive.

In a program consisting of only one module (that is, one source code file), the **END** directive should always specify the start address for the program. In a program consisting of more than one module, only the **END** directive in the module containing the instruction at which the program is to start should specify the start address; the **END** directives in all other modules should appear as **END**, and nothing more. Think of it this way: Every program needs a place to start—but it would make no sense to have two or more places to start. Make sure you have one—and only one—start address per program. (By the way, if you do have two addresses in your program, TLINK will use the first one it finds and ignore the other.)

Operands

Instruction mnemonics and directives tell Turbo Assembler what to do. Operands, on the other hand, tell Turbo Assembler what registers, parameters, memory locations, and so on to associate with each instance of an instruction or directive. A **MOV** instruction means nothing by itself; operands are necessary to tell Turbo Assembler where to move the value from and where to store it.

Zero, one, two, or more operands are required for various instructions, and virtually any number of operands that will fit on a single line can be accepted by various directives; the correct number of operands depends on the specific instruction or directive. (Occasionally, three operands are allowed.) Possible operands include registers, constant values, labels, memory variables, and text strings.

It's pretty obvious what an instruction with one operand does: It operates on that one operand. For example,

```
push  ax
```

pushes AX onto the stack. Instructions with no operands are more obvious still. However, what about the case of an instruction with *two* operands, one of which is the source and the other the destination? For instance, when the 8086 executes

```
mov   ax,bx
```

which register is it that gets read out, and which register is it that receives that value?

You might think that the English equivalent of this instruction would read, "Move the contents of AX into BX," but that's not the case. Instead, the **MOV** instruction moves the contents of BX into AX. A hint: With **MOV** instructions, mentally substitute an equal sign for the comma between the two operands and then treat the line like a C (or Pascal) assignment statement. With this approach, the **MOV** example would translate into

```
ax = bx;
```

Admittedly, it's a bit confusing having the rightmost operand as the source, but at least 8086 assembly language is consistent in this respect. You'll soon get used to it.

Register Operands

Registers are perhaps the most frequently used operands for instructions. Registers can serve as either source or destination and can even contain an address to jump to under certain circumstances. There's very little that can be done with constants, labels, or memory variables that can't be done with registers; on the other hand, there are a number of instructions that can only use register operands.

Here are some examples of instructions with register operands:

```
mov    di,ax
push   di
xchg   ah,dl
ror    dx,cl
in     al,dx
inc    si
```

Register operands can be mixed with other sorts of operands:

```
mov    al,1
add    [BaseCount],cx
cmp    si,[bx]
```

There's really very little to explain about the use of register operands. To use a register as an operand, you specify that register's name as an operand to an instruction, and the instruction uses that register. If there are two operands, and the register is the rightmost operand, it's the source register; if it's the leftmost operand, it's the destination register and may also be one of the source registers if the instruction requires two sources. For instance, in

```
    .
    .
    .
mov    cx,1
mov    dx,2
sub    dx,cx
    .
    .
    .
```

CX is set to 1, DX is set to 2, and then CX is subtracted from DX with the result, 1, stored back in DX. CX is the rightmost operand to the **SUB** instruction, so it's one source register; DX is the leftmost operand, so it's both the other source and the destination. By the way, the action of the preceding **SUB** instruction is expressed in English as "subtract CX from DX." Using the approach of converting to C code to make sense of two-operand instruction, the previous **SUB** instruction translates to this:

```
dx -= cx;
```

In Pascal, it translates to this: `dx := dx-cx;`

Constant Operands

Registers are fine for storing variable values, but often you just need a constant value for an operand. For example, suppose you want to count SI down by 4 in a loop, repeating the loop until SI reaches zero. You could use

```
         .
         .
         .
CountByFourLoop:
         .
         .
         .
dec    si
dec    si
dec    si
dec    si
jnz    CountByFourLoop
         .
         .
         .
```

but it's much easier to use

```
              .
              .
              .
CountByFourLoop:
              .
              .

              .
    sub    si,4
    jnz    CountByFourLoop

              .
              .
```

Characters can be used as constant operands as well, since a character has a well-defined value. For example, since the character *A* has the decimal value 65, these two instructions are equivalent:

```
          .
          .

          .
  sub    al,'A'
  sub    al,65
          .

          .
          .
```

Constant values can be specified in binary, octal, or hexadecimal notation, as well as in decimal. We'll discuss those notations in a later section entitled "Bits, Bytes, and Bases" (page 120).

Constant operands can never be the leftmost of two operands, since it's clearly not possible for a constant to be the destination operand. Constant operands can, however, be used pretty much anywhere that using a value for a source operand makes sense. The 8086 does impose some limitations on the use of constants; for example, you can't push a constant value (this is only a restriction of 8086/8088). To push the value 5, you must execute two instructions:

```
         .
         .

         .
  mov    ax,5
  push   ax
         .

         .
         .
```

You'll have to learn special cases where constants aren't allowed on a case-by-case basis. Fortunately, there aren't many such instructions, and, of course, Turbo Assembler will let you know right away if you try to use a constant incorrectly.

Expressions

Constant expressions may be used wherever constant values are accepted. Turbo Assembler supports full expression evaluation, including nested parentheses, arithmetic, logical, and relational operators, and a variety of operators for such purposes as extracting the segment and offset components of labels and determining the size of memory variables.

For example, the code

```
        .
        .
        .
MemVar  DB    0
NextVar DB    ?
        .
        .
        .
        mov   ax,SEG MemVar
        mov   ds,ax
        mov   bx,OFFSET MemVar+((3*2)-5)
        mov   BYTE PTR [bx],1
        .
        .
        .
```

uses the **SEG** operator to load the constant value of the segment *MemVar* resides in into AX and then copies that value from AX to DS. Next, this code uses a complex expression, involving the *, +, –, and **OFFSET** operators, that resolves to the value **OFFSET** *MemVar+1*, which is nothing more than the address of *NextVar*. Finally, the **BYTE PTR** operator is used to select a byte-sized operation when storing the constant value 1 to the location pointed to by BX, which is *NextVar*.

An important point about expressions is that all expressions must resolve to a constant value. **OFFSET** *MemVar* is a constant value—the offset of *MemVar* in its segment. After all, while the value stored at *MemVar* may change, *MemVar* itself certainly isn't going to move.

Turbo Assembler can evaluate expressions consisting of constant values as it assembles your code, precisely because constant values are always known. To Turbo Assembler, **OFFSET** *MemVar+2* is just like 5 + 2; since all the component parts of this expression are unchanging and well-defined at assembly time, the expression can be resolved to a single constant value.

Here are the operators that can be used in expressions:

<>, (), [], LENGTH, MASK, SIZE, WIDTH

. (*structure member selector*)

HIGH, LOW

+, – (unary)

: (*segment override*)

OFFSET, PTR, SEG, THIS, TYPE

__*, /, MOD, SHL, SHR__

+, – (binary)

EQ, GE, GT, LE, LT, NE

NOT

AND

OR, XOR

LARGE, SHORT, SMALL, .TYPE

Many operators are self-explanatory, doing just what you'd expect them to do in any arithmetic expression. We'll explain operators as we come to them in this chapter. In the meantime, refer to Chapter 2 of the *Reference Guide* if you've got any questions about specific operators.

Label Operands

Labels can serve as operands to many instructions. Given the proper operators, labels can be used to generate constant values. For example,

```
        .
        .
        .
MemWord DW    1
        .
        .
        .
        mov   al,SIZE MemWord
        .
        .
        .
```

moves 2, the size in bytes of the memory variable *MemWord*, into AL. In this context, a label can become part of an expression, as illustrated in the last section.

Labels may also be used as the destinations of **CALL** and **JMP** instructions. For example, in

```
            .
            .
            .
            cmp    ax,100
            ja     IsAbove100
            .
            .
            .
IsAbove100:
            .
            .
            .
```

the **JA** instruction jumps to the address specified by the operand *IsAbove100* if AX is above 100. Again, in this capacity labels are used as constants, specifying memory addresses to be branched to.

Finally, labels may be used as operands in much the same way as registers are—as source or destination operands to data manipulation instructions. The code

```
            .
            .
            .
TempVar DW     ?
            .
            .
            .
            mov    [TempVar],ax
            sub    ax,[TempVar]
            .
            .
            .
```

invariably leaves AX containing zero, since the first instruction writes the value stored in AX to the memory variable *TempVar*, and the second instruction subtracts the value stored in *TempVar* from AX.

The use of labels as operands is part of the larger topic of memory-addressing modes, which we'll explore next.

Memory-Addressing Modes

When you use a memory operand, exactly how do you specify which memory location you want to work with? The obvious answer is to give the name of the desired memory variable, as we did in the last section. You can subtract the memory variable *Debts* from the memory variable *Assets* with

```
        .
        .
        .
Assets  DW   ?
Debts   DW   ?
        .
        .
        .
        mov  ax,[Debts]
        sub  [Assets],ax
        .
        .
        .
```

There's more to memory-addressing than meets the eye, though. Suppose you have a character string named *CharString*, containing the letters ABCDEFGHIJKLM, which starts at offset 100 in the data segment, as shown in Figure 4.1. How can you read the ninth character, *I*, which is at address 108? In C, you can just use

```
C = CharString[8];
```

An in Pascal, you can use

```
C := CharString[9];
```

But how can you do the same in assembler? Certainly, referencing *Char-String* directly isn't going to do the trick, since the character at *CharString* is *A*.

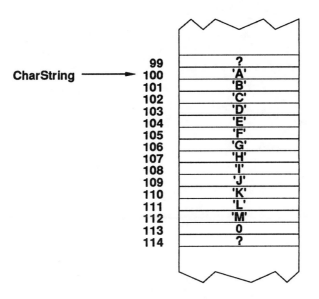

Figure 4.1: The Memory Location of the Character String CharString

Actually, assembly language supports several different ways to handle the addressing of character strings, arrays, and data buffers. The simplest way to read the ninth character of *CharString* is

```
          .
          .
          .
          .DATA
CharString    DB    'ABCDEFGHIJKLM',0
          .
          .
          .
          .CODE
          .
          .
          .
          mov   ax,@data
          mov   ds,ax
          mov   al,[CharString+8]
          .
          .
          .
```

In this case, this is the same as

```
mov  al,[100+8]      (Ideal mode)
mov  al,ds:[100+8]   (MASM mode)
```

since *CharString* starts at offset 100. Turbo Assembler treats everything between square brackets as an address, so the offset of *CharString* and 8 are added together and used as a memory address. The instruction effectively becomes

```
mov  al,[108]        (Ideal mode)
mov  al,ds:[108]     (MASM mode)
```

as shown in Figure 4.2.

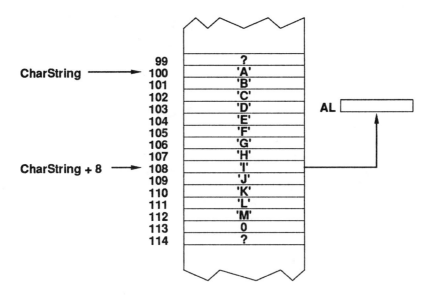

Figure 4.2: Addressing the Character String CharString

This sort of addressing, where a memory location is specified either by its name or by its name plus some constant, is known as *direct* addressing. While direct addressing is straightforward to use, it's not very flexible because it accesses the same memory address every time. Let's look at another, more flexible way to address memory.

Consider the following, which also loads the ninth character of *CharString* into AL:

```
    .
    .
    .
mov  bx,OFFSET CharString+8
```

```
mov  al,[bx]
     .
     .
     .
```

This example uses BX to point to the ninth character. The first instruction loads BX with the offset of *CharString* (remember that the **OFFSET** operator returns the memory offset of a label), plus 8. (This is an expression, with Turbo Assembler doing the **OFFSET** calculation and the addition at assembly time.) The second instruction specifies that AL should be loaded with the contents of the memory offset pointed to by BX, as shown in Figure 4.3.

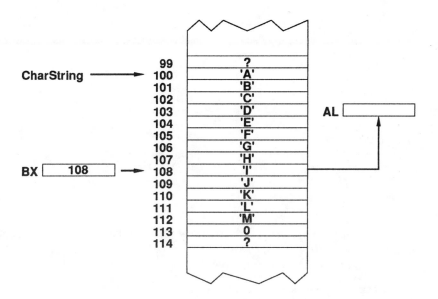

Figure 4.3: Using BX to Address CharString

It's the square brackets that indicate that the memory location pointed to by BX, rather than BX itself, should be the source operand. Don't forget the brackets when using BX as a memory pointer; for example,

```
mov  ax,[bx]    ;load AX from the memory offset pointed to by BX
```

and

```
mov  ax,bx      ;load AX with the contents of BX
```

are two very different instructions.

Why bother to first load BX with the offset of a memory variable and then access memory using BX as a pointer, when a single instruction with a direct operand does the same thing? The special quality of registers used as memory pointers is that, unlike instructions that use direct operands, instructions that use registers as pointers can point to different memory addresses at different times in the execution of a program.

Suppose you want to find the last character of a null-terminated *CharString*. In order to do this, you must start at the first character of *CharString*, search for the zero byte that ends the string, and then back up one character to read the last character. There's no way to do this with direct addressing, since the string could be of any length. Using BX as a pointer register, though, does the trick nicely:

```
          .
          .
          .
        mov    bx,OFFSET CharString      ;point to string start
FindLastCharLoop:
        mov    al,[bx]                   ;get next string char
        cmp    al,0                      ;is this the zero byte?
        je     FoundEndOfString          ;yes, back to last char
        inc    bx                        ;point to next char
        jmp    FindLastCharLoop          ;check the next char
FoundEndOfString:
        dec    bx                        ;point back to last char
        mov    al,[bx]                   ;get the last character in the string
          .
          .
          .
```

If you're going to search through memory for characters or words, if you're going to manipulate arrays, or if you're going to copy blocks of data about, you'll find that pointer registers are invaluable.

BX is not the only register that can be used as a memory pointer. BP, SI, and DI can also be used, along with an optional constant value or label. The general form of a memory operand looks like this:

[*base register+index+register+displacement*]

or

[*base register+index*] [*register+displacement*]

where *base register* is BX or BP, *index register* is SI or DI, and *displacement* is any 16-bit constant value, including expressions and labels. The three components are added together by the 8086 each time an instruction using a memory operand is executed. Each of the three parts of a memory operand is optional, although obviously you must use at least one of the three (or else you'd have no memory address at all!). Here's how the elements of a memory operand look in another format:

$$\begin{matrix} BX & & SI & & \\ or & + & or & + & Displacement \\ BP & & DI & & \end{matrix}$$

(Base)   *(Index)*

It works out that there are 16 ways to specify a memory address:

- [*displacement*]
- [bx]
- [si]
- [di]
- [bx+si]
- [bx+di]
- [bp+si]
- [bp+di]

- [bp+*displacement*]
- [bx+*displacement*]
- [si+*displacement*]
- [di+*displacement*]
- [bx+si+*displacement*]
- [bx+di+*displacement*]
- [bp+si+*displacement*]
- [bp+di+*displacement*]

where, again, *displacement* is anything that works out to a 16-bit constant value.

Sixteen addressing modes certainly seem like a lot, but if you look at the preceding list, you'll see that all those addressing modes are built from nothing more than a few elements combined in a few different ways. Here are some more ways you can load the ninth character of *CharString* into AL, using the various addressing modes:

```
          .
          .
          .
          .DATA
CharString   DB  'ABCDEFGHIJKLM',0
          .
          .
          .
          .CODE
          mov  ax,@data
          mov  ds,ax
          .
          .
          .
          mov  si,OFFSET CharString+8
          mov  al,[si]
          .
          .
          .
```

```
mov   bx,8
mov   al,[CharString+bx]
 .
 .
 .
mov   bx,OFFSET CharString
mov   al,[bx+8]
 .
 .
 .
mov   si,8
mov   al,[CharString+si]
 .
 .
 .
mov   bx,OFFSET CharString
mov   di,8
mov   al,[bx+di]
 .
 .
 .
mov   si,OFFSET CharString
mov   bx,8
mov   al,[si+bx]
 .
 .
 .
mov   bx,OFFSET CharString
mov   si,7
mov   al,[bx+si+1]
 .
 .
 .
mov   bx,3
mov   si,5
mov   al,[bx+CharString+si]
 .
 .
 .
```

Believe it or not, all these instructions reference exactly the same memory
location, [*CharString*]+8.

There are several interesting points about this example. First, you should
understand that a plus (+) sign used inside square brackets has a special
meaning. At assembly time, Turbo Assembler adds together all the constant
values inside square brackets, so that

```
mov   [10+bx+1+si+100],cl
```

effectively becomes

```
mov   [bx+si+111],cl
```

Then, when the instruction is actually executed (when the program is run), the memory-addressing operands are added together on the fly by the 8086. If BX contains 25 and SI contains 52, then CL is stored to the memory address 25 + 52 +111 = 188 when the **MOV** instruction is executed. The key here is that it's the 8086 that adds together the base register, the index register, and the displacement when this instruction is executed. To put it another way, Turbo Assembler adds the constants at assembly time, while the 8086 adds together the base and/or index and/or displacement fields as the instruction is actually executed.

You may have noticed that we haven't used BP in any of the examples so far. That's because BP behaves a little differently from BX. Recall that while BX is used as an offset into the data segment, BP is used as an offset into the *stack* segment. That means that BP can't normally be used to address *CharString*, which resides in the data segment (more on segments shortly).

An explanation of the use of BP to address the stack segment is given in Chapter 2. For now, it's enough to know that BP can be used just as we've used BX in the examples, except that the data addressed must reside in the stack segment when BP is used.

(Actually, BP *can* be made to address the data segment, and BX, SI, and DI can be made to address the stack segment, or the code segment, or the extra segment, by use of *segment override prefixes*. We'll cover segment override prefixes in Chapter 10; most of the time, though, you won't need them, and for now we'll ignore their existence.)

Finally, the square brackets around direct addresses are optional. That is,

```
mov   al,[MemVar]
```

and

```
mov   al,MemVar
```

do exactly the same thing. Nonetheless, we strongly recommend placing square brackets around all memory references, in order to reduce confusion and make your code as clear as possible. At some point, you'll undoubtedly come across code that lacks square brackets, since some people feel that the bracketless code is more intuitive. As usual, it's a matter of taste, and you'll find that your programming goes more smoothly if you choose a single memory-addressing style and use it consistently.

You'll also run across memory-addressing forms like

```
mov   al,CharString[bx]
```

and even

```
mov  al,CharString[bx][si]+1
```

All these forms are the same as putting the memory-addressing elements inside a single pair of square brackets and separating them with plus signs; the last example is the same as

```
mov  al,[CharString+bx+si+1]
```

Again, pick a style for your own code and stick with it.

Square brackets around register pointers to memory are *not* optional. Without square brackets, for instance, BX is treated as an operand, not as a pointer to an operand.

Comments

Last, but surely not least, we come to the comment field. Comments don't actually *do* anything, in the sense that they don't affect the code of the executable file generated by Turbo Assembler, but that doesn't mean they're not important.

Most likely, you already know how to program in some high-level language—C, Pascal, Prolog, or whatever—since few people begin their programming careers with assembly language. As you learned that language, no doubt you were advised time and time again to comment carefully. That's good advice, since both complexity and passing time can make any program inscrutable even to its author.

By comparison with assembly language, though, a Pascal program is virtually self-documenting. Pascal code is full of neatly delineated control structures, strongly typed variables, arithmetic expressions, and procedure and function calls complete with formal and actual parameters.

Assembly language, on the other hand, has no built-in control structures, strong but erratically-enforced data-typing, no arithmetic expressions involving variables, and no inherent parameter-passing mechanism. In short, assembler code is about as far from structured, easily maintained code as you're ever likely to see. This doesn't mean that assembler programs can't be structured, or that they can't be maintained, but rather that you must use comments (and subroutines and macros as well) to raise assembler code above its natural cryptic level.

There are all sorts of ways to comment assembler code. One useful approach is to put a comment at the right margin of each instruction that might benefit from a bit of explanation. For instance, you've certainly got a better shot at understanding

```
       mov   [bx],al      ;store the modified character
```

at a glance than

```
       mov   [bx],al
```

You don't have to comment *every* line; after a while, comments like

```
       .
       .
       .
       mov   ah,1      ;DOS keyboard input function #
       int   21h       ;invoke DOS to get the next key press
       .
       .
       .
```

cease to serve any useful purpose. That doesn't mean you shouldn't comment such lines, though; instead, make your comments short and to the point:

```
       .
       .
       .
       mov   ah,1
       int   21h       ;get the next key press
       .
       .
       .
```

Remember, the purpose of comments is not to explain every bit of your program, but rather to make it easy for you or someone else to look over the code and quickly understand it.

Another good commenting technique is to use lines of only comments to describe blocks of code. These comments can describe code operation at a higher level than comments for individual lines can. For example, consider the following:

```
           .
           .
           .
;
; Generate a checksum byte for the transfer buffer.
;
       mov   bx,OFFSET TransferBuffer
       mov   cx,TRANSFER_BUFFER_LENGTH
       sub   al,al                          ;clear the checksum accumulator
Checksum:
       add   al,[bx]                        ;add in the current byte's value
       inc   bx                             ;point to the next byte
```

```
        loop    Checksum
          .
          .
          .
```

Note that we didn't comment every line. In light of the comment for this
block of code, it's obvious that BX is loaded with the address of the transfer
buffer, and that CX is loaded with the length of the buffer. The key here is
that the comment for this block of seven lines neatly summarizes the
operation of the code, so the comments for the individual lines become less
important. Someone skimming through the code is likely to benefit more
from the block comments than from the line comments.

Another still higher-level commenting technique is that of preceding each
subroutine with a descriptive comment header. Such a header can contain a
description of the subroutine, a summary of inputs and outputs, register
preservation information, and miscellaneous notes on the subroutine's
operation. For example,

```
;
; Function to return the byte-sized checksum of a data buffer.
;
; Input:
;       DS:BX - a pointer to the start of the buffer
;       CX - the length of the buffer
;
; Output:
;       AL - the buffer checksum
;
; Registers destroyed:
;       BX, CX
;
; Note: The buffer must not exceed 64 Kb in length, and must not
; cross a segment boundary.
;
Checksum        PROC    NEAR
        sub     al,al           ;clear the checksum accumulator Checksum:
        add     al,[bx]         ;add in the current byte's value
        inc     bx              ;point to the next byte
        loop    Checksum
        ret
Checksum        ENDP
```

If you think about it, you'll realize that once a subroutine is written and
working properly, there's rarely any reason to ever look at the code of that
subroutine again. What you will want to know is exactly what happens
when you call that subroutine; in other words, you'll often want to know
just how that subroutine interacts with the code that's calling it. A
descriptive header such as the one we've written meets that need very well.

There are many other commenting techniques, and you'll no doubt develop one suited to your programming style. The important thing is to make it a point to comment your code thoroughly from the start, so that commenting becomes an integral part of your programming style.

Segment Directives

In both this chapter and the last, we've spent considerable time discussing what segments are and how they affect the code you write. There's one thing we haven't dealt with yet, though, and that's how Turbo Assembler knows exactly which segment or segments data and code reside in.

Segment control is one of the more complex aspects of 8086 assembly language; accordingly, Turbo Assembler provides not one but two sets of segment control directives. The first set, consisting of the *simplified segment directives*, makes segment control relatively easy and is ideal for linking assembler modules to high-level languages, but supports only some of the segment-related features of which Turbo Assembler is capable. The second set, consisting of the *standard segment directives,* is more complicated to use, but provides the complete segment control required by demanding assembler applications.

Next, we'll look at both the simplified and the standard segment directives. We'll just give you an overview of how to use the segment directives so you'll know enough to write your own programs; a detailed explanation of segment directives is given in Chapter 10, "Advanced Programming in Turbo Assembler."

Simplified Segment Directives

The key simplified segment directives are **.STACK**, **.CODE**, **.DATA**, **.MODEL**, and **DOSSEG**. We'll cover these in two groups in this section, starting with **.STACK**, **.CODE**, and **.DATA**.

.STACK, .CODE, and .DATA

.STACK, **.CODE**, and **.DATA** define the stack, code, and data segments, respectively. **.STACK** controls the size of the stack. For example,

```
.STACK  200h
```

defines a stack 200h (512) bytes long. That's really all you have to do as far as the stack is concerned; just make sure you've got a **.STACK** directive in your program, and Turbo Assembler handles the stack for you. 200h is a good stack size for normal programs, although heavily stack-oriented programs—for instance, programs using recursion—might require larger stacks. (For information about exceptions to using **.STACK**, see the section "Forgetting the Stack or Reserving a Too-Small Stack" on page 247 in Chapter 5.)

.CODE marks the start of your program's code segment. You might think it would be obvious to Turbo Assembler that all your instructions belong in the code segment. Actually, though, Turbo Assembler lets you have many code segments (by using the standard segment directives), and **.CODE** tells Turbo Assembler exactly which code segment to place your instructions in. Defining your code segment is even simpler than defining your stack segment, since there are no operands to **.CODE**. For example,

```
       .
       .
       .
.CODE
sub    ax,ax      ;set the accumulator to zero
mov    cx,100     ;# of loops to execute
       .
       .
       .
```

.DATA is a bit more complex. As you'd expect, **.DATA** marks the start of your data segment. You should place your memory variables in this segment. For example,

```
        .
        .
        .
        .DATA
TopBoundary   DW   100
Counter       DW   ?
ErrorMessage  DB   0dh,0ah,'***Error***',0dh,0ah,'$'
        .
        .
        .
```

That's certainly straightforward. The complex part of **.DATA** (and it's really not that complex) is that you must explicitly load the DS segment register with the symbol **@data** before you can access memory locations in the segment defined by **.DATA**. Since a segment register can be loaded from either a general-purpose register or a memory location, but can't be loaded with a constant, the DS segment register is generally loaded with a two-instruction sequence along the lines of

```
          .
          .
          .
     mov    ax,@data
     mov    ds,ax
          .
          .
          .
```

(Any general-purpose register could be used instead of AX.) The preceding sequence sets DS to point to the data segment that starts with the **.DATA** directive.

The following program displays the text stored at *DataString* on the screen:

```
          .MODEL  small
          .STACK  200h
          .DATA
DataString     DB   'This text is in the data segment$'
          .CODE
ProgramStart:
     mov    bx,@data
     mov    ds,bx            ;set DS to the .DATA segment
     mov    dx,OFFSET DataString  ;point DX to the offset of DataString
                            ; in the .DATA segment
     mov    ah,9             ;DOS print string function #
     int    21h              ;invoke DOS to print string
     mov    ah,4ch           ;DOS terminate program function #
     int    21h              ;invoke DOS to end program
     END    ProgramStart
```

Without the two instructions that set the DS register to the segment defined with **.DATA**, the print string function wouldn't work properly. *DataString* resides in the **.DATA** segment and cannot be accessed unless DS is set to that segment. You might want to think of it this way: When you invoke DOS to print a string, you pass the full segment:offset address of the string in DS:DX. Only after you loaded DS with the **.DATA** segment and DX with the offset of *DataString* did you have a full segment:offset pointer to *Data-String*.

You may well wonder at this point why it is that you have to load DS, but not CS or SS. Then, too, what about ES?

Well, you never have to load CS explicitly because DOS does that for you when you run a program. After all, if CS weren't already set when the time came to execute the first instruction of a program, the 8086 wouldn't know where to find the instruction, and the program would never run. This may not be obvious to you right now, but trust us—CS is automatically set when a program begins, and you never need to load it explicitly.

Likewise, SS is set by DOS before a program begins, and generally stays the same for the duration of the program. While it is *possible* to change SS, it's very rarely desirable, and it's certainly not something you'll want to attempt unless you know exactly what you're doing. So, like CS, SS is automatically set when a program begins, and need not be touched thereafter.

DS is quite different. While CS points to instructions, and SS points to the stack, DS points to data. Programs don't directly manipulate instructions or stacks—but they do constantly manipulate data directly. What's more, programs might want to get at data in any of several different segments at any time; remember that the 8086 allows you to access any memory location in a 1 Mb range, but only in blocks of 64 Kb (relative to a segment register) at a time.

You may well want to load DS with one segment, access data in that segment, and then load DS with another segment in order to access a different block of data. In small- and medium-sized programs, such as those we've presented here, you'll never need more than one data segment, but larger programs often use multiple data segments. Also, you'll need to load DS with different values if you want to access system memory areas, such as the memory locations used by the BIOS.

The upshot of all this is that Turbo Assembler lets you set DS to any segment at any time. In return for this flexibility, you must explicitly set DS to the segment you want—usually **@data**, which is equivalent to the segment that starts with **.DATA**—before you access memory locations in that segment.

The ES segment register is loaded just like DS. Often, you won't need to bother with ES at all, but when you do need to access a memory location in the segment pointed to by ES, you must first load ES with that segment. For example, the following program loads ES with the **.DATA** segment, then loads a character to print from that segment via ES:

```
          .MODEL  small
          .STACK  200h
          .DATA
OutputChar        DB    'B'
          .CODE
ProgramStart:
          mov   dx,@data
          mov   es,dx              ;set ES to the .DATA segment
          mov   bx,OFFSET OutputChar  ;point BX to the offset of OutputChar
          mov   al,es:[bx]         ;get the character to output from the
                                   ; segment pointed to by ES
          mov   ah,2               ;DOS display output function #
          int   21h               ;invoke DOS to print character
```

```
        mov   ah,4ch                  ;DOS terminate program function #
        int   21h                     ;invoke DOS to end program
        END   ProgramStart
```

Note that ES is loaded with the two-instruction sequence

```
     .
     .
     .
   mov  dx,@data
   mov  es,dx
     .
     .
     .
```

just as DS was earlier.

Admittedly, there's no particular reason to use ES rather than DS in this example, and, in fact, using ES meant that we had to use an ES: segment override prefix (as discussed in Chapter 10). However, there are many occasions when it's handy to have ES set to one segment while DS is set to another, particularly when the string instructions are used.

DOSSEG

The **DOSSEG** directive causes the segments in an assembler program to be grouped according to the Microsoft segment-ordering conventions. For now, you don't need to worry about what that means; all you need to know is that almost all stand-alone assembler programs will work just fine if you start them with **DOSSEG**.

While it is not necessary to specify **DOSSEG** when linking assembler modules to a high-level language, since the high-level language automatically selects Microsoft segment-ordering, **DOSSEG** doesn't hurt and is a useful reminder of the sort of segment-ordering that is in effect.

All this means is that the simplest approach is to use **DOSSEG** as the first line in all your programs (unless you have a specific reason not to). That way, you'll be able to rely on a consistent segment order. (For more on **DOSSEG**, see Chapter 3 in the *Reference Guide*.)

.MODEL

The **.MODEL** directive specifies the memory model for an assembler module that uses the simplified segment directives. Note that near code is branched to (jumped to) by loading the IP register only, while far code is branched to by loading both CS and IP. Similarly, near data is accessed with just an offset, while far data must be accessed with a full segment:offset address. In short, far means that full 32-bit segment:offset addresses are used, while near means that 16-bit offsets can be used.

These are the available memory models:

tiny
Both program code and program data must fit within the same 64K segment. Both code and data are near.

small
Program code must fit within a single 64K segment, and program data must fit within a separate 64K segment. Both code and data are near.

medium
Program code may be larger then 64K, but program data must fit within a single 64K segment. Code is far, while data is near.

compact
Program code must fit within a single 64K segment, but program data may be larger than 64K. Code is near, while data is far. No single data array may be greater than 64K.

large
Both program code and program data may be larger than 64K, but no single data array may be larger than 64K. Both code and data are far.

huge
Both program code and program data may be larger than 64K, and data arrays may exceed 64K in size. Both code and data are far. Pointers to elements within an array are far.

Note that, from an assembler point of view, large and huge are identical. Huge model does not automatically support data arrays larger than 64K.

Few assembler programs require more than 64K of code or data, so the small model serves well in most applications. You should use the small model whenever possible, because far code (medium, large, and huge models) makes program execution slower; far data (compact, large, and huge models) is considerably harder to manage in assembler.

The memory models described here correspond to the memory models used by Turbo C (and many other compilers for the PC). Whenever you link an assembler module to a high-level language, be sure to use the correct **.MODEL** directive. **.MODEL** makes sure that assembler segment names correspond to those used by high-level languages, and that labels of type **PROC**, which are used to name subroutines, procedures, and functions, default to the type—near or far—used by high-level languages.

.MODEL is required if you're using the simplified segment directives, since otherwise Turbo Assembler wouldn't know how to set up the segments defined with **.CODE** and **.DATA**. **.MODEL** must precede **.CODE**, **.DATA**, and **.STACK**.

Here's the framework of a program using simplified segment directives:

```
        .MODEL   small
        .STACK   200h
        .DATA
MemVar  DW       0
        .
        .
        .
        .CODE
ProgramStart:
        mov      ax,@data
        mov      ds,ax
        mov      ax,[MemVar]
        .
        .
        .
        mov      ah,4ch
        int      21h
        END      ProgramStart
```

Other Simplified Segment Directives

There are several other less commonly used segment directives. You'll need these only for large or sophisticated assembler programs, so we'll just mention them now to let you know they exist; refer to Chapter 10 for more information.

.DATA? is used just like **.DATA** except that it defines that portion of the data segment containing uninitialized data. This is usually used in an assembler module linked to a high-level language.

.FARDATA lets you define a far data segment, that is, a data segment other than the standard **@data** segment shared by all modules. **.FARDATA** allows an assembler module to define its own data segment of up to 64 Kb in size. If a **.FARDATA** directive has been given, **@fardata** is the name of the far data segment specified by that directive, just as **@data** is the name of the data segment specified by **.DATA**.

.FARDATA? is much like **.FARDATA** except that it defines an uninitialized far segment. As with **.FARDATA** and **@fardata**, if a **.FARDATA?** directive has been given, **@fardata?** is the name of the far data segment specified by that directive.

.CONST defines that portion of the data segment containing constant data. Once again, this only matters when linking assembler code to a high-level language.

Some useful predefined labels are available when the simplified segment directives are used. **@FileName** is the name of the file being assembled. **@curseg** is the name of the segment Turbo Assembler is currently assembling into. **@CodeSize** is 0 in memory models with near code segments (tiny, small, and compact) and 1 in memory models with far code segments (medium, large, and huge). Likewise, **@DataSize** is 0 in memory models with near data segments (tiny, small, and medium), 1 in compact and large memory models, and 2 in the huge model.

Standard Segment Directives

Next, we'll show the same sample program framework from the last section, but this time we'll use the standard segment directives **SEGMENT**, **ENDS**, and **ASSUME**:

```
DGROUP   GROUP    _DATA, STACK
         ASSUME   cs:_TEXT, ds:_DATA, ss:STACK
STACK    SEGMENT  PARA STACK 'STACK'
         DB       200h DUP (?)
STACK    ENDS
_DATA    SEGMENT  WORD PUBLIC 'DATA'
MemVar   DW       0
            .
            .
            .
_DATA    ENDS
_TEXT    SEGMENT  WORD PUBLIC 'CODE'
ProgramStart:
         mov      ax,_DATA
         mov      ds,ax
         mov      ax,[MemVar]
            .
            .
            .
         mov      ah,4ch
         int      21h
_TEXT    ENDS
         END      ProgramStart
```

Now you know why the simplified segment directives are called "simplified"! However, much of what the simplified segment directives do is intended to make it easier to link assembler modules to high-level languages and is unnecessary in stand-alone assembler programs. Here's the *Hello, world* program using standard segment directives:

```
STACK    SEGMENT PARA STACK 'STACK'
         DB      200h DUP (?)
STACK    ENDS

Data     SEGMENT WORD 'DATA'
HelloMessage   DB     'Hello, world',13,10,'$'
Data     ENDS

Code     SEGMENT WORD 'CODE'
         ASSUME  cs:Code, ds:Data
ProgramStart:
         mov    ax,Data
         mov    ds,ax                  ;set DS to the Data segment
         mov    dx,OFFSET HelloMessage  ;DS:DX points to the hello message
         mov    ah,9                   ;DOS print string function #
         int    21h                    ;print the hello string
         mov    ah,4ch                 ;DOS terminate program function #
         int    21h                    ;end the program
Code     ENDS
         END    ProgramStart
```

The last example isn't too terribly complicated, but it's nonetheless clear that the standard segment directives are more complex than the simplified segment directives.

Chapter 10 describes the standard segment directives in detail. In this section, we're only going to give you an idea what each standard segment directive does.

The **SEGMENT** directive defines the start of a segment. The label accompanying the **SEGMENT** directive is the name of the segment; for example,

```
Cseg    SEGMENT
```

defines the start of a segment named *Cseg*. The **SEGMENT** directive may optionally specify a number of segment attributes, including alignment on a byte, word, doubleword, paragraph (16 byte), or page (256 byte) memory boundary. Other attributes include the way in which the segment can be combined with other segments with the same name and the class of the segment.

The **ENDS** directive defines the end of a segment. For example,

```
Cseg    ENDS
```

ends the segment named *Cseg*, which was started earlier with the **SEGMENT** directive. When you use the standard segment directives, you must explicitly end every segment.

The **ASSUME** directive tells Turbo Assembler what segment a given segment register is currently set to. An **ASSUME CS:** directive is required in every program that uses the standard segment directives, since Turbo Assembler needs to know about the code segment in order to set up an executable program. **ASSUME DS:** and **ASSUME ES:** are usually used as well so that Turbo Assembler knows what memory locations you can address at any given time.

ASSUME lets Turbo Assembler check that each access to a named memory variable is valid, given the current segment register settings. For example, consider the following:

```
Data1   SEGMENT WORD 'DATA'
Var1    DW      0
Data1   ENDS
        .
        .
        .

Data2   SEGMENT WORD 'DATA'
Var2    DW      0
Data2   ENDS

Code    SEGMENT WORD 'CODE'
        ASSUME  cs:Code
ProgramStart:
        mov     ax,Data1
        mov     ds,ax      ;set DS to Data1
        ASSUME  ds:Data1
        mov     ax,[Var2]  ;try to load Var2 into AX--this will cause an
                           ; error, since Var2 can't be reached in segment Data1
        .
        .
        .
        mov     ah,4ch     ;DOS terminate program function #
        int     21h        ;end the program
Code    ENDS
        END     ProgramStart
```

Turbo Assembler flags an error in this code because the code tries to access memory variable *Var2* when DS is set to segment *Data1*, and *Var2* can't be addressed unless DS is set to segment *Data2*.

It's important to understand that Turbo Assembler doesn't actually know that DS has been set to *Data1*; rather, by using the **ASSUME** statement, you *told* Turbo Assembler to make that assumption. **ASSUME** is your way to tell Turbo Assembler what the segment registers are set to at any given time, so that Turbo Assembler can let you know when you've attempted the impossible.

Turbo Assembler can't catch all such mistakes, however. Whenever a memory reference involves a named memory variable, such as previous *Var1* or *Var2*, Turbo Assembler can check the validity of that reference, since each named memory variable is explicitly associated with a segment. There's no way Turbo Assembler can know what segment an instruction like

```
mov  al,[bx]
```

is intended to access, though. In such a case, Turbo Assembler must assume that the segment DS is set to is the segment you want to access.

If a segment register doesn't currently point to any named segment, you can use **NOTHING** with **ASSUME** to convey that information to Turbo Assembler. For example,

```
        .
        .
        .
        mov    ax,0b800h
        mov    ds,ax
        ASSUME  ds:NOTHING
        .
        .
        .
```

sets DS to point to the color text screen and then informs Turbo Assembler that DS doesn't point to any named segment. Here's another way to point to the color text screen:

```
        .
        .
        .
ColorTextSeg    SEGMENT AT 0B800h
ColorTextMemory LABEL   BYTE
ColorTextSeg    ENDS
        .
        .
        .
        mov    ax,ColorTextSeg
        mov    ds,ax
        ASSUME  ds:ColorTextSeg
        .
        .
        .
```

Note that the **AT** directive that follows **SEGMENT** provides an explicit starting address for the segment.

One final point about **ASSUME**: It may cause Turbo Assembler to use a different segment register than you expect to access memory in some cases. For example, consider the following code:

```
          .
          .
          .

Data1    SEGMENT WORD 'DATA'
Var1     DW      0
Data1    ENDS

Data2    SEGMENT WORD 'DATA'
Var2     DW      0
Data2    ENDS

Code     SEGMENT WORD 'CODE'
         ASSUME  cs:Code
ProgramStart:
         mov     ax,Data1
         mov     ds,ax       ;set DS to Data1
         ASSUME  ds:Data1
         mov     ax,Data2
         mov     es,ax       ;set ES to Data2
         ASSUME  es:Data2
         mov     ax,[Var2]   ;load Var2 into AX--Turbo Assembler will tell
                             ; the 8086 to load relative to ES,
                             ; since Var2 can't be reached relative to DS

          .
          .
          .

         mov     ah,4ch      ;DOS terminate program function #
         int     21h         ;end the program
Code     ENDS
         END     ProgramStart
```

This example should look familiar; it's a modified version of the code we used earlier to show how **ASSUME** lets Turbo Assembler tell you when you've attempted an impossible memory reference. In this example, though, no error will be reported, but that doesn't mean Turbo Assembler is letting you make a mistake. Instead, Turbo Assembler modifies

```
mov    ax,[Var2]
```

to access *Var2* relative to the ES segment register rather than the DS segment register.

What happens is this: The two **ASSUME** directives have informed Turbo Assembler that DS is set to the *Data1* segment and that ES is set to the *Data2* segment. Then, when the **MOV** instruction attempts to access *Var2*, which is in the *Data2* segment, Turbo Assembler correctly concludes that there's no way *Var2* can be accessed relative to DS; however, *Var2 can* be accessed relative to ES. Consequently, Turbo Assembler inserts a special code known as a *segment override prefix* before the **MOV** instruction in order to tell the 8086 to use the ES rather than the DS segment register.

What does all this mean to you? It means that if you're careful to use **ASSUME** directives to let Turbo Assembler know the current DS and ES settings, Turbo Assembler can automatically help you out by checking that accesses to named memory variables are possible, and can even select the correct segment automatically in some cases.

Segment override prefixes, and the standard segment directives in general, are discussed in Chapter 10.

Simplified Versus Standard Segment Directives

Now that you've seen both the simplified and standard segment directives, the question remains: Which set of segment directives should you use? The answer depends on the sort of assembler programming you need to do.

If you're linking assembler modules to a high-level language, you'll almost always want to use the simplified segment directives. The simplified segment directives do a good job of taking care of the segment-naming and memory-model details associated with the interface to high-level languages.

If you're writing small- or medium-sized stand-alone assembler programs, you'll generally want to use the simplified segment directives, since they're easier to use and make programs more readable.

If you're writing large stand-alone assembler programs with many segments and mixed-model programming (both near and far code and/or near and far data in the same program), you'll need to use the standard segment directives, since only with the standard segment directives do you get full control over segment type, alignment, naming, and the way in which segments are combined.

The rule of thumb is this: Use the simplified segment directives until you find you need the complete control over segment definition that only the standard segment directives can provide.

Allocating Data

Now that you know how to create segments, let's look at how to fill those segments with meaningful data. The stack segment is no problem; the stack resides there, and you can access the stack with **PUSH**, **POP**, and addressing by way of the BP register. The code segment is filled with the instructions generated by the instruction mnemonics in your programs, so that's no problem either.

That leaves the data segment. Turbo Assembler provides you with a variety of ways to define variables in the data segment, both initialized to some value and uninitialized. In order to understand the sorts of data Turbo Assembler lets you define, we must first teach you a bit about the fundamentals of assembler data types.

Bits, Bytes, and Bases

The fundamental unit of storage in a computer is a *bit*. A bit can store either the value 1 or the value 0. A bit, by itself, is not very useful. The 8086 doesn't deal directly with bits; in fact, it deals with nothing smaller than a *byte*, which consists of 8 bits.

Since a bit is effectively a base 2 digit, a byte contains an 8-bit, base 2 number. The largest possible 8-bit, base 2 number follows:

```
2 to the 0th power:       1
2 to the 1st power:       2
2 to the 2nd power:       4
2 to the 3rd power:       8
2 to the 4th power:      16
2 to the 5th power:      32
2 to the 6th power:      64
2 to the 7th power:  + 128
                     ---
                     255
```

This means that a byte can store one value in the range 0-255.

Each of the 8086's 8-bit registers (AL, AH, BL, BH, CL, CH, DL, and DH) stores exactly 1 byte. Each of the 8086's 1,000,000-plus addressable memory locations can also store exactly 1 byte.

The PC's character set (which includes uppercase and lowercase letters, the digits 0-9, special graphics, scientific, and foreign characters, and assorted punctuation and other characters) consists of precisely 256 characters in all. Does that number sound familiar? It should, since the PC's character set was designed so that 1 byte can store 1 character.

So now you know about the byte, which is the smallest unit that the 8086 can address, and which can store one character, one unsigned value between 0 and 255, or one signed value in the range –128 to +127. A byte is clearly inadequate for many assembler programming tasks, such as storing integer and floating-point values and storing memory pointers.

The next larger storage unit of the 8086 is the 16-bit *word*. A word is twice the size of a byte (16 bits). In fact, a word is stored in memory at two consecutive byte locations; the 8086's memory address space can be thought of as 500,000-plus words. Each of the 8086's 16-bit registers (AX, BX, CX, DX, SI, DI, BP, SP, CS, DS, ES, SS, IP, and the flags register) stores one word. A word contains a 16-bit, base 2 number. The largest possible 16-bit base 2 number follows:

```
2 to the 0th power:       1
2 to the 1st power:       2
2 to the 2nd power:       4
2 to the 3rd power:       8
2 to the 4th power:      16
2 to the 5th power:      32
2 to the 6th power:      64
2 to the 7th power:     128
2 to the 8th power:     256
2 to the 9th power:     512
2 to the 10th power:   1024
2 to the 11th power:   2048
2 to the 12th power:   4096
2 to the 13th power:   8192
2 to the 14th power:  16384
2 to the 15th power: + 32768
                      -----
                      65535
```

That's also the maximum size of an unsigned integer—which is no coincidence, since integers are 16 bits long. Signed integers (which can range from –32,768 to +32,767) are stored in words as well.

Since words are 16 bits in size, they can address any offset in a given segment, so word-sized values are large enough to be used as memory pointers. As you'll recall, the word-sized BX, BP, SI, and DI registers are used as memory pointers.

The values stored in 32-bit (4-byte) units are known as *doublewords*, or *dwords*. While the 8086 can't manipulate 32-bit integer values directly, instructions such as **ADC** and **SBB** make it possible to do 32-bit integer arithmetic with two successive 16-bit operations. Doublewords support unsigned integers in the range 0 to 4,294,967,295 and signed integers in the range –2,147,483,648 to +2,147,483,647.

The 8086 can load a segment:offset pointer from a doubleword into both a segment register and a general-purpose register with an **LDS** or **LES** instruction, but that's as far as direct support for doublewords goes. Single-precision floating-point numbers are also stored in doublewords. (Single-precision numbers require 4 bytes and can handle values from 10^{-38} to 10^{38}.)

Each double-precision floating-point value requires a full 8 bytes. Such 64-bit values are known as *quadwords*. The 8086 has no built-in support for quadwords. However, the 8087 numeric coprocessor uses quadwords as its basic data type. (Double-precision numbers handle values that range from 10^{-308} to 10^{308} and have an accuracy up to 16 digits.)

Turbo Assembler supports one more data size for temporary (intermediate) floating-point values, a data element 10 bytes in length. This 10-byte data element can also be used to store packed binary-coded decimal (BCD) values, in which each byte stores two decimal digits.

It's worth noting that the 8086 stores word and doubleword values in memory, *low byte first*. That is, if a word value is stored at address 0, then bits 7-0 of the value are stored at address 0, and bits 15-8 are stored at address 1, as illustrated by Figure 4.4.(*WordVar* contains the value 199Fh; *DwordVar* contains the value 12345678h.)

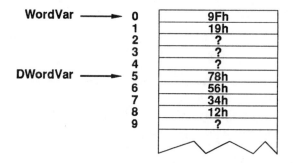

Figure 4.4: Storing WordVar and DwordVar.

Similarly, if a doubleword value is stored at address 5, bits 7-0 are stored at address 5, bits 15-8 are stored at address 6, bits 23-16 are stored at address 7, and bits 31-24 are stored at address 8. This may seem a bit odd, but it's the way that every processor in the iAPx86 family works.

Decimal, Binary, Octal, and Hexadecimal Notation

Now that you know the assembly language data types, the next question is, "How do you represent values?" Decimal (base 10) values are easy, since we've been using decimal notation all our lives. It's certainly easy enough to type

```
mov   cx,100  ;set loop counter to 100
```

and, indeed, Turbo Assembler assumes that values are expressed in decimal unless you indicate otherwise. Unfortunately, decimal is not particularly well suited for many aspects of assembly language because computers are binary (base 2) devices.

Well, then, it seems logical to use binary notation in assembler programs. You can indicate to Turbo Assembler that a number is expressed in binary notation simply by putting a *b* at the end of the number. (Of course, the number must consist only of 0s and 1s because those are the only two digits in binary notation.) For instance, decimal 5 is expressed in binary as 101b.

The problem with binary notation is that base 2 numbers are so *long* that they're hard to use. This occurs because each base 2 digit can store only two possible values, 0 and 1, as shown in the following table:

Decimal	Binary	Octal	Hexadecimal
0	0	0	0
1	1	1	1
2	10	2	2
3	11	3	3
4	100	4	4
5	101	5	5
6	110	6	6
7	111	7	7
8	1000	10	8
9	1001	11	9
10	1010	12	A
11	1011	13	B
12	1100	14	C
13	1101	15	D
14	1110	16	E
15	1111	17	F
16	10000	20	10
17	10001	21	11
18	10010	22	12
19	10011	23	13
20	10100	24	14
21	10101	25	15
22	10110	26	16
23	10111	27	17
24	11000	30	18
25	11001	31	19
26	11010	32	1A
:	:	:	:
256	100000000	400	100
:	:	:	:
4096	1000000000000	10000	1000
:	:	:	:
65536	10000000000000000	200000	10000

For instance, here's the last example in binary notation:

```
mov   cx,1100100b    ;set loop counter to 100 decimal
```

Word and doubleword binary values are even harder to read and use.

If you're not already familiar with these notations, we strongly suggest that you get a good book on the topic, since fluency with binary, octal, and hexadecimal notation is a key element in assembly language programming.

There are two notations, *octal* and *hexadecimal*, that are not only well matched to the underlying binary nature of the computer, but also reasonably compact.

Octal, or base 8, notation uses the digits 0-7, displayed in a 3-bit-per-digit form. Figure 4.5 shows how the bits of the binary value 001100100b (100 decimal) can be collected in groups of three bits to form the octal value 144o.

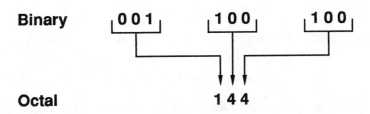

Binary 001 100 100

Octal 1 4 4

Figure 4.5: From Binary 001100100 (Decimal 100) to Octal 144

Consequently, octal numbers are only one third as long as their binary equivalents. In octal, the last example becomes

```
mov   cx,144o    ;set loop counter to 100 decimal
```

Note that the suffix *o* indicates octal notation; you can also use the suffix *q*, which isn't so easily confused with zero.

Octal notation works perfectly well and is widely used in some parts of the computer world. By and large, however, IBM PC programmers almost always use hexadecimal (base 16) notation rather than octal.

Each hexadecimal digit can take on any of 16 values. Here's how you count from zero in hexadecimal:

```
0  1  2  3  4  5  6  7  8  9  A  B  C  D  E  F  10  ....
```

The letters after 9 are the six additional hexadecimal digits *A-F*. (Lowercase *a-f* can also be used.) While it might seem strange to use letters as digits, you've got no choice, since you need 16 digits and there are only 10 traditional decimal digits. Figure 4.6 shows how the bits of the binary value 01100100b (100 decimal) can be collected in groups of 4 bits to form the hexadecimal value 64h.

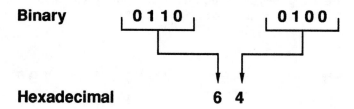

Figure 4.6: From Binary 01100100 (Decimal 100) to Hexadecimal 64

Hexadecimal notation essentially displays values in 4-bits-per-digit form, as shown in Figure 4.6. Consequently, hexadecimal numbers are only one-fourth as long as their binary equivalents. In fact, any offset or other word value can be expressed in just four hexadecimal digits. In hexadecimal, the last example becomes

```
mov   cx,64h  ;set loop counter to 100 decimal
```

Hexadecimal numbers are denoted with an *h* suffix. Additionally, hexadecimal numbers must begin with one of the digits 0-9, since a hexadecimal number like BAD4 could be mistaken for the label *BAD4h*. Here's an example where the hexadecimal value 0BAD4h and the label *BAD4h* coexist:

```
        .
        .
        .
        .DATA
BAD4h   DW    0             ;label BAD4h
        .
        .
        .

        .CODE
        mov   ax,0BAD4h     ;loads AX with a hexadecimal constant
                            ; (the leading 0 dictates that this is a constant)
        .
        .

        mov   ax,BAD4h      ;loads AX from the memory variable BAD4h
                            ; (the lack of a leading 0 dictates that
                            ; this is a label)
        .
        .
        .
```

In general, only an operand starting with a digit 0-9 can be a constant numeric value.

Floating-point numbers can be denoted in one of two ways. First, you can specify a floating-point value in the familiar mantissa/exponent form; for example,

```
  1.1
-12.45
  1.0E12
252.123E-6
```

Turbo Assembler converts the mantissa/exponent form to binary form following floating-point format. If you wish, you may specify floating-point values directly in IEEE or Microsoft binary form by specifying the number in hexadecimal and placing an *r* suffix at the end of the value.

Real numbers can only be used with the **DD**, **DQ**, and **DT** directives, which we discuss later. If you choose to use the *r* suffix, you must specify exactly the maximum number of hexadecimal digits for the data type you're initializing (plus a leading zero, if necessary); for example,

```
DD   40000000r              ;2.0 (exactly 8 long)
DQ   0C014CCCCCCCCCCCCr      ;-5.2 (16 long plus a leading zero)
DT   4037D529AE9E86000000r   ;1.2E17 (exactly 20 long)
```

In general, it's much simpler to use the mantissa/exponent form.

The letter *d* can be used as a suffix to indicate that a number is decimal. Why would you ever need to use the *d* suffix when Turbo Assembler assumes that all numbers are decimal? As you might have guessed, the answer is that you can tell Turbo Assembler to assume that numbers are in some notation other than decimal. This is done with the **.RADIX** directive, which we'll cover shortly.

Finally, character constant values can be used with the characters enclosed in single or double quotes. The value of a character is its ASCII value. For instance, all the following lines load the character *A* into AL:

```
mov   al,65
mov   al,41h
mov   al,'A'
mov   al,"A"
```

Where can values in the various notations we've described be used? Binary, octal, decimal, hexadecimal, and character values can be used anywhere a constant can be used; for example,

```
mov    ax,1001b
add    cx,5bh
sub    [Count],177o
and    al,1
mov    al,'A'
```

Floating-point values can only be used with **DD, DQ,** and **DT;** BCD (Binary Coded Decimal) values can only be used with **DT.**

Default Radix Selection

Most of the time, you'll probably want to use decimal values by default, simply because that's the most familiar notation. Occasionally, however, it's convenient to have numbers without suffixes default to another notation—that's when the **.RADIX** directive is needed. (*Radix* means "base of a numbering system," by the way.)

.RADIX selects the base in which numbers without suffixes are assumed to be specified. For example,

```
.RADIX  16
```

selects base 16, or hexadecimal, as the default notation. The following code illustrates the effect of the **.RADIX** directive:

```
    .
    .
    .
.RADIX  16       ;select base 16, hexadecimal, as the default
mov     ax,100   ;= 100h, or 256 decimal
.RADIX  10       ;select base 10, decimal, as the default
sub     ax,100   ;-100 decimal, result is 256 - 100 = 156 decimal
.RADIX  2        ;select base 2, binary, as the default
add     ax,100   ;+100b, or 4 decimal result is 156 + 4 = 160 decimal
    .
    .
    .
```

.RADIX can select base 2, 8, 10, or 16 as the default. Incidentally, the operand to **.RADIX** is always decimal, no matter what default notation is selected; in other words, one **.RADIX** directive doesn't affect the notation of the next **.RADIX** directive's operand.

There is a potential problem to consider when you use the **.RADIX** directive. No matter what default notation is selected, values specified with **DD, DQ,** and **DT** are assumed to be decimal values unless a suffix is used. This means that in

```
        .
        .
        .
.RADIX  16
DD      1E7
        .
        .
        .
```

1E7 is taken to be 1 times 10 to the seventh power, not 1E7h. In fact, you're best advised to place the *h* suffix on all hexadecimal values even after a **.RADIX 16** directive. Why? Remember that *b* and *d* are valid suffixes, specifying binary and decimal notation, respectively. Unfortunately, *b* and *d* are also valid hexadecimal digits. If **.RADIX 16** is in effect, what is Turbo Assembler to make of numbers like 129D and 101B?

As it happens, Turbo Assembler always pays attention to valid suffixes, so 129D is 129 decimal and 101B is 101 binary, or 5 decimal. What this means is that even when **.RADIX 16** is in effect, any hexadecimal number ending in *b* or *d* must have an *h* suffix. Given that, it's simplest just to put *h* suffixes on all hexadecimal numbers, and given *that*, it becomes clear that, in general, it's not particularly useful to use **.RADIX 16**.

Initialized Data

Now we're ready to look at the ways in which Turbo Assembler lets you define memory variables. First, let's look at the definition of initialized data.

The data definition directives, **DB, DW, DD, DF, DP, DQ**, and **DT**, let you define memory variables of varying data sizes as follows:

DB	1 byte
DW	2 bytes = one word
DD	4 bytes = one doubleword
DF, DP	6 bytes = one far pointer word (386)
DQ	8 bytes = one quadword
DT	10 bytes

For example,

```
        .
        .
        .
        .DATA
ByteVar     DB      'Z'     ;1 byte
WordVar     DW      101b    ;2 bytes (1 word)
```

```
DwordVar      DD      2BFh        ;4 bytes (1 doubleword)
QwordVar      DQ      307o        ;8 bytes (1 quadword)
TwordVar      DT      100         ;10 bytes
              .
              .
              .
              mov     ah,2        ;DOS display output function #
              mov     dl,[ByteVar] ;character to display
              int     21h         ;invoke DOS to display the character
              .
              .
              .
              add     ax,[WordVar]
              .
              .
              .
              add     WORD PTR [DwordVar],ax
              adc     WORD PTR [DwordVar+2],dx
              .
              .
              .
```

defines five initialized memory variables and illustrates how some of those variables might be used.

Initializing Arrays

Multiple values may appear with a single data definition directive. For instance,

```
SampleArray  DW   0, 1, 2, 3, 4
```

creates the five-entry array *SampleArray*, made up of word-sized elements, as shown in Figure 4.7. Any number of values that will fit on a line may be used with the data definition directives.

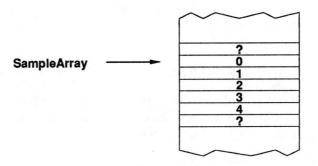

SampleArray

Figure 4.7: Example of Five-Entry Array

What if you want to define an array that's too large to fit on a single line? Just add more lines; it's not required that a label be used with the data definition directives. For instance,

```
         .
         .
         .
SquaresArray   DD    0, 1, 4, 9, 16
               DD    25, 36, 49, 64, 81
               DD    100, 121, 144, 169, 196
         .
         .
         .
```

creates an array of doubleword-sized elements named *SquaresArray*, consisting of the squares of the first 15 integers.

Turbo Assembler lets you define blocks of memory initialized to a given value with the **DUP** operator. For example,

```
BlankArray     DW    100h DUP (0)
```

creates an array *BlankArray*, consisting of 256 (decimal) words initialized to zero. Likewise,

```
ArrayOfA    DB    92 DUP ('A')
```

creates an array of 92 bytes, each initialized to the character *A*.

Initializing Character Strings

What about creating character strings? Characters are valid operands to the data definition directives, so you could define a character string as follows:

```
String DB   'A', 'B', 'C', 'D'
```

You don't have to do all that typing, though, since Turbo Assembler provides a handy shortcut:

```
String DB   'ABCD'
```

If you want to use a C-style string, which is terminated with a zero byte, you have to explicitly put the zero byte at the end. Likewise, if you want carriage-return or linefeed characters, you have to insert them as well. The following defines a string of text followed by a carriage-return character, a linefeed character, and a terminating zero byte:

```
HelloString   DB   'Hello, world',0dh,0ah,0
```

You must print carriage-return/linefeed pairs in order to advance to the left margin of the next line. For example, the program

```
          .MODEL  small
          .STACK  200h
          .DATA
String1 DB      'Line1','$'
String2 DB      'Line2','$'
String3 DB      'Line3','$'
          .CODE
ProgramStart:
          mov   ax,@data
          mov   ds,ax
          mov   ah,9              ;DOS print string function #
          mov   dx,OFFSET String1 ;string to print
          int   21h              ;invoke DOS to print string
          mov   dx,OFFSET String2 ;string to print
          int   21h              ;invoke DOS to print string
          mov   dx,OFFSET String3 ;string to print
          int   21h              ;invoke DOS to print string
          mov   ah,4ch           ;DOS terminate program function
          int   21h
          END   ProgramStart
```

prints the following output:

```
Line1Line2Line3
```

If, however, you add a carriage-return/linefeed pair at the end of each string,

```
String1 DB      'Line1',0dh,0ah,'$'
String2 DB      'Line2',0dh,0ah,'$'
String3 DB      'Line3',0dh,0ah,'$'
```

the output becomes

```
Line1
Line2
Line3
```

Initializing with Expressions and Labels

The initial value of an initialized variable must be a constant, but it doesn't necessarily have to be a number. Expressions are fine:

```
TestVar DW    ((924/2)+1)
```

as are labels:

```
        .
        .
        .
        .DATA
Buffer          DW    16 DUP (0)
BufferPointer   DW    Buffer
        .
        .
        .
```

Whenever a label is used as an operand to a data definition directive, it's the value of the label itself that's used, not the value stored at that label. In the last example, the initial value of *BufferPointer* is the offset in the **.DATA** segment of *Buffer*, not the value zero that's stored at *Buffer*, much as if **OFFSET** *Buffer* had been used to initialize *BufferPointer*. In other words, given the previous initialization of *BufferPointer*, both

```
mov  ax,OFFSET Buffer
```

and

```
mov  ax,[BufferPointer]
```

load AX with the same value, the offset of *Buffer*.

Labels can be used in data definition expressions. For example, the following code initializes the variable *WordArrayLength* to the length in bytes of *WordArray*:

```
              .
              .
              .
          .DATA
WordArray         DW      50 DUP (0)
WordArrayEnd      LABEL   WORD
WordArrayLength DW        (WordArrayEnd - WordArray)
              .
              .
              .
```

If you wanted to calculate the length of *WordArray* in words rather than bytes, you could do it simply by dividing the length in bytes by two:

```
WordArrayLengthInWords  DW   (WordArrayEnd - WordArray) / 2
```

Uninitialized Data

Sometimes it doesn't make sense to assign an initial value to a memory variable. For instance, suppose your program reads the next ten characters typed at the keyboard into an array named *KeyBuffer* as follows:

```
              .
              .
              .
        mov   cx,10                  ;# of characters to read
        mov   bx,OFFSET KeyBuffer
                                     ;the characters will be stored
                                     ; in KeyBuffer
GetKeyLoop:
        mov   ah,1                   ;DOS keyboard input function #
        int   21h                    ;get the next key pressed
        mov   [bx],al                ;save the character
        inc   bx                     ;point to storage location for next key
        loop  GetKeyLoop
              .
              .
              .
```

You could define *KeyBuffer* to be initialized with

```
KeyBuffer   DB  10 DUP (0)
```

but that really doesn't make much sense, since the initial values in *KeyBuffer* are immediately overwritten in *GetKeyLoop*. What you really need is a way to define a memory variable as uninitialized, and Turbo Assembler provides that capability with the question mark (?).

The question mark tells Turbo Assembler you are reserving a storage location, but not initializing it. For example, the proper way to define *KeyBuffer* in the last example is like this:

```
KeyBuffer  DB  10 DUP (?)
```

This line reserves 10 bytes starting at the label *KeyBuffer*, but does not set those bytes to any specific value.

Of course, whenever you use an uninitialized memory variable, you must be sure to initialize it in your program before using it. For instance, it would be a mistake to use the contents of *KeyBuffer* in the last example before filling it, since the initial values stored in *KeyBuffer* are not defined.

Named Memory Locations

So far, we've seen how to name memory locations by preceding a data definition directive such as **DB** with a label. The **LABEL** directive is another handy way to name a memory location, without allocating any storage.

LABEL lets you specify both a label's name and its type without having to define any data. For example, the following is another way to define the array *KeyBuffer* used in the last example:

```
         .
         .
         .
KeyBuffer    LABEL  BYTE
        DB   10 DUP (?)
         .
         .
         .
```

The label types that can be defined with **LABEL** include

BYTE	**PWORD**	**FAR**
WORD	**QWORD**	**PROC**
DWORD	**TBYTE**	**UNKNOWN**
FWORD	**NEAR**	

BYTE, WORD, DWORD, FWORD, PWORD, QWORD, and **TBYTE** are self-explanatory, labeling 1-, 2-, 4-, 6-, 8-, and 10-byte data items, respectively. Here's an example of initializing a memory variable as a pair of bytes but accessing it as a word:

```
              .
              .
              .
              .DATA
WordVar  LABEL    WORD
              DB       1,2
              .
              .
              .
              .CODE
              .
              .
              .
              mov      ax,[WordVar]
              .
              .
              .
```

When this code is executed, AL is loaded with 1 (the first byte of *WordVar*), and AH is loaded with 2.

NEAR and **FAR** are used in code to select the type of call or jump needed to reach a certain label. For example, in

```
              .
              .
              .
              .CODE
              .
              .
              .
FarLabel      LABEL    FAR
NearLabel     LABEL    NEAR
              mov      ax,1
              .
              .
              .
              jmp      FarLabel
              .
              .
              .
              jmp      NearLabel
              .
              .
              .
```

the first **JMP** is a far jump (loading both CS and IP) because it is to a **FAR** label, while the second jump is a near jump (loading only IP) because it is to a **NEAR** label. Note that *FarLabel* and *NearLabel* both describe the same address, that of the **MOV** instruction, but allow you to branch to that location in two different ways.

When you are using the simplified segment directives, **PROC** is a handy way to define a label in the appropriate size, near or far, for the current code model. When the memory model is tiny, small, or compact, **LABEL PROC** is the same as **LABEL NEAR**; when the memory model is medium, large, or huge, **LABEL PROC** is the same as **LABEL FAR**. This means that if you change the memory model, you can change certain labels automatically as well.

For example, in

```
        .MODEL  small
        .
        .
        .
        .CODE
        .
        .
        .
EntryPoint      LABEL   PROC
        .
        .
        .
```

EntryPoint is near, but if you change the memory model to large, *EntryPoint* will become far. Normally, you will use the **PROC** directive (discussed in the section "Subroutines" on page 174), rather than **LABEL**, to define the sort of entry points that you would want to have change as the memory model changes; however, sometimes you'll need more than one entry point into a subroutine and then you'll need **LABEL**, as well as **PROC**.

Finally, we come to **LABEL UNKNOWN**. **UNKNOWN** is simply a way of saying that you're not sure what data type a label is going to be used as. If you're familiar with C, **UNKNOWN** is similar to C's **void** type. As an example of **UNKNOWN**, suppose you have a memory variable, *TempVar*, that's sometimes accessed as a byte and sometimes accessed as a word. The following code does the job by using **LABEL UNKNOWN**:

```
        .
        .
        .
        .DATA
TempVar LABEL   UNKNOWN
        DB      ?,?
        .
        .
        .
```

```
        .CODE
        .
        .
        .
        mov     [TempVar],ax
        .
        .
        .
        add     dl,[TempVar]
        .
        .
```

Moving Data

Up to this point, you've learned a lot about the nature of assembly language, fundamental assembler concepts, and the structure of assembler programs. Now that you've got that solid foundation, it's time to focus on assembler instructions, which form the part of any assembler program that actually puts the 8086 through its paces. Let's start with the most basic of assembler operations—moving data.

MOV is the instruction that moves data on the 8086. Actually, **MOV** is something of a misnomer; **COPY** might be more like it, since **MOV** actually stores a copy of the source operand in the destination operand, without affecting the source. For example,

```
    .
    .
    .
    mov     ax,0
    mov     bx,9
    mov     ax,bx
    .
    .
    .
```

first stores the constant 0 in AX, then stores the constant 9 in BX, and finally copies the contents of BX to AX as shown in these next few diagrams.

After mov ax,0:

AX	0
BX	?

After mov bx,9:

AX	0
BX	9

After mov ax,bx:

AX	9
BX	9

Note that the value 9 is not moved from BX to AX, but is rather copied from BX to AX.

MOV accepts almost any pair of operands that makes sense except when a segment register is an operand. (We'll discuss this situation in the section "Accessing Segment Registers" on page 145.) Any of the following can be used for the source (right-hand) operand to **MOV**: a constant, an expression that resolves to a constant, a general-purpose register, or a memory location accessed with any of the addressing modes discussed in the section "Memory-Addressing Modes" on page 96. Either a general-purpose register or a memory location can be used for the destination (left-hand) operand to **MOV**.

Selecting Data Size

In assembly language, it's possible to copy byte or word values with the **MOV** instruction. Let's look at how Turbo Assembler determines what data size to work with.

In many cases, the operands to **MOV** tell Turbo Assembler exactly what the data size should be. If a register is involved, then the data size must be the size of that register. For example, the data sizes of the following instructions are clear:

```
        .
        .
        .
mov    al,1              ;byte-sized
mov    dx,si             ;word-sized
mov    bx,[di]           ;word-sized
mov    [bp+si+2],al      ;byte-sized
        .
        .
        .
```

Likewise, named memory locations have inherent sizes, so the data sizes of the following instructions are known to Turbo Assembler:

```
        .
        .
        .
        .DATA
TestChar       DB    ?
TempPointer    DW    TestChar
        .
        .
        .
        .CODE
        .
        .
        .
mov    [TestChar],'A'
mov    [TempPointer],0
        .
        .
        .
```

Sometimes, though, you'll have a **MOV** instruction that has no defined size whatsoever. For example, there's no way Turbo Assembler can be sure whether the following instruction should store a byte- or word-sized value:

```
mov    [bx],1
```

and, in fact, Turbo Assembler will complain that it doesn't know how to assemble such an instruction. It would also be handy to be able to handle the case where you want to temporarily access a word-sized variable as a byte, or vice versa.

Turbo Assembler gives you a means to flexibly define data size in the form of the **WORD PTR** and **BYTE PTR** operators. **WORD PTR** tells Turbo Assembler to treat a given memory operand as word-sized, and **BYTE PTR** tells Turbo Assembler to treat a given memory operand as byte-sized, regardless of its predefined size. For example, the last example could be made to store a word-sized value 1 to the word pointed to by BX with

```
mov    WORD PTR [bx],1
```

or could be made to store a byte-sized value 1 to the byte pointed to by BX with

```
mov    BYTE PTR [bx],1
```

Note that **WORD PTR** and **BYTE PTR** make no sense when applied to registers, since registers are always a fixed size; in this case, **WORD PTR** and **BYTE PTR** are ignored. Similarly, **WORD PTR** and **BYTE PTR** are ignored when applied to a constant, which always takes on the same size as the destination operand.

WORD PTR and **BYTE PTR** have another use, which is to temporarily select a different data size for a named memory variable. Why would that be useful? Consider the following:

```
        .
        .
        .
        .DATA
Source1 DD      12345h
Source2 DD      54321h
Sum     DD      ?
        .
        .
        .
        .CODE
        .
        .
        .
        mov    ax,WORD PTR [Source1]     ;get low word of Source1
        mov    dx,WORD PTR [Source1+2]   ;get high word of Source1
        add    ax,WORD PTR [Source2]     ;add to Source2 low word
        adc    dx,WORD PTR [Source2+2]   ;add to Source2 high word
        mov    WORD PTR [Sum],ax         ;store low word of sum
        mov    WORD PTR [Sum+2],dx       ;store high word of sum
        .
        .
        .
```

The variables this example works with are all long integers or doublewords. However, the 8086 can't perform doubleword addition directly, so you have to break up the addition into a series of word-sized operations. **WORD PTR** lets you access parts of *Source1*, *Source2*, and *Sum* as words, even though the variables themselves are doublewords.

While the **FAR PTR** and **NEAR PTR** operators don't strictly affect data size, they are similar to **WORD PTR** and **BYTE PTR**. **FAR PTR** forces a label that is the target of a jump or call to be treated as a far label, causing the jump or call to load both CS and IP. **NEAR PTR,** on the other hand, forces a label to be treated as a near label, which is branched to by loading only IP.

Signed Versus Unsigned Data

Both signed and unsigned numbers are made up of a series of binary digits. The distinction between the two is made by you, the assembler programmer, not by the 8086 itself. For example, the value 0FFFFh can be either 65,535 or –1, depending on how your program chooses to interpret it. How do you know that 0FFFFh is –1? Add 1 to it:

```
   .
   .
   .
mov   ax,0ffffh
add   ax,1
   .
   .
   .
```

and you'll find that the result is 0, which is just what you'd expect to get from adding –1 and 1 together.

The same **ADD** instruction works just fine whether you're considering the operands to be signed or unsigned. For example, suppose you were to subtract 1 from 0FFFFh as follows:

```
   .
   .
   .
mov   ax,0ffffh
sub   ax,1
   .
   .
   .
```

The result would be 0FFFEh, which is either 65,534 (as an unsigned number) or –2 (as a signed number).

If this seems confusing, you should read one of the books recommended at the end of this book in order to learn more about *two's complement* arithmetic, the means by which the 8086 handles signed numbers. Unfortunately, we haven't the space to cover signed arithmetic here, although it's a useful subject for an assembler programmer to understand. Right now, you just need to know that **ADD, SUB, ADC,** and **SBB** work equally well with signed and unsigned numbers, so no special instructions are needed for signed addition and subtraction. Sign does matter for multiplication and division, as you'll see later; it also matters when you're converting between data sizes and when you're executing conditional jumps.

Converting Between Data Sizes

Sometimes it's necessary to convert words to bytes, or vice versa. This is one area where it matters whether the values are signed or unsigned.

First, let's look at converting a word to a byte. That's simple; just toss away the high byte of the word. For example,

```
      .
      .
      .
mov   ax,5
mov   bl,al
      .
      .
      .
```

converts the word value 5 in AX to the byte value 5 in BL. Of course, you must be sure that the value you're converting will fit in a byte; trying to convert 100h to a byte with

```
      .
      .
      .
mov   dx,100h
mov   al,dl
      .
      .
      .
```

would be fruitless, since only the lower byte, which is 0, would be stored in AL.

Converting an unsigned byte to a word is simply a matter of zeroing the upper byte of the word. For example,

```
        •
        •
        •
    mov   cl,12
    mov   al,cl
    mov   ah,0
        •
        •
        •
```

converts the unsigned byte value 12 in CL to the unsigned word value 12 in AX.

Converting a signed byte to a word is a bit more complex, so the 8086 provides you with a special instruction to handle that task: **CBW**. **CBW** converts a signed byte in AL to a signed word in AX. The following code converts the signed byte value –1 in DH to the signed word value –1 in DX:

```
        •
        •
        •
    mov   dh,-1
    mov   al,dh
    cbw
    mov   dx,ax
        •
        •
        •
```

The 8086 also provides a special instruction, **CWD**, for converting a signed word in AX to a signed doubleword in DX:AX (the high word is in DX). The following converts the signed word value +10,000 in AX to the signed doubleword value +10,000 in DX:AX:

```
        •
        •
        •
    mov   ax,10000
    cwd
        •
        •
        •
```

Unsigned word values can be converted to unsigned doubleword values by zeroing the high word of the value.

Accessing Segment Registers

Although the **MOV** instruction can be used to move values to and from segment registers, this is a special case, more limited than other uses of **MOV**. If a segment register is one operand to **MOV**, the other operand must be a general-purpose register or a memory location. It's not possible to load a constant directly into a segment register, and one segment register may not be copied directly to another segment register.

Since segment names are constants, it's necessary to load segment registers by way of a general-purpose register or a memory variable. For example, here are two ways to set ES to the **.DATA** segment:

```
        .
        .
        .
        .DATA
DataSeg DW      @data
        .
        .
        .
        .CODE
        .
        .
        .
        mov     ax,@data
        mov     es,ax
        .
        .
        .
        mov     es,[DataSeg]
        .
        .
        .
```

What you'd like to do, but can't, is this:

```
    mov    es,@data        ;this won't work!
```

In order to copy the contents of one segment register to another segment register, you have to pass the value through a general-purpose register or memory. For example, both

```
        .
        .
        .
    mov   ax,cs
    mov   ds,ax
        .
        .
        .
```

and

```
        .
        .
        .
    push  cs
    pop   ds
        .
        .
        .
```

copy the contents of CS to DS. The first method executes faster, but the second is smaller in code size.

It's worth noting that it's not only the **MOV** instruction that limits you when it comes to the use of segment registers; most instructions can't use segment registers as operands at all. Segment registers can be pushed to and popped from the stack, but that's about it; they can't be used in addition, subtraction, logical operations, or comparisons.

Moving Data To and From the Stack

You've already encountered the stack, the last-in, first-out storage area in the stack segment. The top of the stack is always pointed to by SP. The **MOV** instruction can be used to access data on the stack via memory-addressing modes that use BP as a base pointer; for example,

```
    mov   ax,[bp+4]
```

loads AX with the contents of the word at offset BP+4 in the stack segment. (See Chapter 2 for a discussion of accessing the stack via BP.)

Most often, the stack is accessed with **PUSH** and **POP. PUSH** stores the operand on top of the stack, and **POP** retrieves the value on the top of the stack and stores it in the operand. For example,

```
        .
        .
        .
mov     ax,1
push    ax
pop     bx
        .
        .
        .
```

pushes the value in AX (which is 1) on top of the stack, then pops 1 from
the top of the stack and stores it in BX.

Exchanging Data

The **XCHG** instruction lets you swap the contents of two operands. This is
a convenient way to perform an operation that would otherwise require
three instructions. For example,

```
xchg    ax,dx
```

swaps the contents of AX and DX, an operation that is equivalent to

```
        .
        .
        .
push    ax
mov     ax,dx
pop     dx
        .
        .
        .
```

I/O

So far, we've discussed moving data between constant values, registers,
and the memory address space of the 8086. As you'll recall, the 8086 has a
second, independent address space, known as the input/output, or I/O,
address space. The 65,536 I/O addresses, or ports, are generally used as
control-and-data channels to devices such as disk drives, display adapters,
keyboards, and printers.

Most of the 8086's instructions, including **MOV**, can only access operands
in the memory address space. Only two instructions, **IN** and **OUT**, can
access I/O ports.

IN copies a value from a selected I/O port into AL or AX. The I/O port address that serves as the source can be selected in one of two ways. If the I/O port address is less than 256 (100h), you can specify the address as part of the instruction; for example,

```
in    al,41h
```

copies a byte from I/O port 41h to **AL**.

Alternatively, you can use DX to point to the I/O port to be read:

```
.
.
.
mov   dx,41h
in    al,dx
.
.
.
```

Why bother using DX as an I/O pointer? For one thing, if the I/O port address is greater than 255, you *must* use DX. For another, the use of DX gives you more flexibility in addressing I/O ports; for instance, a subroutine can use a passed I/O port pointer by loading it into DX.

Don't be fooled by the syntax of the **IN** instruction; AL and AX are the *only* possible destination operands. Likewise, DX and a constant value less than 256 are the only possible source operands. Much as you might like to, you can never use an instruction like

```
in    bh,si    ;this won't work!
```

OUT is exactly like **IN**, except that AL or AX is the source operand, and an I/O port pointed to by DX or a constant value less than 256 is the destination operand. The following code sets I/O port 3B4h to 0Fh:

```
.
.
.
mov   dx,3b4h
mov   al,0fh
out   dx,al
.
.
.
```

Operations

Data movement is certainly important, since a computer spends much of its time moving data about from here to there. Still, it's equally important to be able to manipulate the data by performing arithmetic and logical operations on it. Next, we'll take a look at the arithmetic and logical operations supported by the 8086.

Arithmetic Operations

Even if your PC doesn't spend all its time crunching numbers, you know that it *could* if you needed it to. After all, spreadsheets, database programs, and engineering packages all run on the PC. Given that, it's pretty obvious that the 8086 must be a powerful math engine, right?

Well, yes and no. While it's certainly true that software that runs on the 8086 can do wonderful math, the 8086 itself provides surprisingly rudimentary arithmetic capabilities. For starters, the 8086 has no instructions to support any sort of floating-point arithmetic (arithmetic with numbers such as 5.2 and 1.03E17, as opposed to arithmetic with integers), let alone transcendental functions; that's the job of the 8087 numeric coprocessor. This doesn't mean that 8086 programs can't do floating-point arithmetic; certainly, spreadsheets run on PCs without 8087s. However, 8086 programs must perform floating-point arithmetic by a slow, involved series of shift, add, and test instructions, rather than with a single speedy instruction, as can be done with the 8087.

Also, the 8086 provides no arithmetic or logical instructions that can directly handle operands larger than 16 bits.

What arithmetic operations *does* the 8086 have built-in support for, then? Well, the 8086 can perform 8- and 16-bit signed and unsigned addition, subtraction, multiplication, and division, and has special, fast instructions for incrementing and decrementing operands. The 8086 also provides support for addition and subtraction of values larger than 16 bits, although operations on such values require multiple instructions.

Addition and Subtraction

We've already encountered the **ADD** and **SUB** instructions in many of our example programs. They operate much as you'd expect. **ADD** adds the contents of the source (right-hand) operand to the contents of the destination operand, and stores the result back in the destination operand.

SUB is the same except that it subtracts the source operand from the destination.

So, for example,

```
            .
            .
            .
            .DATA
BaseVal DW      99
Adjust  DW      10
            .
            .
            .
            .CODE
            .
            .
            .
            mov    dx,[BaseVal]
            add    dx,11
            sub    dx,[Adjust]
            .
            .
            .
```

first loads the value 99 stored at *BaseVal* into DX, then adds the constant 11 to it, resulting in the value 110 in DX, and finally subtracts the value 10 stored at *Adjust* from DX. The result: 100 is stored in DX.

32-Bit Operands

ADD and **SUB** work with either 8- or 16-bit operands. If you want to add or subtract, say, 32-bit operands, you must break the operation into a series of word-sized operations and use **ADC** or **SBB**.

When you add two operands, the 8086 stores a status in the carry flag (the C bit in the flags register) that indicates whether there was a carry out of the destination; that is, whether the result of the addition was too large to fit in the destination. You're familiar with the concept of carry-in decimal arithmetic; if you add 90 and 10, you get a carry-out to the third digit:

```
   90
+  10
 ────
  100
```

Now consider this addition of two hexadecimal values:

```
   FFFF
+    1
------
 10000
```

The lower word of the result is zero, and the carry is 1, since the result, 10000h, doesn't fit into 16 bits.

ADC is just like **ADD** except that it takes the carry flag (which was presumably set by a previous addition) into account. Whenever you add two values that are larger than a word, add the lower (least significant) words of the values together first with **ADD**, then add the remaining words of the values together with one or more **ADC** instructions, adding the most-significant words last. For example, the following code adds a doubleword value stored in CX:BX to a doubleword value stored in DX:AX:

```
    .
    .
    .
add   ax,bx
adc   dx,cx
    .
    .
    .
```

and the following adds the quadword value at *DoubleLong1* to the quadword value at *DoubleLong2*:

```
    .
    .
    .
mov   ax,[DoubleLong1]
add   [DoubleLong2],ax
mov   ax,[DoubleLong1+2]
adc   [DoubleLong2+2],ax
mov   ax,[DoubleLong1+4]
adc   [DoubleLong2+4],ax
mov   ax,[DoubleLong1+6]
adc   [DoubleLong2+6],ax
    .
    .
    .
```

SBB operates along much the same lines as **ADC**. As **SBB** performs a subtraction, it takes into account any borrow that occurred during the previous subtraction. For example, the following code subtracts a doubleword value stored in CX:BX from a doubleword value stored in DX:AX:

```
        .
        .
        .
sub     ax,bx
sbb     dx,cx
        .
        .
        .
```

With both **ADC** and **SBB**, you must make sure that the carry flag hasn't
changed since the last addition or subtraction, or else the carry/borrow
status stored in the carry flag would be lost. For instance, the following will
not add CX:BX to DX:AX correctly:

```
        .
        .
        .
add     ax,bx     ;add the lower words
sub     si,si     ;set SI to 0 (clears the carry flag)
adc     dx,cx     ;add the upper words...
                  ; this won't work properly, since the
                  ; carry flag from the add has been destroyed!
        .
        .
        .
```

Incrementing and Decrementing

When an assembler program needs to perform an addition, odds are good
that it will be adding the value 1. This is known as *incrementing*. Likewise,
the value 1 is often subtracted from registers and memory variables. This is
known as *decrementing*. For operations such as counting down or counting
up, and for advancing pointer registers through memory, incrementing and
decrementing are all the addition and subtraction that's needed.

In recognition of the frequent need for incrementing and decrementing, the
8086 provides the instructions **INC** and **DEC**. As you might expect, **INC**
adds 1 to a register or memory variable, and **DEC** subtracts 1 from a
register or memory variable.

For example, the following code fills the 10-byte array *TempArray* with the
numbers 0, 1, 2, 3, 4, 5, 6, 7, 8, 9:

```
        .
        .
        .
        .DATA
TempArray    DB    10 DUP (?)
```

```
FillCount    DW    ?
             .
             .
             .
             .CODE
             .
             .
             .
        mov   al,0                    ;first value to store in TempArray
        mov   bx,OFFSET TempArray     ;point BX to TempArray
        mov   [FillCount],10          ;# of elements to fill
FillTempArrayLoop:
        mov   [bx],al                 ;set the current element of TempArray
        inc   bx                      ;point to next element of TempArray
        inc   al                      ;next value to store
        dec   [FillCount]             ;count down # of elements to fill
        jnz   FillTempArrayLoop       ;do another element if we haven't
                                      ; filled all the elements
             .
             .
             .
```

Why would you want to use, say,

```
inc   bx
```

instead of

```
add   bx,1
```

since they do the same thing? Well, where the **ADD** is 3 bytes long, the **INC** is only 1 byte long, and executes faster as well. In fact, it's more compact to perform *two* **INC** instructions than to add 2 to a word-sized register. (Increments and decrements of byte-sized register and memory variables are 2 bytes long—still shorter than adding or subtracting.)

In short, **INC** and **DEC** are the most efficient instructions available for incrementing and decrementing registers and memory variables. Use them whenever you can.

Multiplication and Division

The 8086 can perform certain types of integer multiplication and division. This is one of the strong points of the 8086, since many microprocessors provide no direct support at all for multiplication and division, and it's fairly complex to perform those operations in software.

The **MUL** instruction multiplies two 8- or 16-bit unsigned factors together, generating a 16- or 32-bit product. Let's look at the 8-bit-by-8-bit multiply first.

One of the factors to an 8-bit-by-8-bit **MUL** must be stored in AL; the other may be in any 8-bit general-purpose register or memory operand. **MUL** always stores the 16-bit product in AX. For example,

```
        .
        .
        .
mov     al,25
mov     dh,40
mul     dh
        .
        .
        .
```

multiplies AL times DH, placing the result, 1000, in AX. Note that **MUL** only requires one operand; the other factor is always AL (or AX, in the case of a 16-bit-by-16-bit multiply).

A 16-bit-by-16-bit **MUL** is similar; one factor must be stored in AX, while the other may be in any 16-bit, general-purpose register or memory operand. **MUL** puts the 32-bit product in DX:AX, with the lower (least significant) 16 bits of the product in AX and the upper (most significant) 16 bits of the product in DX. For instance,

```
        .
        .
        .
mov     ax,1000
mul     ax
        .
        .
        .
```

loads AX with 1000 and then squares AX, placing the result, 1,000,000, in DX:AX.

Unlike addition and subtraction, multiplication does care whether the operands are signed or unsigned, so there's a second multiplication instruction, **IMUL**, for multiplying 8- or 16-bit signed factors. Apart from handling signed values, **IMUL** is just like **MUL**. The code

```
        .
        .
        .
mov    al,-2
mov    ah,10
imul   ah
        .
        .
        .
```

stores the value –20 in AX.

The 8086 lets you divide a 32-bit value by a 16-bit value, or a 16-bit value by an 8-bit value, with certain restrictions. Let's look at 16-bit-by-8-bit division first.

In 16-bit-by-8-bit unsigned division, the dividend must be stored in AX. The 8-bit divisor may be in any 8-bit, general-purpose register or memory variable. **DIV** always puts the 8-bit quotient in AL, and the 8-bit remainder in AH. For example,

```
        .
        .
        .
mov    ax,51
mov    dl,10
div    dl
        .
        .
        .
```

results in 5 (51 divided by 10) in AL and 1 (the remainder of 51 divided by 10) in AH.

Note that the quotient is an 8-bit value. This means that the result of a 16-bit-by-8-bit division must be no larger than 255. If the quotient is too large, an interrupt 0 (the divide-by-zero interrupt) is generated. The code

```
        .
        .
        .
mov    ax,0ffffh
mov    bl,1
div    bl
        .
        .
        .
```

generates a divide-by-zero interrupt. (As you might expect, a divide-by-zero interrupt is also generated if zero is used as a divisor.)

For 32-bit-by-16-bit division, the dividend must be stored in DX:AX. The 16-bit divisor may be in any 16-bit, general-purpose register or memory variable. **DIV** always puts the 16-bit quotient in AX, and the 16-bit remainder in DX. For example,

```
        .
        .
        .
mov     ax,2
mov     dx,1       ;load DX:AX with 10002h
mov     bx,10h
div     bx
        .
        .
        .
```

results in 1000h (10002h divided by 10h) in AX and 2 (the remainder of 10002h divided by 10h) in DX.

Again, the quotient is only a 16-bit value, so the result of a 32-bit-by-16-bit division must be no larger than 0FFFFh, or 65,535, else a divide-by-zero interrupt is generated.

Like multiplication, division cares whether signed or unsigned operands are used. **DIV** is used for unsigned operands, and **IDIV** is used for signed operands. For example,

```
            .
            .
            .
        .DATA
TestDivisor     DW    100
            .
            .
            .
        .CODE
            .
            .
            .
mov     ax,-667
cwd                         ;set DX:AX to -667
idiv    [TestDivisor]
            .
            .
            .
```

stores –6 in AX and –67 in DX.

Changing Sign

Finally, we come to the **NEG** instruction, with which you can reverse the sign of the contents of a general-purpose register or memory variable. For example, the code

```
        .
        .
        .
mov     ax,1        ;set AX to 1
neg     ax          ;negate AX, which becomes -1
mov     bx,ax       ;copy AX to BX
neg     bx          ;negate BX, which becomes 1
        .
        .
        .
```

ends up with –1 in AX and 1 in BX.

Logical Operations

Turbo Assembler supports a full set of instructions that perform logical operations, including **AND**, **OR**, **XOR**, and **NOT**. These instructions are very useful for manipulating individual bits within a byte or word, and for performing Boolean algebra.

Given two source bits, the logical instructions produce the results shown in Table 4.2. The logical instructions perform these bit-wise operations on corresponding bits of the source operands; for example,

```
and   ax,dx
```

performs a logical **AND** with bit 0 of AX and bit 0 of DX as the source bits and bit 0 of AX as the destination, and does the same for bit 1, bit 2, and so on, up to bit 15.

Table 4.2: The Operation of the 8086 AND, OR, and XOR Logical Instructions

Source Bit A	Source Bit B	A AND B	A OR B	A XOR B
0	0	0	0	0
0	1	0	1	1
1	0	0	1	1
1	1	1	1	0

The **AND** instruction combines two operands according to the rules shown in Table 4.2, setting each bit in the destination to 1 only if both corresponding source bits are 1. **AND** lets you isolate a specific bit, or force specific bits to 0. For example,

```
        .
        .
        .
mov     dx,3dah
in      al,dx
and     al,1
        .
        .
        .
```

isolates bit 0 of the status byte of the Color/Graphics Adapter (CGA). This code leaves AL set to 1 if display memory on the CGA can be updated without causing snow, and set to 0 otherwise.

The **OR** instruction combines two operands according to the rules shown in Table 4.2, setting each bit in the destination to 1 if either of the corresponding source bits is 1. **OR** lets you force a specific bit(s) to 1. For example,

```
        .
        .
        .
mov     ax,40h
mov     ds,ax
mov     bx,10h
or      WORD PTR [bx],0030h
        .
        .
        .
```

forces both bit 5 and bit 4 of the BIOS equipment flag word to 1, causing the BIOS to support the monochrome display adapter.

The **XOR** instruction combines two operands according to the rules shown in Table 4.2 (page 157), setting each bit in the destination to 1 only if one of the corresponding source bits is 0, and the other is 1. This lets you flip the value of selected bits within a byte. For example,

```
        .
        .
        .
mov     al,01010101b
xor     al,11110000b
        .
        .
        .
```

sets **AL** to 10100101b, or A5h. The key here is that when **AL** is exclusive-ORed with 11110000b, or 0F0h, the 1 bits in 0F0h flip the value of the corresponding bits in **AL**, while the 0 bits in 0F0h leave the corresponding bits in **AL** unchanged. The result is that all bits in the upper nibble of **AL** are changed, while all bits in the lower nibble of **AL** remain the same.

By the way, **XOR** is a handy way to zero a register. For instance, this code set AX to 0:

```
xor    ax,ax
```

Finally, **NOT** simply flips each bit in the operand to the opposite state, just as if an **XOR** with a source operand of 0FFh had been executed. For instance, consider

```
       .
       .
       .
mov    bl,10110001b
not    bl               ;flip BL to 01001110b
xor    bl,0ffh          ;flip BL back to 10110001b
       .
       .
       .
```

Shifts and Rotates

The 8086 provides a variety of means by which to move bits left or right in a register or memory variable. The simplest of these is the logical shift.

SHL (shift left, also known as **SAL**) moves each bit in the destination one place to the left, or toward the most-significant bit. Figure 4.8 shows how the value 10010110b (96h or 150 decimal) stored in AL is shifted left with **SHL AL,1**. The result is the value 00101100b (2Ch or 44 decimal), which is stored back in AL. The carry flag is set to 1.

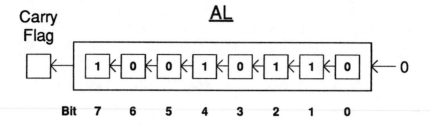

Figure 4.8: Example of a Shift Left

The most-significant bit is shifted out of the operand altogether and into the carry flag, and a 0 is shifted into the least significant bit.

Of what use is a left shift? The most common use of **SHL** is to perform fast multiplies by powers of two, since each **SHL** multiplies the operand by 2. For example, the following code multiplies DX by 16:

```
      .
      .
      .
shl   dx,1    ;DX * 2
shl   dx,1    ;DX * 4
shl   dx,1    ;DX * 8
shl   dx,1    ;DX * 16
      .
      .
      .
```

Multiplying by shifts is much faster than using the **MUL** instruction.

You'll notice that there's a second operand to **SHL** in the previous example, the value 1. This indicates that DX should be shifted left by 1 bit. Unfortunately, the 8086 doesn't support 2, 3, or any constant value other than 1 for a shift amount. However, CL can be used to supply a shift count; for instance,

```
      .
      .
      .
mov   cl,4
shl   dx,cl
      .
      .
      .
```

multiplies DX times 16, just as the last example did.

Turbo Assembler User's Guide

If there's a left shift, it seems logical that there must also be a right shift, and there is—in fact, there are two right shifts. **SHR** (shift right) is much like **SHL**: It shifts the bits in the operand to the right, either by 1 or CL bits, then shifts the least-significant bit into the carry flag and shifts 0 into the most-significant bit. **SHR** is a quick way to do unsigned division by powers of two.

SAR (arithmetic shift right) is just like **SHR**, except that with **SAR**, the most-significant bit of the operand is shifted right to the next bit, and then back to itself. Figure 4.9 shows how the value 10010110b (96h or –106 in signed decimal) stored in AL is shifted right with **SAR AL,1**. The result is the value 11001011b (0CBh or –53 in signed decimal), which is stored back in AL. The carry flag is set to 0.

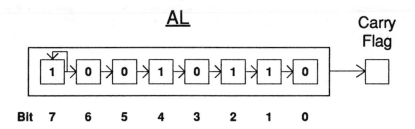

Figure 4.9: Example of SAR (Arithmetic Right Shift)

This has the effect of preserving the sign of the operand, so **SAR** is useful for performing signed division by powers of two. For example,

```
       .
       .
       .
mov    bx,-4
sar    bx,1
       .
       .
       .
```

leaves –2 stored in BX.

There are also four rotate instructions: **ROR, ROL, RCR,** and **RCL. ROR** is like **SHR**, except that the least-significant bit is shifted back into the most-significant bit, as well as to the carry flag. Figure 4.10 shows how the value 10010110b (96h or 150 decimal) stored in AL is rotated right with **ROR AL,1**. The result is the value 01001011b (04Bh or 75 in decimal), which is stored back in AL. The carry flag is set to 0.

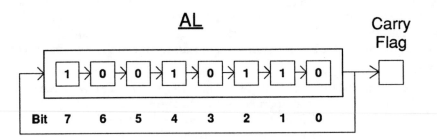

Figure 4.10: Example of ROR (Rotate Right)

ROL reverses the action of **ROR,** shifting the operand in a circular fashion, but to the left, with the most-significant bit shifting back into the least-significant bit. **ROR** and **ROL** are useful for realigning the bits in a byte or word. For example,

```
   .
   .
   .
mov   si,49F1h
mov   cl,4
ror   si,cl
   .
   .
   .
```

leaves 149Fh in SI, moving bits 3-0 to bits 15-12, bits 7-4 to bits 3-0, and so on.

RCR and **RCL** are a bit different. **RCR** is like a right shift in which the most-significant bit is shifted in from the carry flag. Figure 4.11 shows how the value 100101106 (96h or 150 decimal) stored in AL is rotated right through the carry flag, which initially contains the value 1, with **ROR AL,1.** The result is the value 11001011b (0CBh or 203 in decimal), which is stored back in AL. The carry flag is set to 0.

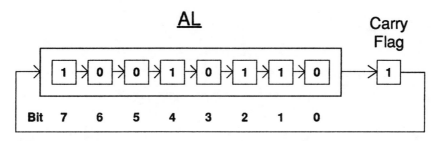

Figure 4.11: Example of RCR (Rotate Right and Carry)

Likewise, **RCL** is like a left shift in which the least-significant bit is shifted in from the carry flag. **RCR** and **RCL** are useful for shifts involving multiple-word operands. For instance, the following multiplies the doubleword value in DX:AX by 4:

```
    .
    .
    .
shl    ax,1    ;bit 15 of AX is shifted into carry
rcl    dx,1    ;carry is shifted into bit 0 of DX
shl    ax,1    ;bit 15 of AX is shifted into carry
rcl    dx,1    ;carry is shifted into bit 0 of DX
    .
    .
    .
```

The rotate instructions, like the shift instructions, can shift an operand either by 1 bit or by the number of bits specified by CL.

Loops and Jumps

Up until now, you've seen the 8086 execute instructions in strict sequence, with each instruction executing immediately after the instruction at the preceding address. Given the code

```
        .
        .
        .
mov    ax,[BaseCount]
add    ax,4
        .
        .
        .
push   ax
        .
        .
        .
```

you could be very sure that the **ADD** would execute immediately after the **MOV**, and the **PUSH** some time after that.

If that were all the 8086 could do, it would be a dull computer indeed. A fundamental feature of any useful computer is the presence of an instruction that can jump, or branch, to an instruction other than the one following it in memory. Equally important is the ability to branch conditionally, depending on a status or on the result of an operation. Naturally, the 8086 has instructions for both sorts of branching; in addition, the 8086 provides special branching instructions to facilitate repeated processing of a block of instructions.

Unconditional Jumps

The fundamental branching instruction of the 8086 is the **JMP** instruction. **JMP** instructs the 8086 to execute the instruction at the target label as the next instruction after the **JMP**. For example, when

```
            .
            .
            .
            mov    ax,1
            jmp    AddTwoToAX
AddOneToAX:
            inc    ax
            jmp    AXIsSet
AddTwoToAX:
            inc    ax
AXIsSet:
            .
            .
            .
```

is finished, AX contains 3, and the **ADD** and **JMP** instructions following the label *AddOneToAX* are never executed. Here, the instruction

```
jmp    AddTwoToAX
```

instructs the 8086 to set IP, the instruction pointer, to the offset of the label *AddTwoToAX*, so the next instruction executed is

```
add    ax,2
```

An operator sometimes used with **JMP** is **SHORT**. **JMP** usually uses a 16-bit displacement to point to the destination label; **SHORT** instructs Turbo Assembler to use an 8-bit displacement instead, thereby saving 1 byte per **JMP**. For instance, the last example is 2 bytes shorter as

```
            .
            .
            .
            mov    ax,1
            jmp    SHORT AddTwoToAX
AddOneToAX:
            inc    ax
            jmp    SHORT AXIsSet
AddTwoToAX:
            inc    ax
AXIsSet:
            .
            .
            .
```

The drawback to using **SHORT** is that short jumps can only reach labels within 128 bytes of the **JMP** instruction, so in some cases Turbo Assembler can inform you that it can't reach a given label with a short jump. It only makes sense to use **SHORT** on forward jumps, since Turbo Assembler automatically makes backward jumps short if a short jump will reach the destination, and long otherwise.

JMP can also be used to jump to another code segment, loading both CS and IP with a single instruction. For example,

```
            .
            .
            .
CSeg1    SEGMENT
            ASSUME  cs:Cseg1
            .
            .
            .
FarTarget        LABEL    FAR
            .
            .
            .
```

```
             .
Cseg1    ENDS
             .
             .
             .
Cseg2    SEGMENT
         ASSUME   cs:Cseg2
             .
             .
             .
         jmp      FarTarget    ;this is a far jump
             .
             .
             .
Cseg2    ENDS
             .
             .
             .
```

performs a far jump.

If you wish, you can use the **FAR PTR** operator to force a label to be treated as far; for instance,

```
             .
             .
             .
         jmp    FAR PTR NearLabel
         nop
NearLabel:
             .
             .
             .
```

performs a far jump to *NearLabel*, even though *NearLabel* is in the same code segment as the **JMP** instruction.

Finally, you can jump to an address stored in a register or memory variable. For example,

```
             .
             .
             .
         mov    ax,OFFSET TestLabel
         jmp    ax
             .
             .
             .
```

```
TestLabel:
        .
        .
        .
```

branches to *TestLabel*, as does

```
        .
        .
        .
        .DATA
JumpTarget      DW      TestLabel
        .
        .
        .
        .CODE
        .
        .
        .
        jmp     [JumpTarget]
        .
        .
        .
TestLabel:
        .
        .
        .
```

Conditional Jumps

Jumps such as those described in the last section are only part of what you need to write useful programs. You really need to be able to write code that's capable of making decisions, and that's what the conditional jumps give you.

A conditional jump instruction may either branch or not to a destination label, depending on the state of the flags register. For example, consider the following:

```
        .
        .
        .
        mov     ah,1            ;DOS keyboard input function
        int     21h             ;get the next key press
        cmp     al,'A'          ;was capital "A" pressed?
        je      AWasTyped       ;yes, handle it specially
        mov     [TempByte],al   ;no, store the character
        .
```

```
                .
                .
                .
AWasTyped:
         push    ax              ;save the character on the stack
                .
                .
                .
```

First, this code gets a key press by way of a DOS function. Then it uses the **CMP** instruction to compare the character typed to the character *A*. The **CMP** instruction is like a **SUB** that doesn't affect anything; the whole purpose of **CMP** is to let you compare two operands without changing them. **CMP** does, however, set the flags just as **SUB** would. So, in the preceding code the zero flag is set to 1 only if **AL** contains the character *A*.

Now we come to the crux of the example. **JE** is a conditional jump instruction that branches only if the zero flag is 1. Otherwise, the instruction immediately following **JE**, in this case a **MOV** instruction, is executed. Only if the *A* key is pressed will the zero flag be set in the previous example, and only in that case will the 8086 branch to the instruction at the label *AWasTyped*, a **PUSH** instruction.

The 8086 provides a remarkable variety of conditional jumps, giving you the ability to branch on just about any flag or combination of flags you could imagine (and several more besides). You can jump conditionally on the state of the zero, carry, sign, parity, and overflow flags, and on the combination of flags that indicate the results of operations with signed numbers.

Table 4.3 summarizes the conditional jump instructions.

Table 4.3: Conditional Jump Instructions

Name	Meaning	Flags Checked
JB/JNAE	Jump if below/Jump if not above or equal to	CF=1
JAE/JNB	Jump if above or equal to/Jump if not below	CF=0
JBE/JNA	Jump if below or equal to/Jump if not above	CF=1 or ZF=1
JA/JNBE	Jump if above/Jump if not below or equal to	CF=0 and ZF=0
JE/JZ	Jump if equal to	ZF=1
JNE/JNZ	Jump if not equal to	ZF=0
JL/JNGE	Jump if less than/Jump if not greater than or equal to	SF≠OF
JGE/JNL	Jump if greater than or equal to/Jump if not less than	SF=OF
JLE/JNG	Jump if less than or equal to/Jump if not greater than	ZF=1 or SF≠OF
JG/JNLE	Jump if greater than/Jump if not less than or equal to	ZF=0 or SF=OF
JP/JPE	Jump if parity/Jump if parity even to	PF=1
JNP/JPO	Jump if no parity/Jump if parity odd	PF=0
JS	Jump if sign	SF=1
JNS	Jump if not sign	SF=0
JC	Jump if carry	CF=1
JNC	Jump if not carry	CF=0
JO	Jump if overflow	OF=1
JNO	Jump if not overflow	OF=0

CF = carry flag;   SF = sign flag;   OF = overflow flag;   ZF = zero flag;   PF = parity flag

For more information about synonyms and the conditional jump instructions in general, consult Chapter 5, which also provides detailed information about the ways in which each 8086 instruction can modify the flags register.

Flexible as they are, the conditional jump instructions have a serious limitation: They are always short jumps. In other words, the destination label for a conditional jump instruction must be within 128 bytes of the instruction.

For example, Turbo Assembler can't assemble

```
          .
          .
          .
JumpTarget:
          .
          .
          .
DB     1000 DUP (?)
          .
          .
          .
dec    ax
jnz    JumpTarget
          .
          .
          .
```

since *JumpTarget* is over 1000 bytes away from the **JNZ** instruction. This is what's needed in a case like this:

```
          .
          .
          .
JumpTarget:
          .
          .
          .
DB     1000 DUP (?)
          .
          .
          .
dec    ax
jz     SkipJump
jmp    JumpTarget
SkipJump:
          .
          .
          .
```

where a conditional jump is used to make the decision about whether to make a long unconditional jump.

Looping

One sort of programming construct that can be built with conditional jumps is the loop. A loop is nothing more than a block of code that ends with a conditional jump, so that the code can be executed repeatedly until a termination condition is reached. You may be familiar with looping constructs such as **for** and **while** in C, **while** and **repeat** in Pascal, and FOR in BASIC.

What are loops used for? They're used to manipulate arrays, test the status of I/O ports until a certain state is reached, clear blocks of memory, read strings from the keyboard, display strings on the screen, and more. Loops are the basic means of handling anything that requires repeating a given action. As such, they're used frequently; so frequently, in fact, that the 8086 provides several special instructions just for looping: **LOOP**, **LOOPE**, **LOOPNE**, and **JCXZ**.

Let's look at **LOOP** first. Suppose you wanted to print the 17 characters in the string *TestString*. You could do this with

```
          .
          .
          .
          .DATA
TestString      DB        'This is a test...'
          .
          .
          .
          .CODE
          .
          .
          .
          mov     cx,17
          mov     bx,OFFSET TestString
PrintStringLoop:
          mov     dl,[bx]              ;get the next character
          inc     bx                   ;point to the following char
          mov     ah,2                 ;DOS display output fn #
          int     21h                  ;invoke DOS to print character
          dec     cx                   ;count down the string length
          jnz     PrintStringLoop      ;do the next character, if any remain
          .
          .
          .
```

However, there's a better way. You may remember that earlier we noted that CX is especially useful for code that loops. Here's how

```
     loop  PrintStringLoop
```

does just what

```
     dec   cx
     jnz   PrintStringLoop
```

does, and does it faster and in one less byte. Whenever you have a loop that repeats until a counter reaches 0, just keep the count in CX and use the **LOOP** instruction.

What about loops that have more complex termination conditions than a simple counter counting down? **LOOPE** and **LOOPNE** provide for two such cases.

LOOPE does the same thing **LOOP** does, except **LOOPE** will end the loop (fail to branch) if either CX counts down to 0 or the zero flag is set to 1. (Remember that the zero flag is set to 1 if the last arithmetic result was 0, or if the two operands to the last comparison were not equal.) Similarly, **LOOPNE** will end the loop if either CX counts down to 0 or the zero flag is cleared to 0.

Imagine you want to repeat a loop, saving key presses, until either the *Enter* key has been pressed or 128 characters have been read and stored. The following code uses **LOOPNE** to do the job:

```
          .
          .
          .
          .DATA
KeyBuffer       DB      128 DUP (?)
          .
          .
          .
          .CODE
          .
          .
          .
          mov     cx,128
          mov     bx,OFFSET KeyBuffer
KeyLoop:
          mov     ah,1            ;DOS keyboard input function #
          int     21h             ;read the next key
          mov     [bx],al         ;store the key
          inc     bx              ;set pointer for next key
          cmp     al,0dh          ;was it the enter key?
          loopne  KeyLoop         ;if not, get another key, unless we've
                                  ; already read the maximum number of keys
          .
          .
          .
```

LOOPE is also known as **LOOPZ**, and **LOOPNE** is also known as **LOOPNZ**, just as **JE** is also known as **JZ**.

There's one more loop-related instruction, and that's **JCXZ**. **JCXZ** branches only if CX is 0; this is a useful way to test CX before beginning a loop. For example, the following code, which is called with BX pointing to a block of bytes to be set to 0 and CX containing the length of the block, uses **JCXZ** to skip the entire loop if CX is 0:

```
            .
            .
            .
        jcxz    SkipLoop        ;if CX is 0, there's nothing to do
ClearLoop:
        mov     BYTE PTR [si],0
                                ;set the next byte to 0
        inc     si              ;point to the next byte to clear
        loop    ClearLoop       ;clear the next character, if any
SkipLoop:
            .
            .
            .
```

Why is it desirable to skip the loop if CX is 0? Well, if you execute **LOOP** with CX equal to 0, CX is decremented to 0FFFFh, and the **LOOP** instruction branches to the destination label. Then the loop is executed 65,535 more times! What you want here is a CX setting of 0 to mean that *no* bytes are to be zeroed, not 65,536 bytes. **JCXZ** lets you test for that case quickly and efficiently.

There are a couple of interesting notes about the looping instructions. First, be aware that a looping instruction, like a conditional jump, can only branch to a label within a range of about 128 bytes before or after the looping instruction. Loops larger than about 128 bytes require use of the "conditional jump around an unconditional jump" technique described in the previous section, "Conditional Jumps" (see page 167). Second, it's important to realize that none of the looping instructions affect the flags in any way. This means that

```
    loop  LoopTop
```

isn't *exactly* the same as

```
    dec   cx
    jnz   LoopTop
```

since **DEC** alters the overflow, sign, zero, auxiliary carry, and parity flags, while **LOOP** alters no flags at all. By the same token, the **DEC** instruction isn't exactly the same as

```
    sub   cx,1
    jnz   LoopTop
```

since **SUB** affects the carry flag, while the **DEC** instruction does not. True, these are small differences, but it's important to understand the instruction set thoroughly when programming in assembly language.

Subroutines

So far, we've only looked at programs consisting of a single long chunk of code. Each program has started at the top of the code, executed each instruction in turn (with an occasional detour for looping or decision-making), and then ended at the bottom of the code. That's fine for small programs, but larger programs require a programming construct known as a *subroutine*.

You're probably familiar with subroutines from a high-level language. In C, subroutines are known as functions, and in Pascal and Basic, they're known as procedures and functions. Subroutines, procedures, and functions all amount to the same thing—a separate section of code that accepts well-defined inputs, performs a certain action, and optionally returns a specific result value.

Subroutines let you build programs in a modular fashion, with the subroutines hiding the details of specific tasks so you can focus on the overall flow of the program. Subroutines can also make programs far more compact, since a single subroutine can be called from many places in a program, and can even perform different functions when passed different values. In a large program (whether written in assembler, C, Pascal, or some other language), subroutines are essential to creating orderly, maintainable code.

How Subroutines Work

The fundamental operation of a subroutine is illustrated by Figure 4.12. The code that calls the subroutine executes a **CALL** instruction, which pushes the address of the next instruction onto the stack and then loads IP with the address of the desired subroutine, thereby branching to the subroutine. The subroutine then executes just as any other code would. Subroutines can—and often do—contain calls to other subroutines; in fact, properly designed subroutines can even call themselves, a practice known as *recursion*.

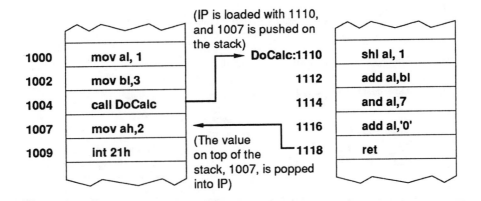

Figure 4.12: The Operation of a Subroutine

When the subroutine has finished its task, it executes a **RET** instruction, which pops into IP the address pushed by the original **CALL** instruction. This causes execution of the calling routine to resume at the instruction following the **CALL** instruction.

For example, the following program prints the three strings:

```
Hello, world!
Hello, solar system!
Hello, universe!
```

by using the subroutine *PrintString*:

```
        .MODEL   small
        .STACK   200h
        .DATA
WorldMessage     DB       'Hello, world!',0dh,0ah,0
SolarMessage     DB       'Hello, solar system!',0dh,0ah,0
UniverseMessage  DB       'Hello, universe!',0dh,0ah,0
        .CODE
ProgramStart     PROC     NEAR
        mov    ax,@data
        mov    ds,ax
        mov    bx,OFFSET WorldMessage
        call   PrintString                 ;print Hello, world!
        mov    bx,OFFSET SolarMessage
        call   PrintString                 ;print Hello, solar system!
        mov    bx,OFFSET UniverseMessage
        call   PrintString                 ;print Hello, universe!
        mov    ah,4ch                      ;DOS terminate program fn #
```

```
        int    21h                           ;...and done
ProgramStart    ENDP
;
; Subroutine to print a null-terminated string on the screen.
;
; Input:
;        DS:BX - pointer to string to print.
;
; Registers destroyed: AX, BX
;
PrintString        PROC      NEAR
PrintStringLoop:
        mov    dl,[bx]                        ;get the next character of the string
        and    dl,dl                          ;is the character's value zero?
        jz     EndPrintString                 ;if so, then we're done with the
                                              ; string
        inc    bx                             ;point to the next character
        mov    ah,2                           ;DOS display output function
        int    21h                            ;invoke DOS to print the character
        jmp    PrintStringLoop                ;print the next character, if any
EndPrintString:
        ret                                   ;return to calling program
PrintString
        ENDP
        END ' ProgramStart
```

There are two things to note here. First, *PrintString* is not hard-wired to print a specific string, but rather prints whatever string the calling program points to by way of BX. Second, two new directives, **PROC** and **ENDP**, are used to bracket *PrintString*.

PROC is used to start a procedure. The label associated with **PROC**, in this case *PrintString*, is the name of the procedure, just as if

```
PrintString    LABEL   PROC
```

had been used. **PROC** does something more, though: It specifies whether near or far **RET** instructions should be used within that procedure.

Let's take a moment to examine the implications of that last statement. Recall that when a near label is branched to, IP is loaded with a new value, while when a far label is branched to, both CS and IP are loaded. If a **CALL** instruction references a far label, both CS and IP are loaded, just as with a jump.

It stands to reason, then, that both CS and IP must be pushed when a far call occurs; otherwise, how could a **RET** instruction have enough information to return to the calling code? Think of it this way: If a far call loaded CS and IP, but pushed only IP, then a return could only load IP from the top of the stack. The result of the **RET** would be a CS:IP consisting of the CS of the called routine paired with the IP of the calling routine, which clearly makes no sense.

Instead, what happens is that both CS and IP are pushed by a call to a far label. How, though, will Turbo Assembler know what type of returns, far or near, to generate in a given subroutine? One way is for you to specify the type of each return explicitly, with the **RETN** (near return) and **RETF** (far return) instructions. However, a better answer lies with the **PROC** and **ENDP** directives.

The **ENDP** directive is used to mark the end of subroutines that start with **PROC** directives. A given **ENDP** marks the end of the subroutine that started with **PROC** and the same label. For example,

```
        .
        .
        .
TestSub     PROC   NEAR
        .
        .
        .
TestSub     ENDP
        .
        .
        .
```

marks the beginning and end of the subroutine *TestSub*.

PROC and **ENDP** don't actually generate any code; they're directives, not instructions. What they *do* do is control the type of **RET** instructions used in a given subroutine.

If the operand to a **PROC** directive is **NEAR**, then all **RET** instructions between that **PROC** directive and the corresponding **ENDP** directive are assembled as near returns. If, on the other hand, the operand to a **PROC** directive is **FAR**, then all **RET** instructions within that procedure are assembled as far returns.

So, for example, to change the type of all **RET** instructions in the *TestSub* example to far, change the **PROC** directive to

```
TestSub   PROC   FAR
```

In general, it's best to use near subroutines whenever possible, since far calls are larger and slower than near calls, and far returns are slower than near returns. However, far subroutines become necessary when you need more than 64 Kb of program code.

If you're using the simplified segment directives, it's better still to use the **PROC** directive without any operand at all, as in

```
TestSub    PROC
```

When Turbo Assembler encounters such a directive, it automatically makes the procedure near or far according to the memory model selected with the **.MODEL** directive. (Small is the default.) Tiny-, small-, and compact-model programs have near calls, while medium-, large-, and huge-model programs have far calls. For example, in

```
            .
            .
            .
        .MODEL   small
            .
            .
            .
TestSub PROC
            .
            .
            .
```

TestSub is near-callable, while in

```
            .
            .
            .
        .MODEL   large
            .
            .
            .
TestSub PROC
            .
            .
            .
```

TestSub is far-callable.

Parameter Passing

Information is often passed to subroutines by the code that calls them (referred to as the "calling code"). For instance, the example program in the last section used the BX register to pass a pointer to the *PrintString* subroutine. This action is known as *parameter-passing*, where the parameters tell the subroutine exactly what to do.

There are two commonly used ways to pass parameters: in the registers and on the stack. Register-passing is often used by pure assembler code, while stack-passing is used by most high-level languages, including Pascal and C, and by assembler subroutines called by those languages.

Passing parameters in registers is as simple as it sounds—just put the parameter values in the appropriate registers and call the subroutine. Each subroutine can have its own parameter requirements, although you'll find it easiest to establish some conventions and stick with them in order to avoid confusion. For example, you might want to make it a rule that the first pointer parameter is always passed in BX, the second in SI, and so on. If you do use register-passing, be sure to carefully comment each subroutine as to which parameters it expects to receive and in which registers they should be placed.

Passing parameters on the stack is a bit more complex. If you decide to use stack-passing, you'll probably want to use the convention established by your favorite high-level language in order to make it easy to link your assembler subroutines to code written in that language. Chapters 6-9 provide detailed descriptions of the parameter-passing conventions of Turbo C, Turbo Pascal, Turbo Basic, and Turbo Prolog, respectively, and provide sample assembler code.

Returning Values

Subroutines often return values to the calling code. In assembler subroutines that are going to be called from a high-level language, you *must* follow that language's conventions for returning values. For example, C-callable functions must return 8- and 16-bit values (**chars**, **ints**, and **near** pointers) in AX, and 32-bit values (**longs** and **far** pointers) in DX:AX. Chapters 6-9 in this book provide detailed descriptions of the return-value conventions of Turbo C, Turbo Pascal, Turbo Basic, and Turbo Prolog, respectively.

In pure assembler code, you have complete freedom about how you'd like to return values; you can put them in any register you wish. In fact, subroutines can even return status information in the flags register, in the form of carry or zero flag settings. However, it's best, once again, to establish and follow some conventions. One useful convention is to return 8-bit values in AL and 16-bit values in AX; that way, you'll get in the habit of not expecting valuable information in AX to remain unchanged by calls.

The major problem with using subroutine return values in assembler is that in the course of returning information, subroutines may destroy information that's important to the calling routine. In assembler, it's easy to code a call to a subroutine without remembering that the subroutine returns a value in, say, SI (or that the subroutine simply alters SI); then you've got a program bug that might be hard to find.

For this reason, it's best to keep the number of values a subroutine returns in the registers to a minimum—preferably no more than one—and to return additional values by storing them at memory locations indicated by passed pointers, as both C and Pascal do.

Preserving Registers

Preserving registers properly during subroutine calls is, in general, a major problem of assembler programming. In modern high-level languages, a subroutine normally can't modify the calling code's variables unless the calling code explicitly makes that possible. Not so in assembler, where the calling code's variables are often stored in the same registers that the subroutine uses. For example, if a subroutine modifies a register that the calling code sets before the call but uses after the call, you've got a bug.

One solution to this problem is for each subroutine, as it's entered, to always push all the registers that that subroutine uses, and then restore the registers by popping them before returning to the calling code. Unfortunately, this is time-consuming and requires a considerable amount of code. Another option is to make it a rule that calling code should never expect subroutines to preserve registers, and so should always preserve any registers it cares about. This is unattractive because a large part of the reason to use assembler is the freedom to use registers efficiently.

In short, there's a conflict between speed and ease of coding in assembly language. If you're going to use assembler, you might as well write fast, compact code, and that means being intelligent about register preservation and playing an active part in making sure each subroutine call produces no register conflicts. Your best approach is to comment each subroutine carefully as to the registers it destroys, and then refer to those comments each time you use a **CALL** instruction.

The sort of attention to detail involved both in keeping an eye on register preservation and in using registers as effectively as possible is an important part of good assembly language programming. High-level languages do those things for you—but then again, high-level languages can't create programs as fast and compact as those you're going to write in assembler.

An Example Assembly Language Program

Let's put together much of what you've learned over the last two chapters in the form of a useful example program. This example program,

WCOUNT.ASM, counts the number of words in a file and displays the count on the screen.

```
;
; Program to count the number of words in a file. Words are delimited by
; whitespace, which consists of spaces, tabs, carriage returns, and linefeeds.
;
; Usage: wc <filename.ext
;
; Select standard segment-ordering
        .MODEL  small                   ;code and data each fit in 64K
        .STACK  200h                    ;512-byte stack
        .DATA
Count           DW      0               ;used to count words
InWhitespace    DB      ?               ;set to 1 when the last
                                        ; character read was whitespace
TempChar        DB      ?               ;temporary storage used by
                                        ; GetNextCharacter
Result          DB      'Word count: ', 5 DUP (?)
                                        ;string printed to report the count
CountInsertEnd  LABEL BYTE              ;used to find the end of the area the
                                        ; count value string is stored in
                DB      0dh,0ah,'$'
                                        ;DOS fn #9 expects strings to end with
                                        ; a dollar sign
        .CODE
ProgramStart:
        mov     ax,@data
        mov     ds,ax                   ;point DS to the .DATA segment
        mov     [InWhitespace],1        ;assume we're in whitespace, since
                                        ; the first non-whitespace we'll find
                                        ; will mark the start of a word
CountLoop:
        call    GetNextCharacter        ;get next character to check
        jz      CountDone               ;...if any
        call    IsCharacterWhitespace   ;is it whitespace?
        jz      IsWhitespace            ;yes
        cmp     [InWhitespace],0        ;character is not
                                        ; whitespace-are we currently in
                                        ; whitespace?
        jz      CountLoop               ;we're not in whitespace, and the
                                        ; character isn't whitespace, so
                                        ; we're done with this character
        inc     [Count]                 ;we are in whitespace, and the
                                        ; character is not whitespace, so
                                        ; we just found the start of a new word
        mov     [InWhitespace],0        ;mark that we're no longer in whitespace
        jmp     CountLoop               ;do the next character
IsWhitespace:
```

```
        mov     [InWhitespace],1         ;mark that we're in whitespace
        jmp     CountLoop                ;do the next character
;
; We're done counting--report the results.
;
CountDone:
        mov     ax,[Count]               ;number to convert to a string
        mov     bx,OFFSET CountInsertEnd-1 ;point to the end of the string to
                                         ; put the number in
        mov     cx,5                     ;number of digits to convert
        call    ConvertNumberToString    ;make the number a string
        mov     bx,OFFSET Result         ;point to result string
        call    PrintString              ;print the count
        mov     ah,4ch                   ;DOS terminate program fn #
        int     21h                      ;end the program
;
; Subroutine to get the next character from the standard input.
;
; Input: None
;
; Output:
;       AL = character, if one was available
;       Z flag = 0 (NZ) if character available,
;              = 1 (Z) if end of file reached
;
; Registers destroyed: AH, BX, CX, DX
;
GetNextCharacter        PROC
        mov     ah,3fh                   ;DOS read from file fn #
        mov     bx,0                     ;standard input handle
        mov     cx,1                     ;read one character
        mov     dx,OFFSET TempChar       ;put the character in TempChar
        int     21h                      ;get the next character
        jc      NoCharacterRead          ;if DOS reports an error, then treat
                                         ; it as the end of the file
        cmp     [TempChar],1ah           ;was it Control-Z?
                                         ; (marks end of some files)
        jne     NotControlZ              ;no
NoCharacterRead:
        sub     ax,ax                    ;mark no character read NotControlZ:
        and     ax,ax                    ;set Z flag to reflect whether a
                                         ; character was read (NZ), or the
                                         ; end of the file was reached (Z).
                                         ; Note that DOS fn #3fh sets AX to
                                         ; the number of characters read
        mov     al,[TempChar]            ;return the character read
        ret                              ;done
GetNextCharacter        ENDP
;
```

```
; Subroutine to report whether a given character is whitespace.
;
; Input:
;       AL = character to check
;
; Output:
;       Z flag = 0 (NZ) if character is not whitespace
;              = 1 (Z) if character is whitespace
;
; Registers destroyed: none
;
IsCharacterWhitespace    PROC
        cmp     al,' '                      ;is it a space?
        jz      EndIsCharacterWhitespace    ;if so, it's whitespace
        cmp     al,09h                      ;is it a tab?
        jz      EndIsCharacterWhitespace    ;if so, it's whitespace
        cmp     al,0dh                      ;is it a carriage return?
        jz      EndIsCharacterWhitespace    ;if so, it's whitespace
        cmp     al,0ah                      ;is it a linefeed? If so,
                                            ; it's whitespace, so return Z;
                                            ; if not, it's not whitespace,
                                            ; so return NZ as set by cmp

EndIsCharacterWhitespace:
        ret
IsCharacterWhitespace    ENDP
;
; Subroutine to convert a binary number to a text string.
;
; Input:
;       AX = number to convert
;       DS:BX = pointer to end of string to store text in
;       CX = number of digits to convert
;
; Output: None
;
; Registers destroyed: AX, BX, CX, DX, SI
;
ConvertNumberToString    PROC
        mov     si,10                       ;used to divide by 10 ConvertLoop:
        sub     dx,dx                       ;convert AX to doubleword in DX:AX
        div     si                          ;divide number by 10. Remainder is in
                                            ; DX--this is a one-digit decimal
                                            ; number. Number/10 is in AX
        add     dl,'0'                      ;convert remainder to a text character
        mov     [bx],dl                     ;put this digit in the string
        dec     bx                          ;point to the location for the
                                            ; next most-significant digit
        loop    ConvertLoop                 ;do the next digit, if any
        ret
```

```
ConvertNumberToString    ENDP
;
; Subroutine to print a string on the display.
;
; Input:
;       DS:BX = pointer to string to print
;
; Output: None
;
; Registers destroyed: None
;
PrintString    PROC
       push    ax
       push    dx                       ;preserve registers in this
subroutine
       mov     ah,9                     ;DOS print string function #
       mov     dx,bx                    ;point DS:DX to the string to print
       int     21h                      ;invoke DOS to print the string
       pop     dx                       ;restore registers we changed
       pop     ax
       ret
PrintString    ENDP
       END     ProgramStart
```

WCOUNT.EXE should be run from the DOS prompt, with input redirected from the file you want to do a word count on. For example, to count the number of words in WCOUNT.ASM, you'd type

```
wcount <wcount.asm
```

at the DOS prompt, and a few seconds later you'd get the result:

```
Word count: 874
```

There are several points of interest regarding WCOUNT.ASM. For one thing, WCOUNT.ASM uses subroutines to handle the details of reading a character, checking whether a character is whitespace, converting the count to a string, and printing a string. This helps keep the main program of WCOUNT.ASM small and easy to understand.

Another advantage of using subroutines is the ease with which you can change the operation of the program. If, for instance, you needed to change the definition of whitespace to include the equal sign, you could alter the *IsWhitespace* subroutine; the main program wouldn't change at all.

Note that both *GetNextCharacter* and *IsWhitespace* return status information in the zero flag; *GetNextCharacter* also returns the character in AL. The zero flag is ideal for returning yes/no sorts of status, while AL (or AX) is good for returning values.

Finally, note the amount of code involved in producing text output in assembler. In order to print the integer word-count value, we had to first convert the count to a text string by repeatedly dividing it by 10 and adding the character "0" to the remainder. Only then could we call DOS to print the text string. That's a far cry from the simple C statement

```
printf("Word count: %d\n",Count);
```

On the other hand, once you've written subroutines, such as *ConvertNumberToString*, you can reuse them as often as necessary in other programs. You'll find that you'll build up a library of useful assembler subroutines, which will help you write future programs more quickly and easily.

5

More About Programming in Turbo Assembler

You've certainly learned a great deal about assembly language over the last two chapters, but there's still much more to learn. And in this chapter, we'll cover some fairly advanced but very useful aspects of Turbo Assembler and assembly language programming.

These are some of the topics we'll cover in this chapter:

- Turbo Assembler's directives **EQU** and **=**, which allow you to assign names to values and text strings
- Turbo Assembler's powerful string instructions
- Turbo Assembler's ability to assemble several source files separately and then use TLINK to link them together into a single program
- Turbo Assembler's ability to include separate source code files into any assembler program
- Turbo Assembler's sophisticated source listing files

It's possible to write assembler programs so that they'll assemble one way under certain circumstances and another way under others. We'll look at why that's useful and the directives that make it possible. Finally, we'll cover some of the more common and subtle pitfalls you're likely to run into as an assembler programmer.

You should at least skim through this chapter, even if everything doesn't sink in right now. You may not need all this information today, but when you do need it, you'll know where to look.

Using Equate Substitutions

We'll begin by looking at using the **EQU** and = directives to assign values and text strings to labels. This feature is very useful in making assembler programs clear and easy to maintain.

The EQU Directive

It's obvious why we use labels to name variables, subroutines, and specific instructions: How could we refer to those program elements as instruction operands if we didn't name them? Perhaps less obvious, but nonetheless important, is the need for labels equated to values and text strings.

EQU allows you to assign a numeric value or text string to a label; a reference to an *EQU* label is translated to the *literal equivalent* of that label. For example, consider the following:

```
        .
        .
        .
END_OF_DATA           EQU  '!'
STORAGE_BUFFER_SIZE EQU  1000
     .DATA
StorageBuffer   DB   STORAGE_BUFFER_SIZE DUP (?)
        .
        .
        .
     .CODE
     mov   ax,@data
     mov   ds,ax
     sub   di,di                 ;set buffer pointer to 0
StorageLoop:
     mov   ah,1
     int   21h                   ;get the next key press
     mov   [StorageBuffer+di],al ;save the next key press
     cmp   al,END_OF_DATA        ;was it the end-of-data key?
     je    DataAcquired          ;yes, go process the data
     inc   di                    ;count this key press
     cmp   di,STORAGE_BUFFER_SIZE ;have we overflowed the buffer?
     jb    StorageLoop           ;no, go get another key
;The buffer overflowed...
        .
        .
        .
;We've acquired the data
```

```
DataAcquired:
        .
        .
        .
```

Here, **EQU** is used to define two labels: *STORAGE_BUFFER_SIZE* and
END_OF_DATA. The *END_OF_DATA* label is equated to the character "!"
and is compared to each key press to see if the end of the data has been
reached. This illustrates one great advantage of using equates: Labels tend
to be far more informative than constant values. After all, the purpose of

```
cmp  al,END_OF_DATA
```

is certainly clearer than the purpose of

```
cmp  al,'!'
```

The use of *STORAGE_BUFFER_SIZE* illustrates another good reason to use
equates. *STORAGE_BUFFER_SIZE*, which is set to the constant value 1000,
is used both to create a storage buffer 1000 bytes long and to check whether
the buffer has overflowed. You could have used the constant 1000 in both
places, although that would have been less informative than the label
STORAGE_BUFFER_SIZE.

Now, however, suppose that you want to change the size of the storage
buffer. You need only change the operand to a single **EQU** directive, and
presto—you've made the change everywhere in the program! Granted, it
wouldn't have been too hard to change two constants, but a given equated
symbol can be used in dozens or even hundreds of places in a single
module, and then it's much easier (and less error-prone) to change a single
equate than to change dozens or hundreds of constants.

The operand to an equated label may itself contain labels, equated or
otherwise. For example,

```
        .
        .
        .
TABLE_OFFSET    EQU   1000h
INDEX_START     EQU   (TABLE_OFFSET+2)
DICT_START      EQU   (TABLE_OFFSET+100h)
        .
        .
        .
        mov  ax,WORD PTR [bx+INDEX_START]    ;get first index entry
        .
        .
        .
```

```
        lea  si,[bx+DICT_START]              ;point to the first dictionary entry
         .
         .
         .
```

is equivalent to

```
         .
         .
         .
        mov  ax,WORD PTR [bx+1000h+2]
        lea  si,[bx+1000h+100h]
         .
         .
         .
```

Equated labels are handy for transforming the myriad interrupts, ports, and memory locations of the PC into readily understood names. The following illustrates some such uses of **EQU**:

```
         .
         .
         .
DOS_INT          EQU 21h           ;the DOS function interrupt
CGA_STATUS       EQU 3dah          ;the CGA status port
VSYNC_MASK       EQU 00001000b     ;isolates the bit in the CGA
                                   ; status port that reports when
                                   ; you can update the screen without snow
BIOS_SEGMENT     EQU 40h           ;the segment the BIOS stores data in
EQUIPMENT_FLAG EQU 10h             ;the offset in the BIOS segment
                                   ; of the equipment flag variable
         .
         .
         .
        mov  ah,2
        mov  dl,'Z'
        int  DOS_INT               ;print a "Z"
         .
         .
         .
;Wait until it's safe to update the screen without causing snow
        mov  dx,CGA_STATUS
WaitForVerticalSync:
        in   al,dx                 ;get the CGA status
        and  al,VSYNC_MASK         ;vertical sync yet?
        jz   WaitForVerticalSync   ;no, wait some more
         .
         .
         .
        mov  ax,BIOS_SEGMENT
```

```
        mov   ds,ax                   ;point DS to the BIOS data segment
        mov   bx,EQUIPMENT_FLAG       ;point to the equipment flag
        and   BYTE PTR [bx],NOT 30h
        or    BYTE PTR [bx],20h       ;force the equipment flag to
                                      ; select 80-column color mode
        .
        .
        .
```

Equated labels that are based on other equated labels extend the concept of using equates to make it easier to change your programs. For instance, if in the previous example you wanted to move all references to the table 10 bytes closer to BX, you'd only have to change the equate for *TABLE_OFFSET* to

```
    TABLE_OFFSET    EQU   (1000h-10)
```

and reassemble, and both *INDEX_START* and *DICT_START* would adjust along with *TABLE_OFFSET*, since their values are based on *TABLE_OFFSET*.

By the way, parentheses around the operand to an **EQU** directive aren't required, but they don't hurt, and they help to visually delimit the operand.

EQU can be used to set a label to contain a text string as well as a value. For example, the following uses an equated label to store a text string to be printed:

```
        .
        .
        .
    EQUATED_STRING EQU  'This text started life in an EQU directive$'
        .
        .
        .
    TextMessage    DB    EQUATED_STRING
        .
        .
        .
        mov   dx,OFFSET TextMessage
        mov   ah,9
        int   21h       ;print TextMessage
        .
        .
        .
```

Labels equated to text strings can appear as operands. For example,

```
             .
             .
             .
REGISTER_BX    EQU  BX
             .
             .
             .
        mov  ax,REGISTER_BX
             .
             .
             .
```

assembles to

```
mov  ax,bx
```

There's no great utility to substituting an equated label for a register, but
you could, for instance, use equated labels or **ARG** to name parameters
passed on the stack, and dynamic storage allocated on the stack:

```
;
; C near model-callable subroutine to add three int parameters
; and return the int result. Function prototype:
;
; int AddThree(int I,int J,int K)
;
Temp EQU  [bp-2]
I    EQU  [bp+4]
J    EQU  [bp+6]
K    EQU  [bp+8]
;
_AddThree PROC
     push bp            ;save caller's BP
     mov  bp,sp         ;point to stack frame
     sub  sp,2          ;allocate space for Temp
     mov  ax,I          ;get I
     add  ax,J          ;calculate I+J
     mov  Temp,ax       ;save I+J
     mov  ax,K          ;get K
     add  ax,Temp       ;calculate I+J+K
     mov  sp,bp         ;deallocate space for Temp
     pop  bp            ;restore caller's BP
     ret
_AddThree ENDP
```

Basically, you can use **EQU** to name any text string you could otherwise
use as an operand. You can actually use an equated label in the instruction/
directive field as well as in the operand field; although, it's hard to imagine
a use for that.

You can use the angle brackets (< and >) to force an operand to **EQU** to be considered a text string rather than an expression. For example,

```
TABLE_OFFSET    EQU  1
INDEX_START     EQU  <TABLE_OFFSET+2>
```

assigns the text string "TABLE_OFFSET+2" to *INDEX_START*, while

```
TABLE_OFFSET    EQU  1
INDEX_START     EQU  TABLE_OFFSET+2
```

assigns the value 3 (the result of 1 + 2) to *INDEX_START*. In general, it's a good practice to put angle brackets around text string operands to **EQU** to make sure those operands aren't evaluated as expressions by accident.

Once a given label is equated to a value or text string with **EQU** in a given source module, it can never be redefined in that module. The following is guaranteed to produce an error:

```
       .
       .
       .
X     EQU  1
       .
       .
       .
X     EQU  101
       .
       .
       .
```

If you need to redefine equated labels (and there are, on occasion, some very good reasons to do so), you'll need to use the = directive, which we'll discuss shortly.

The $ Predefined Symbol

Recall that Turbo Assembler offers several predefined symbols, such as **@data**. Another simple but surprisingly useful predefined symbol is **$**, which is always set to the current value of the location counter; in other words, **$** is always equal to the current offset in the segment that Turbo Assembler is currently assembling into. **$** is a constant offset value, just as **OFFSET** *MemVar* is. This allows **$** to be used in expressions, or anywhere else a constant may be used.

$ is particularly handy for calculating data and code lengths. For example, suppose you want to equate the symbol *STRING_LENGTH* to the length in bytes of a string. Without **$**, you'd have to do the following:

```
         .
         .
         .
StringStart     LABEL     BYTE
     db   0dh,0ah,'Hello, world',0dh,0ah
StringEnd       LABEL     BYTE
STRING_LENGTH EQU (StringEnd-StringStart)
         .
         .
```

with **$**, though, all you need is

```
         .
         .
         .
StringStart     LABEL     BYTE
     db   0dh,0ah,'Hello, world',0dh,0ah
STRING_LENGTH EQU ($-StringStart)
         .
         .
         .
```

Here's how you'd calculate the length in words of an array of words:

```
         .
         .
         .
WordArray DW   90h, 25h, 0, 16h, 23h
WORD_ARRAY_LENGTH    EQU  (($-WordArray)/2)
         .
         .
         .
```

Of course, you could count the individual elements by hand, but with longer arrays and strings, that would quickly become tedious.

Incidentally, three other useful predefined variables are **??date**, **??time**, and **??filename**. **??date** contains the date of assembly, as a quoted text string in the form *01/02/87*. The **??time** variable contains the time of assembly in the form *13:45:06*, and **??filename** contains the name of the file being assembled in the form of an 8-character quoted text string such as *"TEST.ASM"*.

The = Directive

The = directive is like the **EQU** directive in all respects save one. Where labels defined with **EQU** can never be redefined (an error occurs if they are), labels defined with = can be redefined freely. This is very useful for labels that need to be changed on the fly, or that are reused within a single source module.

For example, the following code uses = to generate a lookup table for the first 100 multiples of 10:

```
        .
        .
        .
        .DATA
MultiplesOf10  LABEL    WORD
TEMP =   0
        REPT 100
        DW   TEMP
TEMP =       TEMP+10
        ENDM
        .
        .
        .
        shl  bx,1                    ;BX is # to multiply by 10.
                                     ; Shift left to multiply * 2
                                     ; for lookup in word-sized table
        mov  ax,[MultiplesOf10+bx]   ;get the number * 10
        .
        .
        .
```

All operands to = must resolve to a numeric value; unlike **EQU**, = cannot be used to assign text strings to labels.

The String Instructions

We've come to the most unusual and powerful instructions of the 8086, the string instructions. The string instructions are like no other 8086 instructions in that they can both access memory and increment or decrement a pointer register in a single instruction. A single string instruction can access memory as many as 130,000 times!

As their name implies, the string instructions are particularly useful for manipulating text strings. String instructions are equally adept at handling arrays, data buffers, and any sort of string of bytes or words. You should strive to use the string instructions whenever possible, since they are, as a rule, shorter and faster than equivalent combinations of normal 8086 instructions such as **MOV**, **INC**, and **LOOP**.

We'll examine the string instructions in two functional groups: the string instructions used for data movement (**LODS**, **STOS**, and **MOVS**), and the string instructions used for data scanning and comparison (**SCAS** and **CMPS**).

Data Movement String Instructions

The data movement string instructions are much like the **MOV** instruction, but do more than **MOV** and operate faster. We'll look at **LODS** first. Note that the direction flag controls the direction in which pointer registers are changed for all string instructions.

LODS

LODS, which loads a byte or word from memory into the accumulator, comes in two flavors, **LODSB** and **LODSW**. **LODSB** loads the byte addressed by DS:SI into AL, and either increments or decrements SI, depending on the state of the direction flag. If the direction flag is 0 (set with **CLD**), then SI is incremented, and if the direction flag is 1 (set with **STD**), then SI is decremented. This is not true only of **LODSB**; the direction flag controls the direction in which pointer registers are changed for all string instructions.

For example, the **LODSB** in the following code,

```
   .
   .
   .
cld
mov  si,0
lodsb
   .
   .
   .
```

loads AL with contents of the byte at offset 0 in the data segment and increments SI to 1. That's equivalent to

```
   .
   .
   .
mov  si,0
mov  al,[si]
inc  si
   .
   .
   .
```

However,

```
lodsb
```

is considerably faster (and 2 bytes smaller) than

```
mov  al,[si]
inc  si
```

LODSW is just like **LODSB**, save that the word addressed by DS:SI is loaded into AX, and SI is either incremented or decremented by 2, rather than 1. For example,

```
     .
     .
     .
std
mov  si,10
lodsw
     .
     .
     .
```

loads the word at offset 10 in the data segment into AX, then decrements SI by 2 to 8.

STOS

STOS is the complement to **LODS**, writing a byte or word value in the accumulator to the memory location pointed to by ES:DI, and incrementing or decrementing DI. **STOSB** writes the byte in AL to the memory location ES:DI, then increments or decrements DI, depending on the direction flag. For example,

```
     .
     .
     .
std
mov  di,0ffffh
mov  al,55h
stosb
     .
     .
     .
```

writes the value 55h to the byte at offset 0FFFFh in the segment pointed to by ES, then decrements DI to 0FFFEh.

STOSW does much the same, writing a word value in AX to address ES:DI, then incrementing or decrementing DI by 2. For instance,

```
   .
   .
   .
cld
mov  di,0ffeh
mov  ax,102h
stosw
   .
   .
   .
```

writes the word value 102h in AX to offset 0FFEh in the segment pointed to by ES, then increments DI to 1000h.

LODS and **STOS** work nicely together for copying buffers. For example, the following subroutine copies the zero-terminated string at DS:SI to the string at ES:DI:

```
;
; Subroutine to copy one zero-terminated string to another string.
;
; Input:
;    DS:SI - string to copy from
;    ES:DI - string to copy to
;
; Output: None
;
; Registers destroyed: AL, SI, DI
;
CopyString      PROC
    cld                     ;make SI and DI increment with string instructions
CopyStringLoop:
    lodsb                   ;get source string character
    stosb                   ;store character in destination string
    cmp al,0                ;was the character zero to end the string?
    jnz CopyStringLoop      ;no, do next character
    ret                     ;yes, done
CopyString      ENDP
```

You could equally well use **LODS** and **STOS** to copy blocks of bytes that aren't zero-terminated with a loop like

```
    .
    .
    .
mov  cx,ARRAY_LENGTH_IN_WORDS
mov  si,OFFSET SourceArray
```

```
        mov  ax,SEG SourceArray
        mov  ds,ax
        mov  di,OFFSET DestArray
        mov  ax,SEG DestArray
        mov  es,ax
        cld
CopyLoop:
    lodsw
    stosw
    loop CopyLoop
        .
        .
        .
```

However, there's an even better way to move a byte or word from one memory location to another, and that's with the **MOVS** instruction.

MOVS

MOVS is like **LODS** and **STOS** rolled into one. **MOVS** reads the byte or word stored at DS:SI, then writes that value to the address ES:DI. The byte or word never passes through a register at all, so AX isn't modified. **MOVSB** is as short as any instruction can be, at only 1 byte long, and is even faster than the **LODS/STOS** combination. With **MOVS**, the last example becomes still faster:

```
        .
        .
        .
    mov  cx,ARRAY_LENGTH_IN_WORDS
    mov  si,OFFSET SourceArray
    mov  ax,SEG SourceArray
    mov  ds,ax
    mov  di,OFFSET DestArray
    mov  ax,SEG DestArray
    mov  es,ax
    cld
CopyLoop:
    movsw
    loop CopyLoop
        .
        .
        .
```

Repeating A String Instruction

While the code in the last example looks pretty efficient, you may well be thinking that what you'd really like to do is get rid of that **LOOP** instruction and move the whole array with a single instruction. You're in luck—the 8086 gives you that option with the string instructions in the form of the **REP** prefix.

REP isn't an instruction; instead, it's an *instruction prefix*. Instruction prefixes modify the operation of the following instruction. What **REP** does is tell the following string instruction to execute repeatedly until the CX register reaches zero. (If CX is zero when the repeated instruction begins, the instruction executes zero times—in other words, it doesn't do anything at all.)

Using **REP**, you can replace

```
CopyLoop:
    movsw
    loop CopyLoop
```

in the last example with

```
rep  movsw
```

That single instruction will move a block of as many as 65,535 words (0FFFFh) from memory starting at DS:SI to memory starting at ES:DI.

Of course, a string instruction repeated 65,535 times doesn't execute anywhere near as quickly as an instruction executed once; all those memory accesses take time. However, each repetition of a repeated string instruction executes more quickly than would a single instance of that string instruction, making repeated string instructions a very fast way to read from, write to, or copy memory.

REP can be used with **LODS** and **STOS** as well as with **MOVS** (and also with the **SCAS** and **CMPS** instructions, which we'll discuss next). It's useful to repeat **STOS** to clear or fill blocks of memory; for example,

```
    .
    .
    .
    cld
    mov  ax,SEG WordArray
    mov  es,ax
    mov  di,OFFSET WordArray
    sub  ax,ax
    mov  cx,WORD_ARRAY_LENGTH
```

```
    rep  stosw
        .
        .
        .
```

fills *WordArray* with zeros. There's no correspondingly useful application for repeating **LODS**.

REP can only cause string instructions to repeat. An instruction like

```
    rep  mov  al,[bx]
```

which doesn't make a whole lot of sense anyhow, ignores the **REP** prefix and executes as a plain old

```
    mov  al,[bx]
```

String Pointer Overrun

Note that when a string instruction is executed, it increments or decrements SI, DI, or both *after* memory is accessed. This means that after the instruction the pointer registers don't point to the memory location just accessed; instead, they point to the next memory location to be accessed. This is actually very convenient, since it allows you to build efficient loops such as those in the examples in the last section. It can, however, occasionally cause confusion, especially with the data scanning string instructions, which we'll discuss next.

Data Scanning String Instructions

You've seen the data movement string instructions; now we'll look at the data scanning string instructions, **SCAS** and **CMPS**. These instructions are used for scanning and comparing blocks of memory.

SCAS

SCAS is used to scan memory for a match or non-match of a particular byte or word value. As with all string instructions, **SCAS** comes in two forms, **SCASB** and **SCASW**.

SCASB compares AL to the byte value at address ES:DI, setting the flags to reflect the comparison, just as if a **CMP** instruction had been executed. As with **STOSB**, DI is incremented or decremented by **SCASB**. For example, the following finds the first lowercase *t* in the string *TextString*:

```
        .
        .
        .
        .DATA
TextString           DB    'Test text',0
TEXT_STRING_LENGTH   EQU   ($-TextString)
        .
        .
        .
        .CODE
        .
        .
        .
        mov  ax,@data
        mov  es,ax
        mov  di,OFFSET TextString        ;ES:DI points to the start of TextString
        mov  al,'t'                      ;character to scan for
        mov  cx,TEXT_STRING_LENGTH
                                         ;length of string to scan
        cld                              ;scan with DI incrementing
Scan_For_t_Loop:
        scasb                            ;does ES:DI match AL?
        je   Found_t                     ;yes, we found "t"
        loop Scan_For_t_Loop             ;no, scan next character
;No "t" found
        .
        .
        .
;"t" found
Found_t:
        dec  di                          ;point back to offset of "t"
        .
        .
        .
```

Note that DI is decremented after *t* is found in this example, which reflects the string pointer overrun we discussed earlier. When this code performs the final, successful **SCASB**, DI is incremented after the comparison, since the last thing a string instruction does is increment or decrement its pointer(s). As a result, DI points to the byte after the *t* that was found and must be adjusted to compensate for the overrun and point to the *t*.

You may get a better feel for what **SCASB** does by comparing its use in the last example to similar code that doesn't use the string instructions:

```
        .
        .
        .
Scan_For_t_Loop:
```

```
        cmp  es:[di],al          ;does ES:DI match AL
        je   Found_t             ;yes, we found "t"
        inc  di
        loop Scan_For_t_Loop     ;no, scan next character
        .
        .
        .
```

The last example isn't exactly the same as the **SCASB** example preceding it, however, since **SCASB** increments DI immediately and the last example increments it after the **JE** instruction in order to avoid altering the flags set by **CMP**.

This brings up an important point about string instructions in general. String instructions never set the flags to reflect the changes they make to SI, DI, and/or CX. **LODS**, **STOS**, and **MOVS** don't change any flags, and **SCAS** and **CMPS** only change flags according to the results of the comparisons they make.

It certainly would be handy to be able to reduce the loop in the previous example to a single instruction, and, as you've probably guessed, **REP** lets you do just that. However, you might want to stop the loop on either a match or a non-match. Here are two forms of **REP** to use with **SCAS** (and **CMPS** as well)—**REPE** and **REPNE**.

REPE (also known as **REPZ**) tells the 8086 to repeat **SCAS** (or **CMPS**) until either CX becomes zero or a non-match occurs. You might think of **REPE** as being the "repeat while equal" prefix. Likewise, **REPNE** (also known as **REPNZ**) tells the 8086 to repeat **SCAS** (or **CMPS**) until either CX becomes zero or a match occurs. Think of **REPNE** as being the "repeat while not equal" prefix.

Here's code that uses a single repeated **SCASB** instruction to scan *TextString* for the character *t*:

```
        .
        .
        .
        mov  ax,@data
        mov  es,ax
        mov  di,OFFSET TextString   ;ES:DI points to the start of TextString
        mov  al,'t'                 ;character to scan for
        mov  cx,TEXT_STRING_LENGTH  ;length of string to scan
        cld                         ;scan with DI incrementing
        repne scasb                 ;scan the whole string to see if there's
                                    ; at least one "t"
        je   Found_t                ;yes, we found "t"
;No "t" found

;"t" found
```

```
Found_t:
    dec  di                      ;point back to offset of "t"
    .
    .
    .
```

Like all string instructions, **SCAS** increments its pointer register, DI, if the direction flag is 0 (cleared with **CLD**), and decrements DI if the direction flag is 1 (set with **STD**).

SCASW is a word-sized form of **SCASB**, comparing AX to ES:DI, and incrementing or decrementing DI by two rather than one at the end of each execution. The following code uses **REPE SCASW** to find the last nonzero entry in an array of word-sized integers:

```
    .
    .
    .
    mov  ax,SEG ShortIntArray
    mov  es,ax
    mov  di,OFFSET ShortIntArray+((ARRAY_LEN_IN_WORDS-1)*2)
                                 ;ES:DI points to the end of ShortIntArray
    mov  cx,ARRAY_LEN_IN_WORDS
    sub  ax,ax                   ;search for non-match with zero
    std                          ;search backward from end, decrementing DI
    repe scasw                   ;search until we come to a nonzero word
                                 ; or run out of array
    jne  FoundNonZero
;The whole array is filled with zeros.
    .
    .
    .
;We found a nonzero element--adjust DI for overrun to point to it.
FoundNonZero:
    inc  di
    inc  di
    .
    .
    .
```

CMPS

The **CMPS** string instruction is designed to let you compare two strings of bytes or words. A single repetition of **CMPS** compares two memory locations, then increments both SI and DI. You might think of **CMPS** as being like a **MOVS** that compares two memory locations instead of copying one memory location to another.

CMPSB compares the byte at DS:SI to the byte at ES:DI, sets the flags accordingly, and increments or decrements SI and DI, depending on the direction flag. AX is not modified in any way.

Like the other string instructions, **CMPS** comes in both byte and word sizes, can either increment or decrement SI and DI, and will repeat if preceded by a **REP** prefix. Here's the code to check whether the first 50 elements in two word-sized arrays are identical, using **REP CMPSW**:

```
        .
        .
        .
    mov  si,OFFSET Array1
    mov  ax,SEG Array1
    mov  ds,ax
    mov  di,OFFSET Array2
    mov  ax,SEG Array2
    mov  es,ax
    mov  cx,50              ;compare the first 50 elements, at most
    cld
    repe cmpsw
    jne  ArraysAreDifferent
;First 50 elements are identical.
        .
        .
        .
;At least one element differs between the two arrays.
ArraysAreDifferent:
    dec  si
    dec  si                 ;point back to the element that differed
    dec  di                 ;both arrays
    dec  di
        .
        .
        .
```

Using Operands with String Instructions

We've only looked at the explicit byte and word forms of the string instructions so far; in other words, we've looked at **LODSB** and **LODSW**, but haven't used **LODS**. It's acceptable to use the nonexplicit versions of the string instructions, as long as you provide operands so that Turbo Assembler knows whether you want byte- or word-sized operations.

For example, the following is acceptable and is equivalent to **MOVSB**:

```
            .
            .
            .
        .DATA
String1   LABEL     BYTE
    db    'abcdefghi'
STRING1_LENGTH EQU  ($-String1)
String2   DB    50 DUP (?)
            .
            .
            .
        .CODE
        mov   ax,@data
        mov   ds,ax
        mov   es,ax
        mov   si,OFFSET String1
        mov   di,OFFSET String2
        mov   cx,STRING1_LENGTH
        cld
        rep   movs es:[String2],[String1]
            .
            .
            .
```

Since you specified *String1* and *String2* as operands to **MOVS**, Turbo Assembler makes the data size of the **MOVS** instruction the data size of the operands, which is byte in this case.

There's a catch to using operands with string instructions, however. String instruction operands aren't real operands, in the sense that they're built into the instruction; a string instruction just uses whatever SI and/or DI happen to be when that instruction is executed. The operands are only used to set data size, not to actually load pointers. Look at it this way: When you use an instruction like

```
mov   al,[String1]
```

the offset of *String1* is built right into the machine-language instruction for **MOV**. However, when you use

```
lods [String1]
```

the machine-language instruction assembled is just the single byte for **LODSB**; *String1* is *not* built into the instruction. It's your responsibility to make sure that DS:SI points to the start of *String1* in this case.

Operands to string instructions are sort of like using the **ASSUME** directive for segments. **ASSUME** doesn't actually set a segment register; it just tells Turbo Assembler how you have set a segment register, so Turbo Assembler can do error-checking for you. Similarly, operands to string instructions don't set any registers; they just tell Turbo Assembler what you've set SI and/or DI to, so Turbo Assembler can determine operand size and do error-checking. Refer to the section "Relying on the Operand(s) to a String Instruction" on page 261 for further discussion of operands to string instructions.

In the section "Pitfalls with String Instructions" on page 252, we discuss several points to look out for when using the string instructions.

Multimodule Programs

Sooner or later, you're going to outgrow keeping each program's source code in a single file. Single-file source code is fine for short programs, such as the examples in this manual, but even medium-sized programs must be broken into several files, or modules, that are assembled separately and linked together. The primary advantage of multimodule programs is that after you edit the source code, you only need to reassemble the modules you've changed, rather than every line of the program. Also, it's much easier to find your way around several short files than one massive file.

It's surprisingly easy to create multimodule programs. Turbo Assembler provides three directives to support such programs: **PUBLIC**, **EXTRN**, and **GLOBAL**. We'll look at each in turn, but before we do, we'll look at a sample program consisting of two modules, so that you'll understand the context in which we're discussing the multimodule directives. Here's the main program, MAIN.ASM:

```
        .MODEL    small
        .STACK    200h
        .DATA
String1       DB    'Hello, ',0
String2       DB    'world',0dh,0ah,'$',0
        GLOBAL    FinalString:BYTE
FinalString   DB    50 DUP (?)
        .CODE
        EXTRN     ConcatenateStrings:PROC
ProgramStart:
    mov ax,@data
    mov ds,ax
    mov ax,OFFSET String1
    mov bx,OFFSET String2
    call ConcatenateStrings        ;combine the two strings
                                   ; into a single string
    mov ah,9
    mov dx,OFFSET FinalString
    int 21h                        ;print the resulting string
```

```
        mov   ah,4ch
        int   21h                    ;and done
        END   ProgramStart
```

And here's the other module of the program, SUB1.ASM:

```
        .MODEL    small
        .DATA
        GLOBAL    FinalString:BYTE
        .CODE
;
; Subroutine copies first one string, and then another
; to FinalString.
;
; Input:
;    DS:AX = pointer to first string to copy
;    DS:BX = pointer to second string to copy
;
; Output: None
;
; Registers destroyed: AL, SI, DI, ES
;
        PUBLIC    ConcatenateStrings
ConcatenateStrings  PROC
        cld                          ;strings count up
        mov   di,SEG FinalString
        mov   es,di
        mov   di,OFFSET FinalString
                                     ;ES:DI points to the destination
        mov   si,ax                  ;first string to copy String1Loop:
        lodsb                        ;get string 1 character
        and   al,al                  ;is it 0?
        jz    DoString2              ;yes, done with string 1
        stosb                        ;save string 1 character
        jmp   String1Loop
DoString2:
        mov   si,bx                  ;second string to copy String2Loop:
        lodsb                        ;get string 2 character
        stosb                        ;save string 2 character
                                     ; (including 0 when we find it)
        and   al,al                  ;is it 0?
        jnz   String2Loop            ;no, do next character
        ret                          ;done
ConcatenateString   ENDP
        END
```

These two modules would be assembled separately with

```
    TASM main
```

and

```
        TASM subl
```

and would then be linked into the program MAIN.EXE with

```
tlink main+subl
```

When run with the command

```
main
```

MAIN.EXE displays the output (you guessed it)

```
Hello, world
```

Now that you've seen a multimodule program in action, let's examine the three directives that make multimodule programming possible.

The PUBLIC Directive

What the **PUBLIC** directive does is simple enough: It instructs Turbo Assembler to make the associated label or labels available to other modules. Labels of almost any sort, including procedure names, memory variable names, and equated labels, may be made available to other modules by way of **PUBLIC**. For example,

```
        .
        .
        .
        .DATA
        PUBLIC    MemVar, Array1, ARRAY_LENGTH
ARRAY_LENGTH   EQU  100
MemVar         DW   10
Array1         DB   ARRAY_LENGTH DUP (?)
        .
        .
        .

        .CODE
        PUBLIC    NearProc, FarProc
NearProc  PROC NEAR
        .
        .
        .
NearProc  ENDP
        .
        .
        .
```

```
FarProc    LABEL    PROC
           .
           .
           .
           END
```

Here the names of an equated label, a word variable, an array, a near procedure, and a far procedure are made available to any other module that is linked to this module.

There is one sort of label that cannot be made public, and that's an equated label that is not equal to a 1- or 2-byte constant value. For example, the following labels couldn't be made public:

```
LONG_VALUE    EQU   10000h
TEXT_SYMBOL   EQU   <TextString>
```

Turbo Assembler normally ignores case when assembling, so all public labels are normally converted to uppercase. If you want case-sensitivity for public labels, you must use either the **/ml** or **/mx** command-line switch to Turbo Assembler in all modules that contain or reference public labels.

For example, without **/ml** or **/mx**, other modules won't be able to distinguish between the following two labels:

```
PUBLIC    Symbol1, SYMBOL1
```

When you use the **/mx** command-line switch to allow case sensitivity for public and external symbols, you must be careful to use the proper case for the symbol name in the **PUBLIC** or **EXTRN** directive. Turbo Assembler makes the symbol available to other modules with the name that appears in the **EXTRN** or **PUBLIC** directive, not how it appears where defined or referred to elsewhere in the module. For example,

```
      PUBLIC Abc
abC   Dw
```

causes the name *Abc* to become public, not *abC*.

The EXTRN Directive

In the last section, we used **PUBLIC** to make the labels *MemVar, Array1, ArrayLength, NearProc,* and *FarProc* available to other modules. The next question is, "How do other modules reference those labels?"

The **EXTRN** directive is used to make public labels from other modules available in a given module. Once **EXTRN** has been used to make a public label from another module available, that label may be used just as if it were defined in the current module. Here's how another module would use **EXTRN** to reference the public labels we defined in the last section:

```
        .
        .
        .
.DATA
EXTRN    MemVar:WORD,Array1:BYTE,ARRAY_LENGTH:ABS
        .
        .
        .
.CODE
EXTRN    NearProc:NEAR,FarProc:FAR
        .
        .
        .
mov  ax,[MemVar]
mov  bx,OFFSET Array1
mov  cx,ARRAY_LENGTH
        .
        .
        .
call NearProc
        .
        .
        .
call FarProc
        .
        .
        .
```

Note that all five labels are used as you'd normally use labels; only the **EXTRN** directives differ from single-module assembler source code.

Each label declared with **EXTRN** is followed by a colon and a type. The type is necessary because Turbo Assembler has no way of knowing what sort of label you've declared with **EXTRN** unless you tell it. With one exception, the types that can be used with external labels are the same as those that can be used with the **LABEL** directive. Available types are

ABS	An absolute value
BYTE	A byte-sized data variable
DATAPTR	A near or far data pointer, depending on the current memory model
DWORD	A doubleword-sized (4 byte) data variable
FAR	A far code label (branched to by loading CS:IP)
FWORD	A 6-byte data variable
NEAR	A near code label (branched to by loading IP only)
PROC	A procedure code label, near or far according to .MODEL
QWORD	A quadword-sized (8 byte) data variable
Structure Name	Name of a user-defined **STRUC** type
TBYTE	A 10-byte data variable
UNKNOWN	An unknown type
WORD	A word-sized (2 byte) data variable

The only unfamiliar external data type is ABS, which is used to declare a label that's defined in its original module with **EQU** or =; in other words, a label that is simply a name for a constant value and is not associated with a code or data address.

It's important that you specify the correct data type for external labels, since Turbo Assembler has to generate code on the basis of the data types you specify, and has no way of knowing if you've made an incorrect specification. For instance, if you accidentally typed

```
    .
    .
    .
.CODE
EXTRN     FarProc:NEAR
    .
    .
call FarProc
    .
    .
```

given

```
    .
    .
    PUBLIC   FarProc
FarProc  PROC FAR
    .
    .
```

```
      .
      .
    ret
FarProc   ENDP
      .
      .
      .
```

in another module, Turbo Assembler would generate a near call to *FarProc*, in accordance with the data type you specified with **EXTRN**. This code surely wouldn't work properly, since *FarProc* is actually a far procedure and ends with a far **RET** instruction.

As described in the last section, Turbo Assembler is normally case-insensitive, and public labels are normally converted to uppercase. This means that external labels are normally expected to be uppercase. Use the **/ML** or **/MX** command-line switch if you want case-sensitive external labels.

The GLOBAL Directive

At this point, you may well wonder why it takes two directives, **PUBLIC** and **EXTRN**, to do a single job—sharing labels between modules. Actually, the only reason two directives are required is for compatibility with other assemblers; Turbo Assembler gives you the **GLOBAL** directive, which does everything both **PUBLIC** and **EXTRN** do.

If you declare a label global and then define it (with **DB, DW, PROC, LABEL,** or the like), then that label is made available to other modules, just as if you'd used **PUBLIC** instead of **GLOBAL**. If, on the other hand, you declare a label global and then use it without defining it, then that label is treated as an external label, just as if you'd used **EXTRN**.

For example, consider the following:

```
      .
      .
      .
    .DATA
    GLOBAL    FinalCount:WORD,PromptString:BYTE
FinalCount    DW  ?
      .
      .
      .
    .CODE
    GLOBAL    DoReport:NEAR,TallyUp:FAR
TallyUp   PROC FAR
      .
```

```
        .
        .
        .
     call DoReport
        .
        .
        .
```

Here *FinalCount* and *TallyUp* are defined, so they're made public labels, available to other modules. *PromptString* and *DoReport* aren't defined in this module, so they're made external labels and are assumed to have been made public in some other module.

One particularly handy place to use **GLOBAL** is in an include file. (We'll discuss include files in the next section.) Suppose you have a set of labels that you want to make available to all the modules in a multimodule program. It would be nice to be able to declare all those labels in an include file, and then include that file in each module. Unfortunately, that's impossible using **PUBLIC** and **EXTRN** because **EXTRN** won't work in the module a given label is defined in, and **PUBLIC** will *only* work in the module a given label is defined in. However, **GLOBAL** will work in all modules, so you can make up an include file that declares all the labels of interest to be global, and include that file in all your modules.

Include Files

You'll often find that you'd like to insert the same block of assembler source code in several source modules. You may want to share equates or macros among different parts of a program, or you may simply want to reuse equates or macros in several programs. Then, too, you may have a long program that you don't want to break into several linkable modules (a program that will be stored in ROM, for example), but which is too big to conveniently keep in a single file. The **INCLUDE** directive meets all these needs.

When Turbo Assembler encounters an **INCLUDE** directive, it marks its place in the current assembler module, goes to disk and finds the specified include file, and starts assembling the include file, just as if the lines in the include file were right in the current module. When the end of the include file is reached, Turbo Assembler returns to the line after the **INCLUDE** directive in the current module, and resumes assembly there. The key point is this: The text of the include file is literally inserted into the assembly of the current assembler module at the location of the **INCLUDE** directive.

For instance, if MAINPROG.ASM contains

```
   .
   .
   .
.CODE
mov  ax,1
INCLUDE    INCPROG.ASM
push ax
   .
   .
   .
```

and INCPROG.ASM contains

```
mov  bx,5
add  ax,bx
```

then the result of assembling MAINPROG.ASM is exactly equivalent to

```
   .
   .
   .
.CODE
mov    ax,1
mov    bx,5
add    ax,bx
push   ax
   .
   .
   .
```

Include files can be nested, in other words, an Include file can itself include another file. You can easily tell included lines in a listing file because Turbo Assembler places a number at the left end of included lines, which indicates how deeply the module files are nested. (Include files can be nested arbitarily deep.)

How does Turbo Assembler know where to find Include files? Well, if you specify a drive or path as part of the file name operand to **INCLUDE**, Turbo Assembler looks exactly where you specify, and nowhere else. If you specify only a file name, with no drive or path, Turbo Assembler first searches the current directory for the specified file. If Turbo Assembler can't find the file in the current directory, it searches the directories specified with the –**I** command-line switch, if any. For example, given the Turbo Assembler command line

```
TASM -ic:\include testprog
```

and given the line

```
INCLUDE    MYMACROS.ASM
```

in TESTPROG.ASM, Turbo Assembler will first search the current directory for MYMACROS.ASM, and, failing that, will search the directory C:\INCLUDE. If MYMACROS.ASM isn't in either of those places, Turbo Assembler will report an error.

By the way, backward slashes (\) can be used in **INCLUDE** path specifications. This provides compatibility with MASM.

Include files are useful for making your libraries of macros available to many different assembler modules. Include files are also very useful for sharing equates, global label declarations, and data segments among the various modules of a single program. Include files are rarely used for code, since you can readily link separate code modules together, but it is perfectly acceptable to put code (or, for that matter, any valid assembly line) into an Include file, should you so desire.

The Listing File

Normally, Turbo Assembler produces only one file as the result of assembly: an object (.OBJ) file with the same name as the source (.ASM) file. You can, if you wish, ask Turbo Assembler to produce a listing file with the extension .LST as well, simply by typing two additional commas (or two additional file names) on the command line. For example, where

```
TASM hello
```

assembles HELLO.ASM and produces the object file HELLO.OBJ, the command line

```
TASM hello,,
```

generates the listing file HELLO.LST, as do both

```
TASM hello,hello,hello
```

and

```
TASM /l hello
```

The object and/or listing file names don't have to match the source file name, but there's rarely a reason for your source file to have one name and your object or listing files to have another.

The listing file is basically the source file annotated with a variety of information about the results of the assembly. Turbo Assembler lists the actual machine code for each instruction, along with the offset in the current segment of the machine code for each line. What's more, Turbo Assembler provides tables of information about the labels and segments used in the program, including the value and type of each label, and the attributes of each segment.

Turbo Assembler can also, on demand, generate a cross-reference table for all labels used in a source file, showing you where each label was defined and where it was referenced. (See the /c command-line option in Chapter 3.)

We'll look at the basics of the listing file first—the assembled machine code and offset for each instruction.

Annotated Source Code

Here's the listing file for the original example program, HELLO.ASM:

```
Turbo Assembler  Version 1.0     06-29-88 16:21:27          Page 1

HELLO.ASM

 1                              DOSSEG
 2 0000                         .MODEL small
 3 0000                         .STACK 100h
 4 0100                         .DATA
 5 0000   48 65 6C 6C 6F 2C 20 + HelloMessage DB 'Hello, world',13,10,12
 6        77 6F 72 6C 64 0D 0A +
 7        0C
 8      = 000F                  HELLO_MESSAGE_LENGTH EQU $ - HelloMessage
 9 000F                         .CODE
10 0000   B8 0000s              mov  ax,@data
11 0003   8E D8                 mov  ds,ax                 ;set DS to point to data seg
12 0005   B4 40                 mov  ah,40h                ;DOS write to device function #
13 0007   BB 0001               mov  bx,1                  ;standard output handle
14 000A   B9 000F               mov  cx,HELLO_MESSAGE_LENGTH ;number of characters to print
15 000D   BA 0000r              mov  dx,OFFSET HelloMessage ;string to print
16 0010   CD 21                 int  21h                   ;print "Hello, world"
17 0012   B4 4C                 mov  ah,4ch                ;DOS terminate program function #
18 0014   CD 21                 int  21h                   ;terminate the program
19                              END

Turbo Assembler  Version 1.0     06-29-88 16:21:27          Page 2
Symbol Table

Symbol Name                     Type   Value

??date                          Text   "06-29-88"
??filename                      Text   "HELLO   "
??time                          Text   "16:21:26"
??version                       Number 004A
@code                           Text   _TEXT
@CodeSize                       Text   0
@Cpu                            Text   0101h
```

```
@curseg                             Text    _TEXT
@data                               Text    DGROUP
@DataSize                           Text    0
@FileName                           Text    HELLO
@WordSize                           Text    2
HELLOMESSAGE                        Byte    DGROUP:0000
HELLO_MESSAGE_LENGTH                Number  000F

Groups & Segments                   Bit Size  Align Combine Class

DGROUP                              Group
  STACK                             16  0100  Para  Stack   STACK
  _DATA                             16  000F  Word  Public  DATA
  _TEXT                             16  0016  Word  Public  CODE
```

The top of each page of the listing file displays a header consisting of the version of Turbo Assembler that assembled the file, the date and time of assembly, and the page number within the listing.

There are two parts to the listing file: the annotated source code listing and the symbol tables. The original assembler code is displayed first, with a header containing the name of the file where the source code resides. The assembler source code is annotated with information about the machine code Turbo Assembler assembled from it. Any errors or warnings encountered during assembly are inserted immediately following the line they occurred on.

The code lines in the listing file follow this format:

    <depth> <line number> <offset> <machine code> <source>

- *<depth>* indicates the level of nesting of Include files and macros within your listing file.

- *<line number>* is the number of the line in the listing file (not including header and title lines). Line numbers are particularly useful when the cross-reference feature of Turbo Assembler, which refers to lines by line number, is used. In HELLO.LST, the **DOSSEG** directive is line 1 of the listing file, the **.MODEL** directive is line 2, and so on.

Be aware that the line numbers in the *<line number>* field are not the source module line numbers. For example, if a macro is expanded or a file is included, the line-number field will continue to advance, even though the current line in the source module stays the same. In order to translate a line number (for example, one produced by the cross-referencer) back to the source file, you must look up the line number in the listing file, then find that same line (by eye, not by number) in the source file.

- *<offset>* is the offset in the current segment of the start of the machine code generated by the associated assembler source line. For instance, *HelloMessage* starts at offset 0 in the data segment.

- *<machine code>* is the actual sequence of hexadecimal byte and word values that is assembled from the associated assembler source line. For example, **MOV AX,@data** starts at offset 0 in the code segment. The information just to the right of the offset field for a given instruction is the machine code assembled from that instruction, so the machine code assembled for **MOV AX,@data** is B8 0000s (all in hexadecimal). 0B8h is the machine language instruction to load AX with a constant value, while 0000s is the constant value of **@data**, which is loaded into AX. (Actually, 0000s is just a placeholder for the value of **@data**; we'll get to that in a minute.) Altogether, the instruction **MOV AX,@data** assembles to 3 bytes of machine code.

  Note that the listing file indicates that the instruction following **MOV AX,@data**, which is **MOV DS,AX**, starts at offset 3 in the code segment. This makes perfect sense, given that **MOV AX,@data** starts at offset 0 and is 3 bytes long. The machine code assembled from **MOV DS,AX**—8e D8—is 2 bytes long, so the next instruction should start at offset 5; looking at the listing file, we see that that is the case.

- Finally, *<source>* is simply the original assembler line, comments and all. Some assembler lines, such as those that contain only comments, don't generate any machine code; these lines have no *<offset>* or *<machine code>* fields, but do have a line number.

Recall that we said that the 0000s value for **@data** was only a placeholder for the real value in the instruction

```
mov ax,@data
```

This is because segment values are assigned by the linker, not by Turbo Assembler, so Turbo Assembler can't fill in the correct value. What Turbo Assembler can do, however, is let you know that a given value is a segment value that will be resolved by the linker, and that's done by appending the letter *s* to the end of the machine code generated for

```
mov ax,@data
```

Likewise, the offset in the machine code assembled from

```
mov dx,OFFSET HelloMessage
```

ends with *r*, indicating that the offset may have to be relocated when its segment is combined with other segments by the linker.

Here's the full list of notations used by Turbo Assembler to indicate assembly characteristics (such as relocatability):

Notation	Meaning
r	Indicates offset fixup type for symbols within the module
s	Indicates segment fixup type for symbols within the module
sr	Indicates segment and offset fixup type within the module
e	Indicates offset fixup on an external symbol
se	Indicates pointer fixup on an external symbol
so	Indicates segment-only fixup
+	Indicates object code that has been truncated or wrapped to the next line

In the object code listing, *r*, *s*, and *sr* are used to indicate offset, segment, and pointer (segment and offset) fixup types for symbols within the module. *e* indicates an offset fixup on an external symbol, and *se* indicates a pointer fixup on an external symbol. Segment fixups on external symbols appear as *s*, just like for local symbols. The object code field can also contain a + in the last column, indicating that there is more object code to display, but it has been truncated.

The leftmost field of the listing is the *level counter*, which is blank when assembling from the main file. Include files cause this field to contain a 1 that becomes a 2, 3, and so on, for each nested include level. Likewise, macro expansions put a level counter in this field.

You may have noticed that the listing file shows some of the machine code entries as byte values (two hexadecimal digits) and others as word values. There's a logical pattern here: Whenever Turbo Assembler assembles machine code that represents a word value, such as **OFFSET** *HelloMessage*, which is a 16-bit offset, that value is shown as a word value. This is useful because, otherwise, the low-byte-first approach the 8086 uses for storing words would cause words to appear with the bytes reversed.

For example, the instruction

```
mov  ax,1234h
```

assembles to 3 bytes of machine code: 0B8h, 034h, and 012h, in that order. If Turbo Assembler listed this machine code as 3 bytes, it would appear as

```
B8 34 12
```

with the bytes of the word value swapped. Instead, Turbo Assembler lists this machine code as

```
B8 1234
```

which is certainly easier to read.

When we discussed the *<offset>* field, we talked about the offset in the current segment of the labels and lines in a program. How do you know what segment a given label or line is in? That's the job of the listing tables, which we'll cover next.

Listing Symbol Tables

The second part of the listing file begins with the header "Symbol Table" and consists of two tables: one describing the labels used in the source code and the other describing the segments used.

By the way, if you have no use for the symbol table portion of the listing file, you can instruct Turbo Assembler to generate only the annotated source code portion of the listing with the **/n** command-line switch.

The Table of Labels

The first table, which we'll call the table of labels, lists all the labels in the source code in alphabetical order, along with their types and the values to which they were set. For example, the listing file HELLO.LST contains the following entry:

```
HELLOMESSAGE    BYTE DGROUP:0000
```

HELLOMESSAGE is the name of the label, or symbol; it's in uppercase because Turbo Assembler converts all symbols to uppercase unless you use the **/mx** or **/ml** command-line switch. **BYTE** represents the data size of the data element referred to by the name *HelloMessage*. **DGROUP:0000** is the value of the label *HelloMessage*, meaning that the string pointed to by the label *HelloMessage* starts at offset 0 in the segment group **DGROUP**. (However, remember that the reference to *HelloMessage* in the last section was marked with an *r*, meaning *HelloMessage* may be relocated to another offset by the linker as the other segments in **DGROUP** are linked into the program. The map file produced by the linker is the place to look for information about segment relocation.)

Similarly, *ProgramStart* is listed as a label of type near, with the value **_TEXT:0000**; **_TEXT** is the name of the segment defined with **.CODE**, so *ProgramStart* is at the first address in the code segment. As you can see, we've answered an earlier question about how to find out what segment a given label is in, since the value field of the table of labels reports the segment in which the label resides.

The other labels listed in the HELLO.LST listing file are the labels that are predefined by Turbo Assembler when the simplified segment directives are used. These labels are all set to text strings, and contain values such as **_TEXT** and **DGROUP**.

Labels can be any of the following data types:

ABS	**DWORD**	**NUMBER**	**TBYTE**
ALIAS	**FAR**	**QWORD**	**TEXT**
BYTE	**NEAR**	**STRUCT**	**WORD**

As we discussed at the beginning of this chapter, equated labels may be set to any constant value or may be set to a text string; the value field of the table of labels reports the values of such labels exactly as you set them. For a label associated with memory addresses, such as *HelloMessage*, it's the address of the label that is reported in the value field.

The table of labels is the place to look for type and value information about any label used anywhere in your source code.

The Table of Groups and Segments

The other table in the symbol table portion of the listing is the table of groups and segments. Segment groups such as **DGROUP** are simply reported as groups here, since segment groups have no attributes of their own, but rather consist of one or more segments. The segments making up a group in a given module appear directly under that group's name in the table of groups and segments, indented two columns to show they belong to the group. In HELLO.LST, the segments **STACK** and **_DATA** are members of the **DGROUP** segment group.

Segments do have attributes, and the table of groups and segments lists five attributes for each segment. Reading from the left, the table of groups and segments reports the data size, overall size, alignment, combine type, and class for each segment. We'll take each of these separately.

The data size is always 16 except for **USE32** segments in code assembled for the 80386 processor. (Refer to Chapter 10 for information on **USE32** segments.)

The segment size is given as four hexadecimal digits. For example, the **STACK** segment is 0200h (512 decimal) bytes long.

The alignment type describes what sort of memory boundaries a segment can start on. These are the possible alignment types:

BYTE	Segment can start at any address
DWORD	Segment can start at any address that is a multiple of 4
PAGE	Segment can start at any address that is a multiple of 256
PARA	Segment can start at any address that is a multiple of 16
WORD	Segment can start at any even address

In HELLO.LST, the **STACK** segment starts on a paragraph boundary, while the **_DATA** and **_TEXT** segments are word-aligned. (Take a look at Chapter 10 for more information about alignment.)

The combine type dictates how segments of the same name are combined with a given segment. For example, identically named segments with combine-type **PUBLIC** are concatenated into a larger segment, while those with combine-type **COMMON** are overlaid into a single common segment. (Chapter 10 contains more information about combine types.)

Finally, the segment class specifies the overall class in which a segment belongs, such as **CODE**, **DATA**, and **STACK**. The linker uses this information to order segments when it links the segments into a program. (Again, look at Chapter 10 for information about segment classes.)

The Cross-Reference Table

The symbol table portion of the listing file normally tells you a great deal about labels, groups, and segments, but there are two things it doesn't tell you: where labels, groups, and segments are defined and where they're used. In other words, the symbol tables don't cross-reference your labels, groups, and segments. Cross-referenced symbol information makes it easier to find labels and follow program execution when debugging a program.

There are two ways to instruct Turbo Assembler to produce cross-reference information in the listing file. The **/c** command-line switch is one way to ask Turbo Assembler to place cross-reference information in the listing file; for example,

```
TASM /c hello,,
```

generates cross-reference information in the listing file HELLO.LST. Note, however, that **/c** by itself is not enough to generate cross-reference information; you must also instruct Turbo Assembler to generate a listing file in which the cross-reference information can be placed.

You may also ask Turbo Assembler to generate a listing file containing cross-reference information by adding a fourth field to the command line, as in

```
      TASM hello,hello,hello,hello

or

      TASM hello,,,
```

Suppose we assemble REVERSE.ASM, the second example program you looked at in Chapter 2, with the **/c** command-line switch:

```
      TASM /c reverse,,
```

Turbo Assembler creates the following listing file, REVERSE.LST:

```
REVERSE.ASM

1                               DOSSEG
2                               .MODEL   small
3                               .STACK   200h
4                               .DATA
5          = 03E8               MAXIMUM_STRING_LENGTH  EQU   1000
6  0000    03E8*(??)            StringToReverse DB      MAXIMUM_STRING_LENGTH DUP(?)
7  03E8    03E8*(??)            ReverseString   DB      MAXIMUM_STRING_LENGTH DUP(?)
8                               .CODE
9                       ProgramStart:
10 0000    B8 0000s             mov     ax,@data
11 0003    8E D8               mov     ds,ax    ;set DS to point to the data segment
13 0005    B4 3F               mov     ah,3fh   ;DOS read from handle function #
14 0007    BB 0000             mov     bx,0     ;standard input handle
15 000A    B9 03E8             mov     cx,MAXIMUM_STRING_LENGTH
16                                              ;read up to maximum # of characters
17 000D    BA 0000r            mov     dx,OFFSET StringToReverse
18                                              ;store the string here
19 0010    CD 21               int     21h      ;get the string
20 0012    23 C0               and     ax,ax    ;were any characters read?
21 0014    74 1F               jz      Done     ;no, so we're done
22 0016    8B C8               mov     cx,ax    ;put string length in CX, where
23                                              ; can use it as a count
24 0018    51                  push    cx       ;save the string length
25 0019    BB 0000r            mov     bx,OFFSET StringToReverse
26 001C    BE 03E8r            mov     si,OFFSET ReverseString
27 001F    03 F1               add     si,cx
28 0021    4E                  dec     si       ;point to the end of the reverse
29                                              ; string buffer
30                       ReverseLoop:
31 0022    8A 07               mov     al,[bx] ;get the next character
32 0024    88 04               mov     [si],al ;store the characters in reverse order
33 0026    43                  inc     bx       ;point to next character
34 0027    4E                  dec     si       ;point to previous location in
35                                              ; reverse buffer
36 0028    E2 F8               loop    ReverseLoop ;move next character, if any
37 002A    59                  pop     cx       ;get back the string length
38 002B    B4 40               mov     ah,40h   ;DOS write from handle function #
39 002D    BB 0001             mov     bx,1     ;standard output handle
40 0030    BA 03E8r            mov     dx,OFFSET ReverseString ;print this string
41 0033    CD 21               int     21h      ;print the reversed string
42                       Done:
43 0035    B4 4C               mov     ah,4ch ;DOS terminate program function #
```

```
44 0037  CD 21                    int   21h      ;terminate the program

45                                END   ProgramStart
```

Symbol Table

Symbol Name	Type	Value		Cref defined at #
@code	Text	_TEXT		#2 #8
@curseg	Text	_TEXT		#2 #3 #4 #8
DONE	Near	_TEXT:0035		21 #42
MAXIMUM_STRING_LENGTH	Number	03E8		#5 6 7 15
PROGRAMSTART	Near	_TEXT:0000		#9 45
REVERSELOOP	Near	_TEXT:0022		#30 36
REVERSESTRING	Byte	DGROUP:03E8		#7 26 40
STRINGTOREVERSE	Byte	DGROUP:0000		#6 17 25

Groups & Segments	Bit Size Align	Combine Class		Cref defined at #
DGROUP	Group			#2 2 10
STACK	16 0200 Para	Stack STACK		#3
_DATA	16 07D0 Word	Public DATA		#2 #4
_TEXT	16 0039 Word	Public CODE		#2 2 #8 8

Once again, the listing file contains annotated source code and the symbol tables. There's something new in the symbol tables, however, and that's the cross-reference field.

For each symbol (label, group, or segment), the cross-reference field lists the line numbers of all the lines in the program on which that symbol was referenced. Lines on which a symbol was defined are prefixed with a #.

For example, let's find out where the *MAXIMUM_STRING_LENGTH* label is defined and used. The listing file informs you that it was defined on line 5; if you look at the first part of the listing file, you'll see that this is the case. (Incidentally, notice that the table of labels informs you that the value of *MAXIMUM_STRING_LENGTH* is a number, which is 03E8h—decimal 1000.)

The cross-reference field for *MAXIMUM_STRING_LENGTH* also tells you that the label is referenced (but not defined) on lines 6, 7, and 15. A glance at the first part of the listing file shows that this is correct.

The /c switch allows you to enable cross-referencing for an entire file. You certainly won't always want a cross-reference listing for every symbol—such a listing could be huge for a long source module. Turbo Assembler provides you with directives that let you enable and disable cross-referencing in selected portions of your listings.

The %CREF directive enables cross-referencing for succeeding lines. The %NOCREF directive disables cross-referencing for succeeding lines. Either of these directives overrides the command-line /c switch. If cross-referencing is enabled anywhere in a source module, then the symbol table section reports the lines on which all labels, groups, and segments were defined. However, only those lines on which the labels, groups, and segments were referenced (and for which cross-referencing was enabled) are listed as cross-reference entries.

For example, consider

```
          .
          .
          .
      %NOCREF
ProgramStart    PROC              ;line 1
          .
          .
          .
      jmp  LoopTop                ;line 2
          .
          .
          .
      %CREF
LoopTop:                          ;line 3
          .
          .
          .
      loop LoopTop                ;line 4
      %NOCREF
      mov  ax,OFFSET ProgramStart ;line 5
          .
          .
          .
```

Line 1 will be listed as the definition line (with a #) for *ProgramStart*, even though it was in an area in which cross-referencing is turned off because the definition lines for all labels are listed if cross-referencing is turned on anywhere in a module. Similarly, line 3 will be listed as the definition line for *LoopTop*.

Line 4 will appear as a cross-reference line for *LoopTop* because it occurs after %**CREF** and before %**NOCREF**. However, line 2 will not appear as a cross-reference line for *LoopTop*, because it occurs when cross-referencing is disabled. Likewise, line 5 will not appear as a cross-reference for *ProgramStart*.

For compatibility with other assemblers, **.CREF** and **.XCREF** are provided, controlling cross-referencing in the same way as do %**CREF** and %**NOCREF**, respectively.

Controlling the Listing Contents and Format

Turbo Assembler gives you a remarkable degree of control over which lines of source code should be listed, and over the format of the listing file as a whole. The listing control directives fall into two categories: the line-listing selection directives, which select the information to be included in the listing file, and the listing format control directives, which determine the actual format of the listing file.

The Line-Listing Selection Directives

The line-listing selection directives enable or disable inclusion of certain lines in the listing file. In general, these directives are useful for suppressing from the listing file information that you don't care about at the moment, in order to keep the listing file to a manageable size.

%LIST and %NOLIST

%LIST and **%NOLIST** are the most basic of the line-listing selection directives, enabling and disabling inclusion of succeeding lines in the listing file. For example, given

```
        .
        .
        .
%NOLIST
mov    ax,1
%LIST
mov    bx,2
%NOLIST
add    ax,bx
        .
        .
        .
```

only the middle line, `mov bx, 2`, will be included in the listing file. By default, **%LIST** is selected.

%CONDS and %NOCONDS

%CONDS and **%NOCONDS** allow you to enable and disable the listing of false conditionals and conditional statements. The listing of such conditionals is normally disabled. For example, given the code

```
        .
        .
        .
     %CONDS
IFE IS8086
     shl   ax,7
ELSE
     mov   cl,7
     shl   ax,cl
ENDIF
        .
        .
        .
```

both of the conditional sections, along with the conditional assembly
directives, will be placed in the listing file, rather than just the conditional
section that's true at the time of assembly.

%INCL and %NOINCL

%INCL and %NOINCL allow you to enable and disable the listing of lines
included from other files by way of the INCLUDE directive. The listing of
included text is normally enabled. For example, given the code

```
        .
        .
        .
     %NOINCL
     INCLUDE   HEADER.ASM
     %INCL
     INCLUDE   INIT.ASM
        .
        .
        .
```

the lines included from HEADER.ASM won't be placed in the listing file,
while the lines included from INIT.ASM will appear in the listing file.
(However, both INCLUDE directives will appear in the listing file.)

%MACS and %NOMACS

%MACS and %NOMACS allow you to enable and disable the listing of the
text of macro expansions. The listing of macro expansions is normally
disabled. For example, given the code

```
        .
        .
        .
MAKE_BYTE MACRO  VALUE
    DB      VALUE
    ENDM
        .
        .
        .
    %NOMACS
    MAKE_BYTE 1
    %MACS
    MAKE_BYTE 2
        .
        .
        .
```

the text generated by the first expansion of the *MAKE_BYTE* macro, **DB 1**, won't appear in the listing file, while the text generated by the second expansion of *MAKE_BYTE*, **DB 2**, will appear in the listing file. (However, both **MACRO** directives appear in the listing file.)

%CTLS and %NOCTLS

%CTLS and **%NOCTLS** allow you to enable and disable the listing of listing control directives themselves. The listing of listing control directives is normally disabled. For example, given the code

```
        .
        .
        .
    %NOCTLS
    %NOINCL
    %CTLS
    %NOMACS
        .
        .
        .
```

the listing control directive **%NOINCL** won't appear in the listing file, while the listing control directive **%NOMACS** will.

%UREF and **%NOUREF** allow you to enable and disable the listing of unreferenced symbols—in other words, symbols that are defined but never used—in the symbol tables. The listing of unreferenced symbols is normally enabled. You must specify a cross-reference listing in order for those two options to have any effect.

%SYMS and **%NOSYMS** allow you to enable and disable the inclusion of the symbol tables in the listing file. The inclusion of the symbol tables in the listing file is (quite obviously, given the last few sections of this chapter) normally enabled.

The Listing Format Control Directives

The listing format control directives alter the format of the listing file. You can use these directives to tailor the appearance of the listing file to your tastes and needs.

The **%TITLE** directive selects a title to be printed at the top of each page of the annotated source code portion of the listing file. Only one title may be specified in a given program. The **%SUBTTL** directive selects a subtitle to be printed below the title on each page of the listing. Any number of subtitles may be specified in a program. For example, if the source module SPACEWAR.ASM contained the directives

```
        .
        .
        .
%TITLE    'Space Wars Game Program'
%SUBTTL   'Gravitational Effects Subroutines'
        .
        .
        .
```

each page of the annotated source code would start with the lines

```
Turbo Assembler Version 1.0  10 Feb 88   06-27-88  21:53:35    Page 1
SPACEWAR.ASM
Space Wars Game Program
Gravitational Effects Subroutines
```

%NEWPAGE forces Turbo Assembler to start a new page in the listing file.

%TRUNC instructs Turbo Assembler to truncate fields that exceed their maximum width, while **%NOTRUNC** instructs Turbo Assembler to wrap fields that exceed their maximum width to the next line. Normally, fields that overflow are not truncated. Note that **%NOTRUNC** is on by default.

%PAGESIZE specifies the height in rows and width in columns of the listing pages Turbo Assembler generates. For example,

```
%PAGESIZE 66,132
```

instructs Turbo Assembler to generate pages 132 columns wide by 66 rows high. Note that **%PAGESIZE** does not send page size commands to the printer; rather, you should set up the printer before printing the listing file, then use **%PAGESIZE** to instruct Turbo Assembler to generate pages that match the way you've set up your printer.

Field-Width Directives

Five directives control the width of the five fields of the annotated source code portion of the listing file. The full format of a line in this section of the listing file is

```
<depth> <line number> <offset> <machine code> <source>
```

Earlier we described four of the five fields; the fifth field is the *<depth>* field, which indicates how many macro or include levels deep the current line is nested. For example, if the current line is produced by a macro that itself is called from within a macro, then the depth field will read 2.

The **%DEPTH** directive specifies the width in characters of the *<depth>* field. The **%LINUM** directive specifies the width in characters of the *<line number>* field. The **%PCNT** directive specifies the width of the *<offset>* field. (If you think of this field as the "program counter" field, **%PCNT** is easier to remember.) The **%BIN** directive specifies the width of the *<machine code>* field. Finally, the **%TEXT** directive specifies the width of the *<source>* field.

%PUSHLCTL and %POPLCTL

You might, at times, want to briefly change the current listing control state and then restore it. Perhaps, in order to list every byte of a data table, you need to enable wrapping and adjust the width of the fields, or perhaps you want to enable listing of all types of lines for debugging purposes. After you modify the listing control state, it can be a real nuisance to restore the listing controls to their previous state, especially since some of the listing controls may have been set in an Include file or in some far-distant part of the source module.

Turbo Assembler provides the **%PUSHLCTL** and **%POPLCTL** directives to handle this situation. **%PUSHLCTL** pushes the current listing control state onto an internal stack, and **%POPLCTL** pops the current listing control state from that stack. (Both directives have a maximum of 16 levels.) These two directives only save and restore the listing controls that can be enabled and disabled (like **%TRUNC** and **%NOTRUNC**), and not those that take a numeric argument (like **%BIN**). For example, in the following code, the listing control state is exactly the same after **%POPLCTL** as it was before **%PUSHLCTL**:

```
        .
        .
        .
%LIST
%TRUNC
%PUSHLCTL
%NOLIST
%NOTRUNC
%NEWPAGE
        .
        .
        .
%POPLCTL
        .
        .
        .
```

Other Listing Control Directives

Turbo Assembler provides several other listing control directives in order to provide compatibility with other assemblers. These directives include **TITLE, SUBTTL, PAGE, .LIST, .XLIST, .LFCOND, .SFCOND, .TFCOND, .LALL, .SALL**, and **.XALL**. (Refer to Chapter 2 of the *Reference Guide* for details on these directives.)

Displaying a Message During Assembly

Turbo Assembler provides two directives that allow you to display a string on the console during assembly. These directives can be used to report on the progress of an assembly, either to let you know how far the assembly has progressed or to let you know that a certain part of the code has been reached.

The **DISPLAY** directive displays a quoted string onscreen. The **%OUT** directive displays a nonquoted string onscreen. Otherwise, the two directives are the same. For example, the following code

```
        .
        .
        .
DISPLAY    'This message produced by DISPLAY'
%OUT       This message produced by %OUT
        .
        .
        .
```

displays the following lines onscreen:

```
This message produced by DISPLAY
This message produced by %OUT
```

Assembling Source Code Conditionally

You'll find there are times when it would be very useful to be able to have a single assembler source module assemble to any of several different versions of a program. For example, you might want two versions of a given program: one version that uses standard 8086 instructions and one version that takes advantage of the powerful instructions of the 80186 and 80286. You could maintain two separate source modules, one for each version, but then you'd have a hard time keeping both modules up to date. The simplest solution would be to build both versions into a single source module, with a single equated label that selects which version gets assembled at any given time.

Turbo Assembler's conditional assembly directives give you this capability and more. Consider the following code:

```
        .
        .
        .
IF IS8086
        mov  ax,3dah
        push ax
ELSE
        push 3dah
ENDIF
        call GetAdapterStatus
        .
        .
        .
```

If the value of the label **IS8086** is nonzero, then the parameter value 3dah is pushed on the stack with the two-step process required by the 8086. If, however, **IS8086** is zero, then the parameter value is pushed directly, using a special form of **PUSH** that's available on the 80186 and 80286, but not the 8086. The code in this example uses conditional assembly to support two versions of the same program, one for the 8086 and one for the 80186 and 80286.

Turbo Assembler supports a variety of conditional assembly directives, and also gives you the ability to generate assembly errors in a variety of ways. We'll look at the conditional assembly directives first.

Conditional Assembly Directives

The simplest and most useful conditional assembly directives are **IF** and **IFE**, which are used in conjunction with **ENDIF** and, optionally, **ELSE**. **IFDEF** and **IFNDEF** are also frequently used, while **IFB**, **IFNB**, **IFIDN**, **IFDIF**, **IF1**, and **IF2** are useful in certain situations.

IF and IFE

IF causes the following block of code (up to the matching **ELSE** or **ENDIF**) to be assembled only if the value of the operand is nonzero. The operand may be a constant value or an expression that evaluates to a constant value. For example,

```
        .
        .
        .
IF REPORT_ASSEMBLY_STATUS
     DISPLAY   'Reached assembly checkpoint 1'
ENDIF
        .
        .
        .
```

displays

```
Reached assembly checkpoint 1
```

when the **IF** is reached only if *REPORT_ASSEMBLY_STATUS* is nonzero.

An **IF** conditional may be terminated with either **ENDIF** or **ELSE**. If an **IF** conditional is terminated with **ELSE**, then the code following **ELSE** is assembled only if the operand to the associated **IF** was zero. The block of code following the **ELSE** must be terminated with an **ENDIF**. **IF** conditionals may also be nested. For instance, this code

```
        .
        .
        .
;See whether arrays are to be defined (otherwise, they're
; allocated dynamically)
IF DEFINE_ARRAY
;Make sure the array isn't too long
  IF (ARRAY_LENGTH GT MAX_ARRAY_LENGTH)
ARRAY_LENGTH    =    MAX_ARRAY_LENGTH
  ENDIF
;Set the array to an initial value if that's indicated
  IF INITIALIZE_ARRAY
```

```
Array      DB     ARRAY_LENGTH DUP (INITIAL_ARRAY_VALUE)
   ELSE
Array      DB     ARRAY_LENGTH DUP (?)
  ENDIF
ENDIF
      .
      .
      .
```

nests an **IF** and an **IF....ELSE** inside another **IF**.

IFE is exactly like **IF** except that the following code is assembled only if the operand *is* zero. The code associated with the following **IFE** directive always assembles:

```
      .
      .
      .
IFE  0
      .
      .
      .
ENDIF
      .
      .
      .
```

Like **IF**, **IFE** can have an associated **ELSE** directive.

Understand that the conditional assembly directives operate at assembly time only, not when the program is run. These are not like **if** statements in C, executing different code depending on some run-time condition; instead, they *assemble* different code depending on some assembly-time condition.

IFDEF and IFNDEF

IF and **IFE** are your primary tools for building programs that can assemble into more than one version. Two other directives that are useful in this connection are **IFDEF** and **IFNDEF**.

The block of code between an **IFDEF** directive and its associated **ENDIF** is assembled only if the label that's the operand to **IFDEF** exists; in other words, if the label has already been defined when the **IFDEF** directive is executed. For example, given the code

```
      .
      .
      .
DEFINED_LABEL  EQU  0
```

```
        .
        .
        .
IFDEF DEFINED_LABEL
     DB    0
ENDIF
        .
        .
        .
```

the **DB** directive will assemble; if, however, you were to delete the equate that sets *DEFINED_LABEL* (and assuming *DEFINED_LABEL* isn't set anywhere else in the program), then the **DB** directive would not be assembled. Note that the value of *DEFINED_LABEL* doesn't matter to **IFDEF**.

IFNDEF is the opposite of **IFDEF**, assembling its associated code only if the label that's the operand is not defined.

You may well wonder what **IFDEF** and **IFNDEF** are used for. One use is guarding against attempts to define the same label twice with **EQU** in a complex program; if the label's already defined, you can use **IFDEF** to avoid defining it again and causing an error. Another use is selecting the version of a program to be assembled, much like what was done with **IF** previously; instead of checking to see whether, say, *INITIALIZE_ARRAYS* is zero or nonzero, you could simply check to see whether it is defined at all.

One handy way to select program version is by way of the /**d** command-line switch to Turbo Assembler. /**d** defines the associated label, and optionally assigns that label a value. So, for example, you could use a command line like

```
TASM /dINITIALIZE_ARRAYS=1 test
```

to assemble the program TEST.ASM with the label *INITIALIZE_ARRAYS* set to 1.

While that's undeniably useful, there's a potential problem here. What if you're relying on *INITIALIZE_ARRAYS* being set on the command line, but forget to type the appropriate /**d** switch? Also, suppose you want to initialize arrays as a special case, and don't want to be bothered with typing /*dINITIALIZE_ARRAYS* at other times?

IFNDEF comes to your rescue in this case. You can use **IFNDEF** to test whether *INITIALIZE_ARRAYS* is already defined (from the command line), and then initialize it only if it's not already set. That way, the command-line definition takes precedence, but there's a default state for the label if no command-line definition was specified. Here's the code to define *INITIALIZE_ARRAYS* only if it's not already defined:

```
        .
        .
        .
IFNDEF    INITIALIZE_ARRAYS
INITIALIZE_ARRAYS    EQU  0     ;default to not initializing
ENDIF
        .
        .
        .
```

When you use **IFNDEF** in this way to define a symbol that has not already been defined, you will get a warning message indicating that you are using a pass-dependent construction. You can ignore this message if all you are doing is defining a symbol inside the **IFNDEF** conditional block. The message happens because Turbo Assembler can't tell if you are going to put instructions or directives inside the block, which may not work due to Turbo Assembler's one-pass nature.

Other Conditional Assembly Directives

The **IFB**, **IFNB**, **IFIDN**, and **IFDIF** directives are used for testing parameters passed to macros. (Macros are discussed in Chapter 10, "Advanced Programming in Turbo Assembler.") **IFB** causes its associated code to be assembled if the macro parameter that is its operand is blank, while **IFNB** does the same if its operand is not blank. **IFB** and **IFNB** are sort of the equivalent of **IFNDEF** and **IFDEF** for macro parameters.

For example, consider the macro **TEST**, defined as

```
;
; Macro to define a byte or a word.
;
; Input:
;    VALUE = value of byte or word
;    DEFINE_WORD = 1 to define a word, 0 to define a byte
;
; Note: If PARM2 is not specified, a byte is defined.
;
TEST MACRO      VALUE, DEFINE_WORD
IFB  <DEFINE_WORD>
    DB    VALUE                ;define a byte if PARM2 is blank ELSE
  IF DEFINE_WORD
    DW    VALUE                ;define a word if PARM2 is nonzero
  ELSE
    DB    VALUE                ;define a byte if PARM2 is zero
  ENDIF
```

```
      ENDIF
          ENDM
```

If *TEST* is invoked with

```
      TEST 19
```

then a byte with the value 19 is defined, while if *TEST* is invoked with

```
      TEST 19,1
```

then a word with the value 19 is defined.

IFIDN causes its associated code to be assembled if the two macro parameters that are its operands are identical, while **IFDIF** does the same if its pair of operands are different. For example, the following macro, which converts a signed byte to a signed word in AX, doesn't bother to copy the source operand to AL if the source operand is AL:

```
;
; Macro to convert a signed byte in an 8-bit register or
; named memory location to a signed word in AX.
;
; Input:
;    SIGNED_BYTE - the name of the register or memory location
;         containing the signed byte to convert to a signed word
;
MAKE_SIGNED_WORD    MACRO    SIGNED_BYTE
IFDIFI    <AL>,<SIGNED_BYTE>                    ;make sure the operand isn't AL
     mov  al,SIGNED_BYTE
ENDIF
     cbw
     ENDM
```

IFIDN and **IFDIF** are sensitive to the case of their arguments. Their companion directives **IFIDNI** and **IFDIFI** treat as equivalent uppercase and lowercase letters in their arguments.

Note that angle brackets are required around all operands to **IFB**, **IFNB**, **IFIDN**, and **IFDIF**.

IF1 and **IF2** report whether pass 1 or pass 2 of the assembler is active. This may seem a bit odd, since Turbo Assembler is a one-pass assembler; these directives are provided for compatibility with other assemblers that perform two passes. However, be aware that, in general, Turbo Assembler will not correctly assemble constructions that rely on the two-pass nature of other assemblers.

ELSEIF Family of Directives

Each of the **IF** family of directives (**IF, IFB, IFIDN,** and so on) has a related member in the **ELSEIF** family (for example, **ELSEIF, ELSEIFB, ELSEIFIDN**). They act like a combination of the **ELSE** directive with one of the **IF** directives. You can use them to make your code more readable when you want to test against multiple conditions or values and only assemble a single block of code. Consider the following code fragment:

```
IF BUFLENGTH GT 1000
        CALL DOBIGBUF
ELSE
        IF BUFLENGTH GT 100
                CALL MEDIUMBUF
        ELSE
                IF BUFLENGTH GT 10
                        CALL SMALLBUF
                ELSE
                        CALL TINYBUFP
                ENDIF
        ENDIF
ENDIF
```

You can use the **ELSEIF** directive to improve the readability of this code:

```
IF BUFLENGTH GT 1000
        CALL DOBIGBUF
ELSEIF BUFLENGTH GT 100
        CALL MEDIUMBUF
ELSEIF BUFLENGTH GT 10
        CALL SMALLBUF
ELSE
        CALL TINYBUF
ENDIF
```

This roughly corresponds to the **case** or **switch** statements in Pascal and C. However, this capability is actually far more general, since you don't have to use the same kind of **ELSEIF** test throughout the conditional code block. For example, the following is perfectly valid:

```
PUSHREG MACRO ARG
        IFIDN <ARG>,<INDEX>
                push si
                push di
        ELSEIFB <ARG>
                push ax
        ENDIF
        ENDM
```

Conditional Error Directives

Turbo Assembler allows you to unconditionally or conditionally generate assembly errors with the conditional error directives:

.ERR	.ERRB	.ERRDIFI	.ERRIDNI
.ERR1	.ERRDEF	.ERRE	.ERRNB
.ERR2	.ERRDIF	.ERRIDN	.ERRNDEF
			.ERRNZ

Why on earth would you intentionally generate an assembly error? Well, the conditional error directives allow you to catch a variety of mistakes in your programs, such as equated labels that are too large or too small, labels that aren't defined, and missing macro parameters.

Take another look at the list of conditional error directives. You'll note that the conditional error directives are very similar to the conditional assembler directives, and that's no coincidence, since most of the conditional error directives test the same conditions. For example, **.ERRNDEF** generates an error if the operand label is not defined, just as **IFNDEF** assembles the associated code if the operand label is not defined.

.ERR, .ERR1, and .ERR2

Whenever Turbo Assembler encounters the **.ERR** directive, an error is generated. By itself, that's not a particularly useful function; however, **.ERR** is useful when combined with a conditional assembly directive.

For example, suppose you want to generate an error if the equate for the length of a given array is set to too large a number. The following code would do the job:

```
IF (ARRAY_LENGTH GT MAX_ARRAY_LENGTH)
    .ERR
ENDIF
```

If the array isn't too long, Turbo Assembler won't assemble the code within the **IF** block, so the **.ERR** directive will never be assembled, and no error will be generated.

.ERR1 and **.ERR2** do just what **.ERR** does, but only on pass 1 or pass 2, respectively. Turbo Assembler is a one-pass assembler; these directives are present for compatibility with other assemblers that perform two passes. However, be aware that, in general, Turbo Assembler will not correctly assemble constructions that rely on the two-pass nature of other assemblers.

.ERRE and .ERRNZ

The **.ERRE** directive generates an error if its operand, which must evaluate to a constant expression, is equal to zero. **.ERRE** is equivalent to performing **.IFE** combined with **.ERR**. For example,

```
.ERRE    TEST_LABEL-1
```

is equivalent to

```
IFE  TEST_LABEL-1
    .ERRE
ENDIF
```

.ERRE can be used to generate an error when a relational expression returns false, since the value of a false expression is 0.

Similarly, the **.ERRNZ** directive generates an error if its operand is not equal to zero; this is equivalent to **IF** followed by **.ERR**. **.ERRNZ** can be used to generate an error when a relational expression returns true, since the value of a true expression is nonzero. For example,

```
.ERRNZ    ARRAY_LENGTH GT MAX_ARRAY_LENGTH
```

performs the same action as do the **IF** and **.ERR** directives in the example in the last section.

.ERRDEF and .ERRNDEF

.ERRDEF generates an error if the label that is its operand is defined, while **.ERRNDEF** generates an error if the label that is its operand is undefined. These directives let you perform the equivalent of **IFDEF** or **IFNDEF** and **.ERR** in a single line. For example,

```
.ERRNDEF  MAX_PATH_LENGTH
```

is equivalent to

```
IFNDEF    MAX_PATH_LENGTH
    .ERR
ENDIF
```

Other Conditional Error Directives

The four remaining conditional error directives are intended for use in macros only, and are directly analogous to the four conditional assembly directives intended for use in macros that we discussed in the previous section, "Other Conditional Assembly Directives," on page 237.

.ERRB generates an error if the macro parameter that is its operand is blank, and **.ERRNB** generates an error if the macro parameter that is its operand is not blank. **.ERRIDN** generates an error if the two macro parameters that are its operands are identical, and **.ERRDIF** generates an error if the two macro parameters that are its operands are different.

For example, the following macro generates an error if it's invoked with any number of parameters other than two; this is accomplished by using **.ERRB** and **.ERRNB** to make sure that **PARM2** isn't blank and **PARM3** is blank. The macro also uses **.ERRIDN** to make sure that **PARM2** isn't DX, in which case it would be wiped out when **PARM1** is loaded. Here's the macro:

```
;
; Macro to add two constants, registers, or named memory
; locations and store the result in DX.
;
; Input:
;    PARM1 - one operand to add
;    PARM2 - the other operand to add
;
ADD_TWO_OPERANDS    MACRO    PARM1,PARM2,PARM3
    .ERRB     <PARM2>                         ;there must be two parameters
    .ERRNB    <PARM3>                         ;...but not three
    .ERRIDN   <PARM2>,<DX>                    ;second parameter can't be DX
    mov  dx,PARM1
    add  dx,PARM2
    ENDM
```

Pitfalls in Assembler Programming

Each computer language has its own set of oft-encountered programming problems, and assembly language is certainly no exception. Here are some of the common pitfalls of assembly-language programming, along with tips on how to avoid them.

Forgetting to Return to DOS

In Pascal, C, and other languages, a program ends automatically and returns to DOS when there is no more code to execute, even if no explicit termination command was written into the program. Not so in assembly language, where only those actions that you explicitly request are performed. When you run a program that has no command to return to

DOS, execution simply continues right past the end of the program's code and into whatever code happens to be in the adjacent memory.

For example, consider the following program:

```
        .MODEL   small
        .CODE
DoNothing PROC NEAR
        nop
DoNothing ENDP
        END  DoNothing
```

Past experience might lead you to think that either the **ENDP** directive or the **END** directive properly terminates this program, just as } and **end**. do in C and Pascal, but that's not the case. The executable code generated by assembling and linking this program consists only of a single **NOP** instruction. In assembler, the **ENDP** directive—like all directives—generates no code; it's simply a note to the assembler that the code for the *DoNothing* procedure has ended. Similarly, the **END** *DoNothing* directive merely tells the assembler that the code for this module has ended, and that the program should start execution at *DoNothing*. Nowhere in the source code are instructions generated to transfer control back to DOS when the program is finished; as a result, when the program is run, whatever random instructions happen to be lying in memory at the address following the **NOP** will be executed immediately following the **NOP**. At this point, all bets are off, with a hung computer and a soft or hard reboot far more likely than the desired return to DOS.

While there are several means by which an assembler program can return to DOS, the recommended technique is to execute DOS function 4Ch. The following version of the preceding program will terminate properly:

```
        .MODEL   small
        .CODE
DoNothing PROC NEAR
        nop
        mov  ah,4Ch      ;DOS terminate process function
        int  21h         ;invoke DOS to end program
DoNothing ENDP
        END  DoNothing
```

Always remember that directives don't generate code, and that Turbo Assembler generates programs that do exactly what your source code tells them to do, no more and no less.

Forgetting a RET Instruction

Recall that the proper invocation of a subroutine consists of a call to the subroutine from another section of code, execution of the subroutine, and a return from the subroutine to the calling code. Remember to insert a **RET** instruction in each subroutine, so that the RETurn to the calling code occurs. When typing a program, it's easy to skip a **RET** and end up with code like this:

```
; Subroutine to multiply a value by 80.
; Input: AX - value to multiply by 80
; Output: DX:AX - product
;
MultiplyBy80    PROC NEAR
      mov dx,80
      mul dx
MultiplyBy80    ENDP

; Subroutine to get the next key press.
; Output: AL - next key pressed
; AH destroyed
;
GetKey    PROC NEAR
      mov ah,1
      int 21h
      ret
GetKey    PROC NEAR
```

The *MultiplyBy80* **ENDP** directive can fool you into thinking that *Multiply-By80* has been terminated properly, when in fact a call to *MultiplyBy80* will not only multiply AX by 80 but also continue on into *GetKey* and return the next key typed in AL. The proper code for *MultiplyBy80* is

```
; Subroutine to multiply a value by 80.
; Input: AX - value to multiply by 80
; Output: DX:AX - product
;
MultiplyBy80    PROC NEAR
      mov dx,80
      mul dx
      ret
MultiplyBy80    ENDP
```

Generating the Wrong Type of Return

The **PROC** directive has two effects. First, it defines a name by which a procedure can be called. Second, it controls whether the procedure is a near or far procedure.

The type of a procedure—near or far—is used by the assembler to determine what type of calls to generate when that procedure is called from within the same source file. The type of a procedure is also used to determine the type of **RET** performed when the procedure returns control to the calling code. Consider the following code:

```
; Near subroutine to shift DX:AX right 2 bits.
;
LongShiftRight2    PROC NEAR
    shr  dx,1
    rcr  ax,1          ;shift DX:AX right 1 bit
    shr  dx,1
    rcr  ax,1          ;shift DX:AX right another bit
    ret
LongShiftRight2    ENDP
```

Turbo Assembler makes the **RET** in this code near, since *LongShiftRight2* is a near procedure. If the **PROC** directive is changed to read

```
LongShiftRight2    PROC FAR
```

however, a far **RET** is generated.

So far, everything makes sense. After all, the **RET** instructions in a procedure should match the type of the procedure, shouldn't they?

Yes and no. The problem is that it's possible and often desirable to group several subroutines in the same procedure; since these subroutines lack an associated **PROC** directive, their **RET** instructions take on the type of the overall procedure, which is not necessarily the correct type for the individual subroutines. For example,

```
; Far subroutine to shift DX:AX right 2 bits.
;
LongShiftRight2    PROC FAR
    call LongShiftRight        ;shift DX:AX right 1 bit
    call LongShiftRight        ;shift DX:AX right another bit
    ret
LongShiftRight:
    shr  dx,1
    rcr  ax,1                  ;shift DX:AX right 1 bit
    ret
LongShiftRight2    ENDP
```

does not work properly. *LongShiftRight2* makes near calls to *LongShiftRight*, since they are both in the same code segment. However, since *LongShift-Right* is embedded in the *LongShiftRight2* procedure, the return at the end of *LongShiftRight* subroutine becomes a far **RET**, and matching far calls with near returns is likely to lead to a crash.

One good solution is to make sure that each subroutine has an associated **PROC** directive. Nested **PROC** directives work well:

```
; Far subroutine to shift DX:AX right 2 bits.
;
LongShiftRight2    PROC FAR
     call LongShiftRight        ;shift DX:AX right 1 bit
     call LongShiftRight        ;shift DX:AX right another bit
     ret
LongShiftRight        PROC NEAR
     shr  dx,1
     rcr  ax,1                  ;shift DX:AX right 1 bit
     ret
LongShiftRight     ENDP
LongShiftRight2    ENDP
```

as do sequential **PROC** directives:

```
; Far subroutine to shift DX:AX right 2 bits.
;
LongShiftRight2    PROC FAR
     call LongShiftRight        ;shift DX:AX right 1 bit
     call LongShiftRight        ;shift DX:AX right another bit
     ret
LongShiftRight2    ENDP
LongShiftRight        PROC NEAR
     shr  dx,1
     rcr  ax,1                  ;shift DX:AX right 1 bit
     ret
LongShiftRight     ENDP
```

You can also use **RETN** and **RETF** to explicitly generate a near or far return, respectively. You can use these outside of a procedure defined with the **PROC** directive and rest assured that the correct return will always be generated.

Reversing Operands

To many people, the order of instruction operands in 8086 assembly language seems backward, and there is certainly some justification for this viewpoint. If the line

```
mov  ax,bx
```

meant "move AX to BX," the line would scan smoothly from left to right, and this is the way many microprocessor manufacturers have designed their assembly languages. However, Intel took a different approach with 8086 assembly language; for us the line means "move BX to AX," and that can sometimes cause confusion.

The thinking behind the ordering of Intel's operands is that the operands appear in the same order as they would in C or Pascal code, with the destination on the left. Consequently, one way to think of operand-ordering in 8086 assembly language is to mentally insert an equal sign in place of the comma between operands and reword the line to form an assignment. For example, think of

```
mov  ax,bx
```

as

```
ax = bx
```

Constant operands, such as

```
add  bx,(OFFSET BaseTable * 4) + 2
```

which can be thought of as

```
bx += (OFFSET BaseTable * 4) + 2
```

also lend themselves to this approach.

Forgetting the Stack or Reserving a Too-Small Stack

In most cases, you are treading on thin ice if you don't explicitly allocate space for a stack. Programs without an allocated stack will sometimes run, since the default stack may happen to fall in an unused area of memory. But there is no assurance that these programs will run under all circumstances, since not a single byte is guaranteed to be available for the stack. Most programs should have a **.STACK** directive to reserve space for the stack, and for each program that directive should reserve more than enough space for the deepest stack you can conceive of the program using.

Why more than enough space rather than just enough space? In general, it's difficult to be sure just how much stack space a given program needs, and the sort of bugs that occur when the stack grows into other parts of the program and overwrites them are often very difficult to reproduce and track down. Then, too, many debuggers use a little extra space on the stack when getting control back from a program. So be generous when allocating stack space, and save yourself future headaches. A minimum stack size of 512 bytes is a good rule of thumb.

The only assembler programs that should not have a stack allocated are programs that are going to be made into .COM or .BIN files. .BIN files contain code hard-wired to run at a specific address, and since .BIN files are generally used as interpreted BASIC subroutines, they use BASIC's stack. .COM programs run with the stack at the very top of the program's segment (which is a maximum of 64 Kb long, or less if there's less than 64 Kb available), so the maximum size of the stack is simply the amount of memory left in the program's segment. Beware if any of the .COM programs you write approach 64 Kb in size, since the stack shrinks accordingly. Also be aware that large .COM programs may encounter stack problems when run on computers with little available memory or when run from a DOS shell under another program. Writing .EXE rather than .COM programs and reserving ample stack space is a simple way to avoid these potential problems.

Calling a Subroutine that Wipes Out Needed Registers

When writing assembler code, it's easy to think of the registers as local variables, dedicated to the use of the procedure you're working on at the moment. In particular, there's a tendency to assume that registers are unchanged by calls to other procedures. It just isn't so, though—the registers are global variables, and each procedure can preserve or destroy any or all registers.

As an example, consider the following:

```
        .
        .
        .
mov  bx,[TableBase]      ;point BX to base of table
mov  ax,[Element]        ;get element #
call DivideBy10          ;divide element # by 10
add  bx,ax               ;point to appropriate entry
        .
        .
        .
; Subroutine to divide a value by 10.
; Input: AX - value to divide by 10
; Output: AX - value divided by 10
;         DX - remainder of value divided by 10
; BX destroyed.
;
```

```
DivideBy10    PROC NEAR
    mov  dx,0              ;prepare DX:AX as the 32-bit dividend
    mov  bx,10             ;BX is the 16-bit divisor
    div  bx
    ret
DivideBy10    ENDP
```

The calling routine assumes that BX is preserved by *MultiplyBy80*, when in fact *MultiplyBy80* sets BX to 10. There are a number of possible solutions in this particular case. BX could be pushed and popped either at the start or end of *MultiplyBy80*:

```
    .
    .
    .
    mov  bx,[TableBase]    ;point BX to base of table
    mov  ax,[Element]      ;get element #
    call DivideBy10        ;divide element # by 10
    add  bx,ax             ;point to appropriate entry
    .
    .
    .
; Subroutine to divide a value by 10.
; Input: AX - value to divide by 10
; Output: AX - value divided by 10
;         DX - remainder of value divided by 10
;
DivideBy10    PROC NEAR
    push bx                ;preserve BX
    mov  dx,0              ;prepare DX:AX as the 32-bit dividend
    mov  bx,10             ;BX is the 16-bit divisor
    div  bx
    pop  bx                ;restore original BX
    ret
DivideBy10    ENDP
```

or in the calling routine around the call to *MultiplyBy80*:

```
    .
    .
    .
    mov  bx,[TableBase]    ;point BX to base of table
    mov  ax,[Element]      ;get element #
    push bx                ;preserve table base
    call DivideBy10        ;divide element # by 10
    pop  bx                ;restore table base
    add  bx,ax             ;point to appropriate entry
    .
    .
    .
```

```
; Subroutine to divide a value by 10.
; Input: AX - value to divide by 10
; Output: AX - value divided by 10
;         DX - remainder of value divided by 10
;
DivideBy10    PROC NEAR
    mov  dx,0              ;prepare DX:AX as the 32-bit dividend
    mov  bx,10             ;BX is the 16-bit divisor
    div  bx
    ret
DivideBy10    ENDP
```

or BX could simply be loaded after, rather than before, the call

```
    .
    .
    .

    mov  ax,[Element]     ;get element #
    call DivideBy10       ;divide element # by 10
    mov  bx,[TableBase]   ;point BX to base of table
    add  bx,ax            ;point to appropriate entry
    .
    .
    .

; Subroutine to divide a value by 10.
; Input: AX - value to divide by 10
; Output: AX - value divided by 10
;         DX - remainder of value divided by 10
;
DivideBy10    PROC NEAR
    mov  dx,0              ;prepare DX:AX as the 32-bit dividend
    mov  bx,10             ;BX is the 16-bit divisor
    div  bx
    ret
DivideBy10    ENDP
```

An obvious solution to the general problem of subroutines that accidentally
clobber registers is for all subroutines to preserve all registers as a matter of
course. Unfortunately, pushing and popping registers takes time and code
space, negating some of the advantages of programming in assembler.
Another approach is to preface each subroutine with a comment indicating
which registers are preserved and which are destroyed and then carefully
check that there are no problems in each case where you must assume a
register is preserved across a subroutine call. Yet another approach is to
explicitly preserve needed registers in calling routines.

Using the Wrong Sense for a Conditional Jump

The profusion of conditional jumps in assembly language (JE, JNE, JC, JNC, JA, JB, JG, and so on) allows tremendous flexibility in writing code—and also makes it easy to select the wrong jump for a given purpose. Moreover, since condition-handling in assembly language requires at least two separate lines, one for the comparison and one for the conditional jump (and many more lines for complex conditions), assembly language condition-handling is less intuitive and more prone to errors than condition-handling in C and Pascal.

- One common error is the use of **JA, JB, JAE,** or **JBE** for comparing signed values or, similarly, the use of **JG, JL, JGE,** or **JLE** for comparing unsigned values.

- Another common error is the use of, say, **JA** when **JAE** was intended. Remember that without the *e* on the end of **JAE, JBE, JLE,** or **JGE,** the comparison does not include the case where the two operands are equal.

- And yet another common error is the use of inverted logic, such as **JS** when **JNS** was intended.

One approach that can help minimize errors when using conditional jumps is to comment the tests and conditional jumps in a C-like notation. For example,

```
        .
        .
        .
;
; if ( Length > MaxLength ) {
;
      mov   ax,[Length]
      cmp   ax,[MaxLength]
      jng   LengthIsLessThanMax
        .
        .
        .
      jmp   EndMaxLengthTest
;
; } else {
;
LengthIsLessThanMax:
        .
        .
        .
;
; }
;
```

```
EndMaxLengthTest:
        .
        .
        .
```

Pitfalls with String Instructions

String instructions are uniquely powerful among 8086 instructions, and with that power come some unique problems, which are described next.

Forgetting About REP String Overrun

String instructions have a curious property: After they're executed, the pointers they use wind up pointing to an address 1 byte away (or 2 bytes if a word instruction) from the last address processed. For example, after this code executes

```
        .
        .
        .
cld                     ;make string instructions count up
mov  si,0               ;point to offset 0
lodsb                   ;read the byte at offset 0
        .
        .
        .
```

SI will contain 1, not 0. This makes sense, since the next **LODSB** is likely to want to access address 1, and the **LODSB** after that to access address 2, but it can cause some confusion with repeated string instructions, especially **REP SCAS** and **REP CMPS**. Consider the code

```
        .
        .
        .
cld                     ;make string instructions count up
les  di,[bp+ScanString] ;point ES:DI to the string to scan
mov  cx,MAX_STRING_LEN  ;check up to the longest string
mov  al,0               ;search for the terminating null
repne scasb             ;perform search
        .
        .
        .
```

Suppose ES is 2000h, DI is 0, and the memory starting at 2000:0000 contains

```
41h 61h 72h 64h 00h
```

After this code executes, DI will contain 5, the offset of the byte *after* the 0 byte that was found. In order to return a pointer to the last character in the string, the preceding code would have to read

```
        .
        .
        .
        cld                         ;make string instructions count up
        les  di,[bp+ScanString]     ;point ES:DI to the string to scan
        mov  cx,MAX_STRING_LEN       ;check up to the longest string
        mov  al,0                   ;search for the terminating zero
        repne scasb                 ;perform search
        jne  NoMatch                ;error-terminating zero not found
        dec  di                     ;point back to the zero
        dec  di                     ;point back to last character
        ret
NoMatch:
        mov  di,0                   ;return a null pointer
        mov  es,di
        ret
        .
        .
        .
```

Remember also that when the direction flag is set, causing string instructions to count down, DI will point to the byte before, not after, the last character scanned.

Similar confusion can arise because CX is decremented during **REP SCAS** and **REP CMPS** one more time than might be expected. CX is not only decremented once for each byte that matches the "repeat while" condition (equal or not equal), but also once for the byte that fails to match the "repeat while" condition and thereby causes the instruction to terminate. For instance, if in the last example the byte at 2000:0000 contained zero, after execution CX would contain *MAX_STRING_LEN – 1*, even though not a single nonzero character was found. A subroutine to count the number of characters in a string must account for this:

```
; Returns the length of a zero-terminated string in bytes.
; Input: ES:DI - start of string
; Output: AX - length of string, not including terminating zero
;         ES:DI - points to last byte of string, or
;                 0000:0000 if terminating zero not found
;
StringLength    PROC NEAR
    cld                         ;search counts up
    push cx                     ;preserve CX
    mov  cx,0FFFFh              ;maximum length to search
    mov  al,0                   ;terminating byte to search for
```

```
    repne scasb                    ;search for the terminating zero
    jne  StringLengthError         ;error if end of string not found
    mov  ax,0FFFFh                 ;maximum length searched
    sub  ax,cx                     ;see how many bytes were counted
    dec  ax                        ;don't count the terminating zero
    dec  di                        ;point back to terminating zero
    dec  di                        ;point back to last character
    jmp  short StringLengthEnd
StringLengthError:
    mov  di,0                      ;return a null pointer
    mov  es,di
StringLengthEnd:
    pop  cx                        ;restore the original CX
    ret
StringLength   ENDP
```

Another potential problem arising from CX counting on the byte that terminates a **REP SCAS** or **REP CMPS** is that CX may be zero at the end of the comparison even though the termination condition was found. This code does not correctly evaluate whether two arrays are the same, since CX will count down to zero when comparing two non-equal arrays that differ only at the last byte:

```
    .
    .
    .
repz cmpsb
jcxz ArraysAreTheSame
    .
    .
    .
```

The correct code for testing array equality is

```
    .
    .
    .
repz cmpsb
jz   ArraysAreTheSame
    .
    .
    .
```

In short, CX should be used only as a count of the bytes scanned by **REP SCAS** and **REP CMPS**, not as an indicator of whether the data scanned or compared was equal or non-equal.

If you find yourself having trouble figuring out just what repeated string instructions will do in your programs, one good approach is to use either pencil and paper or a debugger to trace, step-by-step, through the workings of your repeated string code.

Relying on a Zero CX to Cover a Whole Segment

Any repeated string instruction executed with CX equal to zero will do nothing. Period. This can be convenient in that there's no need to check for the zero case before executing a repeated string instruction; on the other hand, there's no way to access every byte in a segment with a byte-sized string instruction. For example, the following code scans the segment at ES for the first occurrence of the letter *A*:

```
        .
        .
        .
        cld                 ;searches count up
        sub  di,di          ;start at offset zero
        mov  al,'A'         ;search for letter 'A'
        mov  cx,0FFFFh      ;first scan the first 64 Kb-1 bytes
        repne SCASb         ;scan the first 64 Kb-1 bytes
        je   AFound         ;found it
        scasb               ;didn't find it yet-scan the last byte
        je   AFound         ;found it at the last byte
                            ;there's no letter 'A' in this segment
        .
        .
        .

AFound:                     ;DI - 1 points to the letter 'A'
        .
        .
        .
```

There's an asymmetry in the 8086 instruction set concerning the use of zero CX values when counting. While repeated string instructions don't do anything if CX is 0, the **LOOP** instruction *does* execute if CX is 0, decrementing CX to 0FFFFh and jumping to the loop address. This means that a full 64 Kb can be processed in a single loop. The preceding example of scanning the segment at ES for the letter *A* can be implemented with **LOOP** as

```
        .
        .
        .
        cld                 ;searches count up
        sub  di,di          ;start at offset zero
        mov  al,'A'
        sub  cx,cx          ;search 64 Kb bytes
```

```
ASearchLoop:
    scasb                   ;check the next byte
    je   AFound             ;it's a letter 'A'
    loop ASearchLoop        ;there's no letter 'A' in this segment
    .
    .
    .
AFound:                     ;DI - 1 points to the letter 'A'
    .
    .
    .
```

On the other hand, the case of CX equal to zero does have to be specially checked for when using **LOOP** in those cases where CX equal to zero really does mean, "Don't do anything"; otherwise, 64 Kb loops instead of zero loops will be executed with potentially disastrous results. The **JCXZ** instruction helps you handle such cases:

```
; Subroutine to fill up to 64 Kb-1 bytes with a given byte value.
; Input: AL - fill value
;        CX - number of bytes to fill
;        DS:BX - first address to fill
; BX, CX altered.
;
FillBytes PROC NEAR
     jcxz FillBytesEnd      ;if the # of bytes to fill is 0, done
FillBytesLoop:
    mov  [bx],al            ;fill a byte
    inc  bx                 ;point to the next byte
    loop FillBytesLoop      ;do for the number of bytes specified
FillBytesEnd:
    ret
FillBytes ENDP
```

Without **JCXZ**, *FillBytes* would fill the entire segment pointed to by ES with AL when CX was zero, instead of leaving memory unchanged.

Using Incorrect Direction Flag Settings

When a string instruction is executed, its associated pointer or pointers—SI or DI or both—increment. Or decrement. It all depends on the state of the direction flag.

The direction flag can be cleared with **CLD** to cause string instructions to increment (count up) and can be set with **STD** to cause string instructions to decrement (count down). Once cleared or set, the direction flag stays in the same state until either another **CLD** or **STD** is executed or the flags are popped from the stack with **POPF** or **IRET**. While it's handy to be able to program the direction flag once and then execute a series of string instructions that all operate in the same direction, the direction flag can also be responsible for intermittent and hard-to-find bugs by causing string instructions to behave differently, depending on code that executed much earlier.

Why is this? In most programs, the direction flag is almost always cleared, since counting up is intuitively easier than counting down and works fine in most cases. There are, however, certain cases where only counting down will do. You can get in the habit of assuming that the direction flag will always be cleared, but forget to clear the flag after one of the few procedures that sets the direction flag. The result will be that parts of your program that require counting up will work perfectly—except after executing that one procedure that leaves the direction flag set.

The remedy is obvious. Always program the direction flag to the desired state before using string instructions if there is any chance at all that the direction flag is not already programmed correctly. In general, it's a good idea to program the direction flag correctly at the beginning of any procedure that uses string instructions.

Using the Wrong Sense for a Repeated String Comparison

The **CMPS** instruction compares two areas of memory, while the **SCAS** instruction compares the accumulator to an area of memory. When prefixed by **REPE**, either of these instructions can perform a comparison until either CX becomes zero or a not-equal comparison occurs. When prefixed by **REPNE**, either instruction can perform a comparison until either CX becomes zero or an equal comparison occurs. Unfortunately, it's easy to become confused about which of the **REP** prefixes does what.

A good way to remember the function of a given **REP** prefix is to mentally insert a "while" after the "rep" portion of the prefix. Then **REPE** becomes "rep while e," or "repeat while equal," and **REPNE** becomes "rep while ne," or "repeat while not equal."

Forgetting About String Segment Defaults

Each string instruction defaults to using a source segment (if any) of DS, and a destination segment (if any) of ES. It's easy to forget this and try to perform, say, a **STOSB** to the data segment, since that's where all the data you're processing with nonstring instructions normally resides. Similarly, it's common to accidentally write code such as

```
        .
        .
        .
        cld                 ;count up while searching
        mov  al,0
        mov  cx,80          ;length of buffer
        repe scasb          ;find first nonzero character, if any
        jz   AllZero        ;no nonzero character
        dec  di             ;point back to first nonzero character
        mov  al,[di]        ;get first nonzero character
        .
        .
        .
AllZero:
        .
        .
        .
```

The problem with this code is that unless DS and ES are the same, the last
MOV won't load the correct byte into AL, since **STOSB** operates relative to
ES and **MOV** operates relative to DS. The correct code would use a
segment override prefix on the move. (Refer to Chapter 10 for an
explanation of segment prefixes.)

```
        .
        .
        .
        cld                 ;count up while searching
        mov  al,0
        mov  cx,80          ;length of buffer
        repe scasb          ;find first nonzero character, if any
        jz   AllZero        ;no nonzero character
        dec  di             ;point back to first nonzero character
        mov  al,es:[di]     ;get first nonzero character (from ES!)
        .
        .
        .
AllZero:
        .
        .
        .
```

Also, remember that while it is possible to override DS as the string source
segment, as, for example, in

```
        .
        .
        .
lods es:[SourceArray]
        .
        .
        .
```

it is not possible to override ES as the string destination segment, so this code won't work:

```
        .
        .
        .
stos ds:[DestArray]
        .
        .
        .
```

(In fact, Turbo Assembler catches this as an error during assembly.)

Converting Incorrectly from Byte to Word Operations

In general, it's desirable to use the largest possible data size (usually word, but dword on an 80386) for a string instruction, since string instructions with larger data sizes often run faster. For example,

```
        .
        .
        .
mov  cx,200     ;number of bytes to move
        .
        .
        .
shr  cx,1       ;convert from # of bytes to # of words
rep  movsw      ;move the block a word at a time
        .
        .
        .
```

runs about 50% faster on an 8088 than

```
        .
        .
        .
mov  cx,200     ;number of bytes to move
        .
        .
```

```
          .
rep  movsb       ;move the block a byte at a time
          .
          .
          .
```

There are a couple of potential pitfalls here, though. First, the conversion from a byte count to a word count by a simple

```
shr cx,1
```

loses a byte if CX is odd, since the least-significant bit is shifted out. Cases where CX might be odd can be handled with the following conditional code:

```
          .
          .
          .
          shr  cx,1        ;convert to word count
          jnc  MoveWord    ;odd byte count?
          movsb            ;yes, odd byte count, so move odd byte
MoveWord:
          rep  movsw       ;move even # of bytes a word at a time
          .
          .
          .
```

Second, make sure you remember **SHR** divides the byte count by two. Using, say, **STOSW** with a byte rather than a word count can wipe out other data and cause all sorts of problems. For example,

```
          .
          .
          .
mov  cx,200           ;number of bytes to move
          .
          .
          .
rep  movsw            ;move the block a word at a time
          .
          .
          .
```

will wipe out the 200 bytes (100 words) immediately following the destination block.

Using Multiple Prefixes

String instructions with multiple prefixes do not work reliably and should generally be avoided. An example is this code

```
        .
        .
        .
rep  movs es:[DestArray],ss:[SourceArray]
        .
        .
        .
```

which has both a **REP** prefix and an **SS** segment override prefix. Multiple prefixes are a problem because string instructions can be interrupted in the middle of repeated execution by a hardware interrupt. On some Intel processors, including the 8086 and 8088, when a string instruction with multiple prefixes resumes after an interrupt has been serviced, all prefixes other than the last are ignored. As a result, the instruction might not be repeated the correct number of times or the wrong segment might be accessed.

If you absolutely must use a string instruction with multiple prefixes, disable interrupts for the duration of the instruction, as follows:

```
        .
        .
        .
cli
rep  movs es:[DestArray],ss:[SourceArray]
sti
        .
        .
        .
```

Relying on the Operand(s) to a String Instruction

The optional operand or operands to a string instruction are used for data sizing and segment overrides only, and do not guarantee that the memory location referenced will actually be accessed. For example,

```
        .
        .
        .
DestArray dw   256 dup (?)
        .
        .
```

```
        .
    cld                         ;count up during fill
    mov  al,'*'                 ;byte to fill with
    mov  cx,256                 ;number of words to fill
    mov  di,0                   ;start address for fill
    rep  stos es:[DestArray]    ;do the fill
        .
        .
        .
```

sets the 256 bytes starting at offset 0 in segment ES to the asterisk character, regardless of where *DestArray* is located. All that **ES:[DestArray]** does is tell the assembler to use a **STOSW**, since *DestArray* is an array of words; it is the contents of SI and/or DI, not the operands, that determine what offsets are accessed by string instructions. Nonetheless, using the optional operand or operands with string instructions can be a useful way of ensuring that you're not accidentally performing, say, word-sized accesses to a byte array.

Similarly, the optional operand to the **XLAT** instruction is used for type-checking and segment overrides only. The code

```
        .
        .
        .
LookUpTable     LABEL  BYTE
        .
        .
        .
ASCIITable      LABEL  BYTE
        .
        .
        .
    mov  bx,OFFSET ASCIITable          ;point to the look-up table
    mov  al,[CharacterToTranslate]     ;get the byte to be looked up
    xlat [LookUpTable]                  ;look the byte up
        .
        .
        .
```

looks up the byte at location AL in *ASCIITable*, not *LookUpTable*, but assembles just fine because all **XLAT** does with its one operand is make sure that it is byte-sized and looks for a segment override. The **XLAT** instruction always looks up the contents of offset BX+AL, regardless of any operand used.

Forgetting About Unusual Side Effects

Since assembler programs are written in the 8086's native language, any changes in the states of the registers and flags of the 8086 are of keen interest to the assembly language programmer. Most of the ways in which assembler programs can alter the state of the processor are obvious and straightforward. For example,

```
add  bx,[Grade]
```

adds the 16-bit value at location *Grade* to BX and updates the overflow, sign, zero, auxiliary carry, parity, and carry flags to reflect the outcome of the addition. Some instructions produce less obvious changes in the state of the processor, though. Here's a quick look at some such instructions.

Wiping Out a Register with Multiplication

Multiplication—whether it be 8-bit by 8-bit, 16-bit by 16-bit, or 32-bit by 32-bit—always destroys the contents of at least one register other than the portion of the accumulator used as a source operand. This is inevitable given that the result of an 8-bit by 8-bit multiplication can be as large as 16 bits in size, the result of a 16-bit by 16-bit multiplication can be 32 bits in size, and the result of a 32-bit by 32-bit multiplication can be 64 bits in size. Multiplication source and destination operands are shown in Table 5.1.

Table 5.1: Source and Destination for the MUL and IMUL Instructions

| Source Operand Size in Bits | Source | | Destination | | |
	Explicit Operand	Implied Operand	High	Low	Example
8 × 8	*reg8**	AL	AH	AL	mul dl
16 × 16	*reg16***	AX	DX	AX	imul bx
32 × 32†	*reg32*‡	EAX	EDX	EAX	mul esi

* *reg8* can be any of AH, AL, BH, BL, CH, CL, DH, or DL.

** *reg16* can be any of AX, BX, CX, DX, SI, DI, BP, or SP.

† 32 × 32 multiples are not supported by the 8086, 8088, 80186, 80188, or 80286.

‡ *reg32* can be any of EAX, EBX, ECX, EDX, ESI, EDI, EBP, or ESP.

While this seems simple enough, there's a glaring lack of detail in the syntax of the **MUL** and **IMUL** instructions, since only one of the two source operands and the size of the operation are explicitly stated; both the portion of the accumulator used as a source operand and the registers used as the destination are merely implied. This lack of detail makes it easy to overlook the extra register that's destroyed. For instance, there are many cases in which the result of, say, a given 16-bit by 16-bit multiplication is known by the programmer to be guaranteed to fit in AX, and in such cases, there's a tendency to forget that DX gets wiped out too. Just remember that every use of **MUL** and **IMUL** wipes out not only AL, AX, or EAX, but also AH, DX, or EDX as well.

Forgetting that String Instructions Alter Several Registers

The string instructions (**MOVS**, **STOS**, **LODS**, **CMPS**, and **SCAS**) can affect several of the flags and as many as three registers during execution of a single instruction. As with the **MUL** instruction, the many effects of the string instructions are not explicitly expressed in the operands to those instructions. When you use string instructions, remember that either SI or DI or both either increment or decrement (depending on the state of the direction flag) on each execution of a string instruction. CX is also decremented at least once and possibly as far as zero each time a string instruction with a **REP** prefix is used.

Expecting Certain Instructions to Alter the Carry Flag

While some instructions affect registers or flags unexpectedly, other instructions don't affect all the flags you might expect them to. For example,

```
inc  ah
```

seems logically equivalent to

```
add  ah,1
```

and so it is—with a single exception. Where **ADD** sets the carry flag if the result is too large for the destination, **INC** does not affect the carry flag in any way. As a result,

```
        .
        .
        .
add ax,1
adc dx,0
        .
        .
        .
```

is a valid way to increment a 32-bit value stored in DX:AX, while

```
        .
        .
        .
inc ax
adc dx,0
        .
        .
        .
```

is not. The same is true of **DEC**, while **LOOP, LOOPZ,** and **LOOPNZ** don't affect any flags at all. Actually, this can sometimes be used to your advantage, since under certain circumstances it can be handy to execute one of these instructions without destroying the current carry flag setting. The important thing is to know exactly what each instruction you use does; if there's any doubt in your mind about how a given instruction affects the flags, look it up.

Waiting Too Long to Use Flags

Flags last only until the next instruction that alters them, which is not very long, by and large. It's a good practice to act on flags as soon as possible after they are set, thereby avoiding all sorts of potential bugs. For example, it's often tempting to test a condition, set a register or two, and only then branch according to the result of the test. The code

```
        .
        .
        .
cmp  ax,1
mov  ax,0
jg   HandlePositive
        .
        .
        .
```

is a perfectly valid way to test the status of AX, then force it to zero before jumping to the code that handles the status. On the other hand, the code

```
         .
         .
         .
cmp   ax,1
sub   ax,ax
jg    HandlePositive
         .
         .
         .
```

which seems appealing because it is both shorter and faster than the first case, does not work because the subtraction wipes out all the flag settings generated by the compare. This is typical of the sort of problem that can result from delaying the use of a flag status.

Confusing Memory and Immediate Operands

An assembler program may refer either to the offset of a memory variable or to the value stored in that memory variable. Unfortunately, assembly language is neither strict nor intuitive about the ways in which these two types of references can be made, and as a result, offset and value references to a memory variable are often confused.

Figure 5.1 illustrates the distinction between the offset and the value of a memory variable. The offset of the word-sized variable *MemLoc* is 5002h, while the value of *MemLoc* is 1234h.

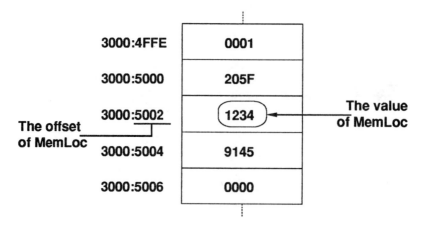

Figure 5.1: Memory Variables: Offset vs. Value

In Figure 5.1, the offset of the word-sized variable *MemLoc* is the constant value 5002h, obtained with the **OFFSET** operator. For example,

```
mov bx,OFFSET MemLoc
```

loads 5002h into BX. The value 5002h is an immediate operand; in other words, it is built right into the instruction and never changes.

The value of *MemLoc* is 1234h, read from the memory at offset 5002h in the data segment. One way to read this value is by loading BX, SI, DI, or BP with the offset of *MemLoc* and using that register to address memory. The code

```
mov  bx,OFFSET MemLoc
mov  ax,[bx]
```

loads the value of *MemLoc*, 1234h, into AX. Alternatively, the value of *MemLoc* can be loaded directly into AX with either

```
mov ax,MemLoc
```

or

```
mov ax,[MemLoc]
```

Here the value 1234h is obtained as a direct, rather than an immediate, operand; the **MOV** instruction has the offset 5002h built into it, and loads AX with the value at 5002h, which in this case happens to be 1234h. Consequently, the value 1234h is not permanently associated with *MemLoc*. For instance,

```
mov  [MemLoc],5555h
mov  ax,[MemLoc]
```

loads the value 5555h, not 1234h, into AX.

The key point is that while the offset of *MemLoc* is a constant value that describes a fixed address in the data segment, the value of *MemLoc* is the changeable number stored at that memory address. The instructions

```
mov  [MemLoc],1
add  [MemLoc],2
```

make the value of *MemLoc* 3, but the instruction

```
add  OFFSET MemLoc,2
```

is equivalent to

```
add  5002h,2
```

which is nonsensical, since it's impossible to add one constant to another.

A surprisingly common problem is that in the heat of coding a program, **OFFSET** is sometimes forgotten, leaving, for example,

```
mov  si,MemLoc
```

when the offset of *MemLoc* is desired. At first glance, this line doesn't look wrong, and since *MemLoc* is a word-sized variable, this line will not cause an assembly-time error. However, at run-time SI will be loaded with the data at *MemLoc* (1234h in Figure 5.1 on page 266), rather than the offset of *MemLoc* (5002h in Figure 5.1)—with unpredictable results.

There is no sure-fire way to avoid this problem, but you might want to make it a rule to enclose all references to memory in square brackets. Then references to address constants will be prefixed with **OFFSET** and references to memory will be enclosed in square brackets, thus eliminating the ambiguous use of memory variable names. This convention makes the functions of

```
mov  si,OFFSET MemLoc
```

and

```
mov  si,[MemLoc]
```

instantly clear, while

```
mov  si,MemLoc
```

should set off mental alarms.

Causing Segment Wraparound

One of the most difficult aspects of programming the 8086 is that memory isn't accessible as one long array of bytes, but is rather made available in chunks of 64 Kb relative to segment registers. Segments can introduce subtle bugs, since if a program attempts to access an address past the end of a segment, it actually ends up wrapping back to access the start of that segment instead.

As an example, suppose that the memory starting at 10000h contains the data shown in Figure 5.2. When DS is set to 1000h, code that accesses the string *"Testing"* at 1000:FFF9 wraps back to address the byte at 1000:0000 as the next byte addressed after the *g* at 1000:FFFF because offsets cannot exceed 0FFFFh, the maximum 16-bit value.

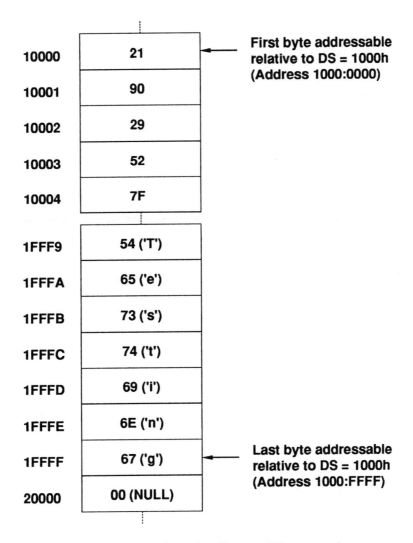

10000	21	
10001	90	
10002	29	
10003	52	
10004	7F	
1FFF9	54 ('T')	
1FFFA	65 ('e')	
1FFFB	73 ('s')	
1FFFC	74 ('t')	
1FFFD	69 ('i')	
1FFFE	6E ('n')	
1FFFF	67 ('g')	
20000	00 (NULL)	

First byte addressable relative to DS = 1000h (Address 1000:0000)

Last byte addressable relative to DS = 1000h (Address 1000:FFFF)

Figure 5.2: An Example of Segment Wraparound

Now suppose that the following subroutine is called with DS:SI equal to 1000:FFF9 in order to convert the string *"Testing"* at 1000:FFF9 to upper-case:

```
; Subroutine to convert a zero-terminated string to uppercase.
; Input: DS:SI - pointer to string.
;
ToUpper    PROC NEAR
```

```
      mov  al,[si]        ;get the next character
      cmp  al,0           ;if zero...
      jz   ToUpperDone    ;...done with string
      cmp  al,'a'         ;is it a lowercase letter?
      jb   ToUpperNext    ;not lowercase
      cmp  al,'z'
      ja   ToUpperNext    ;not lowercase
      and  al,NOT 20h     ;it is lowercase, so make it uppercase
      mov  [si],al        ;save the uppercase version
ToUpperNext:
      inc  si             ;point to the next character
      jmp  ToUpper
ToUpperDone:
      ret
ToUpper  ENDP
```

After *ToUpper* processes the first seven characters of the string, SI will increment from 0FFFFh to 0. (Recall that SI is only a 16-bit register and so can't count higher than 0FFFFh.) The zero byte stored at address 20000h that terminates the string is never reached; instead *ToUpper* starts to convert the unrelated bytes at 10000h to uppercase, and doesn't stop until it happens to encounter a 0 byte. At some later point, these altered bytes may cause this program to perform incorrectly. Often, it is very difficult to trace bugs caused by such accidentally altered bytes back to the routine that wrapped off the end of a segment, since the cause can be far distant from the symptom in time and may be in a totally unrelated portion of the source code.

There's no simple rule of thumb here, other than always making sure your code doesn't unwittingly try to run off the end of a segment. It is also very dangerous (to your sanity, at least) to try to access a word at offset 0FFFFh; the machine will hang.

Failing to Preserve Everything in an Interrupt Handler

An interrupt handler is a routine that is jumped to whenever a given hardware interrupt, such as the keyboard interrupt, occurs. Interrupt handlers perform a variety of actions, such as buffering keys or updating the system clock. An interrupt may occur at any time, in the middle of any code, so an interrupt handler must leave the registers and flags of the processor in exactly the same state on exit from the handler as they were in on entry to the handler. Were this not done, the code executing when an interrupt occurs might suddenly find that the state of the processor has changed unpredictably.

For instance, if the code

```
    .
    .
    .
mov  ax,[ReturnValue]
ret
    .
    .
    .
```

were executing, an interrupt could occur between the two instructions. If the interrupt handler fails to preserve the contents of AX, the value returned to the calling program would be based on what the interrupt handler did rather than on the contents of the *ReturnValue* variable.

Consequently, every interrupt handler should explicitly preserve the contents of all registers. While it is valid to explicitly preserve only those registers that the handler modifies, it's good insurance to just push all registers on entry to an interrupt handler and pop all registers on exit. After all, you might go back someday and change the code of the interrupt handler—so that it modifies additional registers—but forget to add instructions to preserve those registers.

It is not necessary to save the flags in an interrupt handler. When an interrupt occurs, the flags are automatically pushed on the stack, and when the interrupt handler executes an **IRET** to return to the interrupted program, the flags are automatically restored from the stack.

A corollary to the absolute necessity of preserving all registers in an interrupt handler is this: *Make no assumptions about the state of the registers or flags when an interrupt handler is entered.* A classic example of this is an interrupt handler that executes string instructions without first explicitly setting the direction flag. Remember, any sort of code can be executing when an interrupt occurs, so after you save the interrupted code's registers, you must immediately set up the registers (including segment registers) and flags as needed by your code before doing anything else.

Forgetting Group Overrides in Operands and Data Tables

The concept of a segment group is simple and useful: You specify that several segments belong in the same group, and the linker combines those segments into a single segment, with all the data in all the grouped segments addressable relative to the same segment register. Figure 5.3 illustrates three segments, *Seg1*, *Seg2*, and *Seg3*, grouped into *GroupSeg*; all three segments are addressable simultaneously, relative to a single segment register loaded with the base address of *GroupSeg*.

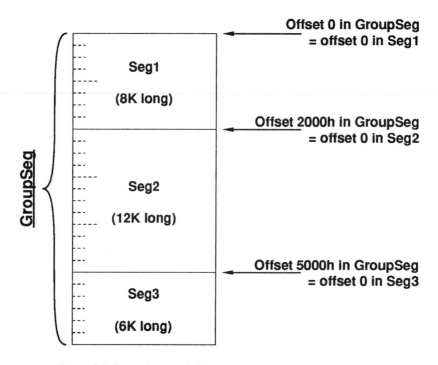

Figure 5.3: Three Segments Grouped into One Segment Group

Segment groups allow you to logically partition data into a number of areas without having to load a segment register every time you want to switch from one of those logical data areas to another.

Unfortunately, there are a few problems with the way the Microsoft Macro Assembler (MASM) handles segment groups, so until Turbo Assembler came along, segment groups were quite a nuisance in assembler. They were, however, an unavoidable nuisance, for they are required in order to link assembler code to high-level languages such as C.

Turbo Assembler Ideal mode has none of the problems with group overrides described in this section. This is yet another good reason to make the switch from MASM-style coding to Ideal mode.

One problem MASM has with segment groups is that MASM treats all offsets obtained with the **OFFSET** operator in a given grouped segment as offsets into that segment, rather than as offsets into the segment group. For example, given the segment grouping shown in Figure 5.3, the assembler would assemble

```
mov  ax,OFFSET Var1
```

into

```
mov  ax,0
```

since *Var1* is at offset 0 in *Seg2*, even though *Var1* is at offset 2000h in *GroupSeg*. Since data in segment groups is always intended to be addressed relative to the segment group rather than the individual segments, this creates quite a problem.

There is a solution to this problem, and that's using a group override prefix. The line

```
mov  ax,OFFSET GroupSeg:Var1
```

does assemble the offset of *Var1* correctly, calculating it relative to the segment group, *GroupSeg*.

MASM has another, similar problem concerning data tables used with segment groups. Just as with the **OFFSET** operator, offsets assembled into data tables are generated relative to segments, not segment groups. The following code shows an example of this problem.

```
Stack      SEGMENT WORD STACK 'STACK'
     DB    512 DUP(?)                  ;reserve space for a 1/2K stack
Stack      ENDS

;
; Define data segment group DGROUP, consisting of Data1 & Data2.
;
DGROUP     GROUP     Data1, Data2

;
; The first segment in DGROUP.
;
Data1      SEGMENT WORD PUBLIC 'DATA'
Scratch    DB    100h DUP(0)           ;a 256-byte scratch buffer
Data1      ENDS

;
; The second segment in DGROUP.
;
Data2      SEGMENT WORD PUBLIC 'DATA'
Buffer     DB    100h DUP('@')         ;a 256-byte buffer, set to at-signs
BufferPtr DW     Buffer                ;a pointer to Buffer
Data2      ENDS

Code SEGMENT PARA PUBLIC 'CODE'
     ASSUME    CS:Code, DS:DGROUP
```

```
;
Start    PROC NEAR
    mov  ax,DGROUP
    mov  ds,ax                  ;point DS to DGROUP
    mov  bx,OFFSET DGROUP:BufferPtr  ;point to buffer pointer
                                ; Note: The DGROUP: group override
                                ; is required to get the correct offset
    mov  bx,[bx]                ;point to the buffer itself
;
; (Code to handle the buffer would go here.)
;
    mov  ah,4Ch                 ;DOS terminate function
    int  21h                    ;terminate & return to DOS
Start    ENDP
Code ENDS
    END  Start
```

In this code, the offset of *BufferPtr* in

```
mov  bx,OFFSET DGROUP:BufferPtr
```

assembles correctly, since the **DGROUP:** group override prefix is used. However, the other reference to an offset, in

```
BufferPtr DW   Buffer
```

which should cause the value of *BufferPtr* to be initialized to the offset of *Buffer*, does not assemble correctly, since the offset of *Buffer* is taken relative to the *Data2* segment rather than relative to the **DGROUP** segment group. The solution is again a **DGROUP** override prefix; change

```
BufferPtr DW   Buffer
```

to

```
BufferPtr DW   DGROUP:Buffer    ;a pointer to Buffer
                                ; Note: The DGROUP: group override is
                                ; required to get the correct offset
```

Omission of group override prefixes when using segment groups in MASM/Quirks mode can lead to some nasty bugs, since your programs may read, modify, or jump to the wrong area of memory. As a general rule, don't use groups in assembler with MASM/Quirks mode unless you have to. When you have to use groups in MASM/Quirks mode, as when interfacing to high-level languages, constantly remind yourself to prefix group overrides when specifying the offsets of all grouped data. The group overrides are easy enough to use—the trick is remembering to use them.

A useful technique for dealing with grouped segments in MASM/Quirks mode is using **LEA** instead of **MOV OFFSET**. For example,

```
lea  ax,Var1
```

has the same effect as

```
mov   ax,OFFSET GroupSeg:Var1
```

without requiring a group override prefix. However, **LEA** is a byte larger and a little slower than **MOV OFFSET**.

By the way, segment group problems occur only with offsets, not with memory accesses. Lines such as

```
mov   ax,[Var1]
```

do not require group override prefixes.

Interfacing Turbo Assembler with Turbo C

While many programmers can—and do—develop entire programs in assembly language, many others prefer to do the bulk of their programming in a high-level language, dipping into assembly language only when low-level control or very high-performance code is required. Still others prefer to program primarily in assembler, taking occasional advantage of high-level language libraries and constructs.

Turbo C lends itself particularly well to supporting mixed C and assembler code on an as-needed basis, providing not one but two mechanisms for integrating assembler and C code. The inline assembly feature of Turbo C provides a quick and simple way to put assembler code directly into a C function. For those who prefer to do their assembler programming in separate modules written entirely in assembly language, Turbo Assembler modules can be assembled separately and linked to Turbo C code.

First, we'll cover the use of inline assembly in Turbo C. Next, we'll discuss the details of linking separately assembled Turbo Assembler modules to Turbo C, and explore the process of calling Turbo Assembler functions from Turbo C code. Finally, we'll cover calling Turbo C functions from Turbo Assembler code. (**Note:** When we refer to Turbo C, we mean versions 1.5 and greater.) Let's begin.

Using Inline Assembly in Turbo C

If you were to think of an ideal way to use assembler to fine-tune a C program, you would probably ask for the ability to insert assembler instructions at just those critical places in C code where the speed and low-level control of assembler would result in a dramatic improvement in performance. While you're at it, you might as well wish away the traditional complexities of interfacing assembler with C. Better still, you'd like to be able to do all this without changing any other C code one bit, so that already-working C code won't have to be altered.

Turbo C fulfills every item on your wish list with inline assembly. Inline assembly is nothing less than the ability to place virtually any assembler code anywhere in your C programs, with full access to C constants, variables, and even functions. In truth, inline assembly is good for more than just fine-tuning, since it's very nearly as powerful as programming strictly in assembler; for instance, the high-performance code in Turbo C's libraries is written in inline assembly. Inline assembly lets you use just as much or as little assembler in your C programs as you'd like, without having to worry about the details of mixing the two.

Consider the following C code, which is an example of inline assembly:

```
    .
    .
    .
i = 0;                    /* set i to 0 (in C) */
asm  dec  WORD PTR i;     /* decrement i (in assembler) */
i++;                      /* increment i (in C) */
    .
    .
    .
```

The first and last lines look normal enough, but what is that middle line? As you've probably guessed, the line starting with **asm** is *inline assembly code.* If you were to use a debugger to look at the executable code this C source compiles to, you would find

```
    .
    .
    .
mov  WORD PTR [bp-02],0000
dec  WORD PTR [bp-02]
inc  WORD PTR [bp-02]
    .
    .
    .
```

with the inline assembly **DEC** instruction nestled between the compiled code for

```
i = 0;
```

and

```
i++;
```

Basically, each time the Turbo C compiler encounters the **asm** keyword that indicates inline assembly, it drops the associated assembler line directly into the compiled code with only one change: References to C variables are transformed into the appropriate assembler equivalent, just as the reference to *i* in the preceding example was changed to WORD PTR [BP-02]. In short, the **asm** keyword lets you insert virtually any assembler code anywhere in your C code. (There are a few limitations on what inline assembler code is allowed to do; we'll cover those limitations in the "Limitations of Inline Assembly" section on page 295.)

The ability to drop assembler code directly into the code Turbo C generates may sound a bit dangerous, and, in truth, inline assembly does have its risks. While Turbo C takes care to compile its code so as to avoid many potentially hazardous interactions with inline assembly, there's no doubt that ill-Behaved inline assembly code can cause serious bugs.

On the other hand, any poorly written assembler code, whether it's inline or in a separate module, has the potential to run amuck; that's the price to be paid for the speed and low-level control of assembly language. Besides, bugs are far less common in inline assembly code than in pure assembler code, since Turbo C attends to many programming details, such as entering and exiting functions, passing parameters, and allocating variables. All in all, the ability to easily fine-tune and turbo-charge portions of your C code with inline assembly is well worth the trouble of having to iron out the occasional assembler bug.

Important notes about inline assembly:

1. You must invoke TCC.EXE, the command-line version of Turbo C, in order to use inline assembly. TC.EXE, the user-interface version of Turbo C, does not support inline assembly.

2. It's very possible that the version of TLINK that came with your copy of Turbo Assembler is not the same version that came with your copy of Turbo C. Since important enhancements were made to TLINK in order to support Turbo Assembler, and since further enhancements will no doubt be made, it is important that you link Turbo C modules containing inline assembly with the most recent version of TLINK that you have. The safest way to accomplish this is to make sure that there's only one TLINK.EXE file on the disk you use to run the linker; that

TLINK.EXE file should have the latest version number of all the TLINK.EXE files you've received with other Borland products.

How Inline Assembly Works

Normally, Turbo C compiles each file of C source code directly to an object file, then invokes TLINK to tie the object files together into an executable program. Figure 6.1 shows such a compile-and-link cycle. To start this cycle, you enter the command line

```
tcc filename
```

which instructs Turbo C to first compile FILENAME.C to FILENAME.OBJ and then invoke TLINK to link FILENAME.OBJ into FILENAME.EXE.

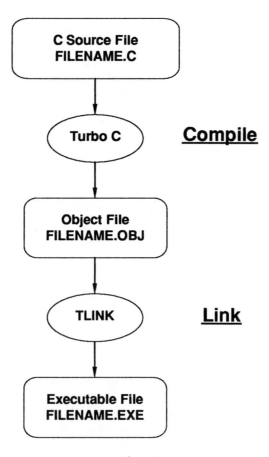

Figure 6.1: Turbo C Compile and Link Cycle

When inline assembly is used, however, Turbo C automatically adds one extra step to the compile-and-link sequence.

Turbo C handles each module containing inline assembly code by first compiling the whole module to an assembly language source file, then invoking Turbo Assembler to assemble the resulting assembler code to an object file, and finally invoking TLINK to link the object files together. Figure 6.2 illustrates this process, showing how Turbo C produces an executable file from a C source file containing inline assembly code. You start this cycle with the command line

```
tcc -B filename
```

which instructs Turbo C to first compile FILENAME.ASM, then invoke Turbo Assembler to assemble FILENAME.ASM to FILENAME.OBJ, and finally invoke TLINK to link FILENAME.OBJ into FILENAME.EXE.

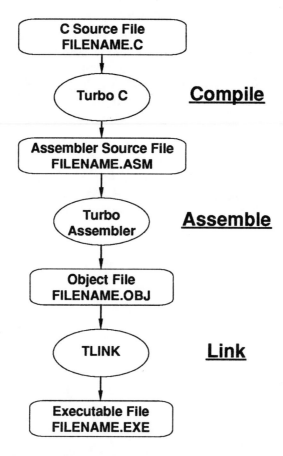

Figure 6.2: Turbo C Compile, Assembly, and Link Cycle

Inline assembly code is simply passed along by Turbo C to the assembly language file. The beauty of this system is that Turbo C need not understand anything about assembling the inline code; instead, Turbo C compiles C code to the same level—assembler code—as the inline assembly code and lets Turbo Assembler do the assembling.

To see exactly how Turbo C handles inline assembly, enter the following program under the name PLUSONE.C:

```
#include <stdio.h>

int  main(void)

{
    int  TestValue;
```

```
        scanf("%d",&TestValue);          /* get the value to increment */
        asm  inc  WORD PTR TestValue;     /* increment it (in assembler) */
        printf("%d",TestValue);          /* print the incremented value */
}
```

and compile it with the command line

```
tcc -S plusone
```

The **–S** option instructs Turbo C to compile to assembler code and then stop, so the file PLUSONE.ASM should now be on your disk. In PLUSONE.ASM you should find

```
           ifndef  ??version
?debug     macro
           ENDM
           ENDIF
           name    Plusone
_TEXT      SEGMENT BYTE PUBLIC 'CODE'
DGROUP     GROUP   _DATA,_BSS
           ASSUME  cs:_TEXT,ds:DGROUP,ss:DGROUP
_TEXT      ENDS
_DATA      SEGMENT WORD PUBLIC 'DATA'
_d@        LABEL   BYTE
_d@w       LABEL   WORD
_DATA      ENDS
_BSS       SEGMENT WORD PUBLIC 'BSS'
_b@        LABEL   BYTE
_b@w       LABEL   WORD
           ?debug C E90156E11009706C75736F6E652E63
           ?debug C E90009B9100F696E636C7564655C737464696F2E68
           ?debug C E90009B91010696E636C7564655C7374646172672E68
_BSS       ENDS
_TEXT      SEGMENT BYTE PUBLIC 'CODE'
;          ?debug L 3
_main      PROC    NEAR
           push    bp
           mov     bp,sp
           dec     sp
           dec     sp
;          ?debug L 8
           lea     ax,WORD PTR [bp-2]
           push    ax
           mov     ax,OFFSET DGROUP:_s@
           push    ax
           call    NEAR PTR _scanf
           pop     cx
           pop     cx
;          ?debug L 9
           inc     WORD PTR [bp-2]
```

```
;           ?debug  L 10
            push    WORD PTR [bp-2]
            mov     ax,OFFSET DGROUP:_s@+3
            push    ax
            call    NEAR PTR _printf
            pop     cx
            pop     cx
@1:
;           ?debug  L 12
            mov     sp,bp
            pop     bp
            ret
_main       ENDP
_TEXT       ENDS
_DATA       SEGMENT WORD PUBLIC 'DATA'
_s@         LABEL   BYTE
            DB      37
            DB      100
            DB      0
            DB      37
            DB      100
            DB      0
_DATA       ENDS
_TEXT       SEGMENT BYTE PUBLIC 'CODE'
            EXTRN   _printf:NEAR
            EXTRN   _scanf:NEAR
_TEXT       ENDS
            PUBLIC  _main
            END
```

(This code should give you a strong appreciation for all the work Turbo C saves you by supporting inline assembly!) Under the comment

```
;    ?debug  L 8
```

you can see the assembler code for the **scanf** call, followed by

```
;    ?debug  L 9
     inc    WORD PTR [bp-2]
```

which is the inline assembler instruction to increment *TestValue*. (Notice that Turbo C automatically took care of the translation from the C variable *TestValue* to the equivalent assembler addressing of that variable, [*BP-2*].) Following the inline assembly instruction is the assembler code for the **printf** call.

The point is that Turbo C compiled the **scanf** call to assembly language, dropped the inline assembly code directly into the assembler output file, and then compiled the **printf** call to assembler. The resulting file is a valid assembler source file, ready to be assembled with Turbo Assembler.

Had you not used the –S option, Turbo C would have proceeded to invoke Turbo Assembler to assemble PLUSONE.ASM and would then have invoked TLINK to link the resultant object file, PLUSONE.OBJ, into the executable file PLUSONE.EXE. This is the normal mode of operation of Turbo C with inline assembler; we used –S for explanatory purposes only, so that we could examine the intermediate assembly language step Turbo C uses when supporting inline assembly. The –S option is not particularly useful when compiling code to be linked into executable programs, but provides a handy means by which to examine both the instructions surrounding your inline assembly code and the code generated by Turbo C in general. If you're ever uncertain about exactly what code you're generating with inline assembly, just examine the .ASM file produced with the –S option.

How Turbo C Knows to Use Inline Assembly Mode

Normally, Turbo C compiles C code directly to object code. There are several ways to tell Turbo C to support inline assembly by compiling to assembly language and then invoking Turbo Assembler.

The **–B** command-line option instructs Turbo C to generate object files by way of compiling to assembler code, then invoking Turbo Assembler to assemble that code.

The **–S** command-line option instructs Turbo C to compile to assembler code, and then stop. The .ASM file generated by Turbo C when the –S option is specified can then be separately assembled and linked to other C and assembler modules. Except when debugging or simply exploring, there's generally no reason to use –S in preference to –B.

The **#pragma** directive

```
#pragma inline
```

has the same effect as the **–B** command-line option, instructing Turbo C to compile to assembly and then invoke Turbo Assembler to assemble the result. When Turbo C encounters **#pragma inline**, compilation restarts in assembler output mode. Consequently, it's best to place the **#pragma inline** directive as close to the start of the C source code as possible, since any C source code preceding **#pragma inline** will be compiled twice, once in normal C-to-object mode and again in C-to-assembler mode. While this doesn't hurt anything, it does waste time.

Finally, if Turbo C encounters inline assembly code in the absence of –**B**, –**S**, and **#pragma inline**, the compiler issues a warning like

```
Warning test.c 6: Restarting compile using assembly in function main
```

and then restarts compilation in assembler-output mode, just as if a **#pragma inline** directive had been encountered at that point. Make it a point to avoid this warning by using the **–B** option or **#pragma inline**, since restarting compilation on encountering inline assembly makes for relatively slow compiles.

Invoking Turbo Assembler for Inline Assembly

In order for Turbo C to be able to invoke Turbo Assembler, Turbo C must first be able to *find* Turbo Assembler. Exactly how this happens varies with different versions of Turbo C.

Versions of Turbo C later than 1.5 expect to find Turbo Assembler under the file name TASM.EXE in either the current directory or one of the directories pointed to by the DOS PATH environment variable. Basically, Turbo C can invoke Turbo Assembler under the same circumstances in which you could type the command

```
TASM
```

and run Turbo Assembler from the command-line prompt. So, if you have Turbo Assembler in the current directory or anywhere in your command search path, Turbo C will automatically find it and run it to perform inline assembly.

Versions 1.0 and 1.5 of Turbo C behave a little differently. Since these versions of Turbo C were written before Turbo Assembler existed, they invoke MASM, the Microsoft Macro Assembler, to perform inline assembly. Consequently, these versions of Turbo C search the current directory and the command search path for the file MASM.EXE, rather than the file TASM.EXE, and so do not automatically use Turbo Assembler.

Note: See the README file on the Turbo Assembler distribution disk for information about how to patch those versions of TCC in order to use TASM.

Where Turbo C Assembles Inline Assembly

Inline assembly code can end up in either Turbo C's code segment or Turbo C's data segment. Inline assembly code located within a function is assembled into Turbo C's code segment, while inline assembly code located outside a function is assembled into Turbo C's data segment.

For example, the C code

```
/* Table of square values */

asm  SquareLookUpTable  label  word;
asm  dw  0, 1, 4, 9, 16, 25, 36, 49, 64, 81, 100;

/* Function to look up the square of a value between 0 and 10 */

int LookUpSquare(int Value)
{
   asm  mov  bx,Value;              /* get the value to square */
   asm  shl  bx,1;                  /* multiply it by 2 to look up in
                                       a table of word-sized elements */

   asm  mov  ax,[SquareLookUpTable+bx];  /* look up the square */
   return(_AX);                     /* return the result */
}
```

puts the data for *SquareLookUpTable* in Turbo C's data segment and the inline assembly code inside *LookUpSquare* in Turbo C's code segment. The data could equally well be placed in the code segment; consider the following version of *LookUpSquare,* where *SquareLookUpTable* is in Turbo C's code segment:

```
/* Function to look up the square of a value between 0 and 10 */
int LookUpSquare(int Value)
{
   asm  jmp  SkipAroundData          /* jump past the data table */

   /* Table of square values */
   asm  SquareLookUpTable  label  word;
   asm  dw  0, 1, 4, 9, 16, 25, 36, 49, 64, 81, 100;

SkipAroundData:
   asm  mov  bx,Value;              /* get the value to square */
   asm  shl  bx,1;                  /* multiply it by 2 to look up in
                                       a table of word-sized elements */

   asm  mov  ax,[SquareLookUpTable+bx];  /* look up the square */
   return(_AX);                     /* return the result */
}
```

Since *SquareLookUpTable* is in Turbo C's code segment, it would seem that a CS: segment override prefix should be required in order to read from it. In fact, this code automatically assembles with a CS: prefix on the access to *SquareLookUpTable;* Turbo C generates the correct assembler code to let Turbo Assembler know which segment *SquareLookUpTable* is in, and Turbo Assembler then generates segment override prefixes as needed.

Use the –1 Switch for 80186/80286 Instructions

If you want to use assembler instructions unique to the 80186 processor, such as

```
shr  ax,3
```

and

```
push  1
```

it's easiest to use the **–1** command-line option to Turbo C as in this example:

```
tcc -1 -B heapmgr
```

where HEAPMGR.C is a program that contains inline assembly instructions unique to the 80186.

The primary purpose of the **–1** option is to instruct Turbo C to take advantage of the full 80186 instruction set when compiling, but the **–1** option also causes Turbo C to insert the **.186** directive at the start of the output assembler file; this instructs Turbo Assembler to assemble the full 80186 instruction set. Without the **.186** directive, Turbo Assembler will flag inline assembly instructions unique to the 80186 as errors. If you want to assemble 80186 instructions without having Turbo C use the full 80186 instruction set, just insert the line

```
asm  .186;
```

at the start of each Turbo C module containing inline 80186 instructions. This line will be passed through to the assembler file, where it will instruct Turbo Assembler to assemble 80186 instructions.

While Turbo C provides no built-in support for 80286, 80386, 80287, and 80387 processors, inline assembly that supports the 80286, 80287, 80386, and 80387 can be enabled in a similar manner, with the **asm** keyword and the **.286**, **.286C**, **.286P**, **.386**, **.386C**, **.386C**, **.287**, and **.387** Turbo Assembler directives.

The line

```
asm  .186;
```

illustrates an important point about inline assembly: *Any* valid assembler line can be passed to the assembler file by use of the **asm** prefix, including segment directives, equates, macros, and so on.

The Format of Inline Assembly Statements

Inline assembly statements are much like normal assembler lines, but there are a few differences. The format of an inline assembly statement is

```
asm [<label>] <instruction/directive> <operands> <; or newline>
```

where

- The **asm** keyword must start every inline assembly statement.
- [*<label>*] is a valid assembler label. The square brackets indicate that *label* is optional, just as it is in assembler. (See the later section "Memory and Address Operand Limitations" on page 296 for information about C versus assembler labels.)
- *<instruction/directive>* is any valid assembler instruction or directive.
- *<operands>* contains the operand(s) acceptable to the instruction or directive; it can also reference C constants, variables, and labels within the limitations described in the section "Limitations of Inline Assembly" on page 295.
- *<; or newline>* is a semicolon or a newline, either of which signals the end of the **asm** statement.

Note: See "Memory and Address Operand Limitations" (page 296) for important information regarding *label*.

Semicolons in Inline Assembly

One aspect of inline assembly that no C purist could miss is that, alone among C statements, inline assembly statements do not require a terminating semicolon. A semicolon *can* be used to terminate each statement, but the end of the line will do just as well. So, unless you're planning to put multiple inline assembly statements on each line (which is not a good practice from the perspective of clarity), semicolons are purely optional. While this may not seem to be in the spirit of C, it is in keeping with the convention adopted by several UNIX-based compilers.

Comments in Inline Assembly

The previous description of the format of an inline assembly statement lacks one key element—a comment field. While semicolons can be placed at the end of inline assembly statements, they only mark the end of inline assembly statements, just as with other C statements; semicolons do not begin comment fields in inline assembly code.

How, then, are you to comment your inline assembly code? Strangely enough, with C comments. Actually, that's not strange at all, for the C preprocessor processes inline assembly code along with the rest of your C code. This has the advantage of allowing you to use a uniform commenting style throughout your C programs containing inline assembly, and also makes it possible to use C-defined symbolic names in both C and inline assembly code. For example, in

```
    .
    .
    .
#define CONSTANT 51
    int i;
    .
    .
    .
    i = CONSTANT;                 /* set i to constant value */
    asm  sub  WORD PTR i,CONSTANT;  /* subtract constant value from i */
    .
    .
    .
```

both C and inline assembly code use the C-defined symbol *CONSTANT*, and *i* winds up equal to 0.

The last example illustrates one wonderful feature of inline assembly, which is that the operand field may contain direct references not only to C-defined symbolic names but also to C variables. As you will see later in this chapter, accessing C variables in assembler is normally a messy task, and convenient reference to C variables is a primary reason why inline assembler is the preferred way to integrate assembler and C for most applications.

Accessing Structure/Union Elements

Inline assembly code can directly reference structure elements. For example,

```
    .
    .
    .
struct Student {
   char Teacher[30];
   int Grade;
} JohnQPublic;
    .
    .
    .
    asm  mov  ax,JohnQPublic.Grade;
    .
    .
    .
```

loads AX with the contents of member *Grade* of the *Student* type structure *JohnQPublic*.

Inline assembly code can also access structure elements addressed relative to a base or index register. For instance,

```
      .
      .
      .
asm   mov   bx,OFFSET JohnQPublic;
asm   mov   ax,[bx].Grade;
      .
      .
      .
```

also loads AX with member *Grade* of *JohnQPublic*. Since *Grade* is at offset 30 in the *Student* structure, the last example actually becomes

```
      .
      .
      .
asm   mov   bx,OFFSET JohnQPublic;
asm   mov   ax,[bx]+30
      .
      .
      .
```

The ability to access structure elements relative to a pointer register is very powerful, since it allows inline assembly code to handle arrays of structures and passed pointers to structures.

If, however, two or more structures that you're accessing with inline assembly code have the same member name, you must insert the following:

```
asm mov  bx,[di].(struct tm) tm_hour > alt
```

For example,

```
      .
      .
      .
struct Student {
   char Teacher[30];
   int Grade;
} JohnQPublic;
      .
      .
      .
struct Teacher {
   int Grade;
```

```
    long Income;
};
        •
        •
        •
asm  mov  ax,JohnQPublic.(struct Student) Grade
        •
        •
        •
```

An Example of Inline Assembly

So far, you've seen a variety of code fragments that use inline assembly, but no real working inline assembly programs. This section remedies that situation by presenting a program that employs inline assembly to greatly speed the process of converting text to uppercase. The code presented in this section serves both as an example of what inline assembly can do and as a template to which you can refer to as you develop your own inline assembly code.

Take a moment to examine the programming problem to be solved by the sample program. We'd like to develop a function, named *StringToUpper*, that copies one string to another string, converting all lowercase characters to uppercase in the process. We'd also like to have this function work equally well with all strings in all memory models. One good way to do this is to have far string pointers passed to the function, since pointers to near strings can always be cast to pointers to far strings, but the reverse is not always true.

Unfortunately, we run into a performance issue here. While Turbo C handles far pointers perfectly well, far pointer-handling in Turbo C is much slower than near pointer-handling. This isn't a shortcoming of Turbo C, but rather an unavoidable effect when programming the 8086 in a high-level language.

On the other hand, string and far pointer-handling is one area in which assembler excels. The logical solution, then, is to use inline assembly to handle the far pointers and string copying, while letting Turbo C take care of everything else. The following program, STRINGUP.C, does exactly that:

```
/* Program to demonstrate the use of StringToUpper().
   Calls StringToUpper to convert TestString to uppercase in
   UpperCaseString, then prints UpperCaseString and its length. */

#pragma inline
#include <stdio.h>
```

```
/* Function prototype for StringToUpper() */
extern unsigned int StringToUpper(
unsigned char far * DestFarString,
unsigned char far * SourceFarString);

#define MAX_STRING_LENGTH 100

char *TestString = "This Started Out As Lowercase!";

char UpperCaseString[MAX_STRING_LENGTH];

main()
{
   unsigned int StringLength;

   /* Copy an uppercase version of TestString to UpperCaseString */
   StringLength = StringToUpper(UpperCaseString, TestString);

   /* Display the results of the conversion */
   printf("Original string:\n%s\n\n", TestString);
   printf("Uppercase string:\n%s\n\n", UpperCaseString);
   printf("Number of characters: %d\n\n", StringLength);
}

/* Function to perform high-speed translation to uppercase from
   one far string to another

   Input:
        DestFarString   - array in which to store uppercased
                          string (will be zero-terminated)
        SourceFarString - string containing characters to be converted
                          to all uppercase (must be zero-terminated)

   Returns:
        The length of the source string in characters, not counting
        the terminating zero. */
unsigned int StringToUpper(unsigned char far * DestFarString,
                           unsigned char far * SourceFarString)
{
   unsigned int  CharacterCount;

   #define LOWER_CASE_A 'a'
   #define LOWER_CASE_Z 'z'
      asm ADJUST_VALUE  EQU  20h;     /* amount to subtract from lowercase
                                         letters to make them uppercase */
      asm  cld;
      asm  push ds;                   /* save C's data segment */
      asm  lds  si,SourceFarString;   /* load far pointer to source string */
      asm  les  di,DestFarString;     /* load far pointer to destination string */
      CharacterCount = 0;             /* count of characters */
   StringToUpperLoop:
```

```
    asm  lodsb;                    /* get the next character */
    asm  cmp  al,LOWER_CASE_A;     /* if < a then it's not a lowercase letter */
    asm  jb   SaveCharacter;
    asm  cmp  al,LOWER_CASE_Z;     /* if > z then it's not a lowercase letter */
    asm  ja   SaveCharacter;
    asm  sub  al,ADJUST_VALUE;     /* it's lowercase; make it uppercase */
SaveCharacter:
    asm  stosb;                    /* save the character */
    CharacterCount++;              /* count this character */
    asm  and  al,al;               /* is this the ending zero? */
    asm  jnz  StringToUpperLoop;   /* no, process the next character, if any */
    CharacterCount--;              /* don't count the terminating zero */
    asm  pop  ds;                  /* restore C's data segment */
    return(CharacterCount);
```

When run, STRINGUP.C displays the output

```
Original string:
This Started Out As Lowercase!

Uppercase string:
THIS STARTED OUT AS LOWERCASE!

Number of characters: 30
```

demonstrating that it does indeed convert all lowercase letters to uppercase.

The heart of STRINGUP.C is the function *StringToUpper*, which performs the entire process of string copying and conversion to uppercase. *StringToUpper* is written in both C and inline assembly, and accepts two far pointers as parameters. One far pointer points to a string containing text; the other far pointer points to another string, to which the text in the first string is to be copied with all lowercase letters converted to uppercase. The function declaration and parameter definition are all handled in C, and, indeed, a function prototype for *StringToUpper* appears at the start of the program. The main program calls *StringToUpper* just as if it were written in pure C. In short, all the advantages of programming in Turbo C are available, even though *StringToUpper* contains inline assembly code.

The body of *StringToUpper* is written in a mixture of C and inline assembly. Assembler is used to read each character from the source string, to check and, if need be, translate the character to uppercase, and to write the character to the destination string. Inline assembly allows *StringToUpper* to use the powerful **LODSB** and **STOSB** string instructions to read and write the characters.

In writing *StringToUpper*, we knew that we wouldn't need to access any data in Turbo C's data segment, so we simply pushed DS at the start of the function, then set DS to point to the source string and left it there for the rest of the function. One great advantage that inline assembly has over a pure C implementation is this ability to load the far pointers once at the start of the function and then never reload them until the function is done. By contrast, Turbo C and other high-level languages generally reload far pointers every time they are used. The ability to load far pointers just once means that *StringToUpper* processes far strings as rapidly as if they were near strings.

One other interesting point about *StringToUpper* is the way in which C and assembler statements are mixed. **#define** is used to set *LOWER_CASE_A* and *LOWER_CASE_Z*, while the assembler **EQU** directive is used to set *ADJUST_VALUE*, but all three symbols are used in the same fashion by the inline assembly code. Substitution for the C-defined symbols is done by the Turbo C preprocessor, while substitution for *ADJUST_VALUE* is done by Turbo Assembler, but both can be used by inline assembly code.

C statements to manipulate *CharacterCount* are sprinkled throughout *StringToUpper*. This was done only to illustrate that C code and inline assembly code can be intermixed. *CharacterCount* could just as easily have been maintained directly by inline assembly code in a free register, such as CX or DX; *StringToUpper* would then have run faster.

Freely intermixing C code and inline assembly code carries risks if you don't understand exactly what code Turbo C generates in between your inline assembly statements. Using the Turbo C's **–S** compiler option is the best way to explore what happens when you mix inline assembly and C code. For instance, you can learn exactly how the C and inline assembly code in *StringToUpper* fit together by compiling STRINGUP.C with the **–S** option and examining the output file STRINGUP.ASM.

STRINGUP.C vividly demonstrates the excellent payback that judicious use of inline assembly provides. In *StringToUpper*, the insertion of just 15 inline assembly statements approximately doubles string-handling speed over equivalent C code.

Limitations of Inline Assembly

There are very few limitations as to how inline assembly may be used; by and large, inline assembly statements are simply passed through to Turbo Assembler unchanged. There are, however, notable limitations involving certain memory and address operands, and a few other restrictions concerning register usage rules and the lack of default sizing of automatic C variables used in inline assembly.

Memory and Address Operand Limitations

The only alterations Turbo C makes to inline assembly statements is to convert memory and memory address references, such as variable names and jump destinations, from their C representations to the assembler equivalents. These alterations introduce two limitations: Inline assembly jump instructions may only reference C labels, while inline assembly non-jump instructions may reference anything *but* C labels. For example,

```
       .
       .
       .
   asm  jz  NoDec;
   asm  dec cx;
NoDec:
       .
       .
       .
```

is fine, but

```
     .
     .
     .
 asm  jnz NoDec;
 asm  dec cx;
 asm  NoDec:
     .
     .
     .
```

will not compile properly. Similarly, inline assembly jumps may not have function names as operands.

Inline assembly instructions other than jumps can have any operands except C labels. For example,

```
     .
     .
     .
 asm  BaseValue  DB  '0';
     .
     .
     .
 asm  mov  al,BYTE PTR BaseValue;
     .
     .
     .
```

compiles, but

```
         .
         .
         .
BaseValue:
   asm  DB  '0';
         .
         .
         .
   asm  mov  al,BYTE PTR BaseValue;
         .
         .
         .
```

does not compile. Note that a call is not considered a jump, so valid operands to inline assembly calls include C function names and assembler labels, but not C labels. If a C function name is referenced in inline assembly code, it must be prefixed with an underscore; see the section "Underscores" on page 312 for details.

Lack of Default Automatic Variable Sizing in Inline Assembly

When Turbo C replaces a reference to an automatic variable in an inline assembly statement with an operand like [*BP-02*], it does not place a size operator, such as **WORD PTR** or **BYTE PTR**, into the altered statement. This means that

```
     .
     .
     .
int i;
     .
     .
     .
asm  mov  ax,i;
     .
     .
     .
```

is output to the assembler file as

```
   mov  ax,[bp-02]
```

In this case, there's no problem, since the use of AX tells Turbo Assembler that this is a 16-bit memory reference. Moreover, the lack of a size operator gives you complete flexibility in controlling operand size in inline assembly. However, consider

```
    .
    .
    .
int i;
    .
    .
    .
asm  mov  i,0;
asm  inc  i;
    .
    .
    .
```

which becomes

```
mov  [bp-02],0
inc  [bp-02]
```

Neither of these instructions has an inherent size, so Turbo Assembler can't assemble them. Consequently, when you refer to an automatic variable in Turbo Assembler without a register as either the source or the destination, be sure to use a size operator. The last example works just fine as

```
    .
    .
    .
int i;
    .
    .
    .
asm  mov  WORD PTR i,0;
asm  inc  BYTE PTR i;
    .
    .
    .
```

The Need to Preserve Registers

At the end of any inline assembly code you write, the following registers *must* contain the same values as they did at the start of the inline code: BP, SP, CS, DS, and SS. Failure to observe this rule can result in frequent program crashes and system reboots. AX, BX, CX, DX, SI, DI, ES, and the flags may be freely altered by inline code.

Preserving Calling Functions and Register Variables

Turbo C requires that SI and DI, which are used as register variables, not be destroyed by function calls. Happily, you don't have to worry about explicitly preserving SI or DI if you use them in inline assembly code. If Turbo C detects any use of those registers in inline assembly, it preserves them at the start of the function and restores them at the end—yet another of the conveniences of using inline assembly.

Suppressing Internal Register Variables

Since register variables are stored in SI and DI, there would seem to be the potential for conflict between register variables in a given module and inline assembly code that uses SI or DI in that same module. Again, though, Turbo C anticipates this problem; any use of SI or DI in inline code will disable the use of that register to store register variables.

Turbo C version 1.0 did not guarantee avoidance of conflict between register variables and inline assembly code. If you are using version 1.0, you should either explicitly preserve SI and DI before using them in inline code or update to the latest version of the compiler.

Disadvantages of Inline Assembly Versus Pure C

We've spent a good bit of time exploring how inline assembly works and learning about the potential benefits of inline assembly. While inline assembly is a splendid feature for many applications, it does have certain disadvantages. Let's review those disadvantages, so you can make informed decisions about when to use inline assembly in your programs.

Reduced Portability and Maintainability

The very thing that makes inline assembly code so effective—the ability to program the 8086 processor directly—also detracts from a primary strength of C, portability. If you use inline assembly, it's a pretty safe bet that you won't be able to port your code to another processor or C compiler without changes.

Similarly, inline assembly code lacks the clear and concise formatting C provides, and is often unstructured as well. Consequently, inline assembly code is generally more difficult to read and maintain than C code.

When you use inline assembly code, it's a good practice to isolate the inline code in self-contained modules, and to structure the inline code carefully with plenty of comments. That way, it's easy to maintain the code, and it's a relatively simple matter to find the inline assembly code and rewrite it in C if you need to port the program to a different environment.

Slower Compilation

Compilation of C modules containing inline assembly code is considerably slower than compilation of pure C code, primarily because inline assembly code must effectively be compiled twice, first by Turbo C and then again by Turbo Assembler. If Turbo C has to restart compilation because neither the **–B** option, the **–S** option, nor **#pragma inline** was used, compilation time for inline assembly becomes longer still. Fortunately, slow compilation of modules containing inline assembly is less of a problem now than it was in the past, since Turbo Assembler is so much faster than earlier assemblers.

Available with TCC Only

As we mentioned earlier, the inline assembly feature is unique to TCC.EXE, the command-line version of Turbo C. TC.EXE, the integrated development environment version of Turbo C, does not support inline assembly.

Optimization Loss

When inline assembly is used, Turbo C loses some control over the code of your programs, since you can directly insert any assembler statements into any C code. To some extent, you, as the inline assembly programmer, must compensate for this, by avoiding certain disruptive actions, such as failing to preserve the DS register or writing to the wrong area of memory.

On the other hand, Turbo C doesn't require you to follow all its internal rules when you program in inline assembler; if it did, you'd scarcely be better off using inline assembly than if you programmed in C and let Turbo C generate the code. What Turbo C does do is turn off some of its optimizations in functions containing inline assembly statements, thereby allowing you a relatively free hand in coding inline assembly. For example, some portions of the jump optimizer are turned off when inline assembly is used, and register variables are disabled if the inline code uses SI and DI. This partial loss of optimization is worth considering, given that you are presumably using inline assembly in order to boost code quality to its maximum.

If you are greatly concerned about producing the fastest or most compact code with inline assembly, you might want to write your functions that contain inline assembly code entirely in inline assembly—that is, don't mix C and inline assembly code within the same function. That way, you have control of the code in the inline assembly functions, Turbo C has control of the code in the C functions, and both you and Turbo C are free to generate the best possible code without restrictions.

Error Trace-Back Limitations

Since Turbo C does little error-checking of inline assembly statements, errors in inline assembly code are often detected by Turbo Assembler, not Turbo C. Unfortunately, it can sometimes be difficult to relate the error messages produced by Turbo Assembler back to the original C source code, since the error messages and the line numbers they display are based on the .ASM file output by Turbo C and not the C code itself.

For example, in the course of compiling TEST.C, a C program containing inline assembly code, Turbo Assembler might complain about an incorrectly sized operand on line 23; unfortunately, "23" refers to the number of the error-producing line in TEST.ASM, the intermediate assembler file Turbo C generated for Turbo Assembler to assemble. You're on your own when it comes to figuring out what line in TEST.C is ultimately responsible for the error.

Your best bet in a case like this is to first locate the line causing the error in the intermediate .ASM file, which is left on the disk by Turbo C whenever Turbo Assembler reports assembly errors. The .ASM file contains special comments that identify the line in the C source file from which each block of assembler statements was generated; for example, the assembler lines following

```
; ?debug  L 15
```

were generated from line 15 of the C source file. Once you've located the line that caused the error in the .ASM file, you can then use the line-number comments to map the error-generating line back to the C source file.

Debugging Limitations

Versions of Turbo C up to and including version 1.5 can't generate source-level debugging information (information required to let you see C source code as you debug) for modules containing inline assembly code. When inline assembly is used, Turbo C versions 1.5 and earlier generate plain assembler code with no embedded debugging information. Source-level debugging capabilities are lost, and only assembler-level debugging of C modules containing inline code is possible.

Later versions of Turbo C take advantage of special Turbo Assembler features to provide state-of-the-art, source-level debugging when used with Turbo Debugger to debug modules containing inline assembly code (and pure C modules too, of course).

Develop in C and Compile the Final Code with Inline Assembly

In light of the disadvantages of inline assembly we've just discussed, it may seem that inline assembly should be used as sparingly as possible. Not so. The trick is to use inline assembly at the right point in the development cycle—at the end.

Most of the disadvantages of inline assembly boil down to a single problem: Inline assembly can slow down the edit/compile/debug cycle considerably. Slower compilation, inability to use the integrated user-interface environment, and difficulty in finding compilation errors all mean that development of code containing inline assembly statements will probably be slower than development of pure C code. Still, the proper use of inline assembly can result in dramatic improvements in code quality. What to do?

The answer is simple. Initially, develop each program entirely in C, taking full advantage of the excellent development environment provided by TC.EXE. When a program reaches full functionality, with the code debugged and running smoothly, switch to TCC.EXE and begin to convert critical portions of the program to inline assembly code. This approach allows you to develop and debug your overall program efficiently, then isolate and enhance selected sections of the code when it comes time to fine-tune the program.

Calling Turbo Assembler Functions from Turbo C

C and assembler have traditionally been mixed by writing separate modules entirely in C or assembler, compiling the C modules and assembling the assembler modules, and then linking the separately compiled modules together. Turbo C modules can readily be linked with Turbo Assembler modules in this fashion. Figure 6.3 shows how to do this.

The executable file is produced from mixed C and assembler source files. You start this cycle with

```
tcc filenam1 filenam2.asm
```

This instructs Turbo C to first compile FILENAM1.C to FILENAM1.OBJ, then invoke Turbo Assembler to assemble FILENAM2.ASM to FILENAM2.OBJ, and finally invoke TLINK to link FILENAM1.OBJ and FILENAM2.OBJ into FILENAM1.EXE.

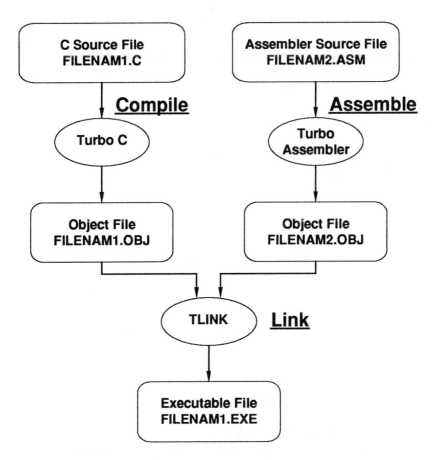

Figure 6.3: Compile, Assemble, and Link with Turbo C, Turbo Assembler, and TLINK

Separate compilation is very useful for programs that have sizable amounts of assembler code, since it makes the full power of Turbo Assembler available and allows you to do your assembly language programming in a pure assembler environment, without the **asm** keywords, extra compilation time, and C-related overhead of inline assembly.

There is a price to be paid for separate compilation: The assembler programmer must attend to all the details of interfacing C and assembler code. Where Turbo C handles segment specification, parameter-passing, reference to C variables, register variable preservation, and the like for inline assembly, separately compiled assembler functions must explicitly do all that and more.

There are two major aspects to interfacing Turbo C and Turbo Assembler. First, the various parts of the C and assembler code must be linked together properly, and functions and variables in each part of the code must be made available to the rest of the code as needed. Second, the assembler code must properly handle C-style function calls. This includes accessing passed parameters, returning values, and following the register preservation rules required of C functions.

Let's start by examining the rules for linking together Turbo C and Turbo Assembler code.

The Framework for Interfacing Turbo C and Turbo Assembler

In order to link Turbo C and Turbo Assembler modules together, three things must happen: The Turbo Assembler modules must use a Turbo C-compatible segment-naming scheme, the Turbo C and Turbo Assembler modules must share appropriate function and variable names in a form acceptable to Turbo C, and TLINK must be used to combine the modules into an executable program. This says nothing about what the Turbo Assembler modules actually *do*; at this point, we're only concerned with creating a framework within which C-compatible Turbo Assembler functions can be written.

Memory Models and Segments

For a given assembler function to be callable from C, that function must use the same memory model as the C program and must use a C-compatible code segment. Likewise, in order for data defined in an assembler module to be accessed by C code (or for C data to be accessed by assembler code), the assembler code must follow C data segment-naming conventions.

Memory models and segment-handling can be quite complex to implement in assembler. Fortunately, Turbo Assembler does virtually all the work of implementing Turbo C-compatible memory models and segments for you in the form of the simplified segment directives. (See "Standard Segment Directives" in Chapter 4, page 114, for an introduction to the simplified segment directives.)

Simplified Segment Directives and Turbo C

The **DOSSEG** directive instructs Turbo Assembler to order segments according to the Intel segment-ordering conventions, the same conventions followed by Turbo C (and many other popular language products, including those from Microsoft).

The **.MODEL** directive tells Turbo Assembler that segments created with the simplified segment directives should be compatible with the selected memory model (tiny, small, compact, medium, large, or huge), and controls the default type (near or far) of procedures created with the **PROC** directive. Memory models defined with the **.MODEL** directive are compatible with the equivalently named Turbo C models.

Finally, the **.CODE, .DATA, .DATA?, .FARDATA, .FARDATA?,** and **.CONST** simplified segment directives generate Turbo C-compatible segments.

For example, consider the following Turbo Assembler module, named DOTOTAL.ASM:

```
; select Intel-convention segment ordering
        .MODEL  small             ;select small model (near code and data)
        .DATA                     ;TC-compatible initialized data segment
        EXTRN   _Repetitions:WORD ;externally defined
        PUBLIC  _StartingValue    ;available to other modules
_StartingValue DW  0
        .DATA?                    ;TC-compatible uninitialized data segment
RunningTotal   DW  ?
        .CODE                     ;TC-compatible code segment
        PUBLIC  _DoTotal
_DoTotal        PROC              ;function (near-callable in small model)
        mov     cx,[_Repetitions] ;# of counts to do
        mov     ax,[_StartingValue]
        mov     [RunningTotal],ax ;set initial value
TotalLoop:
        inc     [RunningTotal]    ;RunningTotal++
        loop    TotalLoop
        mov     ax,[RunningTotal] ;return final total
        ret
```

```
_DoTotal        ENDP
        END
```

(Underscores (_) prefix many of the labels in the *DoTotal* procedure because they are normally required by Turbo C. This is covered in more detail in the section "Underscores" on page 312.)

The assembler procedure *_DoTotal* is readily callable from a small-model Turbo C program with the statement

```
DoTotal();
```

Note that *_DoTotal* expects some other part of the program to define the external variable *Repetitions*. Similarly, the variable *StartingValue* is made public, so other portions of the program can access it. The following Turbo C module, SHOWTOT.C, accesses public data in DOTOTAL.ASM and provides external data to DOTOTAL.ASM:

```
extern int StartingValue;
extern int DoTotal(void);
int Repetitions;
main()
{
    int i;
    Repetitions = 10;
    StartingValue = 2;
    printf("%d\n", DoTotal());
}
```

To create the executable program SHOWTOT.EXE from SHOWTOT.C and DOTOTAL.ASM, enter the command line

```
tcc showtot dototal.asm
```

If you wanted to link *_DoTotal* to a compact-model C program, you would simply change the **.MODEL** directive to **.MODEL** *COMPACT*. If you wanted to use a far segment in DOTOTAL.ASM, you could use the **.FARDATA** directive.

In short, generating the correct segment ordering, memory model, and segment names for linking with Turbo C is a snap with the simplified segment directives.

Old-Style Segment Directives and Turbo C

Simply put, it's a nuisance interfacing Turbo Assembler code to C code using the old-style segment directives. For example, if you replace the simplified segment directives in DOTOTAL.ASM with old-style segment directives, you get

```
DGROUP    GROUP     _DATA,_BSS
_DATA     SEGMENT   WORD PUBLIC 'DATA'
          EXTRN     _Repetitions:WORD          ;externally defined
          PUBLIC    _StartingValue             ;available to other modules
_StartingValue      DW 0
_DATA     ENDS
_BSS      SEGMENT   WORD PUBLIC 'BSS'
RunningTotal        DW  ?
_BSS      ENDS
_TEXT     SEGMENT   BYTE PUBLIC 'CODE'
          ASSUME    cs:_TEXT,ds:DGROUP,ss:DGROUP
          PUBLIC    _DoTotal
_DoTotal            PROC                       ;function (near-callable
                                               ; in small model)
          mov       cx,[_Repetitions]          ;# of counts to do
          mov       ax,[_StartingValue]
          mov       [RunningTotal],ax          ;set initial value
TotalLoop:
          inc       [RunningTotal]             ;RunningTotal++
          loop      TotalLoop
          mov       ax,[RunningTotal]          ;return final total
          ret
_DoTotal ENDP
_TEXT     ENDS
          END
```

The version with old-style segment directives is not only longer, but also
much harder to read and harder to change to match a different C memory
model. When you're interfacing to Turbo C, there's generally no advantage
to using the old-style segment directives. If you still want to use the old-
style segment directives when interfacing to Turbo C, you'll have to
identify the correct segments for the memory model your C code uses. For
an overview of Turbo C segment usage, refer to the *Turbo C User's Guide*.

The easiest way to determine the appropriate old-style segment directives
for linking with a given Turbo C program is to compile the main module of
the Turbo C program in the desired memory model with the **–S** option,
which causes Turbo C to generate an assembler version of the C code. In
that C code, you'll find all the old-style segment directives used by Turbo
C; just copy them into your assembler code. For example, if you enter the
command

```
tcc -S showtot.c
```

the file SHOWTOT.ASM is generated, containing

```
          ifndef    ??version
?debug    macro
          ENDM
```

```
        ENDIF
        NAME    showtot
_TEXT   SEGMENT BYTE PUBLIC 'CODE'
DGROUP  GROUP   _DATA,_BSS
        ASSUME  cs:_TEXT,ds:DGROUP,ss:DGROUP
_TEXT   ENDS
_DATA   SEGMENT WORD PUBLIC 'DATA'
_d@     LABEL   BYTE
_d@w    LABEL   WORD
_DATA   ENDS
_BSS    SEGMENT WORD PUBLIC 'BSS'
_b@     LABEL   BYTE
_b@w    LABEL   WORD
        ?debug  C E91481D5100973686F77746F742E63
_BSS    ENDS
_TEXT   SEGMENT BYTE PUBLIC 'CODE'
;       ?debug  L 3
_main   PROC    NEAR
;       ?debug  L 6
        mov     WORD PTR DGROUP:_Repetitions,10
;       ?debug  L 7
        mov     WORD PTR DGROUP:_StartingValue,2
;       ?debug  L 8
        call    NEAR PTR _DoTotal
        push    ax
        mov     ax,offset DGROUP:_s@
        push    ax
        call    NEAR PTR _printf
        pop     cx
        pop     cx
@1:
;       ?debug  L 9
        ret
_main   ENDP
_TEXT   ENDS
_BSS    SEGMENT WORD PUBLIC 'BSS'
_Repetitions    LABEL   WORD
        DB      2 dup (?)
        ?debug  C E9
_BSS    ENDS
_DATA   SEGMENT WORD PUBLIC 'DATA'
_s@     LABEL   BYTE
        DB      37
        DB      100
        DB      10
        DB      0
_DATA   ENDS
        EXTRN   _StartingValue:WORD
_TEXT   SEGMENT BYTE PUBLIC 'CODE'
```

```
         EXTRN    _DoTotal:NEAR
         EXTRN    _printf:NEAR
  _TEXT  ENDS
         PUBLIC  _Repetitions
         PUBLIC  _main
         END
```

The segment directives for **_DATA** (the initialized data segment), **_TEXT** (the code segment), and **_BSS** (the uninitialized data segment), along with the **GROUP** and **ASSUME** directives, are in ready-to-assemble form, so you can use them as is.

(Chapter 10 covers segment directives in detail.)

Segment Defaults: When Is It Necessary to Load Segments?

Under some circumstances, your C-callable assembler functions may have to load DS and/or ES in order to access data. It's also useful to know the relationships between the settings of the segment registers on a call from Turbo C, since sometimes assembler code can take advantage of the equivalence of two segment registers. Let's take a moment to examine the settings of the segment registers when an assembler function is called from Turbo C, the relationships between the segment registers, and the cases in which an assembler function might need to load one or more segment registers.

On entry to an assembler function from Turbo C, the CS and DS registers have the following settings, depending on the memory model in use (SS is always used for the stack segment, and ES is always used as a scratch segment register):

Table 6.1: Register Settings when Turbo C Enters Assembler

Model	CS	DS
Tiny	_TEXT	DGROUP
Small	_TEXT	DGROUP
Compact	_TEXT	DGROUP
Medium	filename_TEXT	DGROUP
Large	filename_TEXT	DGROUP
Huge	filename_TEXT	calling_filename_DATA

filename is the name of the assembler module, and *calling_filename* is the name of the module calling the assembler module.

In the tiny model, **_TEXT** and **DGROUP** are the same, so CS equals DS on entry to functions. Also in the tiny, small, and medium models, SS equals DS on entry to functions.

So, when is it necessary to load a segment register in a C-callable assembler function? For starters, you should never have to (or want to) directly load the CS or SS registers. CS is automatically set as needed on far calls, jumps, and returns, and can't be tampered with otherwise. SS always points to the stack segment, which should never change during the course of a program (unless you're writing code that switches stacks, in which case you had best know *exactly* what you're doing!).

ES is always available for you to use as you wish. You may use ES to point at far data, or you may load ES with the destination segment for a string instruction.

That leaves the DS register. In all Turbo C models other than the huge model, DS points to the static data segment (**DGROUP**) on entry to functions, and that's generally where you'll want to leave it. You can always use ES to access far data, although you may find it desirable to instead temporarily point DS to far data that you're going to access intensively, thereby saving many segment override instructions in your code. For example, you could access a far segment in either of the following ways:

```
        .
        .
        .
        .FARDATA
Counter DW      0
        .
        .
        .
        .CODE
        PUBLIC  _AsmFunction
_AsmFunction    PROC
        .
        .
        .
        mov     ax,@fardata
        mov     es,ax           ;point ES to far data segment
        inc     es:[Counter]    ;increment counter variable
        .
        .
        .
_AsmFunction    ENDP
        .
        .
        .
```

or

```
          .
          .
          .
          .FARDATA
Counter   DW        0
          .
          .
          .
          .CODE
          PUBLIC    _AsmFunction
_AsmFunction        PROC
          .
          .
          .
          ASSUME    ds:@fardata
          mov       ax,@fardata
          mov       ds,ax           ;point DS to far data segment
          inc       [Counter]       ;increment counter variable
          ASSUME    ds:@data
          mov       ax,@data
          mov       ds,ax           ;point DS back to DGROUP
          .
          .
          .
_AsmFunction        ENDP
          .
          .
          .
```

The second version has the advantage of not requiring an ES: override on
each memory access to the far data segment. If you do load DS to point to a
far segment, be sure to restore it as in the preceding example before
attempting to access any variables in **DGROUP**. Even if you don't access
DGROUP in a given assembler function, be sure to restore DS before
exiting, since Turbo C assumes that functions leave DS unchanged.

Handling DS in C-callable huge model functions is a bit different. In the
huge model, Turbo C doesn't use **DGROUP** at all. Instead, each module
has its own data segment, which is a far segment relative to all the other
modules in the program; there is no commonly shared near data segment.
On entry to a function in the huge model, DS should be set to point to that
module's far segment and left there for the remainder of the function, as
follows:

```
          .
          .
          .
          .FARDATA
          .
```

```
            .
            .
        .CODE
        PUBLIC  _AsmFunction
_AsmFunction    PROC
        push    ds
        mov     ax,@fardata
        mov     ds,ax
            .
            .
            .
        pop     ds
        ret
_AsmFunction    ENDP
            .
            .
            .
```

Note that the original state of DS is preserved with a **PUSH** on entry to
AsmFunction and restored with a **POP** before exiting; even in the huge
model, Turbo C requires all functions to preserve DS.

Publics and Externals

Turbo Assembler code may call C functions and reference external C
variables, and Turbo C code may likewise call public Turbo Assembler
functions and reference public Turbo Assembler variables. Once Turbo C-
compatible segments are set up in Turbo Assembler, as described in the
preceding sections, only the following few simple rules need be observed in
order to share functions and variables between Turbo C and Turbo
Assembler.

Underscores

Normally, Turbo C expects all external labels to start with an underscore
character (_). Turbo C automatically prefixes an underscore to all function
and external variable names when they're used in C code, so you only need
to attend to underscores in your assembler code. You must make sure that
all assembler references to Turbo C functions and variables begin with
underscores, and you must begin all assembler functions and variables that
are made public and referenced by Turbo C code with underscores.

For example, the following C code:

```
extern int ToggleFlag();
int Flag;
main()
{
    ToggleFlag();
}
```

links properly with the following assembler program:

```
        .MODEL  small
        .DATA
        EXTRN   _Flag:WORD
        .CODE
        PUBLIC  _ToggleFlag
_ToggleFlag     PROC
        cmp     [_Flag],0         ;is the flag reset?
        jz      SetFlag           ;yes, set it
        mov     [_Flag],0         ;no, reset it
        jmp     short EndToggleFlag ;done
SetFlag:
        mov     [_Flag],1         ;set flag
EndToggleFlag:
        ret
_ToggleFlag     ENDP
        END
```

Note that labels that are not referenced by C code, such as *SetFlag*, need not have leading underscores.

By the way, it *is* possible to tell Turbo C not to use underscores by using the **–u-** command-line option. While this may seem like an attractive option, all the Turbo C run-time libraries are compiled with underscores enabled. Therefore you'd have to purchase the run-time library source from Borland and recompile the libraries with underscores disabled in order to use the **–u-** option. (See "Pascal Calling Conventions" on page 330 for information on the **–p** option, which disables the use of underscores and case-sensitivity.)

The Significance of Uppercase and Lowercase

Turbo Assembler is normally insensitive to case when handling symbolic names, making no distinction between uppercase and lowercase letters. Since C is case-sensitive, it's desirable to have Turbo Assembler be case-sensitive, at least for those symbols that are shared between assembler and C. **/ml** and **/mx** make this possible.

The **/ml** command-line switch causes Turbo Assembler to become case-sensitive for all symbols. The **/mx** command-line switch causes Turbo

Assembler to become case-sensitive for public (**PUBLIC**), external (**EXTRN**), global (**GLOBAL**), and communal (**COMM**) symbols only.

Label Types

While assembler programs are free to access any variable as data of any size (8 bit, 16 bit, 32 bit, and so on), it is generally a good idea to access variables in their native size. For instance, it usually causes problems if you write a word to a byte variable:

```
            .
            .
            .
SmallCount  DB   0
            .
            .
            .
        mov  WORD PTR [SmallCount],0ffffh
            .
            .
            .
```

Consequently, it's important that your assembler **EXTRN** statements that declare external C variables specify the right size for those variables, since Turbo Assembler has only your declaration to go by when deciding what size access to generate to a C variable. Given the statement

```
    char c
```

in a C program, the assembler code

```
            .
            .
            .
EXTRN   c:WORD
            .
            .
            .
inc    [c]
            .
            .
            .
```

could lead to nasty problems, since every 256th time the assembler code incremented c, c would turn over and, since c is erroneously declared as a word variable, the byte at **OFFSET** $c + 1$ would incorrectly be incremented, with unpredictable results.

Correspondence between C and assembler data types is as follows:

C Data Type	Assembler Data Type
unsigned char	byte
char	byte
enum	word
unsigned short	word
short	word
unsigned int	word
int	word
unsigned long	dword
long	dword
float	dword
double	qword
long double	tbyte
near *	word
far *	dword

Far Externals Must be Outside Any Segment

If you're using the simplified segment directives, **EXTRN** declarations of symbols in far segments must not be placed within any segment, since Turbo Assembler considers symbols declared within a given segment to be associated with that segment. This has its drawbacks; Turbo Assembler cannot check the addressability of symbols declared **EXTRN** outside any segment, and so can neither generate segment overrides as needed nor inform you when you attempt to access that variable when the correct segment is not loaded. Turbo Assembler still assembles the correct code for references to such external symbols, but can no longer provide the normal degree of segment addressability checking.

If you want to (even though we discourage you), you can use the old-style segment directives to explicitly declare the segment each external symbol is in and then place the **EXTRN** directive for that symbol inside the segment declaration. However, this is a good bit of work; if you don't mind taking responsibility for making sure that the correct segment is loaded when you access far data, it's easiest to just put **EXTRN** declarations of far symbols outside all segments. For example, suppose that FILE1.ASM contains

```
        .
        .
        .
        .FARDATA
File1Variable   DB    0
        .
        .
        .
```

Then if FILE1.ASM is linked to FILE2.ASM, which contains

```
        .
        .

        .
        .DATA
        EXTRN   File1Variable:BYTE
        .CODE
Start   PROC
        mov     ax,SEG File1Variable
        mov     ds,ax
        .
        .
        .
```

SEG *File1Variable* will not return the correct segment. The **EXTRN** directive is placed within the scope of the **DATA** directive of FILE2.ASM, so Turbo Assembler considers *File1Variable* to be in the near **DATA** segment of FILE2.ASM, rather than in the **FARDATA** segment.

The following code for FILE2.ASM allows **SEG** *File1Variable* to return the correct segment:

```
        .
        .

        .
        .DATA
@curseg ENDS
        EXTRN   File1Variable:BYTE
        .CODE
Start   PROC
        mov     ax,SEG File1Variable
        mov     ds,ax
        .
        .
        .
```

The trick here is that the **@curseg ENDS** directive ENDS the .**DATA** segment, so no segment directive is in effect when *File1Variable* is declared external.

Linker Command Line

The simplest way to link Turbo C modules with Turbo Assembler modules is to enter a single Turbo C command line and let Turbo C do all the work. Given the proper command line, Turbo C will compile the C code, invoke Turbo Assembler to do the assembling, and invoke TLINK to link the object files into an executable file. Suppose, for example, that you have a program consisting of the C files MAIN.C and STAT.C and the assembler files SUMM.ASM and DISPLAY.ASM. The command line

```
tcc main stat summ.asm display.asm
```

compiles MAIN.C and STAT.C, assembles SUMM.ASM and DISPLAY.ASM, and links all four object files, along with the C start-up code and any required library functions, into MAIN.EXE. You only need remember the .ASM extensions when typing your assembler file names.

If you use TLINK in stand-alone mode, the object files generated by Turbo Assembler are standard object modules and are treated just like C object modules.

Interactions Between Turbo Assembler and Turbo C

Now that you understand how to build and link C-compatible assembler modules, you need to learn what sort of code you can put into C-callable assembler functions. There are three areas to examine here: receiving passed parameters, using registers, and returning values to the calling code.

Parameter-Passing

Turbo C passes parameters to functions on the stack. Before calling a function, Turbo C first pushes the parameters to that function onto the stack, starting with the rightmost parameter and ending with the leftmost parameter. The C function call

```
    .
    .
    .
Test(i, j, 1);
    .
    .
    .
```

compiles to

```
        mov    ax,1
        push   ax
        push   WORD PTR DGROUP:_j
        push   WORD PTR DGROUP:_i
        call   NEAR PTR _Test
        add    sp,6
```

in which you can clearly see the rightmost parameter, 1, being pushed first, then *j*, and finally *i*.

Upon return from a function, the parameters that were pushed on the stack are still there, but are no longer of any use. Consequently, immediately following each function call, Turbo C adjusts the stack pointer back to the value it contained before the parameters were pushed, thereby discarding the parameters. In the previous example, the three parameters of 2 bytes each take up 6 bytes of stack space altogether, so Turbo C adds 6 to the stack pointer to discard the parameters after the call to *Test*. The important point here is that under C calling conventions, the *calling* code is responsible for discarding the parameters from the stack. (See "Pascal Calling Conventions" on page 330.)

Assembler functions can access parameters passed on the stack relative to the BP register. For example, suppose the function *Test* in the previous example is the following assembler function:

```
        .MODEL   small
        .CODE
        PUBLIC   _Test
_Test   PROC
        push     bp
        mov      bp,sp
        mov      ax,[bp+4]     ;get parameter 1
        add      ax,[bp+6]     ;add parameter 2 to parameter 1
        sub      ax,[bp+8]     ;subtract parameter 3 from sum
        pop      bp
        ret
_Test   ENDP
        END
```

You can see that *Test* is getting the parameters passed by the C code from the stack, relative to BP. (Remember that BP addresses the stack segment.) But just how are you to know *where* to find the parameters relative to BP?

Figure 6.4 shows what the stack looks like just before the first instruction in *Test* is executed:

```
i = 25;
j = 4;
Test(i, j, 1);
```

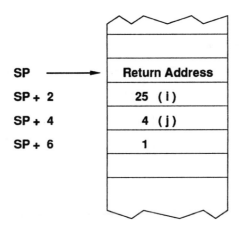

Figure 6.4: State of the Stack Just Before Executing Test's First Instruction

The parameters to *Test* are at fixed locations relative to SP, starting at the stack location 2 bytes higher than the location of the return address that was pushed by the call. After loading BP with SP, you can access the parameters relative to BP. However, you must first preserve BP, since the calling C code expects you to return with BP unchanged. Pushing BP changes all the offsets on the stack. Figure 6.5 shows the stack after these lines of code are executed:

```
    .
    .
    .
push  bp
mov   bp,sp
    .
    .
    .
```

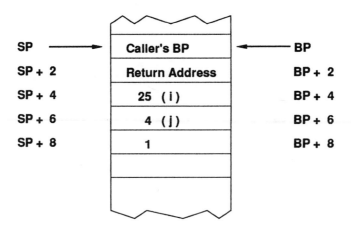

Figure 6.5: State of the Stack after PUSH and MOV

This is the standard C stack frame, the organization of a function's parameters and automatic variables on the stack. As you can see, no matter how many parameters a C program may have, the leftmost parameter is always stored at the stack address immediately above the pushed return address, the next parameter to the right is stored just above the leftmost parameter, and so on. As long as you know the order and type of the passed parameters, you always know where to find them on the stack.

Space for automatic variables can be reserved by subtracting the required number of bytes from SP. For example, room for a 100-byte automatic array could be reserved by starting *Test* with

```
    .
    .
    .
push  bp
mov   bp,sp
sub   sp,100
    .
    .
    .
```

as shown in Figure 6.6.

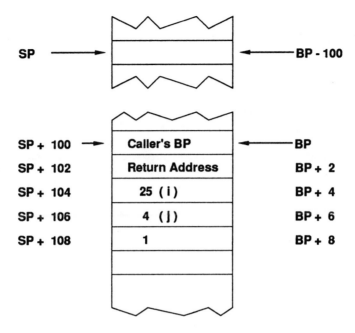

Figure 6.6: State of the Stack after PUSH, MOV, and SUB

Since the portion of the stack holding automatic variables is at a lower address than BP, negative offsets from BP are used to address automatic variables. For example,

```
mov  BYTE PTR [bp-100],0
```

would set the first byte of the 100-byte array you reserved earlier to zero. Passed parameters, on the other hand, are always addressed at positive offsets from BP.

While you can, if you wish, allocate space for automatic variables as shown previously, Turbo Assembler provides a special version of the **LOCAL** directive that makes allocation and naming of automatic variables a snap. When **LOCAL** is encountered within a procedure, it is assumed to define automatic variables for that procedure. For example,

```
LOCAL  LocalArray:BYTE:100,LocalCount:WORD = AUTO_SIZE
```

defines the automatic variables *LocalArray* and *LocalCount*. *LocalArray* is actually a label equated to [*BP-100*], and *LocalCount* is actually a label equated to [*BP-102*], but you can use them as variable names without ever needing to know their values. *AUTO_SIZE* is the total number of bytes of automatic storage required; you must subtract this value from SP in order to allocate space for the automatic variables.

Here's how you might use **LOCAL**:

```
           .
           .
           .
_TestSub  PROC
      LOCAL      LocalArray:BYTE:100,LocalCount:WORD=AUTO_SIZE
      push bp                       ;preserve caller's stack frame pointer
      mov  bp,sp                    ;set up our own stack frame pointer
      sub  sp,AUTO_SIZE             ;allocate room for automatic variables
      mov  [LocalCount],10          ;set local count variable to 10
                                    ; (LocalCount is actually [BP-102])

           .
           .
           .
      mov  cx,[LocalCount]          ;get count from local variable
      mov  al,'A'                   ;we'll fill with character "A"
      lea  bx,[LocalArray]          ;point to local array
                                    ; (LocalArray is actually [BP-100])
FillLoop:
      mov  [bx],al                  ;fill next byte
      inc  bx                       ;point to following byte
      loop FillLoop                 ;do next byte, if any
      mov  sp,bp                    ;deallocate storage for automatic
                                    ; variables (add sp,AUTO_SIZE would
                                    ; also have worked)
      pop  bp                       ;restore caller's stack frame pointer
      ret
_TestSub  ENDP
           .
           .
           .
```

In this example, note that the first field after the definition of a given automatic variable is the data type of the variable: **BYTE, WORD, DWORD, NEAR,** and so on. The second field after the definition of a given automatic variable is the number of elements of that variable's type to reserve for that variable. This field is optional and defines an automatic array if used; if it is omitted, one element of the specified type is reserved. Consequently, *LocalArray* consists of 100 byte-sized elements, while *LocalCount* consists of 1 word-sized element.

Also note that the **LOCAL** line in the preceding example ends with =*AUTO_SIZE*. This field, beginning with an equal sign, is optional; if present, it sets the label following the equal sign to the number of bytes of automatic storage required. You must then use that label to allocate and deallocate storage for automatic variables, since the **LOCAL** directive only generates labels, and doesn't actually generate any code or data storage. To put this another way: **LOCAL** doesn't allocate automatic variables, but simply generates labels that you can readily use to both allocate storage for and access automatic variables.

A very handy feature of **LOCAL** is that the labels for both the automatic variables and the total automatic variable size are limited in scope to the procedure they're used in, so you're free to reuse an automatic variable name in another procedure.

As you can see, **LOCAL** makes it much easier to define and use automatic variables. Note that the **LOCAL** directive has a completely different meaning when used in macros as discussed in Chapter 10. (Refer to Chapter 3 in the *Reference Guide* for additional information about both forms of the **LOCAL** directive.)

By the way, Turbo C handles stack frames in just the way we've described here. You may well find it instructive to compile a few Turbo C modules with the –S option and look at the assembler code Turbo C generates to see how Turbo C creates and uses stack frames.

So far, so good, but there are further complications. First of all, this business of accessing parameters at constant offsets from BP is a nuisance; not only is it easy to make mistakes, but if you add another parameter, all the other stack frame offsets in the function must be changed. For example, suppose you change *Test* to accept four parameters:

```
Test(Flag, i, j, 1);
```

Suddenly *i* is at offset 6, not offset 4, *j* is at offset 8, not offset 6, and so on. You can use equates for the parameter offsets:

```
        .
        .
        .
Flag        EQU   4
AddParm1    EQU   6
AddParm2    EQU   8
SubParm1    EQU   10
        mov   ax,[bp+AddParm1]
        add   ax,[bp+AddParm2]
        sub   ax,[bp+SubParm1]
        .
        .
        .
```

but it's still a nuisance to calculate the offsets and maintain them. There's a more serious problem, too: The size of the pushed return address grows by

2 bytes in far code models, as do the sizes of passed code pointers and data pointer in far code and far data models, respectively. Writing a function that can be easily assembled to access the stack frame properly in any memory model would thus seem to be a difficult task.

Fear not. Turbo Assembler provides you with the **ARG** directive, which makes it easy to handle passed parameters in your assembler routines.

The **ARG** directive automatically generates the correct stack offsets for the variables you specify. For example,

```
arg  FillArray:WORD,Count:WORD,FillValue:BYTE
```

specifies three parameters: *FillArray*, a word-sized parameter; *Count*, a word-sized parameter, and *FillValue*, a byte-sized parameter. **ARG** actually sets the label *FillArray* to [*BP+4*] (assuming the example code resides in a near procedure), the label *Count* to [*BP+6*], and the label *FillValue* to [*BP+8*]. However, **ARG** is valuable precisely because you can use **ARG**-defined labels without ever knowing the values they're set to.

For example, suppose you've got a function *FillSub*, called from C as follows:

```
main()
{
#define ARRAY_LENGTH 100
   char TestArray[ARRAY_LENGTH];

   FillSub(TestArray,ARRAY_LENGTH,'*');
}
```

You could use **ARG** in *FillSub* to handle the parameters as follows:

```
_FillSub  PROC NEAR
     ARG  FillArray:WORD,Count:WORD,FillValue:BYTE
     push bp                 ;preserve caller's stack frame
     mov  bp,sp              ;set our own stack frame
     mov  bx,[FillArray]     ;get pointer to array to fill
     mov  cx,[Count]         ;get length to fill
     mov  al,[FillValue]     ;get value to fill with
FillLoop:
     mov  [bx],al            ;fill a character
     inc  bx                 ;point to next character
     loop FillLoop           ;do next character
     pop  bp                 ;restore caller's stack frame
     ret
_FillSub  ENDP
```

That's really all it takes to handle passed parameters with **ARG**! Better yet, **ARG** automatically accounts for the different sizes of near and far returns. Another convenience is that the labels defined with **ARG** are limited in scope to the procedure they're used in when you declare them using the local label prefix (see **LOCALS** in the *Reference Guide*). So you need never worry about conflict between parameter names in different procedures.

Take a look at Chapter 3 in the *Reference Guide* for additional information about the **ARG** directive.

Preserving Registers

As far as Turbo C is concerned, C-callable assembler functions can do anything they please, as long as they preserve the following registers: BP, SP, CS, DS, and SS. While these registers can be altered during the course of an assembler function, when the calling code is returned, they must be exactly as they were when the assembler function was called. AX, BX, CX, DX, ES, and the flags may be changed in any way.

SI and DI are special cases, since they're used by Turbo C as register variables. If register variables are enabled in the C module calling your assembler function, you must preserve SI and DI, but if register variables are not enabled, SI and DI need not be preserved. It's a good practice to always preserve SI and DI in your C-callable assembler functions, regardless of whether register variables are enabled. You never know when you might link a given assembler module to a different C module, or recompile your C code with register variables enabled, without remembering that your assembler code needs to be changed as well.

Returning Values

A C-callable assembler function can return a value, just like a C function. Function values are returned as follows:

Return Value Type	Return Value Location
unsigned char	AX
char	AX
enum	AX
unsigned short	AX
short	AX
unsigned int	AX
int	AX
unsigned long	DX:AX
long	DX:AX
float	8087 top-of-stack (TOS) register (ST(0))
double	8087 top-of-stack (TOS) register (ST(0))
long double	8087 top-of-stack (TOS) register (ST(0))
near *	AX
far *	DX:AX

In general, 8- and 16-bit values are returned in AX, and 32-bit values are returned in DX:AX, with the high 16 bits of the value in DX. Floating-point values are returned in ST(0), which is the 8087's top-of-stack (TOS) register, or in the 8087 emulator's TOS register if the floating-point emulator is being used.

Structures are a bit more complex. Structures that are 1 or 2 bytes in length are returned in AX, and structures that are 4 bytes in length are returned in DX:AX. Three-byte structures and structures larger than 4 bytes must be stored in a static data area, and a pointer to that static data must then be returned. As with all pointers, near pointers to structures are returned in AX, and far pointers to structures are returned in DX:AX.

Let's look at a small model C-callable assembler function, *FindLastChar*, that returns a pointer to the last character of a passed string. The C prototype for this function would be

```
extern char * FindLastChar(char * StringToScan);
```

where *StringToScan* is the nonempty string for which a pointer to the last character is to be returned.

Here's *FindLastChar*:

```
        .MODEL  small
        .CODE
        PUBLIC  _FindLastChar
_FindLastChar   PROC
        push    bp
        mov     bp,sp
        cld                     ;we need string instructions to count up
```

```
        mov     ax,ds
        mov     es,ax           ;set ES to point to the near data segment
        mov     di,             ;point ES:DI to start of passed string
        mov     al,0            ;search for the null that ends the string
        mov     cx,0ffffh       ;search up to 64K-1 bytes
        repnz   scasb           ;look for the null
        dec     di              ;point back to the null
        dec     di              ;point back to the last character
        mov     ax,di           ;return the near pointer in AX
        pop     bp
        ret
_FindLastChar   ENDP
        END
```

The final result, the near pointer to the last character in the passed string, is returned in AX.

Calling a Turbo Assembler Function from Turbo C

Now look at an example of Turbo C code calling a Turbo Assembler function. The following Turbo Assembler module, COUNT.ASM, contains the function *LineCount*, which returns counts of the number of lines and characters in a passed string:

```
; Small model C-callable assembler function to count the number of
; lines and characters in a zero-terminated string.
;
; Function prototype:
;       extern unsigned int LineCount(char * near StringToCount,
;               unsigned int near * CharacterCountPtr);
; Input:
;       char near * StringToCount: pointer to the string on which a
;       line count is to be performed
;
;       unsigned int near * CharacterCountPtr: pointer to the
;               int variable in which the character count is to be stored
;
NEWLINE EQU     0ah                     ;the linefeed character is C's
                                        ; newline character

        DOSSEG
        .MODEL  small
        .CODE
        PUBLIC  _LineCount
_LineCount      PROC
        push    bp
        mov     bp,sp
        push    si                      ;preserve calling program's register
                                        ; variable, if any
```

```
            mov     si,[bp+4]           ;point SI to the string
            sub     cx,cx               ;set character count to 0
            mov     dx,cx               ;set line count to 0
LineCountLoop:
            lodsb                       ;get the next character
            and     al,al               ;is it null, to end the string?
            jz      EndLineCount        ;yes, we're done
            inc     cx                  ;no, count another character
            cmp     al,NEWLINE          ;is it a newline?
            jnz     LineCountLoop       ;no, check the next character
            inc     dx                  ;yes, count another line
            jmp     LineCountLoop
EndLineCount:
            inc     dx                  ;count the line that ends with the
                                        ; null character
            mov     bx,[bp+6]           ;point to the location at which to
                                        ; return the character count
            mov     [bx],cx             ;set the character count variable
            mov     ax,dx               ;return line count as function value
            pop     si                  ;restore calling program's register
                                        ; variable, if any
            pop     bp
            ret
_LineCount  ENDP
            END
```

The following C module, CALLCT.C, is a sample invocation of the *Line-Count* function:

```
char * TestString="Line 1\nline 2\nline 3";
extern unsigned int LineCount(char * StringToCount,
        unsigned int * CharacterCountPtr);
main()
{
    unsigned int LCount;
    unsigned int CCount;

    LCount = LineCount(TestString, &CCount);
    printf("Lines: %d\nCharacters: %d\n", LCount, CCount);
}
```

The two modules are compiled and linked together with the command line

```
tcc -ms callct count.asm
```

As shown here, *LineCount* will only work when linked to small-model C programs, since pointer sizes and locations on the stack frame change in other models. Here's a version of *LineCount*, COUNTLG.ASM, that will work with large-model C programs (but not small-model ones, unless far pointers are passed, and *LineCount* is declared far):

```
; Large model C-callable assembler function to count the number
; of lines and characters in a zero-terminated string.
;
; Function prototype:
;       extern unsigned int LineCount(char * far StringToCount,
;               unsigned int * far CharacterCountPtr);
;       char far * StringToCount: pointer to the string on which
;                               a line count is to be performed
;
;       unsigned int far * CharacterCountPtr: pointer to the int variable
;                                           in which the character count
;                                           is to be stored
;
NEWLINE EQU     0ah                     ;the linefeed character is C's newline
                                        ; character

        .MODEL  large
        .CODE
        PUBLIC  _LineCount
_LineCount      PROC
        push    bp
        mov     bp,sp
        push    si                      ;preserve calling program's register
                                        ; variable, if any
        push    ds                      ;preserve C's standard data seg
        lds     si,[bp+6]               ;point DS:SI to the string
        sub     cx,cx                   ;set character count to 0
        mov     dx,cx                   ;set line count to 0
LineCountLoop:
        lodsb                           ;get the next character
        and     al,al                   ;is it null, to end the string?
        jz      EndLineCount            ;yes, we're done
        inc     cx                      ;no, count another character
        cmp     al,NEWLINE              ;is it a newline?
        jnz     LineCountLoop           ;no, check the next character
        inc     dx                      ;yes, count another line
        jmp     LineCountLoop
EndLineCount:
        inc     dx                      ;count line ending with null character
        les     bx,[bp+10]              ;point ES:BX to the location at
                                        ; which to return character count
        mov     es:[bx],cx              ;set the character count variable
        mov     ax,dx                   ;return the line count as
                                        ; the function value
        pop     ds                      ;restore C's standard data seg
        pop     si                      ;restore calling program's
                                        ; register variable, if any
        pop     bp
        ret
_LineCount      ENDP
```

```
            END
```

COUNTLG.ASM can be linked to CALLCT.C with the following command line:

```
tcc -ml callct countlg.asm
```

Pascal Calling Conventions

Thus far, you've seen how C normally passes parameters to functions by having the calling code push parameters right to left, call the function, and discard the parameters from the stack after the call. Turbo C is also capable of following the conventions used by Pascal programs in which parameters are passed from left to right and the *called* program discards the parameters from the stack. In Turbo C, Pascal conventions are enabled with the **–p** command-line option or the **pascal** keyword.

Here's an example of an assembler function that uses Pascal conventions:

```
;
; Called as: TEST(i, j, k);
;
i       equ     8               ;leftmost parameter
j       equ     6
k       equ     4               ;rightmost parameter
;
        .MODEL  small
        .CODE
        PUBLIC  TEST
TEST    PROC
        push    bp
        mov     bp,sp
        mov     ax,[bp+i]       ;get i
        add     ax,[bp+j]       ;add j to i
        sub     ax,[bp+k]       ;subtract k from the sum
        pop     bp
        ret     6               ;return, discarding 6 parameter bytes
TEST    ENDP
        END
```

Figure 6.7 shows the stack frame after **MOV BP,SP** has been executed.

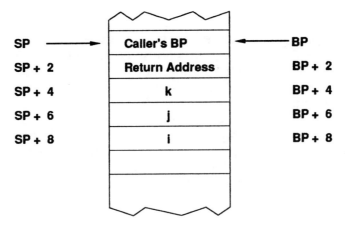

Figure 6.7: State of the Stack Immediately after MOV BP, SP

Note that **RET 6** is used by the called function to clear the passed parameters from the stack.

Pascal calling conventions also require all external and public symbols to be in uppercase, with no leading underscores. Why would you ever want to use Pascal calling conventions in a C program? Code that uses Pascal conventions tends to be somewhat smaller and faster than normal C code, since there's no need to execute an **ADD SP** *n* instruction to discard the parameters after each call. Refer to the Chapter 7 for more information about Pascal calling conventions.

Calling Turbo C from Turbo Assembler

Although it's most common to call assembler functions from C to perform specialized tasks, you may on occasion want to call C functions from assembler. As it turns out, it's actually easier to call a Turbo C function from a Turbo Assembler function than the reverse, since no stack-frame handling on the part of the assembler code is required. Let's take a quick look at the requirements for calling Turbo C functions from assembler.

Link in the C Startup Code

As a general rule, it's a good idea to only call Turbo C library functions from assembler code in programs that link in the C startup module as the first module linked. This "safe" class includes all programs that are linked from TC.EXE or with a TCC.EXE command line, and programs that are linked directly with TLINK that have C0T, C0S, C0C, C0M, C0L, or C0H as the first file to link.

You should generally not call Turbo C library functions from programs that don't link in the C startup module, since some Turbo C library functions will not operate properly if the startup code is not linked in. If you really want to call Turbo C library functions from such programs, we suggest you look at the startup source code (the file C0.ASM on the Turbo C distribution disks) and purchase the C library source code from Borland, so you can be sure to provide the proper initialization for the library functions you need. Another possible approach is to simply link each desired library function to an assembler program, called X.ASM for instance, which does nothing but call each function, linking them together with a command line like this:

```
tlink x,x,,cm.lib
```

where *m* is the first letter of the desired memory model (*t* for tiny, *s* for small, and so on). If TLINK reports any undefined symbols, then that library function can't be called unless the C startup code is linked into the program.

Note: Calling user-defined C functions that in turn call C library functions falls into the same category as calling library functions directly; lack of the C startup can potentially cause problems for *any* assembler program that calls C library functions, directly or indirectly.

Make Sure You've Got the Right Segment Setup

As we learned earlier, you must make sure that Turbo C and Turbo Assembler are using the same memory model and that the segments you use in Turbo Assembler match those used by Turbo C. Refer to the previous section, "The Framework for Interfacing Turbo C and Turbo Assembler," (page 304) if you need a refresher on matching memory models and segments. Also, remember to put **EXTRN** directives for far symbols either outside all segments or inside the correct segment.

Performing the Call

You've already learned how Turbo C prepares for and executes function calls in the section "Calling Turbo Assembler Functions from Turbo C" on page 302. We'll briefly review the mechanics of C function calls, this time from the perspective of calling Turbo C functions from Turbo Assembler.

All you need to do when passing parameters to a Turbo C function is push the rightmost parameter first, then the next rightmost parameter, and so on, until the leftmost parameter has been pushed. Then just call the function. For example, when programming in Turbo C, to call the Turbo C library function **strcpy** to copy *SourceString* to *DestString*, you would enter

```
strcpy(DestString, SourceString);
```

To perform the same call in assembler, you would use

```
lea    ax,SourceString      ;rightmost parameter
push   ax
lea    ax,DestString         ;leftmost parameter
push   ax
call   _strcpy               ;copy the string
add    sp,4                  ;discard the parameters
```

Don't forget to discard the parameters by adjusting SP after the call.

If you're calling a C function that uses Pascal calling conventions, push the parameters left to right and don't adjust SP afterward:

```
lea    ax,DestString         ;leftmost parameter
push   ax
lea    ax,SourceString      ;rightmost parameter
push   ax
call   STRCPY                ;copy the string; don't adjust the stack
```

Of course, the last example assumes that you've recompiled **strcpy** with the –**p** switch, since the standard library version of **strcpy** uses C rather than Pascal calling conventions. C functions return values as described in the section "Returning Values" (page 325); 8- and 16-bit values in AX, 32-bit values in DX:AX, floating-point values in the 8087 TOS register, and structures in various ways according to size.

Rely on C functions to preserve the following registers and *only* the following registers: SI, DI, BP, DS, SS, SP, and CS. Registers AX, BX, CX, DX, ES, and the flags may be changed arbitrarily.

Calling a Turbo C Function from Turbo Assembler

One case in which you might wish to call a Turbo C function from Turbo Assembler is when you need to perform complex calculations, since it's much easier to denote calculations in C than in assembler. This is especially true when mixed integer and floating-point calculations are involved; while it's certainly possible to perform such operations in assembler, it's simpler to let C handle the details of type conversion and floating-point arithmetic.

Let's look at an example of assembler code that calls a Turbo C function in order to get a floating-point calculation performed. In fact, let's look at an example in which a Turbo C function passes a series of integer numbers to a Turbo Assembler function, which sums the numbers and in turn calls another Turbo C function to perform the floating-point calculation of the average value of the series.

The C portion of the program in CALCAVG.C is

```
extern float Average(int far * ValuePtr, int NumberOfValues);
#define NUMBER_OF_TEST_VALUES 10
int TestValues[NUMBER_OF_TEST_VALUES] = {
   1, 2, 3, 4, 5, 6, 7, 8, 9, 10
};

main()
{
   printf("The average value is: %f\n",
          Average(TestValues, NUMBER_OF_TEST_VALUES));
}
float IntDivide(int Dividend, int Divisor)
{
   return( (float) Dividend / (float) Divisor );
}
```

and the assembler portion of the program in AVERAGE.ASM is

```
;
; Turbo C-callable small-model function that returns the average
; of a set of integer values. Calls the Turbo C function
; IntDivide() to perform the final division.
;
; Function prototype:
;     extern float Average(int far * ValuePtr, int NumberOfValues);
;
; Input:
;     int far * ValuePtr:          ;the array of values to average
;     int NumberOfValues:          ;the number of values to average
        .MODEL  small
        EXTRN   _IntDivide:PROC
        .CODE
        PUBLIC  _Average
_Average        PROC
        push    bp
        mov     bp,sp
        les     bx,[bp+4]          ;point ES:BX to array of values
        mov     cx,[bp+8]          ;# of values to average
        mov     ax,0               ;clear the running total
AverageLoop:
        add     ax,es:[bx]         ;add the current value
```

```
        add     bx,2                ;point to the next value
        loop    AverageLoop
        push    WORD PTR [bp+8]     ;get back the number of values passed to
                                    ; IntDivide as the rightmost parameter
        push    ax                  ;pass the total as the leftmost parameter
        call    _IntDivide          ;calculate the floating-point average
        add     sp,4                ;discard the parameters
        pop     bp
        ret                         ;the average is in the 8087's TOS register
_Average        ENDP
        END
```

The C **main** function passes a pointer to the array of integers *TestValues* and the length of the array to the assembler function *Average*. *Average* sums the integers, then passes the sum and the number of values to the C function *IntDivide*. *IntDivide* casts the sum and number of values to floating-point numbers and calculates the average value, doing in a single line of C code what would have taken several assembler lines. *IntDivide* returns the average to *Average* in the 8087 TOS register, and *Average* just leaves the average in the TOS register and returns to **main**.

CALCAVG.C and AVERAGE.ASM could be compiled and linked into the executable program CALCAVG.EXE with the command

```
tcc calcavg average.asm
```

Note that *Average* will handle both small and large data models without the need for any code change, since a far pointer is passed in all models. All that would be needed to support large code models (huge, large, and medium) would be use of the appropriate **.MODEL** directive.

7

Interfacing Turbo Assembler with Turbo Pascal

Turbo Assembler provides extensive and powerful facilities to let you add assembly language code to your Turbo Pascal programs. In this chapter, we'll tell you everything you need to know to make full use of these facilities, including lots of examples and "inside" information.

Why use Turbo Assembler with Turbo Pascal? Most of the programs you're likely to write can be written entirely in Turbo Pascal. Unlike most Pascals, Turbo Pascal lets you access virtually all of your machine's resources directly through the *Port[]*, *Mem[]*, *MemW[]*, and *MemL[]* arrays, and you can call the BIOS and operating system with the *Intr()* and *MsDos()* procedures.

Why, then, would you want to use assembly language with Turbo Pascal? The two most likely reasons: to perform the relatively few operations that are not directly available from Turbo Pascal and to take advantage of the raw speed that only assembly language can provide. (Turbo Pascal itself is so quick because it is written in assembly language.) This chapter will show you how and when to harness the power of assembly language with Turbo Pascal.

Note: Unless a version number is stated specifically, when referring to Turbo Pascal, we mean versions 4.0 and greater.

The Turbo Pascal Memory Map

Before you can begin writing assembly language code to work with Turbo Pascal programs, it's important to understand how the compiler lays information out in memory. The Turbo Pascal memory model embodies aspects of both the medium and large models, which are described in Chapter 4. There is a single global data segment, allowing fast access to global variables and typed constants through DS. However, each unit has its own code segment, and the heap can grow to use all of available memory. Addresses in Turbo Pascal are always passed as far (32-bit) pointers so that they can reference objects anywhere in memory.

The memory map of a Turbo Pascal program looks like this:

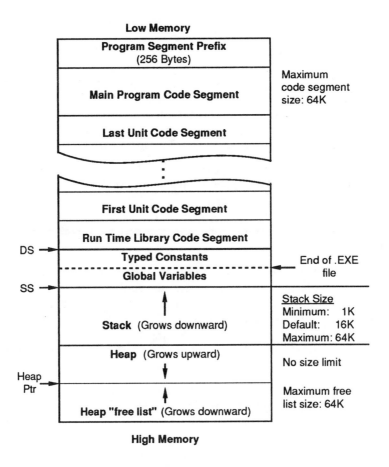

Figure 7.1: Memory Map of a Turbo Pascal 5.0 Program

The Program Segment Prefix

The Program Segment Prefix (PSP) is a 256-byte area created by MS-DOS when the program is loaded. Among other things, it contains information about command-line parameters used to invoke the program, the amount of available memory, and the *DOS environment* (a list of string variables used by DOS).

In Turbo Pascal 3.0, the segment address of the PSP was the same as that of all the rest of the code. This is no longer the case. In Turbo Pascal versions 4.0 and later, the main program, the units it uses, and the run-time library all occupy different segments. Turbo Pascal therefore stores the segment address of the PSP in a predeclared global variable called *PrefixSeg*, so that you can gain access to PSP information.

Code Segments

Every Turbo Pascal program has at least two code segments: one for the code of the main program and one for the run-time library. In addition, each unit's code occupies a separate code segment. Since each code segment can be up to 64 Kb in size, your program can occupy as much memory as you want (subject, of course, to what is available on the machine). Programmers who formerly used overlays to generate programs larger than 64 Kb can now keep all the code in memory for faster execution. The code segment into which an assembly language module is linked has the name **CODE**, or **CSEG**, when viewed from Turbo Assembler.

The Global Data Segment

Turbo Pascal's global data segment follows the run-time library code segment. It contains up to 64 Kb of initialized and uninitialized data: *typed constants* and *global variables*. As in Turbo Pascal 3.0, typed constants are really not constants at all, but variables that start with a pre-initialized value when the program is loaded. But unlike Turbo Pascal 3.0, Turbo Pascal 4.0 does not place typed constants in the code segment. Instead, Turbo Pascal 4.0 places typed constants in the global data segment, where it can access them even more quickly than Turbo 3.0 could. The global data segment has the name **DATA**, or **DSEG**, when referenced from a Turbo Assembler module.

The Stack

In Turbo Pascal 4.0 and later, the global data segment is above the stack. Note that this arrangement is different from the one used in Turbo Pascal 3.0. The stack and heap do not grow toward each other. Instead, a fixed amount of memory is allocated for the stack. The default size, 16K, is more than enough for the vast majority of programs; however, you can specify a stack size as small as 1K (for short programs) or as large as 64K (for programs with a lot of recursion). Stack and heap sizes can be selected with the $M compiler directive.

As in most 80x86 programs, the stack pointer starts at the top of the stack segment and grows downward. Whenever a procedure or function is called, Turbo Pascal normally checks to make sure that the stack is not exhausted. This check can be turned off with the {$S-} compiler directive.

The Heap

At the top of the Turbo Pascal memory map is the heap. By default, the heap takes up all memory not allocated for the code, data, and stack segments, but the $M directive can be used to limit the maximum size of the heap. (It can also be used to prevent the program from running if a minimum amount of heap space is not available.)

Storage is allocated dynamically on the heap, beginning from the bottom, each time you do a *New()* or *GetMem()*. Space is freed when you do a *Dispose, Release,* or *FreeMem*. When *Dispose* and *FreeMem* are used, Turbo Pascal 4.0 keeps track of free areas in the middle of the heap using a data structure called a *free list*. The free list, which can be up to 64K in size, grows downward from the very top of the heap area.

Register Usage in Turbo Pascal

Like Turbo Pascal 3.0, Turbo Pascal 4.0 imposes a minimum of restrictions on register usage. When a call is made to a function or procedure, the values of only three registers must be preserved: stack segment (SS), data segment (DS), and base pointer (BP). DS points to the global data segment (called **DATA**), and SS points to the stack segment. BP is used by each procedure or function to reference its *activation record*—the stack space it uses for parameters, local variables, and temporary storage. All subprograms must also adjust the stack pointer (SP) before exiting, so that the parameters no longer remain on the stack.

Near or Far?

Because a Turbo Pascal program contains multiple code segments, it uses a mixture of near and far calls to access procedures and functions. What's the difference? Well, a near call can only be used to access a subprogram that resides in the same code segment where the call is made, while a far call can access a subprogram anywhere in memory. This flexibility incurs a small penalty, however: A far call takes a bit more time and space than a near call.

Each subprogram in your Turbo Pascal program must be written (either by the compiler or by you) to be called in only one of these two ways. Which should you choose? Subprograms declared in the **interface** section of a unit must always be far so that they can be called from other units. But subprograms declared in the main program, or declared only in the **implementation** section of a unit, are usually near. (Any subprogram can be forced to be far by the {$F+} compiler directive.)

When writing assembly language routines to interface with Turbo Pascal, you must check to make sure that your routine has the correct "distance." Turbo Pascal will not report an error if you declare a **PROC** as near in assembly language when the corresponding **external** procedure declaration is positioned in such a way that it needs to be far.

Sharing Information with Turbo Pascal

The $L Compiler Directive and External Subprograms

The two keys to using Turbo Assembler with Turbo Pascal are the {$L} compiler directive and the **external** subprogram declaration. The directive {$L MYFILE.OBJ} causes Turbo Pascal to look for MYFILE.OBJ, a file in standard MS-DOS *linkable object format*, and link it into your Turbo Pascal program. If the file name given in the {$L} directive does not have an extension, .OBJ is assumed.

Each Turbo Assembler procedure or function that you want to be visible within the Turbo Pascal program must be declared as a PUBLIC symbol, and must have a corresponding external declaration within that program. The syntax of an **external** procedure or function declaration in Turbo Pascal is very similar to that of a **forward** declaration:

```
procedure AsmProc(a : integer; b : real); external;

function AsmFunc(c : word; d : byte); external;
```

These declarations might correspond to the following declarations within
your Turbo Assembler program:

```
CODE     SEGMENT BYTE PUBLIC
AsmProc  PROC NEAR
         PUBLIC AsmProc
            .
            .
            .
AsmProc  ENDP

AsmFunc  PROC FAR
         PUBLIC Bar
            .
            .
            .
AsmFunc  ENDP
CODE     ENDS
```

A Turbo Pascal **external** procedure declaration must be at the outermost
level of the program or unit; that is, it may not be nested within another
procedure declaration. An attempt to declare an **external** procedure at any
other level will cause a compile-time error.

Turbo Pascal does not check to make sure that **PROCs** declared with the
near and far attributes correspond to near and far subprograms in your
Turbo Pascal program. In fact, it does not even check to see whether the
public labels *AsmProc* and *AsmFunc* are the names of **PROCs**. It is up to you
to make sure that the assembly language and Pascal declarations are
consistent.

The PUBLIC Directive: Making Turbo Assembler Information Available to Turbo Pascal

Only labels that are declared **PUBLIC** in an assembly language module are
visible to Turbo Pascal. Labels are the only objects that can be exported
from assembly language to Turbo Pascal. Further, every label that is made
PUBLIC must have a corresponding procedure or function declaration in
the Turbo Pascal program, or the compiler will report an error. A public
label need not be part of a **PROC** declaration. As far as Turbo Pascal is
concerned,

```
AsmLabel  PROC FAR
          PUBLIC Bar
```

and

```
AsmLabel:
        PUBLIC Bar
```

are equivalent.

The EXTRN Directive: Making Turbo Pascal Information Available to Turbo Assembler

A Turbo Assembler module can access any Turbo Pascal procedure, function, variable, or typed constant that is declared at the outermost level of the program or unit to which it is linked. (Note that this includes variables declared after the {$L} compiler directive and the **external** declaration(s) associated with the module.) Turbo Pascal labels and ordinary constants are not visible to the assembly language.

Suppose your Turbo Pascal program declares the following global variables:

```
var
    a : byte;
    b : word;
    c : shortInt;
    d : integer;
    e : real;
    f : single;
    g : double;
    h : extended;
    i : comp;
    j : pointer;
```

You can access any of these variables inside your assembly language program with **EXTRN** declarations, as follows:

```
EXTRN A : BYTE      ;1 byte
EXTRN B : WORD      ;2 bytes
EXTRN C : BYTE      ;Assembly language treats signed and unsigned alike
EXTRN D : WORD      ;Ditto
EXTRN E : FWORD     ;6-byte software real
EXTRN F : DWORD     ;4-byte IEEE floating point
EXTRN G : QWORD     ;8-byte IEEE double-precision floating point
EXTRN H : TBYTE     ;10-byte IEEE temporary floating point
EXTRN I : QWORD     ;8087 8-byte signed integer
EXTRN J : DWORD     ;Turbo Pascal pointer
```

You can access Turbo Pascal procedures and functions—including library routines—in a similar manner. Suppose you have a Turbo Pascal unit that looks like this:

```
unit Sample;
{ Sample unit that defines several pascal procedures that are
  called from an assembly language procedure. }

interface

procedure TestSample;

procedure PublicProc;              { Must be far since it is visible outside }

implementation

var
  A : word;

procedure AsmProc; external;
{$L ASMPROC.OBJ}

procedure PublicProc;
  begin { PublicProc }
    Writeln('In PublicProc');
  end; { PublicProc }

procedure NearProc;                { Must be near }
  begin { NearProc }
    Writeln('In NearProc');
  end; { NearProc }

{$F+}
procedure FarProc;                 { Must be far due to compiler directive }
  begin { FarProc }
    Writeln('In FarProc');
  end; { FarProc }

{$F-}

procedure TestSample;
  begin { TestSample }
    Writeln('In TestSample');
    A := 10;
    Writeln('Value of A before ASMPROC = ',A);
    AsmProc;
    Writeln('Value of A after ASMPROC = ',A);
  end { TestSample };

end.
```

The procedure *AsmProc* can call procedures *PublicProc, NearProc,* or *FarProc*
by using **EXTRN** directives as follows:

```
DATA     SEGMENT WORD PUBLIC
         ASSUME DS:DATA
         EXTRN  A:WORD              ;variable from the unit
DATA     ENDS
```

```
CODE      SEGMENT BYTE PUBLIC
          ASSUME CS:CODE
          EXTRN  PublicProc : FAR    ;far procedure (exported by the unit)
          EXTRN  NearProc : NEAR     ;near procedure (local to unit)
          EXTRN  FarProc  : FAR      ;far procedure (local but forced far)

AsmProc   PROC NEAR
          PUBLIC AsmProc
          call   FAR PTR PublicProc
          call   NearProc
          call   FAR PTR FarProc
          mov    cx,ds:A             ;pull in variable A from the unit
          sub    cx,2                ;do something to change it
          mov    ds:A,cx             ;store it back
          ret
AsmProc   ENDP
CODE      ENDS
          END
```

The main program that tests this Pascal unit and assembler code follows:

```
program TSample;
uses Sample;
begin
  TestSample;
end.
```

To build the sample program with the command-line compiler and the assembler, use the following batch file commands:

```
TASM ASMPROC
TPC /B TSAMPLE
TSAMPLE
```

Since an external subprogram must be declared at the outermost procedural level of your Turbo Pascal program, you can't use **EXTRN** declarations to access objects that are local to a procedure or function. However, your Turbo Assembler subprogram can receive these objects as value or **var** parameters when called from Turbo Pascal.

Restrictions on Using EXTRN Objects

Turbo Pascal's *qualified identifier syntax,* which uses a unit name plus a period to access an object in a specific unit, is not compatible with Turbo Assembler's syntax rules and will therefore be rejected. The declaration

```
EXTRN SYSTEM.Assign : FAR
```

will produce a Turbo Assembler error message.

There are two other minor restrictions on the use of **EXTRN** objects with Turbo Pascal. The first is that references to procedures and functions cannot use address arithmetic. Thus, if you declare

```
EXTRN PublicProc : FAR
```

you can't write a statement such as

```
call PublicProc + 42
```

The second restriction is that the Turbo Pascal linker will not recognize operators that chop words into bytes, so you cannot apply these operators to **EXTRN** objects. For instance, if you declare

```
EXTRN i : WORD
```

you can't use the expressions *LOW i* or *HIGH i* in your Turbo Assembler module.

Using Segment Fixups

Turbo Pascal generates .EXE files, which can be loaded at any available address in your PC's memory. Since the program cannot know in advance where a given segment of your program will be loaded, the linker tells the DOS .EXE loader to fix up all references to segments in your program when it is loaded. After the fixups are done, all references to segments (such as **CODE** and **DATA**) contain the correct values.

Your Turbo Assembler code can use this facility to obtain the segment addresses of objects at run time. For instance, suppose your program needs to change the value of DS, but you don't want to spend the cycles required to save the original contents on the stack or move them to a temporary location. Instead, you can use the Turbo Assembler **SEG** operator as follows:

```
        .
        .
        .
mov ax,SEG DATA    ;get the actual address of Turbo Pascal's global DS
mov ds,ax          ;put it in DS for Turbo Pascal to use
        .
        .
        .
```

When your Turbo program is loaded, DOS will plug the correct value for **SEG DATA** right into the immediate operand field of the **MOV** instruction. This is the fastest way to reload the segment register.

This technique is also necessary to allow interrupt service routines to save information in Turbo Pascal's global data segment. DS will not necessarily contain Turbo Pascal's DS at interrupt time, but the preceding sequence can be used to gain access to Turbo Pascal variables and typed constants.

Dead Code Elimination

Turbo Pascal features *dead code elimination,* which means that it does not include code for routines that are never executed when it writes the final .EXE file. But, because it does not have complete information about the contents of your Turbo Assembler modules, Turbo Pascal can only perform limited optimization on them.

Turbo Pascal will eliminate the code of an .OBJ module *if and only if* no calls are made to any visible procedure or function in that module. Conversely, if any routine in the module is referenced, the entire module stays.

To make the most efficient use of Turbo's dead code elimination feature, it's a good idea to break up your assembly language into small modules with only a few routines each. Doing so will allow Turbo to "trim the fat" from your finished program, if it can.

Turbo Pascal Parameter-Passing Conventions

Turbo Pascal passes parameters using the CPU's stack (or, in the case of single, double, extended, or comp value parameters, the numeric processor's stack). Parameters are always evaluated and pushed on the stack in the order they appear in the declaration of the subprogram, from left to right. In this section, we'll explain how these parameters are represented.

Value Parameters

A *value parameter* is a parameter whose value cannot be changed by the subprogram to which it is passed. Unlike many compilers, Turbo Pascal does not blindly copy every value parameter onto the CPU stack; the method used depends on the type, as we explain in this and the next few pages.

Scalar Types

Value parameters of all the scalar types (boolean, char, shortInt, byte, integer, word, longInt, subrange types, and enumerated types) are passed as values on the CPU stack. If an object is 1 byte in size, it is pushed as a full 16-bit word; however, the most-significant byte of that word contains no useful information. (This byte cannot be relied on to be 0, as it could in Turbo Pascal versions 3.0 and earlier.) If the object is 2 bytes in size, it is simply pushed as is. If the object is 4 bytes long (a longInt), it is pushed as two 16-bit words. As is standard on the 8088 family of processors, the most-significant word is pushed first and occupies the higher address on the stack.

Note that the comp type, while an integer type, is not considered to be a scalar type for the purposes of parameter-passing. Thus, in Turbo Pascal 4.0, value parameters of this type are passed on the 8087 stack, not the CPU stack. In Turbo Pascal 5.0, values of the comp type are passed on the main CPU stack.

Reals

Value parameters of the type real (Turbo Pascal's 6-byte software floating-point type) are passed as 6 bytes on the stack. This is the only type larger than 4 bytes that is ever passed on the stack.

Single, Double, Extended, and Comp: The 8087 Types

In Turbo Pascal 4.0, value parameters of the 8087 types are passed on the coprocessor stack, not the CPU stack. Since the 8087 stack is only eight levels deep, a Turbo Pascal 4.0 subprogram cannot have more than eight 8087-type value parameters. All 8087-type parameters must be popped from the numeric processor stack before the subprogram returns.

Turbo Pascal 5.0 uses the same parameter-passing conventions for 8087 values as Turbo C does: They are passed on the main CPU stack with the other parameters.

Pointers

Value parameters of all pointer types are pushed directly on the stack as far pointers—first a word containing the segment, then another containing the offset. The segment occupies the higher address, in accordance with Intel conventions. Your Turbo Assembler program can use the **LDS** or **LES** instruction to retrieve a pointer parameter.

Strings

String parameters, regardless of size, are usually never pushed on the stack. Instead, Turbo Pascal pushes a far pointer to the string. It's the responsibility of the called subprogram not to change the string referenced by the pointer; the subprogram must make and work on a copy of the string, if necessary.

The only exception to this rule is when a routine in overlaid unit *A*, passes a string constant as a value parameter to a routine in overlaid unit *B*. In this context, an overlaid unit means any unit compiled with {$O+} (**Overlays Allowed**). In this case, temporary storage is reserved on the stack for the string constant before the call is made and the stack address is passed to the routine in unit *B*. For more information, refer to Chapter 6, "Overlays," in the *Turbo Pascal User's Guide* (5.0).

Records and Arrays

Records and arrays that are exactly 1, 2, or 4 bytes long are duplicated directly onto the stack when passed as value parameters. If an array or record object is any other size (including 3 bytes), a pointer to it is pushed instead. In the case of records and arrays that aren't 1, 2, or 4 bytes long, the subprogram must make a local copy of the structure if it modifies it.

Sets

Sets, like strings, are usually never pushed verbatim on the stack. Instead, a pointer to the set is pushed. The pointer received by the subprogram will point to a "normalized" 32 byte representation of the set. The first bit of the lowest byte of this set will always correspond to the element of the base type (or its parent type) with the ordinal value 0.

The only exception to this rule is when a routine in overlaid unit *A*, passes a set constant as a value parameter to a routine in overlaid unit *B*. In this context, an overlaid unit means any unit compiled with {$O+} (**Overlays Allowed**). In this case, temporary storage is reserved on the stack for the set constant before the call is made and the stack address is passed to the routine in unit B. For more information, refer to Chapter 6, "Overlays," in the *Turbo Pascal User's Guide* (5.0).

Variable Parameters

All **var** parameters are passed exactly the same way: as far pointers to their actual locations in memory.

Stack Maintenance

Turbo Pascal expects that all parameters on the main CPU stack will be removed before a subprogram returns.

There are two ways to adjust the stack. You can use the **RET N** instruction (where *N* is the number of bytes of parameters pushed), or you can save the return address in registers (or in memory) and pop the parameters off one by one. The popping technique is useful when optimizing for speed on the 8086 and 8088 (the slowest processors in the family), where base-plus-offset addressing costs eight cycles (minimum) per access. It can also save space, since a **POP** instruction only takes a single byte.

Note: If you use the **.MODEL, PROC,** and **ARG** directives, the assembler will automatically add the number of parameter bytes to be popped to all **RET** instructions.

Accessing Parameters

When your Turbo Assembler routine receives control, the top of the stack will contain a return address (two or four words, depending on whether the routine is near or far) and, above it, any parameters being passed. **Note:** When computing the locations of parameters, remember to take into account any registers, such as BP, whose contents you might have pushed.

There are three basic techniques for accessing the parameters passed to your Turbo Assembler routine by Turbo Pascal. You can

- use the BP register to address the stack
- use another base or index register to get the parameters
- pop the return address, then pop the parameters

The first and second techniques are more complicated, and we cover them in the next two sections. The third technique involves popping the return address into a safe place and then popping the parameters into registers.

This technique works best when your routine does not require any local variable space.

Using BP to Address the Stack

The first (and most often used) technique for accessing the parameters passed from Turbo Pascal to Turbo Assembler is to use the BP register to address the stack, like this:

```
CODE     SEGMENT
         ASSUME cs:CODE
MyProc   PROC FAR                 ;procedure MyProc(i,j : integer);
         PUBLIC MyProc
j        EQU WORD PTR [bp+6]      ;j above saved BP and return address
i        EQU WORD PTR [bp+8]      ;i just above j
         push bp                  ;must preserve caller's BP
         mov  bp,sp               ;make BP point to the top of the stack
         mov  ax,i                ;address i via BP
         .
         .
         .
```

When computing the stack offsets of parameters to be accessed in this way, remember to allow 2 bytes for the saved BP register.

Note the use of *text equates* for the parameters in this example. These help to make the code more mnemonic. They have but one minor drawback: Because only the **EQU** directive can be used to do this kind of equate (not the = directive), you will not be able to redefine the symbols *i* and *j* again in the same Turbo Assembler source file. One way to get around this is to use more descriptive parameter names so that they do not repeat; another is to assemble each routine separately.

The ARG Directive

When you access your parameters via the BP register, however, Turbo Assembler provides an alternative to calculating stack offsets and performing text equates—the **ARG** directive. When used inside a **PROC**, the **ARG** directive automatically determines the offsets of the parameters relative to BP. It also calculates the size of the parameter block for use in the **RET** instruction. Because the symbols created by the **ARG** directive are only defined within the surrounding **PROC**, you do not need unique parameter names for each procedure or function.

Here's how the preceding example looks when rewritten with the **ARG** directive:

```
CODE    SEGMENT
        ASSUME cs:CODE
MyProc  PROC    FAR             ;procedure MyProc(i,j : integer); external;
        PUBLIC MyProc
        ARG j : WORD, i: WORD = RetBytes
        push bp                 ;must preserve caller's BP
        mov  bp,sp              ;make BP point to the top of the stack
        mov  ax,i               ;address i via BP
        .
        .
        .
```

Turbo Assembler's **ARG** directive creates local symbols for the parameters
i and *j*. The line

```
ARG j: WORD, i : WORD = RetBytes
```

automatically equates the symbol *i* to **[WORD PTR BP+6]**, the symbol *j* to
[WORD PTR BP+8], and the symbol *RetBytes* to the number 4 (the size in
bytes of the parameter block) for the duration of the procedure. The values
take into account both the pushed BP and the size of the return address; if
MyProc were a **NEAR PROC**, *i* would have been equated to [*BP+4*], *j* to
[*BP+6*], and *RetBytes* would still have contained the value 4 (so that, in
either case, *MyProc* could end with the instruction **RET** *RetBytes*).

When using the **ARG** directive, remember to list the parameters in reverse
order. You would place the *last* parameter in the Turbo Pascal procedure (or
function) header *first* in the **ARG** directive, and vice versa.

Another precaution is in order when using the **ARG** directive with Turbo
Pascal. Unlike some other languages, Turbo Pascal always pushes a byte-
sized value parameter as a full 16-bit word—and you are responsible for
telling Turbo Assembler about the extra byte. For instance, suppose you
wrote a function whose Pascal declaration looked like this:

```
function MyProc(i,j : char) : string; external;
```

The **ARG** directive for this procedure would have to look something like
this:

```
ARG j : BYTE : 2, i : BYTE : 2 = RetBytes RETURNS result : DWORD
```

The : 2 after each argument is necessary to tell Turbo Assembler that each
character is pushed as an array of 2 bytes (where, in this case, the upper
byte of each pair holds no useful information).

In a function that returns a string (like the previous one), the **RETURNS**
option in the **ARG** directive lets you define a variable that equates to a
place on the stack that points to the temporary function result (discussed
shortly). The variable in the **RETURNS** portion of **ARG** doesn't affect the

size (in bytes) of the parameter block. See Chapter 3 in the *Reference Guide* for complete information on the **ARG** directive.

.MODEL and Turbo Pascal

The **.MODEL** directive with a parameter of *TPASCAL* sets up simplified segmentation, memory model, and language support. Previously, you've seen how to set up an assembler program for Pascal procedures and functions. Here's the same example recoded to use the **.MODEL** and **PROC** directives:

```
       .MODEL TPASCAL
       .CODE
MyProc PROC   FAR i:BYTE,j:BYTE RETURNS result:DWORD
       PUBLIC MyProc
       mov    ax,i
         .
         .
         .
       ret
```

Notice that now you don't specify the parameters in reverse order and a lot of other statements are not required. Using *TPASCAL* with the **.MODEL** directive sets up Pascal calling conventions, defines the segment names, does the **PUSH BP** and **MOV BP,SP**, and it also sets up the return with **POP BP** and **RET** *N* (where *N* is the number of parameter bytes).

Using Another Base or Index Register

The second way to access parameters is to use another base or index register—BX, SI, or DI—to get them from the stack. Remember, however, that the default segment for these registers is DS, not SS; you will have to use a segment override or change a segment register to use them.

Here's how to use BX to get at your parameters:

```
CODE    SEGMENT
        ASSUME cs:CODE
MyProc  PROC FAR                   ;procedure MyProc(i,j : integer);
          PUBLIC MyProc
j         EQU WORD PTR ss:[bx+4]   ;j above return address
i         EQU WORD PTR ss:[bx+6]   ;i just above j
          mov  bx,sp               ;make BX point to top of stack
```

```
        mov  ax,i                ;address i via BX
          .
          .
          .
```

In routines where a small number of references are made to parameters, this technique saves time and space. Why? Because BX, unlike BP, need not be restored at the end of the routine.

Function Results in Turbo Pascal

Turbo Pascal functions return their results in different ways depending on the result type.

Scalar Function Results

Function results of scalar types are returned in CPU registers. Values of 1 byte are returned in AL, 2-byte values in AX, and 4-byte values in DX:AX (most-significant word in DX).

Real Function Results

Function results of Turbo Pascal's 6-byte software real type are returned in three CPU registers. The most-significant word goes in DX, the middle word in BX, and the least-significant word in AX.

8087 Function Results

Function results of 8087 types are returned in the 8087's "top-of-stack" register, ST(0) (or just ST).

String Function Results

Function results of a string type are returned in a temporary area allocated by Turbo Pascal before the call. A far pointer to this area is pushed on the stack before the first parameter is pushed. Note that this pointer is not part of the parameter list.

Note: Don't remove the function result pointer from the stack, as Turbo Pascal will expect it to be available after the call.

Pointer Function Results

Pointer function results are returned in DX:AX (segment:offset).

Allocating Space for Local Data

Your Turbo Assembler routines can allocate space for their own variables—both *static* (remaining between calls) and *volatile* (disappearing after a call). We'll discuss how to do both in the next two sections.

Allocating Private Static Storage

Turbo Pascal allows your Turbo Assembler program to reserve space for static variables in the global data segment (**DATA**, or **DSEG**). To allocate the space, simply use directives such as DB, DW, and so on, like this:

```
DATA    SEGMENT PUBLIC
MyInt   DW ?              ;Reserve a word
MyByte  DB ?              ;Reserve a byte
  .
  .
  .
DATA    ENDS
```

Two important restrictions apply to variables allocated by Turbo Assembler in the global data segment. First, these variables are "private"—they cannot be made visible to your Turbo Pascal program (though you can pass pointers to them). Second, they can't be pre-initialized, as typed constants are. The statement

```
MyInt  DW 42      ;this will NOT initialize MyInt to 42
```

will not cause an error when the module is linked into your Turbo program, but *MyInt* will not actually start with the value 42 when the program is run.

You can get around these restrictions by declaring Turbo Pascal variables or typed constants and using the **EXTRN** directive to make them visible to Turbo Assembler.

Allocating Volatile Storage

Your Turbo Assembler routines can also allocate volatile storage (local variables) on the stack for the duration of each call. This storage must be reclaimed and the BP register restored before the routine returns. In the following example, the procedure *MyProc* reserves space for two integer variables, *a* and *b*:

```
CODE    SEGMENT
        ASSUME cs:CODE
MyProc  PROC FAR                              ;procedure MyProc(i : Integer);
        PUBLIC MyProc
        LOCAL a : WORD, b : WORD = LocalSpace ;a at [bp-2], b at [bp-4]
i       EQU WORD PTR [bp+6]                   ;parameter i above saved BP
                                              ; and return address
        push bp                               ;must preserve caller's BP
        mov  bp,sp                            ;make BP point to the top
                                              ; of the stack
        sub  sp,LocalSpace                    ;make room for the two words
        mov  ax,42                            ;load A's initial value into AX
        mov  a,ax                             ;and thence into A
        xor  ax,ax                            ;clear AX
        mov  b,ax                             ;and initialize B to 0
        .                                     ;do whatever needs to be done
        .
        .
        mov  sp,bp                            ;this restores the original SP
        pop  bp                               ;this restores the original BP
        ret  2                                ;this pops the word parameter
MyProc  ENDP
CODE    ENDS
        END
```

Note that Turbo Assembler's **LOCAL** directive is used to create symbols and allocate space for local variables. The statement

```
LOCAL a : WORD, b : WORD = LocalSpace
```

equates the symbol *a* to [*BP-2*], the symbol *b* to [*BP-4*], and the symbol *LocalSpace* to the number 4 (the size of the local variable area) for the duration of the procedure. There is no corresponding statement to create symbols that reference parameters, so you must still equate *i* to [*BP+6*].

A more clever way to initialize local variables is to push their values instead of decrementing SP. Thus, you might replace the **SUB SP,** *LocalSpace* with

```
mov  ax,42   ;get the initial value for A
push ax      ;put it in A
xor  ax,ax   ;zero AX
push ax      ;and move the zero into B
```

If you use this method, be sure to keep careful track of the stack! The symbols *a* and *b* should not be referenced before the pushes are performed.

Other optimizations include using the **PUSH CONST** instructions to initialize local variables (available on the 80186, 80286, and 80386), or saving BP in a register instead of pushing it (if there is a register to spare).

Examples of Assembly Language Routines for Turbo Pascal

In this section, we've provided some examples of assembly language routines that you can call from a Turbo Pascal program.

General-Purpose Hex Conversion Routine

The bytes at *num* are converted to a string of hex digits of length (*byteCount* * 2). Since each byte produces two characters, the maximum value of *byteCount* is 127 (not checked). For speed, we use an *add-daa-adc-daa* sequence to convert each nibble to a hex digit (1 nibble equals 4 bits).

HexStr is written to be called with a far call. This means that it should be declared either in the **interface** section of a Turbo Pascal unit or with the $*F*+ compiler directive active.

```
CODE      SEGMENT
          ASSUME cs:CODE,ds:NOTHING

; Parameters (+2 because of push bp)

byteCount EQU BYTE PTR  ss:[bp+6]
num       EQU DWORD PTR ss:[bp+8]

; Function result address (+2 because of push bp)

resultPtr EQU DWORD PTR ss:[bp+12]


HexStr    PROC FAR
          PUBLIC HexStr

          push bp
          mov bp,sp                ;get pointer into stack
          les di,resultPtr         ;get address of function result
          mov dx,ds                ;save Turbo's DS in DX
          lds si,num               ;get number address
          mov al,byteCount         ;how many bytes?
          xor ah,ah                ;make a word
          mov cx,ax                ;keep track of bytes in CX
          add si,ax                ;start from MS byte of number
```

```
            dec si
            shl ax,1                 ;how many digits? (2/byte)
            cld                      ;store # digits (going forward)
            stosb                    ;in destination string's length byte
HexLoop:
            std                      ;scan number from MSB to LSB
            lodsb                    ;get next byte
            mov ah,al                ;save it
            shr al,1                 ;extract high nibble
            shr al,1
            shr al,1
            shr al,1
            add al,90h               ;special hex conversion sequence
            daa                      ;using ADDs and DAA's
            adc al,40h
            daa                      ;nibble now converted to ASCII
            cld                      ;store ASCII going up
            stosb
            mov al,ah                ;repeat conversion for low nibble
            and al,0Fh
            add al,90h
            daa
            adc al,40h
            daa
            stosb
            loop HexLoop             ;keep going until done
            mov ds,dx                ;restore Turbo's DS
            pop bp
            ret 6                    ;parameters take 6 bytes
HexStr      ENDP
CODE        ENDS
            END
```

The sample Pascal program that uses *HexStr* follows:

```
program HexTest;
var
  num : word;

{$F+}

function HexStr (var num; byteCount : byte) : string; external;

{$L HEXSTR.OBJ}

{$F-}
begin
  num := $face;
  Writeln('The Converted Hex String is "',HexStr(num,sizeof(num)),'"');
end.
```

Use the following batch file commands to build and run the example Pascal and assembly program:

```
TASM HEXSTR
TPC HEXTEST
HEXTEST
```

If you use the **.MODEL** directive, the program *HexStr* could be written like this:

```
        .MODEL   TPASCAL
        .CODE
HexStr  PROC FAR num:DWORD,byteCount:BYTE RETURNS resultPtr:DWORD
        PUBLIC HexStr
        les di,resultPtr        ;get address of function result
        mov dx,ds               ;save Turbo's DS in DX
        lds si,num              ;get number address
        mov al,byteCount        ;how many bytes?
        xor ah,ah               ;make a word
        mov cx,ax               ;keep track of bytes in CX
        add si,ax               ;start from MS byte of number
        dec si
        shl ax,1                ;how many digits? (2/byte)
        cld                     ;store # digits (going forward)
        stosb                   ;in destination string's length byte
HexLoop:
        std                     ;scan number from MSB to LSB
        lodsb                   ;get next byte
        mov ah,al               ;save it
        shr al,1                ;extract high nibble
        shr al,1
        shr al,1
        shr al,1
        add al,90h              ;special hex conversion sequence
        daa                     ;using ADDs and DAA's
        adc al,40h
        daa                     ;nibble now converted to ASCII
        cld                     ;store ASCII going up
        stosb
        mov al,ah               ;repeat conversion for low nibble
        and al,0Fh
        add al,90h
        daa
        adc al,40h
        daa
        stosb
        loop HexLoop            ;keep going until done
        mov ds,dx               ;restore Turbo's DS
        ret
HexStr  ENDP
```

```
CODE      ENDS
          END
```

You can use the same sample Pascal program and just assemble the
alternative *HexStr*, recompiling the sample program with the same batch
file commands.

Exchanging Two Variables

With this procedure, you can exchange two variables of size *count*. If *count*
is 0, the processor will attempt to exchange 64K.

```
CODE      SEGMENT
          ASSUME cs:CODE,ds:NOTHING

; Parameters (note that offset are +2 because of push bp)

var1      EQU    DWORD PTR ss:[bp+12]
var2      EQU    DWORD PTR ss:[bp+8]
count     EQU    WORD PTR  ss:[bp+6]


Exchange  PROC FAR
          PUBLIC Exchange
          cld                            ;exchange goes upward
          mov    dx,ds                   ;save DS
          push   bp
          mov    bp,sp                   ;get stack base
          lds    si,var1                 ;get first address
          les    di,var2                 ;get second address
          mov    cx,count                ;get number of bytes to move
          shr    cx,1                    ;get word count (low bit -> carry)
          jnc    ExchangeWords           ;if no odd byte, enter loop
          mov    al,es:[di]              ;read odd byte from var2
          movsb                          ;move a byte from var1 to var2
          mov    [si-1],al               ;write var2 byte to var1
          jz     Finis                   ;done if only one byte to exchange
ExchangeWords:
          mov    bx,-2                   ;BX is a handy place to keep -2
ExchangeLoop:
          mov    ax,es:[di]              ;read a word from var2
          movsw                          ;do a move from var1 to var2
          mov    [bx][si],ax             ;write var2 word to var1
          loop   ExchangeLoop            ;repeat "count div 2" times
Finis:
          mov    ds,dx                   ;get back Turbo's DS
          pop    bp
          ret    10
Exchange  ENDP
```

```
CODE     ENDS
         END
```

The sample Pascal program that uses *Exchange* follows:

```pascal
program TextExchange;

type
  EmployeeRecord = record
                     Name    : string[30];
                     Address : string[30];
                     City    : string[15];
                     State   : string[2];
                     Zip     : string[10];
                   end;
var
  OldEmployee, NewEmployee : EmployeeRecord;

{$F+}

procedure Exchange(var var1,var2; count : word); external;
{$L XCHANGE.OBJ}
{$F-}
begin
  with OldEmployee do
  begin
    Name := 'John Smith';
    Address := '123 F Street';
    City := 'Scotts Valley';
    State := 'CA';
    Zip := '90000-0000';
  end;
  with NewEmployee do
  begin
    Name := 'Mary Jones';
    Address := '9471 41st Avenue';
    City := 'New York';
    State := 'NY';
    Zip := '10000-1111';
  end;
  Writeln('Before: ',OldEmployee.Name,'  ',NewEmployee.Name);
  Exchange(OldEmployee,NewEmployee,sizeof(OldEmployee));
  Writeln('After:  ',OldEmployee.Name,'  ',NewEmployee.Name);
  Exchange(OldEmployee,NewEmployee,sizeof(OldEmployee));
  Writeln('After:  ',OldEmployee.Name,'  ',NewEmployee.Name);
end.
```

To build and run the example Pascal and assembler program, use the following batch file commands:

```
        TASM XCHANGE
        TPC XCHANGE
        XCHANGE
```

Using the **.MODEL** directive, the *Exchange* assembly language program
would be written as

```
                .MODEL  TPASCAL
                .CODE
Exchange    PROC FAR var1:DWORD,var2:DWORD,count:WORD
                PUBLIC Exchange;
                cld                              ;exchange goes upward
                mov     dx,ds                    ;save DS
                lds     si,var1                  ;get first address
                les     di,var2                  ;get second address
                mov     cx,count                 ;get number of bytes to move
                shr     cx,1                     ;get word count (low bit -> carry)
                jnc     ExchangeWords            ;if no odd byte, enter loop
                mov     al,es:[di]               ;read odd byte from var2
                movsb                            ;move a byte from var1 to var2
                mov     [si-1],al                ;write var2 byte to var1
                jz      Finis                    ;done if only one byte to exchange
ExchangeWords:
                mov     bx,-2                    ;BX is a handy place to keep -2
ExchangeLoop:
                mov     ax,es:[di]               ;read a word from var2
                movsw                            ;do a move from var1 to var2
                mov     [bx][si],ax              ;write var2 word to var1
                loop    ExchangeLoop             ;repeat "count div 2" times
Finis:
                mov     ds,dx                    ;get back Turbo's DS
                ret
Exchange    ENDP
CODE        ENDS
                END
```

You can use the same sample Pascal program and just assemble the
alternative *Exchange*, recompiling the sample program with the same batch
file commands.

Scanning the DOS Environment

With the *EnvString* function, you can scan the DOS environment for a
string of the form *"s=SOMESTRING"* and return *SOMESTRING* if it is
found.

```
DATA        SEGMENT PUBLIC
                EXTRN prefixSeg : WORD        ;gives location of PSP
```

```
DATA        ENDS
CODE        SEGMENT PUBLIC
            ASSUME cs:CODE,ds:DATA

EnvString PROC FAR
            PUBLIC  EnvString
            push    bp
            cld                              ;work upward
            mov     es,[prefixSeg]           ;look at PSP
            mov     es,es:[2Ch]              ;ES:DI points at environment
            xor     di,di                    ;which is paragraph-aligned
            mov     bp,sp                    ;find the parameter address
            lds     si,ss:[bp+6]             ;which is right above the return address
            ASSUME ds:NOTHING
            lodsb                            ;look at length
            or      al,al                    ;is it zero?
            jz      RetNul                   ;if so, return
            mov     ah,al                    ;otherwise, save in AH
            mov     dx,si                    ;DS:DX contains pointer
                                             ; to first parm char
            xor     al,al                    ;make a zero
Compare:
            mov     ch,al                    ;we want ch=0 for next count, if any
            mov     si,dx                    ;get back pointer to string sought
            mov     cl,ah                    ;get length
            mov     si,dx                    ;get pointer to string sought
            repe    cmpsb                    ;compare bytes
            jne     Skip                     ;if compare fails, try next string
            cmp     byte ptr es:[di],'='     ;compare succeeded. Is next char '='?
            jne     NoEqual                  ;if not, still no match
Found:
            mov     ax,es                    ;make DS:SI point to string we found
            mov     ds,ax
            mov     si,di
            inc     si                       ;get past the equal (=) sign
            les     bx,ss:[bp+10]            ;get address of function result
            mov     di,bx                    ;put it in ES:DI
            inc     di                       ;get past the length byte
            mov     cl,255                   ;set up a maximum length
CopyLoop:
            lodsb                            ;get a byte
            or      al,al                    ;zero test
            jz      Done                     ;if zero, we're done
            stosb                            ;put it in the result
            loop    CopyLoop                 ;move up to 255 bytes
Done:       not     cl                       ;we've been decrementing CL from
                                             ; 255 during save
            mov     es:[bx],cl               ;save the length
            mov     ax,SEG DATA
```

```
            mov     ds,ax               ;restore DS
            ASSUME  ds:DATA
            pop     bp
            ret     4
            ASSUME  ds:NOTHING
Skip:
            dec     di                  ;check for null from this char on
NoEqual:
            mov     cx,7FFFh            ;search a long way if necessary
            sub     cx,di               ;environment never >32K
            jbe     RetNul              ;if we're past end, leave
            repne   scasb               ;look for the next null
            jcxz    RetNul              ;exit if not found
            cmp     byte ptr es:[di],al ;second null in a row?
            jne     Compare             ;if not, try again
RetNul:
            les     di,ss:[bp+10]       ;get address of result
            stosb                       ;store a zero there
            mov     ax,SEG DATA
            mov     ds,ax               ;restore DS
            ASSUME  ds:DATA
            pop     bp
            ret     4
EnvString ENDP
CODE        ENDS
            END
```

The sample Pascal program that uses *EnvString* follows:

```
program EnvTest;
{ program looks for environment strings }

var
  EnvVariable : string;
  EnvValue : string;

{$F+}

function EnvString(s:string) : string; external;
{$L ENVSTR.OBJ}
{$F-}
begin
  EnvVariable := 'PROMPT';
  EnvValue := EnvString(EnvVariable);
  if EnvValue='' then EnvValue := '*** not found ***';
  Writeln('Environment Variable: ',EnvVariable,'  Value: ',EnvValue);
end.
```

To build and run the example Pascal and assembler program, use the following batch file commands:

```
TASM ENVSTR
TPC ENVTEST
ENVTEST
```

If you used the **.MODEL** directive, the *EnvString* assembly language program would be written like this:

```
          .MODEL  TPASCAL
          .DATA
          EXTRN prefixSeg : WORD         ;gives location of PSP
          .CODE
EnvString PROC FAR  EnvVar:DWORD  RETURNS EnvVal:DWORD
          PUBLIC  EnvString
          cld                            ;work upward
          mov     es,[prefixSeg]         ;look at PSP
          mov     es,es:[2Ch]            ;ES:DI points at environment
          xor     di,di                  ;which is paragraph-aligned
          mov     bp,sp                  ;find the parameter address
          lds     si,EnvVar              ;which is right above the return address
          ASSUME  ds:NOTHING
          lodsb                          ;look at length
          or      al,al                  ;is it zero?
          jz      RetNul                 ;if so, return
          mov     ah,al                  ;otherwise, save in AH
          mov     dx,si                  ;DS:DX contains pointer to
                                         ; first parm char
          xor     al,al                  ;make a zero
Compare:
          mov     ch,al                  ;we want ch=0 for next count, if any
          mov     si,dx                  ;get back pointer to string sought
          mov     cl,ah                  ;get length
          mov     si,dx                  ;get pointer to string sought
          repe    cmpsb                  ;compare bytes
          jne     Skip                   ;if compare fails, try next string
          cmp     byte ptr es:[di],'='   ;compare succeeded. Is next char '='?
          jne     NoEqual                ;if not, still no match
Found:
          mov     ax,es                  ;make DS:SI point to string we found
          mov     ds,ax
          mov     si,di
          inc     si                     ;get past the equal (=) sign
          les     bx,EnvVal              ;get address of function result
          mov     di,bx                  ;put it in ES:DI
          inc     di                     ;get past the length byte
          mov     cl,255                 ;set up a maximum length
CopyLoop:
          lodsb                          ;get a byte
          or      al,al                  ;zero test
          jz      Done                   ;if zero, we're done
          stosb                          ;put it in the result
```

```
        loop    CopyLoop            ;move up to 255 bytes
Done:   not     cl                  ;we've been decrementing CL from
                                    ; 255 during save
        mov     es:[bx],cl          ;save the length
        mov     ax,SEG DATA
        mov     ds,ax               ;restore DS
        ASSUME  ds:DATA
        ret
        ASSUME  ds:NOTHING
Skip:
        dec     di                  ;check for null from this char on
NoEqual:
        mov     cx,7FFFh            ;search a long way if necessary
        sub     cx,di               ;environment never >32K
        jbe     RetNul              ;if we're past end, leave
        repne   scasb               ;look for the next null
        jcxz    RetNul              ;exit if not found
        cmp     byte ptr es:[di],al ;second null in a row?
        jne     Compare             ;if not, try again
RetNul:
        les     di,EnvVal           ;get address of result
        stosb                       ;store a zero there
        mov     ax,SEG DATA
        mov     ds,ax               ;restore DS
        ASSUME  ds:DATA
        ret
EnvString ENDP
CODE    ENDS
        END
```

You can use the same sample Pascal program and just assemble the alternative *EnvString*, recompiling the sample program with the same batch file commands.

8

Interfacing Turbo Assembler with Turbo Basic

Turbo Assembler's upward compatibility with Microsoft's Macro Assembler makes life easier for the Turbo Basic programmer. In this chapter, we'll expand on some Turbo Basic examples currently in the Turbo Basic manual and supply others that illustrate how Turbo Assembler can extend the power of Turbo Basic.

Note: When we refer to Turbo Basic, we mean versions 1.0 and greater.

Turbo Basic provides three general ways to call an assembler routine:

- You can use CALL to call a procedure containing inline code.
- You can use CALL ABSOLUTE to a particular address in memory.
- You can use CALL INTERRUPT and Turbo Basic's support for the processor's interrupt-handling to branch to a routine.

Whichever calling method you select, you must be sure to preserve the values of certain registers. CALL INTERRUPT is the least demanding in this respect: You need only be sure to save SS (stack segment) and SP (stack pointer). The other two methods require that you save the DS (data segment) and BP (base pointer) registers, as well as SS and SP.

"Preserving the registers" doesn't necessarily mean you must push all the registers on the stack, though that is the most typical way of ensuring their safety. Simple routines might not modify any of the registers, in which case, you *might* not need to take any precautions.

We use the word "might" because it's generally a very good idea to avoid making assumptions, especially where assembler programming is concerned. Though your MS-DOS manual might specifically state that a particular interrupt will not alter the contents of the stack pointer or base pointer (or any one of the other registers), that might not always be the case. MS-DOS does change, and some combinations of interrupts might contradict the information in the MS-DOS manual. It's better to be safe than sorry under such circumstances. Taking care to save the required registers will not adversely affect the performance of your routine, considering the risks and added portability for new releases of MS-DOS.

Passing Parameters

Turbo Basic passes parameters to assembler routines on the stack. All such calls are far; the last 4 bytes on the stack are the return address used by Turbo Basic when your routine is finished. The address of the first parameter you pass to your routine will be at [SP+4]; add two to that value for each register you push on the stack. Remember, stacks grow downward in memory to lower-numbered addresses.

Each simple variable (other than arrays) passed on the stack will cause the stack to grow by 4 bytes; Turbo Basic passes both the segment (2 bytes) and the offset (2 bytes) of such variables. This will be an important advantage later, as you will see.

Parameters passed by value (as in constants and expressions) also take precisely 4 bytes on the stack. In this case, the value on the stack is not the value of the expression: It is the address of the temporary location in memory where the value is stored. This may seem roundabout, but it has two appreciable advantages. First, all assembler routines can handle passed values in precisely the same way. Second, routines that modify the value of a parameter mistakenly passed by value instead of by reference cannot alter an important area of memory.

This way of using the stack can increase the standardization of your routines. The following example shows why this is advantageous. Suppose the value of the integer variable x% is precisely 4, and you have an assembler routine MYROUTINE that expects an integer to be passed. This routine will work exactly the same whether you invoke it with CALL MYROUTINE(x%) or CALL MYROUTINE(4%). If the routine were invoked with CALL MYROUTINE(4%) and tried to modify the value of the passed parameter, it would modify an area of memory where the integer value 4 was temporarily stored and no harm would be done.

Note that the type was explicitly stated in the second case (4%). This is not absolutely necessary, though it is good practice. If Turbo Basic happened to assume that the value 4 is a single-precision number, your routine will use a bad value (2 bytes from a 4-byte, single-precision number) and run incorrectly. To make sure that your routines are passed the correct variable type, it is best to indicate the type of the variables or values every time the routine is invoked.

If you pass an array to a routine, the stack will grow by 60 bytes—most of the information that's passed to you is probably irrelevant. The Turbo Basic manual recommends that you pass the relevant array parameters as integers instead of passing the entire array. Passing a few selected parameters rather than the whole array will save stack space, decrease the time needed to call your routine, and make your routine more portable to later versions of Turbo Basic.

For example, suppose you have a simple routine that needs to push only the base pointer, BP. In that case, the value or address of the first parameter will be at [SP+6]. If you had pushed two registers, the address or value of the first parameter would be at [SP+8].

Let's suppose the first parameter is an integer value and is passed by value to the assembler routine. In that case, you can put the integer value into the CX register by simply writing

```
push bp              ;save the base pointer
mov  bp,sp           ;make the base pointer equal the stack pointer
les  di,[bp+6]       ;ES contains the segment, DI the offset of the value
mov  cx,es:[di]      ;now put the value into CX
```

Note: The value will not be in the same segment as ordinary variables. You must take care to use the correct and complete address to access the value. We'll say more about variables that are not in the current data segment later.

On the other hand, if you knew the integer variable had been passed by reference instead of by value, [BP+6] would contain the offset address of the variable within its data segment. To put the value of that integer into the CX register you could write

```
push bp              ;save the base pointer
mov  bp,sp           ;make the base pointer equal the stack pointer
mov  bx,[bp+6]       ;put the address of the value in BX
mov  cx,[bx]         ;put the passed value into CX
```

This routine assumes that the variable is located in the current data segment, and that only the variable's offset within that segment is needed to update the variable's value.

Passing variables is safer if you always assume the pass is done by value. If the variable is actually passed by reference, you will have lost nothing; the complete variable address will include the current data segment. On the other hand, if your routine assumes that the variable was passed by reference and it was not, the address you obtain will not be the correct complete address because the segment will be wrong. Therefore, the routine will either retrieve the wrong value or, if you attempt to alter the value of the passed variable, will alter an incorrect area of memory with unpredictable results.

Passing variables by reference is much easier for variables such as strings, arrays, and floating-point numbers. Those variables can be long enough to cause problems if they were actually passed on the stack. In addition, it takes nearly as much overhead to read a long variable from the stack as to obtain its address from the stack and manipulate the variable at a memory location. For string variables (unless the string is very short, indeed) it's unlikely there would be enough register space available to process the string without performing memory accesses anyway.

Variables Not in the Current Data Segment

If the variable passed is not in the current data segment, then you'll need both the segment and the offset of the variable to access the value of the variable within your assembler program. Turbo Basic always passes both the segment and the offset of each variable on the stack; therefore, the complete address of each variable is always available to the programmer.

The segment part of the address is in the 2 bytes immediately following the offset of the parameter. The most convenient way to use this information in your assembler programs is via the instruction **LES**.

LES will load the indicated register with the offset value of the variable and load the ES register with the segment part of the address. This guarantees you the full address of any variable, regardless of which data segment it is in.

Again, suppose your routine needs to store the value of an integer variable into the CX register. Since the ES register needn't be preserved, you can make use of **LES**:

```
push bp           ;save the base pointer
mov  bp,sp        ;make the base pointer equal the stack pointer
les  di,[bp+6]    ;ES contains the segment, DI the offset
mov  cx,es:[di]   ;put the value of the variable in CX
```

By passing the complete address of each variable, Turbo Basic makes it possible for the assembler programmer to write routines that are independent of where the data is stored. If you rewrite your program and put variables or arrays into different data segments, you won't need to rewrite your assembler routines if you use the complete variable address and the **LES** instruction.

What Kind of CALL?

There are two kinds of CALLs: *far* and *near*. Far CALLs leave the current code segment; near CALLs do not.

In Turbo Basic, only CALL ABSOLUTE can cause any problems because it can be located anywhere in memory. Therefore, Turbo Basic requires CALL ABSOLUTE routines to terminate with a far return, and automatically generates a far CALL when passing control to such routines.

CALL INTERRUPT can implicitly generate a far call, but Turbo Basic handles that internally. If you have written your own interrupt handlers, you only need to use an **IRET** (return from interrupt) instruction to pass control back to the Turbo Basic program.

Inline assembler is inserted into your program when it is compiled. The code will generally be within the current code segment, but Turbo Basic doesn't assume that; such routines also terminate with a far return. Turbo Basic will automatically generate the CALL and the return, so don't use a **RET** instruction in your code. If you want to terminate the routine somewhere before the end of the code, simply jump to a label at the end of the code.

Note: Since Turbo Basic doesn't use the DOS LINK program, you won't need to concern yourself with declaring your routines **PUBLIC**, nor will you need to declare them external within your program.

Popping the Stack

Before the end of your routine, you should make sure that all the registers you have pushed onto the stack have been popped from the stack. It's easy to make a mistake in this area, especially if your routine conditionally **PUSH**es and **POP**s registers.

If you pop too few registers, your routine will probably never return after it is called, since Turbo Basic assumes that the last item on the stack is the address to which it should return. If you pop too many, the same thing will probably happen.

Don't load or pop trash values into the segment registers because this can make your source code incompatible with future versions of DOS (protected mode OS/2, for example).

Creating an Assembler Program for Turbo Basic

If you have created an assembler program and want to convert it into a .COM file for use in a Turbo Basic program, you can still use the example batch file in the Turbo Basic manual:

```
TASM %1;
Tlink /t %1;
```

You should not include a stack segment because the assembler routine will use the stack furnished by Turbo Basic when running anyway.

Turbo Assembler will default to a starting address of 100h if you do not provide an explicit **ORG 100h** statement at the beginning of your program. Still, it is better to explicitly state the **ORG** for later reference.

If your routine is intended to run on an 80186, 80286, or 80386 processor, you can also use the **.186**, **.286**, and **.386** directives at the beginning of your assembler code. Turbo Assembler will then allow you to use opcodes applicable for those processors. This can be a very big advantage, as you will see.

CALLing an Inline Assembler Procedure

Suppose you have created an assembler routine and converted it into a .COM file with Turbo Assembler. There are two ways you can use the result within your Turbo Basic program: with the $INLINE COM directive or with the $INCLUDE directive.

The most direct way is to use the `$INLINE COM filename` method and have Turbo Basic insert the .COM file in the place you've indicated. This method is relatively simple to implement, but has several disadvantages:

- Turbo Basic has a limit of 16 $INLINE directives per procedure. This can cause problems if you're doing something rather complex (but it's rather unlikely).

- A more serious problem comes from the fact that the .COM files do not include documentation. You can include remarks in the calling program, of course, but it would be better if the .COM file included some documentation of its own.

- $INLINE .COM files can proliferate, too. Placing several of them in one file would be useful, especially if you often use a number of them together. (That's one of the reasons for using a library of assembler routines; unfortunately, it's not easy to create a library of .COM files.)

- Finally, $INLINE .COM files must be modified and reassembled if you alter them. This can be aggravating if the changes are relatively minor.

Because of the way $INCLUDE COM works, you might want to convert the .COM files into a sequence of hexadecimal numbers that you can insert into programs via the $INCLUDE directive. Such routines can also be read from disk using the Turbo Basic editor's Read File command (*Ctrl-K R*); that way, your source file will explicitly show what is being included. This can be a big advantage for the Turbo Basic programmer.

Since the hexadecimal codes are editable text, you can include or add comments. You can also use the Turbo Basic editor to make small changes in the inline code without having to re-assemble it, and you can put several routines into one file. By combining these techniques, you can effectively create a library of assembler routines for use with a family of programs. You might be able to maintain such a library more easily than if you had a formal library manager.

If the routine is very long, the hexadecimal code file will be very large and might make the source file too large to edit comfortably. There is a limit of 64 Kb on the largest file you can edit in one piece. If that becomes a problem, you can incorporate the hexadecimal file in your program as an $INCLUDE file. (Something that large wouldn't make your program more readable anyway.)

Here is a small Turbo Basic program that will convert .COM files into hexadecimal files:

```
'COM2INC.BAS
'This program converts COM files to $INCLUDE files with the Turbo
'Basic $INLINE meta-command for easy insertion in Basic programs.
DEFINT A-Z
'All variables will be integers
F$=COMMAND$
'Check to see if there's a command line
WHILE F$=""
  PRINT"This program will convert COM files to $INCLUDE files"
  PRINT"for use with Turbo Basic. The default file type of"
  PRINT"the source file is COM. The default file type of the"
  PRINT"output file is INC. You may override either default"
  PRINT"by entering a specific file-type specification."
  PRINT"If you enter no name for the output file, it will be"
  PRINT"named the same as the input file, but will have a file"
  PRINT"type specification of INC."
  LINE INPUT"Enter the name of the file to convert: ";F$
WEND
```

```
IF COMMAND$="" THEN
   LINE INPUT"Enter the name of the desired output file: ";O$
END IF

IF INSTR(F$,".")=0 THEN F$=F$+".COM"      'fix input spec
IF O$="" THEN
   O$=LEFT$(F$,INSTR(F$,".")))+"INC"       'fix output spec,
   ELSE
      IF INSTR(O$,".")=0 THEN O$=O$+".INC"  'both ways
END IF

OPEN"R",#1,F$,1        'input file will be read one byte
FIELD #1,1 AS A$       'at a time into A$

LASTBYTE&=LOF(1)        'end of file position
OPEN"O",2, O$           'output file is opened
FOR I&=1 TO LASTBYTE&-1
   GET 1,I&
   X%=ASC(A$)
   IF ((I&-1) MOD 5=0) THEN PRINT #2,"":PRINT #2,"$INLINE ";
   PRINT #2,"&H";HEX$(X%);
   IF ((I&-1) MOD 5<>4) THEN PRINT #2,",";
NEXT I&
GET 1,LASTBYTE&
PRINT #2,"&H";HEX$(ASC(A$))
PRINT"Conversion complete. ";LASTBYTE&;" bytes read."
PRINT O$;" contains ";LOF(2);" bytes."
CLOSE
END
```

This program will output a file with up to five hex codes per line. Each line will begin with the $INLINE directive, and the resulting file should have enough room in it for comments you might want to add. If you want to put more or fewer hex codes on a single line, you need only change the references to MOD 5 to MOD *N*, where *N* is greater or less than 5.

If you want to make small changes to the routines you have written and converted to hex codes, you should be able to do so without having to recreate the whole routine from scratch, provided the changes are small enough and your documentation is complete.

Locating A Turbo Basic Routine in Memory

There are three general ways of finding the location of a routine in memory:

■ You can have the routine itself return its address.

- You can group a series of routines together and have a single routine return an address applicable for all of them.
- You can look for a special sequence of bytes within the computer's memory.

To create a routine that will return its address, you could use code similar to the following:

```
xy:  mov  ax,cs            ;move the code segment register to AX
     push bp               ;save the base pointer
     mov  bp,sp            ;and copy the stack pointer into BP
     les  di,[bp+6]        ;ES contains the segment, DI the offset
     mov  es:[di],ax       ;store the CS value to first parameter
     mov  dx, offset xy    ;get the current offset
     les  di,[bp+0ah]      ;address of second parameter
     mov  es:[di],dx       ;store offset value to second parameter
     jmp  fin              ;jump around "real" code
                           ;real code would be here
fin: pop  bp              ;restore BP and return
```

You will need to pass two integers to this routine's variables; it will return the code segment in the first and the offset in the second. The problem: All that code is useless after it has been used once. In fact, it's worse than useless because the code must be removed before the routine can be run normally.

Unless the routine you want to use can gain a lot of speed from the modification you make, it's likely that making the modification will cost more time than you'll save. The modification had better be good; unless your routine is completely relocatable, the working code will be preceded by a lot of **NOPs**.

You can still determine the address of the routine, however. If you had grouped several routines together and put labels in your Turbo Basic program so you could call the one you wanted, wouldn't that allow you to include a "tell me the address" routine in with the others?

The answer is no. Remember, Turbo Basic handles the **RET** instruction for you. Since the routines are given different names, Turbo Basic will assume each is relocatable code. There is no guarantee that the separate routines will be in the same area of memory in the final .EXE file. Even if the routines are in the same area of memory and in the same order, you won't know how many bytes of code Turbo Basic put between them, and so you won't know where to go in each to make the changes you want.

The third method of determining a routine's address is the *signature method*. To use this, you search the computer's memory for a memory location containing the particular sequence of bytes that identify the routine you want to change.

The signature method also has problems. First, such a search will take a good deal of time. Second, there is no guarantee that you have definitely located the routine even if you match the signature. Third, each routine must contain a different signature; this wastes code space and adds to the time needed to modify all routines.

To make routines the program can modify, you need a better way of determining the address of the routine, and you need an easier way of altering the instructions in the routine.

To find a solution to these problems, read the next section, where we consider a special way to use routines that you can modify from within your Turbo Basic program.

Hiding Strings

Turbo Basic allows a maximum of 64 Kb for string space. Sometimes you will need every byte of that space, but quoted string constants (such as those used for menus and prompts) also take up string space.

Code space, however, is limited only to a maximum of 16 segments, each up to 64K long. Life would be grand if you were allowed to store some of those string constants in code space, where they wouldn't reduce the space available for dynamic string data. Fortunately, this is not too hard to do.

Consider the following routine:

```
;This routine takes two integer parameters and returns
;the segment and offset of the text in the body of the program.
;
        push    sp
        mov     bp,sp
        mov     dx,offset show      ;location of string
        mov     ax,cs               ;code segment to AX
        les     di,[bp+6]           ;ES:DI point to parameter
        mov     es:[di],dx          ;report string location
        les     di,[bp+0ah]         ;next parameter
        mov     es:[di],ax          ;report the code segment
        jmp     fini                ;and go back show
        DB      'Any text we like here and as much as we want'
        DB      'For as long as we want, terminated with any'
        DB      'character we like. Here, a null.',0
fini    pop     bp
```

The effect of this routine is somewhat different than the ones we proposed earlier for program-modifiable inline code. For one thing, you're not storing code (though Turbo Basic will process the resulting .COM file as if it were all code); instead, you're storing data.

The routine is returning the current address of the data stored within it. If you wanted to know the length of the data, you could have the routine report that, too, though you'd have to pass a third integer parameter.

Since you know where the text is in memory, you can use the PEEK instruction to read the string data into string space any time you want to print the message. When you've finished printing the message, you can throw away the now unneeded string; it will still be available in code space if you need it again.

You can determine the number of bytes available in this routine. In particular, you can determine the number of bytes preceding the text. Just replace all but the final instruction with your own code: Since you know where the routine is and how big it is, you can use BLOAD to overwrite it. As far as the Turbo Basic .EXE file is concerned, nothing will have changed—even though the whole routine is now different.

Usually, this technique is not necessary. Saving strings in code space is sometimes useful, but replacing a whole routine with another is better done by using CALL ABSOLUTE.

CALL ABSOLUTE

CALL ABSOLUTE is given a short mention in the Turbo Basic manual for several reasons. The first one is that Turbo Basic has less control over such routines. Second, such routines are commonly used because they were written for the Basic interpreter: Turbo Basic is different enough from the Basic interpreter that those routines might not work. Third, future operating systems may not allow CALL ABSOLUTE routines to be used. In particular, operating systems that make a clear distinction between code space and data space might refuse to allow the processor to execute instructions located in data space. Fourth, routines called by CALL ABSOLUTE may only be passed simple integer variables. This is not as much of a restriction as it seems, since simple integer variables can contain segment and offset addresses of any type of variable. Still, it can make parameter-passing somewhat more time-consuming.

For this discussion, we'll assume you're using MS-DOS 2.0 or greater and that the operating system permits the processor to execute instructions anywhere in memory.

CALL ABSOLUTE to Fixed Memory Locations

If you have a family of programs that share the same set of routines, it makes sense to put those routines in a fixed location. Then, each program that needs to use those routines can call them at a particular address. Turbo Basic allows you to safeguard addresses in high memory for this purpose with the MEMSET command.

ENDMEM is frequently used with MEMSET. ENDMEM will return a long integer that will be the last memory location the compiled Turbo Basic program can use. Routines are commonly placed in high memory at some fixed location beginning below this limit.

If you have such a set of routines, you will need to call them with the CALL ABSOLUTE command. To put them into high memory, use BLOAD. You will need to use DEF SEG to set the segment address into which the routines should be loaded, and specifically declare the offset address at which they should be loaded.

When you create these routines with Turbo Assembler, you should take care to follow these rules:

1. Unless the routine is intended to run at one and only one address, all transfers (JMPs and CALLs) in the program should be completely relocatable. (A complete discussion of relocatable code is beyond the scope of this chapter.)
2. If the program is intended to be run at only one address, you must specify that address in the **ORG** directive in the assembler source code.

CALL ABSOLUTE to Other Locations in Memory

Turbo Basic will also allow you to use CALL ABSOLUTE to memory locations that might vary each time you run a program. The most typical way to do this is to load the assembler routine into an array outside of normal data space.

Consider the following code fragment:

```
DEFINT a-z
$DYNAMIC                                'arrays will be dynamic
DIM RoutineArray(10000)                 '20,002 bytes allocated
'miscellaneous code here
whereseg% = VARSEG(ROUTINEARRAY(0))     'segment address
whereoffset% = VARPTR(ROUTINEARRAY(0))  'offset address
DEF SEG = whereseg%                     'set default segment
BLOAD"COMFILE", whereoffset%            'read routine in
```

```
CALL ABSOLUTE whereoffset%(parameter%)   'call the routine
DEF SEG                                  'return to default
```

If you want to use a number of routines, you could load each in turn into the same array. If you wanted to use special versions of the routines, you could select which ones to load, and load each into a different array. Finally, if you wanted to alter portions of the array, you could do so by simply changing the values of selected array elements.

As you can see, routines designed for use by CALL ABSOLUTE can be far more easily located and modified than $INLINE ones. The difficulty with the CALL ABSOLUTE routines is that they must be fully relocatable if they are to be generally useful. For short routines, this might not be a problem; for complex routines, it can be quite difficult to write fully relocatable code.

You can also BLOAD routines into string variables. Here, you must be especially careful. If you attempt to BLOAD a routine longer than the string variable, you will overwrite some other string. If that string is modified, part of your BLOADed routine might also be modified.

String variables can move, too. Even if the routine is loaded correctly into a string, you should take care to use VARSEG and VARPTR to establish the address of the string immediately before attempting to call the routine.

Turbo Basic strings are not stored the same way numeric variables are. If you perform VARPTR(*A%*), you'll get the address of the integer variable *A%*. If you do VARPTR(*A$*), you'll get the address of the string descriptor for *A$*. The memory location 2 bytes further along will contain the actual address of the string in string space. To come up with the same result as VARPTR(*A%*), you'd have to do something equivalent to this:

```
A% = VARPTR(A$)
A% = A%+2
StringAddress% = CVI(CHR$(PEEK(A%)) + CHR$(PEEK(A%+1)))
```

Though putting assembler routines into character strings used to be quite popular, it's a lot less appealing now that integer arrays can be dimensioned and erased. It would be better to use integer arrays for CALL ABSOLUTE routines and avoid the extra difficulties of accessing constantly moveable string data.

If you want to avoid using BLOAD, it's also possible to load .COM files into strings by using binary file I/O; that is, open the .COM file as type binary and read the correct number of bytes into the string. You can use the same approach to read the data into an integer array. BLOAD is faster and easier, however.

Other Problems with CALL ABSOLUTE

Code read from disk for use by CALL ABSOLUTE suffers from several important disadvantages, the most important being the requirement for relocatability, which we mentioned previously.

Another serious problem is that the routines must be read from disk separately from the main program, introducing several possibilities for error. The required code might not be present on the disk, or might be present but damaged.

A third problem is that the time spent reading the code from disk might remove the very reason to have the routine in assembler—rather than in Turbo Basic—in the first place.

Despite these stumbling blocks, the flexibility of pulling in different routines, of having code that can be modified under program control, and of reducing the amount of code that needs to be present in memory at any time can be strong enough reasons to consider using the CALL ABSOLUTE construction.

CALL INTERRUPT

The third and final way to access assembler routines from within Turbo Basic is perhaps both the easiest way to avoid assembler and the most difficult way to use assembler.

Most programmers will use CALL INTERRUPT to access the normal MS-DOS services. In this situation, there is really no assembler to worry. Instead, you need to remember the following:

Name	Register
REG 0	Flags
REG 1	AX
REG 2	BX
REG 3	CX
REG 4	DX
REG 5	SI
REG 6	DI
REG 7	BP
REG 8	DS
REG 9	ES

To set the value of a register, use the REG statement:

```
REG 3,&H0F01
```

This sets the value of the CX register to hexadecimal 0F01. Register CH will be hexadecimal 0F, and CL will be 01.

To read the value of a register, use the REG function:

```
A%=REG(3)
```

This assigns the current value of the CX register to *A%*.

The following example causes the screen to do a reverse scroll, from line 1 to 24:

```
REG 3,0              'row zero, column zero for top.
REG 4,&H175F         'row 23, column 79 for bottom
REG 2,&H70           'color 7,0
REG 1,&H0701         'bios function 7, scroll 1 line
CALL INTERRUPT &H10  'video interrupt 10h
```

The equivalent routine is more difficult to write in assembler and won't work any better. In fact, the CALL INTERRUPT form is easier to modify when needed.

The whole procedure is normally very easy. However, for more advanced programmers, interrupts can be used for other than the normal MS-DOS services.

Interrupts are often used to manage devices (such as temperature sensors, remote recorders, timers, and samplers). To use such an interrupt, you must first find an unused interrupt. (Many are used by MS-DOS, and others may be used by devices such as tape drives and storage devices such as the Bernoulli Box.)

Within the Turbo Basic program, you will point the interrupt vector to the routine written with Turbo Assembler. As noted in the Turbo Basic manual, the interrupt routine should preserve the values of the SS and SP registers; any of the others can be modified. At the end of the routine, control is passed back to the Turbo Basic program via an **IRET** instruction.

It is possible to use the techniques mentioned already to determine the location of a routine and to put that location in the interrupt vector, but it's better to put interrupt routines either in high memory or to BLOAD them like routines for CALL ABSOLUTE.

Interrupt routines included in your programs via the $INLINE command will need to be located somehow. BLOADed routines stored in integer arrays might not be in the same location from time to time, but at least the location will be known. Still, putting interrupt handlers into such arrays will mean that all of the code in the interrupt routine must be fully relocatable.

For that reason, interrupt routines are usually put in fixed locations in high memory. If you decide to use that approach, be sure to include the proper **ORG** command in your Turbo Assembler source code.

Sample Program

```
FILLIT2$ = CHR$(&HFC)+CHR$(&HF3)+CHR$(&HAB)+CHR$(&HCB)
'         cld        rep        stosw       ret
DIM a%(100)                           'integer array whose elements are all zero
WHERE%=VARPTR(FILLIT2$)               'this locations stores the length
WHERE%=WHERE%+2                       'and this is where the string location is
CLS:PRINT PEEK(WHERE%),PEEK(WHERE%+1)
HERE%=PEEK(WHERE%)+256*PEEK(WHERE%+1) 'and this is the string location
DEF SEG                               'not necessary here, but good programming
                                      ' practice

WHERE%=PEEK(0)+256*PEEK(1)
DEF SEG=WHERE%                        'string segment is the first word in
                                      ' default DS

REGES%=VARSEG(a%(0))
REGSI%=VARPTR(a%(0))
REG 1,5%                             'put the fill value into AX
REG 3,101%                           'number of elements to fill, 0 to 100
                                     ' inclusive into CX

REG 9,REGES%                         'segment of the array to fill into ES
REG 6,REGSI%                         'offset to first array element into SI
CALL ABSOLUTE HERE%                  'fill the array with the value 5

DEF SEG
FOR i%=0 TO 100:PRINT a%(i%);:NEXT i%
PRINT
PRINT REG(1),REG(3),REG(9),REG(6):STOP

CALL FILLIT(a%(0),-1%,101%)          'fill the array with the value -1
FOR i%=0 TO 100:PRINT a%(i%);:NEXT i%
PRINT
END

SUB FILLIT INLINE
$INLINE &H55,&H8B,&HEC,&HC4,&H7E
$INLINE &HE,&H26,&H8B,&HD,&HC4
$INLINE &H7E,&HA,&H26,&H8B,&H5
$INLINE &HC4,&H7E,&H6,&HFC,&HF3
$INLINE &HAB,&H5D
END SUB
```

```
;Routine to transfer an arbitrary number of elements with an arbitrary value
;into an integer array for call absolute.  Calling syntax is:
;REG 1,FILLVALUE%                          'AX has the fill value
;REG 3,FILLCOUNT%                          'CX has the number of elements to fill
;REG 9,VARSEG(ARRAY(0))                    'ES has the segment of the array
;REG 6,VARPTR(ARRAY(0))                    'DI is the offset to first array element
;CALL ABSOLUTE FILLIT2
;FILLIT2 is the address of the absolute routine and DEF SEG will have set the
;default program segment to that of FILLIT2 before the CALL ABSOLUTE.

PROGRAM SEGMENT
START    PROC FAR                          ;this will force a far return
    ASSUME cs:PROGRAM
    push bp                                ;save the base pointer
    cld                                    ;clear direction flag
    rep                                    ;next instruction repeats until CX is 0
    stosw                                  ;store AX to ES:DI and increment DI by 2
    pop bp                                 ;restore base pointer
    ret                                    ;intersegment (far) return
START    ENDP
PROGRAM ENDS                               ;end of segment
    END

;Routine to transfer an arbitrary number of elements with an
;arbitrary value into an integer array. Calling syntax is:
;CALL FILLIT(ARRAY(0),FILLVALUE,NUMTIMES)

    ORG 100h
PROGRAM SEGMENT
    ASSUME cs:PROGRAM
    push bp                      ;save the base pointer
    mov  bp,sp                   ;move stack pointer to BP
    les  di,[bp+0eh]             ;get offset address of # of elements to fill
    mov  cx,es:[di]              ;number of elements to fill into CX
    les  di,[bp+0ah]             ;get offset address of fill value
    mov  ax,es:[di]              ;put fill value in AX
    les  di,[bp+6]               ;offset address of array to fill
    cld                          ;clear direction flag
    rep                          ;next instruction repeats until CX is zero
    stosw                        ;store AX to ES:DI and increment DI by two
    pop bp                       ;restore base pointer
PROGRAM ENDS                     ;end segment--no RET instruction
    END
```

Turbo Assembler User's Guide

9

Interfacing Turbo Assembler with Turbo Prolog

Turbo Prolog offers the programmer a wealth of predicates that provide a rich set of high-level functions, from screen window management to B+ tree database management. What Turbo Assembler adds to Turbo Prolog is a low-level programming facility.

In this chapter, we'll first take a look at the interface between Turbo Prolog and Turbo Assembler. Then we'll build some simple examples of interfacing assembly routines to Turbo Prolog. Finally, we'll discuss calling Turbo Prolog predicates from assembly code, using Turbo Prolog library calls and passing compound structures.

Note: When referring to Turbo Prolog, we mean versions 1.0 and greater.

Declaring External Predicates

Turbo Prolog allows interfacing with other languages through the use of a **global predicates** declaration. A language specification is appended to the declaration so that Turbo Prolog knows a global predicate is implemented in another language:

```
global predicates
    add(integer,integer,integer) - (i,i,o),(i,i,i) language asm
    scanner(string,token) - (i,o) language Pascal
```

Turbo Prolog makes the interfaced language explicit to simplify the problems of activation record and parameter format, calling and returning conventions, segment definition, linking, and initialization.

Calling Conventions and Parameters

The 8086 processor family gives the programmer a choice between near and far subroutine calls. Turbo Prolog creates large memory model programs and requires that all calls to and returns from subroutines be far.

Turbo Prolog supports a number of calling conventions; C, Pascal, and assembler. When interfacing to a routine written using the C calling convention, the parameters are pushed onto the stack in reverse order and, after returning, the stack pointer is automatically adjusted. When interfacing to other languages, the parameters are pushed in the normal order, and the called function is responsible for removing the parameters from the stack.

In many language compilers for the 8086 family, there is a choice between 16-bit and 32-bit pointers, where the 16-bit pointers refer to a default segment. Turbo Prolog always uses 32-bit pointers to access all memory.

Turbo Prolog types are implemented in the following way:

integer	2 bytes
real	8 bytes (IEEE format)
char	1 byte (2 bytes when pushed on the stack)
string	4-byte *dword* pointer to a null-terminated string
symbol	4-byte *dword* pointer to a null-terminated string
compound	4-byte *dword* pointer to a record

An output parameter is pushed as a 32-bit pointer to a location where the return value must be assigned. For input parameters, the value is pushed directly, and the size of the parameter depends on its type.

Naming Conventions

The same predicate in Turbo Prolog can have several type variants and several flow variants. Each type and flow variant must have its own procedure that's assigned a unique name. This is done by numbering the different procedures with the same predicate name from 0 upward. For example, given the declaration

```
global predicates
    add(integer,integer,integer)-(i,i,o),(i,i,i) language asm
```

the first variant—with flow pattern (i,i,o)—is named *add_0*, and the second—with flow pattern (i,i,i)—is named *add_1*.

Turbo Prolog also allows the programmer to declare an explicit name for a global predicate. This is done by succeeding the declaration with an "as *public name*" part. In the following example, the global predicate *pred* will be resolved by an identifier name *my_pred*, not *pred_0*.

```
global predicates
    pred(integer,integer)-(i,o) language asm as "my_pred"
```

This method is good when you're naming predicates that have only one flow pattern. If more than one flow pattern exists, you'll have to provide a name for each variant. Using the *add* predicate as an example, the predicate definition might read

```
global predicates
    add(integer,integer,integer)-(i,i,o) language asm as "doadd"
    add(integer,integer,integer)-(i,i,i) language asm as "add_check"
```

The first variant—with flow pattern (i,i,o)—is named *doadd*, and the second—with flow pattern (i,i,i)—is named *add_check*. Note that this naming method requires the variants to be declared separately.

Writing Assembly Language Predicates

Perhaps the simplest predicates to write are those that have only input flow patterns. Suppose you wanted to scroll the contents of the current Turbo Prolog window horizontally. You could create the predicate *scroll_left* that scrolls a region of the screen one column to the left. In the SCROLLH.PRO example, *scroll_left* will take four integer arguments and one flow pattern.

The Turbo Prolog module SCROLLH.PRO contains a **global predicates** declaration for the predicate *scroll_left*. The *scroll_left* predicate is defined as an assembly predicate.

```
/* SCROLLH.PRO */

global predicates
    scroll_left(integer,integer,integer,integer) - (i,i,i,i) language asm

predicates
    scrollh
```

clauses

```
scrollh :-
    makewindow(_,_,_,_,Row,Col,Nrows,Ncols),
    scroll_left(Row,Col,Nrows,Ncols),
    readchar(C),
    char_int(C,CI),
    not(CI = 27),
    scrollh.
```

goal

```
makewindow(1,7,7," A SCROLLING MESSAGE ",10,20,4,60),
write("This message will scroll across the window"),nl,
write("Look at it go!"),
readchar(_),
scrollh,
readchar(_).
```

The following assembly language source is the implementation of the *scroll_left* predicate. Notice that the name given to the predicate is *SCROLL_LEFT_0*. This name conforms (as it must) to the naming conventions discussed earlier in this chapter.

```
;   SCROL.ASM
;
    name    scrol
;
;   scroll_left(integer,integer,integer,integer) - (i,i,i,i) language asm
;
SCROL_TEXT      SEGMENT  BYTE PUBLIC 'CODE'
    ASSUME      cs:SCROL_TEXT

PUBLIC SCROLL_LEFT_0

SCROLL_LEFT_0  PROC FAR
;
; parameters
arg  NCOLS:WORD, NROWS:WORD, COL:WORD, ROW:WORD = ARGLEN
;
; local variable
local       SSEG :WORD = LSIZE
    push  bp
    mov   bp,sp
    sub   sp,lsize              ;room for local variables
    push  si
    push  di

    mov   SSEG, 0B800h

    sub   NCOLS, 3             ;NCOLS = NCOLS - 3

    mov   ax, ROW             ;DEST = ROW*160 + (COL+1)*2
    mov   dx,160
```

```
        mul    dx
        mov    dx, COL
        inc    dx                  ;added
        shl    dx,1
        add    dx,ax

        push   ds
        push   es

        mov    bx , NROWS          ;loop NROWS times using BX as counter
        dec    bx                  ;NROWS = NROWS - 2
        dec    bx

Top: cmp     bx ,0
        je     Done

        add    dx, 160             ;dest = dest + 160

        mov    ax,NCOLs            ;lastchar = dest + nc*2
        shl    ax,1
        add    ax,dx
        push   ax                  ;push lastchar offset on stack

        mov    ax,SSEG             ;load screen segment into ES, DS
        mov    es,ax
        mov    ds,ax

        mov    di,dx               ;set up SI and DI for movs
        mov    si,di               ;source is 2 bytes above DEST
        add    si,2

        mov    ax,[di]             ;save the char in col 0 in AX

        mov    cx,NCOLS            ;mov NCOLS words
        cld
        rep    movsw

        pop    di                  ;pop lastchar offset to DI
        mov    [di],ax             ;put char in AX to last column

        dec    bx
        jmp    TOP
Done:pop      es
        pop    ds
        pop    di
        pop    si
        mov    sp,bp
        pop    bp
        ret    ARGLEN
SCROLL_LEFT_0  ENDP
SCROL_TEXT     ENDS
        END
```

To create an executable file from SCROLLH.PRO and SCROL.ASM, first compile the Turbo Prolog file to an .OBJ file using Turbo Prolog. (When

Turbo Prolog compiles a module, it creates an .OBJ file and a .SYM file.) Then assemble SCROL.ASM to an .OBJ file with Turbo Assembler, and link the modules together with the following TLINK command line:

```
TLINK init scrollh scrol scrollh.sym,scroll,,prolog
```

The resultant executable file will be named SCROLL.EXE.

Implementing the double Predicate

Suppose an assembly language routine is to be called into operation via the clause

```
double(MyInVar,MyOutVar)
```

with *MyInVar* bound to an integer value before the call so that, after the call, *MyOutVar* is bound to twice that value.

The activation record placed on top of the stack when **double** is activated will take the form shown in Figure 9.1.

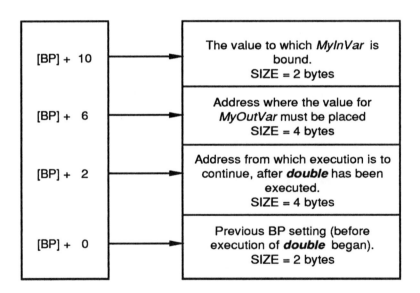

Figure 9.1: Activation Record for double

The following assembly language function implements the **double** predicate:

```
;
; MYASM.ASM
;
```

```
A_PROG      SEGMENT BYTE
            ASSUME cs:a_prog
            PUBLIC double_0
double_0    PROC    FAR
            push    bp
            mov     bp,sp

            mov     ax, [bp]+6          ;get the value to which MyInVar is bound
            add     ax,ax              ;double that value
            lds     si,DWORD PTR [bp]+10
            mov     [si],ax            ;store the value to which MyOutVar is to
                                       ; be bound in the appropriate address

            pop     bp
            mov     sp,bp
            ret     6
double_0    ENDP
A_PROG      ENDS
```

The Turbo Prolog program containing the call to *double* must contain the following **global predicates** declaration:

global predicates
```
    double(integer,integer) - (i,o) language asm
```

Otherwise, the Turbo Prolog program is no different from any other program.

The following program uses this *double*:

```
/* MYPROLOG.PRO */
```

global predicates
```
    double(integer,integer) - (i,o) language asm
```
goal
```
    write("Enter an integer "),
    readint(I),
    double(I,Y),
    write(I," doubled is ",Y).
```

If this assembly language program module is assembled into the file MYASM.OBJ, and the calling Turbo Prolog object module is MYPROLOG.OBJ, the two can be linked via this command line

```
    TLINK init myprolog myasm myprolog.sym,double,,prolog
```

and produce an executable, stand-alone program in the file DOUBLE.EXE (using the Turbo Prolog library in PROLOG.LIB). It is important that MYPROLOG.SYM appear as the last file name before the first comma in the TLINK command.

In general, the format of an activation record will depend on the number of parameters in the calling Turbo Prolog predicate and the domain types corresponding to those parameters. For instance, if you wanted to define

```
add(Val1,Val2,Sum)
```

with *Val1*, *Val2*, and *Sum* belonging to *integer* domains, the activation record would take the form shown in Figure 9.2.

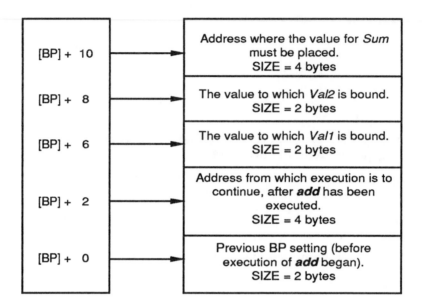

Figure 9.2: Activation Record for add

Notice that each parameter occupies a corresponding number of bytes. For output parameters, the size is always 4 bytes (used for segment address and offset). For input parameters, the size is determined by the value actually pushed onto the stack, so it is dependent on the corresponding domain.

Val1 and *Val2*, belonging to an *integer* domain and being used with an (i) flow pattern, both occupy 2 bytes; *Sum*, being used with an (o) flow pattern, occupies 4 bytes.

Note also that, within the Turbo Prolog compiler, a call to an external predicate takes the form

```
mov  ax,SEGMENT data
mov  ds,ax
call FAR PTR external_predicate_implementation
```

so the data segment that's addressed while a procedure for an external predicate is being executed is the segment called **DATA**.

Implementing Predicates with Multiple Flow Patterns

When implementing predicates with multiple flow patterns, you must be careful that the assembly language functions adhere to the Turbo Prolog naming convention. For example, suppose you want to implement the predicate *add*, which has multiple flow patterns. *add* will find the missing value in the equation $X + Y = Z$ when any two of the three arguments are bound at the time of the call to *add*.

The following Turbo Prolog program, ADDPRO.PRO, declares the global assembly language predicate *add*. Notice that *add* has three flow patterns, (i,i,o), (i,o,i), and (o,i,i).

```
/* ADDPRO.PRO */

global predicates
    add(integer,integer,integer) - (i,i,o),(i,o,i),(o,i,i) language asm

goal
    add(2,3,X), write("2 + 3 = ",X),nl,
    add(2,Y,5), write("5 - 2 = ",Y),nl,
    add(Z,3,5), write("5 - 3 = ",Z),nl.
```

The following assembly language program, ADD.ASM, contains the code to implement *add*. **ADD_0** corresponds to the (i,i,o) flow pattern, **ADD_1** corresponds to (i,o,i), and **ADD_2** to (o,i,i).

```
        name     add

ADD_TEXT         SEGMENT   BYTE PUBLIC 'CODE'
        ASSUME   cs:ADD_TEXT
        PUBLIC   ADD_0                              ;(i,i,o) flow pattern
ADD_0   PROC     FAR
        arg      Z:DWORD, Y:WORD, X:WORD = ARGLEN1
        push     bp
        mov      bp,sp
        mov      ax,X
        add      ax,Y
        les      bx,Z
        mov      WORD PTR es:[bx],ax
        pop      bp
        ret      ARGLEN1
ADD_0   ENDP
```

```
        PUBLIC    ADD_1                              ;(i,o,i) flow pattern
ADD_1   PROC      FAR
arg     Z:WORD,   Y:DWORD, X:WORD = ARGLEN2
        push      bp
        mov       bp,sp
        mov       ax, Z
        sub       ax, X
        les       bx, Y
        mov       WORD PTR es:[bx],ax
        pop       bp
        ret       ARGLEN2
ADD_1   ENDP

        PUBLIC    ADD_2                              ;(o,i,i) flow pattern
ADD_2   PROC      FAR
arg     Z:WORD,   Y:WORD, X:DWORD = ARGLEN3
        push      bp
        mov       bp,sp
        mov       ax, Z
        sub       ax, Y
        les       bx, X
        mov       WORD PTR es:[bx],ax
        pop       bp
        ret       ARGLEN3
ADD_2   ENDP

ADD_TEXT          ENDS
        END
```

After ADDPRO.PRO and ADD.ASM have been translated to .OBJ files, you can create an .EXE file with the following command line:

```
TLINK init addpro add addpro.sym,addpro,,prolog
```

Calling Turbo Prolog Predicates from Assembly Functions

Now that we've discussed calling assembly language functions from Turbo Prolog, we'll cover it in reverse—calling Turbo Prolog predicates from assembly language.

When a predicate is declared as a global predicate, the predicate's variants become global functions that can be called by any other module. The naming and calling conventions are the same as for predicates defined in assembly language.

The following Turbo Prolog module defines two global predicates: *popmessage* and *from_asm*. *popmessage* is declared as a C language predicate and *from_asm* is declared as an assembly language predicate.

To build SHOWMESS, compile SHOWMESS.PRO to .OBJ from the Turbo Prolog development environment. Then compile FROM_ASM.ASM with

```
tasm from_asm
```

and link with

```
TLINK init showmess from_asm showmess.sym,showmess,,prolog
```

Here's SHOWMESS:

```
/* SHOWMESS.PRO */

global predicates
    popmessage(string) - (i) language c              /* predicate called from
                                                        assembly language procedure */
    from_asm - language asm              /* assembly language procedure */

clauses
    popmessage(S) :-          /* can be called as a c function named popmessage_0 */
        str_len(S,L),
        LL = L + 4,
        makewindow(13,7,7,"",10,10,3,LL),
        write(S),
        readchar(_),
        removewindow.

goal
    from_asm.                                         /* external */
```

The following assembly code implements *from_asm* and issues a call to *popmessage*:

```
            EXTRN   PopMessage_0:FAR
DGROUP  GROUP   _DATA
            ASSUME  cs:SENDMESS_TEXT,ds:DGROUP
_DATA   SEGMENT WORD PUBLIC 'DATA'
mess1   DB      "Report: Condition Red",0
_DATA   ENDS

SENDMESS_TEXT   SEGMENT   BYTE PUBLIC 'CODE'
            PUBLIC  FROM_ASM_0
FROM_ASM_0      PROC    FAR
        push    ds
        mov     ax,OFFSET DGROUP:mess1
        push    ax
        call    FAR PTR PopMessage_0
        pop     cx
        pop     cx
```

```
            ret
FROM_ASM_0       ENDP
SENDMESS_TEXT    ENDS
        END
```

A program follows, using high-level assembly extensions to build the same executable program. To build it, compile SHOWNEW.PRO to .OBJ from the Turbo Prolog development environment, then compile FROM_ASM.ASM with

```
tasm /jmasm51 /jquirks from_new
```

and link with

```
TLINK init shownew from_new shownew.sym,show2,,prolog
```

Here's SHOWNEW:

```
/* SHOWNEW.PRO */

global predicates
    popmessage(string) - (i) language c        /* predicate called from assembly
                                                        language procedure */
   from_asm - language c as "_from_asm"         /* define public name of the
                                                   assembly language procedure */

clauses
    popmessage(S) :-
        str_len(S,L),
        LL=L+4,
        makewindow(13,7,7,"window",10,10,3,LL),
        write(S),
        readchar(_),
        removewindow.

goal
    from_asm.                           /* call assembly language procedure */
```

The following assembly code implements *from_asm* and issues a call to *popmessage* (like in the preceding example).

```
; FROM_NEW.ASM

        EXTRN   PopMessage_0:far
        .MODEL large,c
        .CODE

FROM_ASM    PROC
    push ds
    mov  ax, OFFSET DGROUP:mess1
    push ax
    call FAR PTR PopMessage_0
    pop  cx
    pop  cx
```

```
        ret
FROM_ASM    ENDP
        .DATA
mess1 DB        "Report: Condition Red",0
        END
```

Lists and Functors

In this section, we'll discuss the method used to pass lists and functors to assembly language predicates. As mentioned previously, compound Turbo Prolog objects are not passed directly; instead, Turbo Prolog passes a 4-byte pointer to a structure.

The record structure used for both lists and functors is simple and straightforward. Suppose you had the following Turbo Prolog domains:

```
domains
    ilist = integer*
    ifunc = int(integer)
```

The corresponding list-node structure for the *ilist* domain would be as follows:

```
STRUC ILIST
    NodeType DB ?
    Value    DW ?
    NextNode DD ?
ENDS
```

As you can see from this structure, a list node has three parts:

■ the node type (a byte)

■ the node value (depends on the type)

■ the pointer to the next node (4 bytes)

The node type can contain two meaningful values: *Value 1* means that the node is a list node, while *Value 2* means that the node is an end-of-list node. (An end-of-list node contains no other meaningful information.) The node value can be any Turbo Prolog domain.

The corresponding structure for the *ifunc* functor would be as follows:

```
STRUC IFUNC
    FuncType DB ?
    Value    DW ?
ENDS
```

A functor structure has two parts: the functor type and the functor record. The functor type is an integer associated with the position of the functor variant in the list of alternates. The first alternate is type 1, the second is type 2, and so on.

In the following Turbo Prolog and Turbo Assembler modules, we've implemented a predicate that returns a functor to Turbo Prolog:

Here's the Turbo Prolog module:

```
/* FUNC.PRO */

domains
    ifunc = int(integer)

global predicates
    makeifunc(integer,ifunc) - (i,o) language c

goal
    makeifunc(4,H),
    write(H).
```

And this is the Turbo Assembler module:

```
;
; IFUNC.ASM
;
        EXTRN    _alloc_gstack:FAR              ;_alloc_gstack returns
                                                ; pointer to memory block

STRUC IFUNC
   FuncType  DB ?
   Value     DW ?
ENDS

IFUNC_TEXT      SEGMENT  WORD PUBLIC 'CODE'
        ASSUME   cs:IFUNC_TEXT

        PUBLIC   Makeifunc_0
Makeifunc_0     PROC FAR
     arg        __inval:WORD, __outp:DWORD
     push       bp
     mov        bp,sp
     mov        ax,3                            ;allocate 3 bytes
     push       ax
     call       FAR PTR _alloc_gstack
     pop        cx
     les        bx,__outp
     mov        [WORD PTR es:bx+2],dx
     mov        [WORD PTR es:bx],ax
     mov        ax,__inval
```

```
;;     les       bx,__outp
       les       bx,[DWORD PTR es:bx]
       mov       [(IFUNC PTR es:bx).VALUE],ax     ;value = __inval
       mov       [(IFUNC PTR es:bx).FUNCTYPE],1   ;type  = 1
       pop       bp
       ret
Makeifunc_0    ENDP
IFUNC_TEXT     ENDS
       END
```

This example used only one functor type for *ifunc*. If you were to declare another functor, like so:

```
myfunc = int(integer); char(char); r(real); d2(integer,real)
```

the structure would become somewhat more complicated. The structure would still have two parts, but the second part would be a union of the data structures required to define all the variants for *myfunc*. The following structure is a possible implementation of *myfunc* in Turbo Assembler:

```
STRUC MyFunc
       FuncType DB ?
       UNION
          STRUC
             _int DW ?
          ENDS
          STRUC
             _char DB ?
          ENDS
          STRUC
             _real DQ ?
          ENDS
          STRUC
             v1    DW ?
             v2    DQ ?
          ENDS
       ENDS
ENDS
```

The types associated with functor alternates would be

int(integer)	1
char(char)	2
r(real)	3
d2(integer,real)	4

To help put lists and functors into focus, take a look at the earlier **domains** declaration of *ilist*. Why are the valid node types 1 and 2? Because Turbo Prolog treats *ilist* as a structure that could have been just as easily declared as

```
ilist = listnode(integer,listnode); end_of_list.
```

Keep in mind that when you pass compound objects, you pass a pointer to a structure. More specifically: An input flow pattern list or functor is passed by reference; an output flow pattern list or functor is passed as a pointer to a reference to a structure. (Turbo Prolog passes the address of a pointer to the returned structure.) All structures returned to Turbo Prolog should use memory allocated with Turbo Prolog's memory allocation functions. (Refer to the *Turbo Prolog User's Guide* and the *Turbo Prolog Reference Guide*.)

10

Advanced Programming in Turbo Assembler

Over the course of the first 9 chapters of this manual, we've covered the essentials of assembler programming, and then some. Now we're ready to get into several advanced features of Turbo Assembler.

In this chapter, we'll explore several aspects of assembler programming that we've only touched on so far, such as segment override prefixes, macros, the segment directives, and writing programs that contain multiple code and data segments. We'll also look at some useful features that you haven't seen before, including local labels, automatic jump-sizing, forward references, and the data structure directives.

Segment Override Prefixes

Most of the time, memory operands specify memory locations in the segment pointed to by the DS segment register. For example, the instruction sequence

```
        .
        .
        .
mov   bx,10h
mov   si,5
mov   ax,[bx+si+1]
        .
        .
        .
```

loads the word stored at offset 16h in the segment pointed to by DS into AX. Another way to put this is to say that AX is loaded from the memory address DS:0016.

One exception to the rule of loading from the segment pointed to by DS is that the **STOS** and **MOVS** string instructions write to the segment pointed to by ES, and the **SCAS** and **CMPS** string instructions take source operands from the segment pointed to by ES. (One of the source operands to **CMPS** is in the data segment, and one is in the extra segment.)

Another exception is that any memory operand involving BP accesses the segment pointed to by SS. For example,

```
     .
     .
     .
mov   bp,1000h
mov   al,[bp+6]
     .
     .
     .
```

loads AL with the contents of memory location SS:1006.

Suppose, however, you'd like to access a location in the CS segment as a memory operand; that's useful for jump tables, especially in multisegment programs. Or suppose you'd like to access a location on the stack with BX, or a location in DS with BP, or a location in ES with a nonstring instruction. Can you do that?

The answer is yes. You can use *segment override prefixes* to make many instructions access the segment of your choice. For example,

```
     .
     .
     .
mov   bx,100h
mov   cl,ss:[bx+10h]
     .
     .
     .
```

loads CL with the contents of offset 110h in the stack segment, and

```
      .
      .
      .
   mov  bp,200h
   mov  si,cs:[bp+1]
      .
      .
      .
```

loads SI with the contents of offset 201h in the code segment.

Basically, all you need to do to cause a given instruction to access a segment other than its default segment is put a segment override prefix—CS:, DS:, ES:, or SS:—in front of the memory operand for that instruction.

Incidentally, segment override prefixes aren't called "prefixes" because they prefix memory operands in the instruction line. Rather, a segment override prefix is actually an instruction prefix byte, which modifies the operation of the instruction that follows it, just as the **REP** prefix that we discussed in Chapter 5 is an instruction prefix byte. So, for example, when the 8086 encounters the instruction bytes

```
   A0 00 00
```

which form the instruction

```
   mov  al,[0]
```

it loads AL with the contents of offset 0 in the data segment. However, since the value of the ES: segment override prefix is 26h, when the 8086 encounters

```
   26 A0 00 00
```

which forms the instruction

```
   mov  al,es:[0]
```

it loads AL with the contents of offset 0 in the extra segment, not the data segment.

An Alternate Form

Turbo Assembler supports an alternate segment override prefix form, where you put the segment override prefix on a separate line. The separate line-segment overrides are **SEGCS** for a CS: segment override, **SEGDS** for a DS: segment override, **SEGES** for an ES: segment override, and **SEGSS** for an SS: segment override. Each of these will override the next line of code only, not all subsequent lines. For example, the following stores DX to offset 999h in the extra segment:

```
    .
    .
    .
mov  si,999h
seges
mov  [si],dx
    .
    .
    .
```

This alternate form is useful for putting segment override prefixes on instructions that have no operands, such as **LODSB**. The following loads AL from SS:SI:

```
    .
    .
    .
segss
lodsb
    .
    .
    .
```

When Segment Override Prefixes Don't Work

Segment override prefixes don't work with all instructions. For example, string instruction accesses to the extra segment can't be overridden. That is,

```
lods es:[ByteVar]
```

is fine, loading AL from ES:SI, but

```
stos ds:[ByteVar]
```

can't work. If you do try to override a string instruction access to the extra segment as shown above, Turbo Assembler will let you know that's not allowed. However, if you use **SEGCS** or the like to create a segment override, Turbo Assembler doesn't know what instruction you're going to override and so can't generate an error in such cases. For example,

```
    .
    .
    .
segds
```

```
stosb
     .
     .
     .
```

won't generate an assembly error, but **STOSB** will still write to the extra segment, not the data segment.

Along the same lines, be aware that segment override prefixes can never affect accesses to the stack. Pushes to the stack always go to the stack segment, and pops from the stack always come from the stack segment. For instance, an instruction such as

```
     .
     .
     .
segcs
push [bx]
     .
     .
     .
```

uses the segment override prefix to select the segment from which the value to be pushed should be fetched; that value is written to offset SP-2 in the stack segment, as always. Likewise, instructions are always fetched from the segment pointed to by CS.

You should generally avoid mixing segment override prefixes with **REP** prefixes, since problems can result if an instruction using both overrides is interrupted. (See Chapter 5 for details.)

Accessing Multiple Segments

Segment override prefixes are useful whenever you need to access multiple segments. This necessity can arise, for example, if you need to access data stored both on the stack and in the data segment, which commonly occurs when the stack is used for dynamically allocated variables, and the data segment is used for static variables. Another possibility is that a program simply has more than 64 Kb of data, so accesses to any of several segments may be needed at any time.

One particularly useful application for segment override prefixes occurs when you need to mix string and nonstring instructions. For example, suppose that for a given string you want to convert all characters with values less than 20h to spaces. The following code uses a segment override prefix to perform that task efficiently:

```
        .
        .
        .
        mov  ax,SEG StringToConvert
        mov  es,ax
        mov  di,OFFSET StringToConvert    ;ES:DI points to the string to convert
        cld                               ;make STOSB increment DI
ConvertLoop:
        mov  al,es:[di]                   ;get the next character
        and  al,al                        ;is it the end of the string?
        jz   ConvertLoopDone              ;yes, done
        cmp  al,20h                       ;do we need to convert it?
        jnb  SaveChar                     ;no, save it
        mov  al,' '                       ;make it a space
SaveChar:
        stosb                             ;save this character and point to the next
        jmp  ConvertLoop                  ;check the next character
ConvertLoopDone:
        stosb                             ;end the string with a zero
        .
        .
        .
```

Local Labels

Local labels—labels with limited scope—are one of the pleasures of using Turbo Assembler. Let's look at why you might need them.

Suppose you have several sections of code in a source module that perform similar functions. For example, consider the following:

```
        .
        .
        .
Sub1 PROC
        sub  ax,ax
IntCountLoop:
        add  ax,[bx]
        inc  bx
        inc  bx
        loop IntCountLoop
        ret
Sub1 ENDP
        .
        .
        .
Sub2 PROC
```

```
        sub  ax,ax
        mov  dx,ax
LongCountLoop:
        add  ax,[bx]
        adc  dx,[bx+2]
        add  bx,4
        loop LongCountLoop
        ret
Sub2 ENDP
        .
        .
        .
```

When two sections of code perform similar functions, it often follows that they'll contain similar labels. For example, *Sub1* and *Sub2* each contain a label that marks the top of a counting loop.

When there are only a few labels in a whole program, you can easily make sure that all the labels are different. In large programs, however, it can become a nuisance to avoid having identical labels. Then, too, it's common practice to take a subroutine that works, block-copy it and rename it, and modify it into a new subroutine. The problem with this is that it's easy to forget to change a label here or there, causing the new subroutine to jump to a label in the old subroutine. For example, if you copied and modified *Sub1* to make *Sub2*, you could inadvertently end up with

```
        .
        .
        .
Sub2 PROC
        sub  ax,ax
        mov  dx,ax
LongCountLoop:
        add  ax,[bx]
        adc  dx,[bx+2]
        add  bx,4
        loop IntCountLoop
        ret
Sub2 ENDP
        .
        .
        .
```

which would jump to the middle of *Sub1*—with potentially disastrous results.

What you really need, then, is a type of label that is limited in scope to a single subroutine, so it won't conflict with labels in other subroutines.

That's just what local labels are. Local labels, which by default usually start with two at-signs (@@), are limited in scope to the range of instructions between two non-local labels. (Non-local labels are those defined with **PROC** and labels ending with colons that don't start with two at-signs.) As far as Turbo Assembler is concerned, local labels don't even exist outside the range delimited by the nearest non-local labels.

Symbols that you define with the **LABEL** directive do not cause a new local symbol block to start.

For example, you can use local labels to change the example at the beginning of this section with

```
       .
       .
       .
       LOCALS
Sub1 PROC
       sub  ax,ax
@@CountLoop:
       add  ax,[bx]
       inc  bx
       inc  bx
       loop @@CountLoop
       ret
Sub1 ENDP
       .
       .
       .
Sub2 PROC
       sub  ax,ax
       mov  dx,ax
@@CountLoop:
       add  ax,[bx]
       adc  dx,[bx+2]
       add  bx,4
       loop @@CountLoop
       ret
Sub2 ENDP
       .
       .
       .
```

Here you need not worry about the loop label in one subroutine conflicting with the label in the other subroutine, and there's no chance that one subroutine will accidentally jump to a label in the other subroutine.

You'll note that we used the **LOCALS** directive before we used any local labels. In MASM mode, local labels are disabled by default, and must be enabled with **LOCALS** before you can use them. In Ideal mode, local labels are normally enabled, although you can disable them with **NOLOCALS** if you want.

Local labels are also useful when you've got several short conditional jumps in a subroutine, and you don't want to have to spend time thinking of unique names for them. For example, you might want to use local labels when you're testing for any of several values:

```
        .
        .
        .
        LOCALS
        cmp  al,'A'
        jnz  @@P1
        jmp  HandleA
@@P1:
        cmp  al,'B'
        jnz  @@P2
        jmp  HandleB
@@P2:
        cmp  al,'C'
        jnz  @@P3
        jmp  HandleC
@@P3:
        .
        .
        .
```

With local labels, you don't have to worry about whether labels like *P1* are used elsewhere in the program.

Remember, *any* non-local label delimits the scope of a local label. For instance, the following wouldn't assemble:

```
        .
        .
        .
Sub1 PROC NEAR
        .
        .
        .
        LOCALS
@@CountLoop:
        add  ax,[bx]
        jnz  NotZero
        inc  dx
NotZero:
        inc  bx
        inc  bx
```

```
loop @@CountLoop
    .
    .
    .
```

The problem here is that the non-local label *NotZero* lies between the **LOOP** instruction's reference to the local label *@@CountLoop* and the definition of *@@CountLoop*. The scope of a local variable only extends to the nearest non-local label, so when Turbo Assembler assembles the **LOOP** instruction, the local label *@@CountLoop* is nowhere to be found.

You can change the local symbol prefix from the normal two at-signs (@@) to any other two characters that can be used at the start of a symbol name. You do this by putting the new prefix characters as an argument to the **LOCALS** directive:

```
LOCALS _ _
```

This sets the local symbol prefix to two underscore characters. This can be useful if you want to start using local symbols in a module that already has symbols that start with the default local symbol prefix.

When you change the local symbol prefix in this manner, local symbols are automatically enabled at the same time, exactly as if you had used the **LOCALS** directive without any argument. Also, if you subsequently use the **NOLOCALS** directive to disable local symbols, Turbo Assembler remembers the prefix characters that you specified. This lets you simply use **LOCALS** with no arguments to restore local symbols with the prefix you previously specified.

Automatic Jump-Sizing

Many years ago, the designers of the 8086 decided that the conditional jump instructions would only support 1-byte jump displacements. This meant that each conditional jump would only be capable of jumping to a destination within about 128 bytes of the conditional jump instruction itself.

Today, of course, those conditional jumps are with us still, and they're both a blessing and a curse. While the 8086's conditional jump instructions sometimes make for compact code (since the conditional jump instructions are only 2 bytes long), they also often make for awkward, inefficient code, since 5-byte instruction sequences like this

```
        .
        .
        .
    jnz   NotZero
    jmp   IsZero
NotZero:
        .
        .
        .
```

are required when conditional jump destinations are too far away to reach with a 1-byte displacement.

Worse, there's no way to know beforehand whether a given conditional jump will reach a given label, so you're put in the position of trying to jump to the label directly, thereby risking an assembly error, or coding a conditional jump around an unconditional jump, thereby possibly wasting 3 bytes and slowing execution. Still more annoying is the all-too-common occurrence of a Relative jump out of range error when you add an instruction or two inside a loop.

While Turbo Assembler can't solve all the conditional-jump problems of the 8086, it comes close by way of the **JUMPS** directive. Once you've specified **JUMPS**, Turbo Assembler *automatically* turns normal conditional jumps into conditional jumps around unconditional jumps whenever that's what it takes to reach the destination label.

How does automatic jump-sizing work? Consider the following code:

```
        .
        .
        .
    JUMPS
RepeatLoop:
    jmp   SkipOverData
    DB    100h DUP (?)
SkipOverData:
        .
        .
        .
    dec   dx
    jnz   RepeatLoop
        .
        .
        .
```

Clearly, the **JNZ** at the bottom of the loop can't reach *RepeatLoop*, since over 256 bytes lie between the two. Since **JUMPS** was specified, however, no assembly-time error will result. Instead, Turbo Assembler actually assembles this code into the equivalent of

```
        .
        .
        .
RepeatLoop:
        jmp  SkipOverData
        DB   100h DUP (?)    ;temporary data storage in CS
SkipOverData:
        .
        .
        .
        dec  dx
        jz   $+5
        jmp  RepeatLoop
        .
        .
        .
```

automatically using a **JZ** and a **JMP** in place of the **JNZ** at the bottom of the loop.

Don't think that Turbo Assembler always generates a conditional/ unconditional jump pair when **JUMPS** is active; the conditional jump you specify is always used if it will reach the destination. For instance, the following assembles with **JNZ** at the bottom of the loop, since here the destination label is near enough to reach with a 1-byte displacement:

```
        .
        .
        .
        JUMPS
RepeatLoop:
        add  BYTE PTR [bx],1
        inc  bx
        dec  dx
        jnz  RepeatLoop
        .
        .
        .
```

As we mentioned earlier, Turbo Assembler's automatic jump-sizing doesn't solve *all* of the 8086's problems with conditional jumps. Turbo Assembler always handles automatic sizing of backward jumps (jumps to labels earlier in the code than a given jump instruction) perfectly, with nary a wasted byte or instruction.

Turbo Assembler also handles automatic sizing of forward jumps, but not so perfectly as with backward jumps. The good news is that forward conditional jumps to near labels will always assemble if automatic jump-sizing is enabled; the bad news is that several extra **NOP** instructions will be inserted if it turns out that a conditional jump could have reached the destination label after all. (This occurs because Turbo Assembler is a single-pass assembler.)

A moment's thought will make it clear why automatic sizing of forward jumps can't always generate optimal code. When Turbo Assembler reaches a conditional jump instruction that makes a forward reference, there's no way to know how far away that label is; after all, Turbo Assembler hasn't even encountered that label yet. With automatic jump-sizing enabled, Turbo Assembler would like to generate a conditional jump (a 2-byte instruction) if the destination is near enough to read directly, and a conditional jump around an unconditional jump (a 2-byte instruction followed by a 3-byte instruction) otherwise. Unfortunately, Turbo Assembler doesn't yet know whether a 2-byte instruction or a 5-byte pair of instructions is necessary when it encounters a conditional forward jump.

Still, Turbo Assembler has to pick *some* size right away, in order to know where to assemble the following instructions. Consequently, Turbo Assembler has no alternative but to make the safe choice and reserve 5 bytes for a conditional/unconditional jump pair. Then, if Turbo Assembler later reaches the destination label and decides that a 2-byte instruction will do the trick, it will assemble a conditional jump, followed by three **NOP** instructions that fill out the 5 reserved bytes.

Suppose Turbo Assembler is assembling the following:

```
    .
    .
    .
JUMPS
jz   DestLabel
inc  ax
    .
    .
    .
```

If **JZ** can't reach *DestLabel* directly, Turbo Assembler assembles the equivalent of the following:

```
    .
    .
    .
jnz  $+5         ;2 bytes long
jmp  DestLabel   ;3 bytes long
```

```
inc  ax
.
.
.
```

If, on the other hand, **JZ** can reach *DestLabel* directly, Turbo Assembler assembles the following:

```
.
.
.
jz   DestLabel      ;2 bytes long
nop                 ;each nop is 1 byte long
nop
nop
inc  ax
.
.
.
```

The key here is that Turbo Assembler must take up 5 bytes for each automatically sized forward conditional jump, so three **NOP** instructions are inserted in automatically sized forward conditional jumps that can reach their destinations. Those three **NOP** instructions take up space and take time to execute (3 cycles each on an 8086). Consequently, you're best advised to use automatically sized forward conditional jumps sparingly whenever you're particularly sensitive to code size and performance issues.

If you're writing a program containing high-performance code, you might want to enable automatic jump-sizing for noncritical sections of your program, but disable automatic jump-sizing in the key code sections. Alternatively, you might want to enable automatic jump-sizing for backward jumps but disable it for forward jumps. You can do this by pairing the **JUMPS** instruction with the **NOJUMPS** instruction, which turns off automatic jump-sizing.

For example, the following uses automatic jump-sizing for the backward jump, but not for the forward jump:

```
.
.
.
LoopTop:
.
.
.
lodsb
cmp  al,80h
NOJUMPS
```

```
        jb   SaveByteValue
        neg  al
SaveByteValue:
     stosb
        .

        .

        .

     dec  dx
     JUMPS
     jnz  LoopTop
        .

        .

        .
```

Here, we've directly specified a 2-byte conditional jump for the forward jump to *SaveByteValue*, but let Turbo Assembler select the best code for the backward jump to *LoopTop*.

By the way, **NOJUMPS** is always selected at the start of assembly; if you want to use automatic jump-sizing, you must explicitly enable it with the **JUMPS** directive.

Forward References to Code and Data

In the last section, you saw an example of how forward conditional jumps can make Turbo Assembler generate less efficient code when automatic jump-sizing is enabled. The truth of the matter is that all sorts of forward references can cause problems for Turbo Assembler, so you should avoid forward references—that is, references to labels farther on in the code—whenever possible.

Why? Well, as Turbo Assembler assembles a source module, it makes a single pass through the code, progressing steadily from the first line in the source module to the last. This means that Turbo Assembler assembles the first line in a module, then the second line, then the third line, and so on. While that may seem obvious, the implication of the order in which Turbo Assembler assembles lines may be less obvious: Turbo Assembler doesn't know *anything* about a line until it reaches it, and so forward references force Turbo Assembler to make assumptions, which might turn out to be incorrect. If those assumptions are indeed incorrect, Turbo Assembler might generate less than maximally efficient code. Even if Turbo Assembler can generate efficient code, it might be necessary to go back to earlier lines and make corrections, and so assembly might take more time than it otherwise would.

Consider the following:

```
          .
          .
          .
     jmp  DestLabel
          .
          .
          .

DestLabel:
          .
          .
          .
```

When Turbo Assembler encounters the line

```
   jmp  DestLabel
```

it hasn't reached the definition of the label *DestLabel* yet; consequently, Turbo Assembler has no idea whether *DestLabel* is near or far, and, if it's near, whether it can be reached with a 1-byte displacement or whether a full 2-byte displacement is needed. Consequently, Turbo Assembler needs to make an assumption about the nature of *DestLabel* in order to continue assembling.

Turbo Assembler could assume that *DestLabel* is far and reserve 5 bytes for a far **JMP** instruction; however, most jumps are 3-byte near jumps, and it would be a shame to waste 2 bytes on every forward-referenced near jump. At the opposite end of the spectrum, Turbo Assembler could assume *DestLabel* can be reached with a single-byte displacement and reserve just 2 bytes for a **JMP SHORT** instruction; the problem here is that many jumps are not short, and if Turbo Assembler reserved only 2 bytes, an error would occur if the jump proved to be either near or far.

As a compromise, Turbo Assembler assumes that all forward jumps are near, unless you specify otherwise with either the **SHORT** or the **FAR PTR** operator. Three bytes are always reserved for forward jumps. If a forward jump turns out to be far, an error results; you must always use **FAR PTR** to allow forward jumps to far labels to assemble. That's a bit of a nuisance, but if you forget the **FAR PTR**, Turbo Assembler will simply inform you that a data type override is required, and you can insert the required **FAR PTR** operator and reassemble.

If, on the other hand, a forward jump proves to be short, Turbo Assembler assembles a short jump, but inserts a **NOP** instruction to pad out the 3 bytes that were reserved for the jump, thereby wasting a byte. For example, Turbo Assembler assembles this:

```
              .
              .
              .
        jmp  DestLabel
DestLabel:
              .
              .
              .
```

into this:

```
              .
              .
              .
        jmp  SHORT DestLabel
        nop
DestLabel:
              .
              .
              .
```

While the jump works perfectly well, and executes quickly, it is larger than it needs to be. Of course, you can use the **SHORT** operator to turn any forward-referenced jump into a true 2-byte instruction, but that's not as convenient as if Turbo Assembler were able to generate the appropriate jump automatically.

It's important to understand that it's the forward reference that's the culprit here. If Turbo Assembler knew the distance to the destination label, the most efficient jump could be assembled. But with forward references, Turbo Assembler can't know the distance to the destination until it reaches it, and it can't reach the destination until it assembles the forward-referenced jump. Turbo Assembler resolves this dilemma by making a simplifying assumption that allows assembly to proceed, but at the possible cost of larger code than is necessary.

Whenever Turbo Assembler does know the type of a jump—**SHORT, NEAR,** or **FAR**—the most efficient possible code can be generated. Consequently, it's a good idea to use the **SHORT** operator on short forward jumps (and, of course, **FAR PTR** is required for far forward jumps).

Jumps aren't the only instructions that you should avoid using with forward references; forward references to data can easily generate in-efficient code as well. Consider the following:

```
              .
              .
              .
        .CODE
```

```
        .
        .
        .
mov  bl,Value
        .
        .
        .
Value     EQU  1
        .
        .
        .
```

When Turbo Assembler reaches the **MOV** instruction, there's no way to know whether *Value* is an equated label or a memory variable. If *Value* is a memory variable, a 4-byte instruction will be required, while if *Value* is an equated label (one that's used as a constant), a 2-byte instruction will do the job.

As usual, Turbo Assembler must assume the worst in order to continue assembling, so 4 bytes are reserved for the **MOV** instruction. Then, when *Value* is reached and discovered to be an equated label rather than a memory variable, Turbo Assembler must go back to the **MOV** instruction and make it a 2-byte instruction with a constant operand, and must insert two **NOP** instructions to fill out the third and fourth bytes that were reserved. Note that none of this would have happened if *Value* had been defined before the **MOV** instruction, since Turbo Assembler would have known that *Value* wasn't a memory variable.

In fact, backward references present none of the problems of forward references, since Turbo Assembler always knows everything there is to know about backward-referenced labels. As a result, Turbo Assembler always automatically assembles the most efficient possible code for instructions that involve only backward-referenced operands. This makes it highly desirable to avoid forward references whenever possible.

You might wonder if the forward-referencing problems with calls are as severe as they are for jumps. The answer is no. Forward-referenced far calls must have **FAR PTR** type overrides, since Turbo Assembler assumes forward calls are near. Since there is no such thing as a short call; inefficient code for calls is never generated.

Many forward references result in an assembly error rather than inefficient code. For example, forward references to equated labels can't be assembled, and forward references to far labels can't be assembled without a type override.

Even when Turbo Assembler can generate efficient code for forward references, assembly is slower than for backward references. This happens because whenever it encounters a label that has previously been forward-referenced, Turbo Assembler must return to each instruction that performed a forward reference to that label and assemble it properly, now that the value and type of that label are known. Note that this is true even if you used a type override on forward references to that label.

The conclusion is clear: Avoid forward references in your code whenever possible, to let Turbo Assembler generate the best possible code as quickly as possible. For example, put data definitions at the beginning of your source modules before the code that references them. When you can't avoid forward references, always use a type override operator to let Turbo Assembler know exactly what type of label you're working with.

Using Repeat Blocks and Macros

One of the things a computer does well is repetitive work. You might get bored with typing dozens of values for **DB** directives, or with entering slight variations on the same code over and over, but your computer will never tire of such work. Turbo Assembler provides repeat blocks and macros to free you from just that sort of monotonous work.

Repeat Blocks

A repeat block starts with the **REPT** directive and ends with the **ENDM** directive. The code within the repeat block is assembled the number of times specified by the operand to the **REPT** directive. For example,

```
        .
        .
        .
REPT 10
DW    0
ENDM
        .
        .
        .
```

generates the same code as

```
        .
        .
        .
DW    0
DW    0
DW    0
```

```
DW    0
DW    0
DW    0
DW    0
DW    0
DW    0
DW    0
  .
  .
  .
```

That doesn't seem earthshaking, particularly given that

```
DW    10 DUP (0)
```

does the same thing, but now let's combine repeat blocks and the = directive to make a table of the first ten integers:

```
      .
      .
      .
IntVal    =  0
    REPT 10
      DW   IntVal
IntVal    =  IntVal+1
    ENDM
      .
      .
      .
```

This generates the equivalent of

```
  .
  .
  .
DW    0
DW    1
DW    2
DW    3
DW    4
DW    5
DW    6
DW    7
DW    8
DW    9
  .
  .
  .
```

Try doing that with **DUP**! Better yet, if you want the first 100 integers, all you need do is change the operand to **REPT** to 100; that's certainly a lot easier than typing 100 lines.

One excellent application for **REPT** is in the generation of tables used for fast multiplication and division. For example, the following multiplies a number between 0 and 99 (stored in BX) by 10—very rapidly—and places the result in AX.

```
    .DATA
TableOfMultiplesOf10     LABEL     WORD
BaseVal   =    0
    REPT 100
    DW   BaseVal
BaseVal   =    BaseVal+10
    ENDM
    .
    .
    .
    .CODE
    .
    .
    .
    shl  bx,1                        ;prepare for look up in table
                                     ; of word-sized entries
    mov  ax,[TableOfMultiplesOf10+bx]  ;look up the result of
                                     ; multiplication times 10
    .
    .
    .
```

Keep in mind that the text in a repeat block is simply assembled as many times as the operand to **REPT** dictates. There's no difference between executing a repeat block 10 times and making 9 additional copies of the code in a repeat block and then assembling all 10 instances of the code.

This means that any valid assembler code, including instructions, can be placed within a repeat block. For example, the following generates code to divide the 32-bit unsigned value in DX:AX by 16:

```
     .
     .
     .
REPT 4
shr  dx,1
rcr  ax,1
ENDM
     .
     .
     .
```

Repeat blocks can be nested. For instance, the following generates 10 **NOP** instructions:

```
     .
     .
     .
REPT 5
REPT 2
nop
ENDM
ENDM
     .
     .
     .
```

Repeat Blocks and Variable Parameters

IRP and **IRPC** provide two means by which to provide a variable parameter to each pass of a repeat block.

IRP substitutes the first entry in a list for a parameter on the first repetition of a repeat block, the second entry on the second repetition, and so on until the list is used up. For example,

```
     .
     .
     .
IRP  PARM,<0,1,4,9,16,25>
DB   PARM
ENDM
     .
     .
     .
```

generates

```
        .
        .
        .
    DB    0
    DB    1
    DB    4
    DB    9
    DB    16
    DB    25
        .
        .
        .
```

IRPC is similar, save that it substitutes one character from a string on each repetition of a repeat block. The following code sets the zero flag if AL is equal to any of the characters in the string that's the second argument to **IRPC**:

```
            .
            .
            .
    IRPC  TEST_CHAR,azklg
    cmp   al,'&TEST_CHAR&'
    jz    EndCompare
    ENDM
EndCompare:
            .
            .
            .
```

The last example uses the ampersand (&) to force evaluation of the repeat block parameter *TEST_CHAR*, even within quotes. The ampersand is a macro operator that works in a repeat block because repeat blocks are actually a type of macro. Other macro features, such as the **LOCAL** and **EXITM** directives, also work in repeat blocks. We'll discuss macros next.

Macros

The basic operation of a macro is quite simple: You assign a name to a block of text, or a *macro*; then, when Turbo Assembler encounters that macro name later in your source code, the block of text associated with the name is assembled. You might think of the macro name being *expanded* into the full text of the macro; hence the term *macro expansion* is often used to describe the substitution of macro text for a macro name.

A useful analogy is that of an include file. When Turbo Assembler encounters an **INCLUDE** directive, the text in the specified file is immediately assembled, just as if it were in the source module containing the **INCLUDE**. If a second **INCLUDE** of the same file is encountered, Turbo Assembler assembles that text again.

Macros are similar to include files in that the text, or body, of the macro is assembled each time the macro name is encountered. Macros are actually a great deal more flexible than include files, however, since they can optionally be passed parameters and can contain local labels. They are much faster than include files, since the text of a macro does not have to be read from disk. Let's take a look at basic macro operation.

The following code uses the macro *MULTIPLY_BY_4* to multiply the value in AX by 4, storing the result in DX:AX:

```
            .
            .
            .
MULTIPLY_BY_4  MACRO
      sub  dx,dx
      shl  ax,1
      rcl  dx,1
      shl  ax,1
      rcl  dx,1
      ENDM
            .
            .
            .
      mov  ax,[MemVar]
      MULTIPLY_BY_4
      mov  WORD PTR [Result],ax
      mov  WORD PTR [Result+2],dx
            .
            .
            .
```

When Turbo Assembler encounters *MULTIPLY_BY_4*, it assembles the four instructions that make up the body of that macro on the spot. It's almost as if a new instruction has been defined, *MULTIPLY_BY_4*, which you can use just as you use **MOV** and **MUL**. Of course, that new macro instruction consists of five 8086 instructions, but it's certainly easier to read the previous code with the macro than without.

You could just as well have used a subroutine named *MultiplyBy4* instead of a macro in this example, as follows:

```
            .
            .
            .
MultiplyBy4    PROC
```

```
        sub  dx,dx
        shl  ax,1
        rcl  dx,1
        shl  ax,1
        rcl  dx,1
        ret
MultiplyBy4     ENDP
        .
        .
        .
        mov  ax,[MemVar]
        call MultiplyBy4
        mov  WORD PTR [Result],ax
        mov  WORD PTR [Result+2],dx
        .
        .
        .
```

How do you choose between subroutines and macros? Well, you'll generally produce *smaller code* by using a subroutine, since with subroutines the code for a specific task is assembled only once, with calls to that code sprinkled throughout the program. However, you'll produce *faster code* with macros, since macros avoid the overhead of **CALL** and **RET** instructions. Moreover, a single macro can be tailored to generate slightly different code for a number of similar tasks, while a subroutine can't.

In general, you'll want to use subroutines for minimum code size, and macros for speed and flexibility.

What sort of flexibility does a macro provide? Macro flexibility is limited only by your imagination, since macros can accept parameters and can contain conditional assembly directives. Macro parameters appear as operands to the **MACRO** directive. For example, *VALUE* and *LENGTH* are parameters to the macro *FILL_ARRAY*, defined as follows:

```
        .
        .
        .
FILL_ARRAY    MACRO    VALUE,LENGTH
        REPT LENGTH
        DB   VALUE
        ENDM
        ENDM
        .
        .
        .
```

When a macro is invoked, parameters to the macro can be placed as operands to the macro invocation. For example, *FILL_ARRAY* could be invoked as

```
      .
      .
      .
ByteArray LABEL    BYTE
      FILL_ARRAY   2,9
      .
      .
      .
```

The parameters that appear in the macro invocation (2 and 9 in the previous code) are known as *actual parameters*. The parameters that appear in the macro definition (*VALUE* and *LENGTH* in the preceding code) are known as *formal parameters*. Each time a macro is invoked, the formal parameters are set to the values of the corresponding actual parameters before the macro is expanded, so

```
      .
      .
      .
ByteArray LABEL    BYTE
      FILL_ARRAY   2,9
      .
      .
      .
```

causes the following code to assemble:

```
      .
      .
      .
ByteArray LABEL    BYTE
      REPT 9
      DB   2
      ENDM
      .
      .
      .
```

The values of the actual parameters to a macro invocation are substituted for the formal parameters in the macro definition, so you can generate different macro code simply by changing the actual parameters used in a macro invocation. For instance, if you wanted to initialize *ByteArray* to be 8 bytes in length, initialized to 0FFh, and *ByteArray2* to be 100h bytes long, initialized to 0, all you'd need would be

```
        .
        .
        .
ByteArray   LABEL    BYTE
     FILL_ARRAY  0ffh,8
ByteArray2 LABEL    BYTE
     FILL_ARRAY  0,100h
        .
        .
        .
```

Formal parameters can be used anywhere in a macro. However, there's a problem when formal parameters are mixed with other text. For example, in the macro

```
        .
        .
        .
PUSH_WORD_REG  MACRO    RLETTER
     push RLETTERx
     ENDM
        .
        .
        .
```

Turbo Assembler can't know whether the string *RLETTER* embedded in *RLETTERx* is the name of the formal parameter or part of the operand to **PUSH**, so it assumes it's part of the operand. Alas, pushing *RLETTERx* isn't likely to succeed unless you happen to have memory variable of that name, and the desired result of pushing a register wouldn't be achieved in any case.

The solution is to enclose the formal parameter name in a pair of ampersands (&&). When Turbo Assembler encounters macro text enclosed in ampersands, it checks first to see whether that text is the name of a formal parameter; if so, it substitutes the value of that parameter. (If such text isn't the name of a formal parameter, Turbo Assembler ignores the ampersands.)

For example, the following expansion of *PUSH_WORD_REG*,

```
        .
        .
        .
PUSH_WORD_REG      MACRO    RLETTER
     push &RLETTER&x
     ENDM
        .
        .
```

```
        .
     PUSH_WORD_REG  b
        .
        .
        .
```

assembles to

```
     push bx
```

Ampersands are only required when there might be a question about a reference to a formal parameter; for example, they're not needed in

```
        .
        .
        .
     PUSH_WORD_REG    MACRO    REGISTER
         push REGISTER
         ENDM
        .
        .
        .
```

However, it never hurts to use ampersands, so use them whenever you're in doubt about whether they're needed.

Nesting Macros

You've already seen that macros can contain repeat blocks. Macros can invoke other macros as well; this is known as nesting macros. For example, in

```
        .
        .
        .
     PUSH_WORD_REG      MACRO    REGISTER
         push REGISTER
         ENDM
        .
        .
        .
     PUSH_ALL_REGS      MACRO
         IRP  REG,<AX,BX,CX,DX,SI,DI,BP,SP>
         PUSH_WORD_REG REG
         ENDM
         ENDM
        .
        .
        .
```

the macro *PUSH_ALL_REGS* contains a repeat block, which in turn contains an invocation of the macro *PUSH_WORD_REG*.

Macros and Conditionals

Perhaps the most powerful feature of macros is their capability to contain conditional assembly directives. This allows a single macro to assemble different sorts of code depending on the state of equated labels and parameters to each macro invocation.

For example, we'll return to the earlier example of a macro that performs multiplication. In this case, however, if the factor passed as a parameter to the new *MULTIPLY* macro is any power of two, we'll multiply by using the faster shift and rotate instructions; otherwise, we'll use the **MUL** instruction. Here's the macro:

```
        .
        .
        .
MULTIPLY  MACRO     FACTOR
;
; Check FACTOR against each of the 16 possible powers of two.
;
IS_POWER_OF_TWO =   0
COUNT           =   15
POWER_OF_TWO    =   8000h
        REPT 16
IF POWER_OF_TWO EQ FACTOR
IS_POWER_OF_TWO =   1                 ;FACTOR is a power of two
        EXITM
ENDIF
COUNT           =   COUNT-1
POWER_OF_TWO    =   POWER_OF_TWO SHR 1
        ENDM

IF IS_POWER_OF_TWO
        sub  dx,dx
        REPT COUNT
        shl  ax,1
        rcl  dx,1
        ENDM
ELSE
        mov  dx,FACTOR
        mul  dx
ENDIF
```

```
        ENDM
        .
        .
        .
```

MULTIPLY actually checks on the fly whether the multiplication is by a power of two and assembles the appropriate code. So the code

```
    MULTIPLY  10
```

assembles to

```
        .
        .
        .
    mov   dx,10
    mul   dx
        .
        .
        .
```

but the code,

```
    MULTIPLY   8
```

assembles to

```
        .
        .
        .
    sub   dx,dx
    shl   ax,1
    rcl   dx,1
    shl   ax,1
    rcl   dx,1
    shl   ax,1
    rcl   dx,1
        .
        .
        .
```

Bear in mind that macros are expanded at assembly time, not at run-time. *MULTIPLY* assembles new code each time it is invoked; the **IF** directive in *MULTIPLY* determines which instructions get assembled. Don't confuse macros with subroutines, and don't confuse conditional assembly with **if** statements and the like in high-level languages.

Stopping Expansion with EXITM

The next example contains a directive you haven't seen before: **EXITM**. The **EXITM** directive instructs Turbo Assembler to stop expanding the current macro or repeat block. If, however, the current macro or repeat block is nested inside another macro or repeat block, expansion of the nesting macro or repeat block continues.

In this example, **EXITM** terminates expansion of the repeat block containing the **EXITM** directive; however, expansion of the macro *MULTIPLY*, which contains the repeat block, continues. In fact, in this example, **REPT** and **EXITM** are used together to produce something similar to a **while** loop in C. Again, though, the while loop in *MULTIPLY* is an assembly-time loop that determines which code should be assembled, not a run-time loop.

Defining Labels within Macros

One potential problem with macros arises when you define a label within a macro. For example, the following causes an error due to the redefinition of *SkipLabel*, since each expansion of the macro *DO_DEC* defines *SkipLabel*:

```
        .
        .
        .
DO_DEC    MACRO
        jcxz SkipLabel
        dec  cx
SkipLabel:
        ENDM
        .
        .
        .
        DO_DEC
        .
        .
        .
        DO_DEC
        .
        .
        .
```

Fortunately, Turbo Assembler provides a simple solution in the form of the **LOCAL** directive. A **LOCAL** directive in a given macro causes the scope of the specified label or labels to be restricted to that macro. For example, **LOCAL** can be used as follows to allow the last example to assemble:

```
         .
         .
         .
DO_DEC   MACRO
    LOCAL      SkipLabel
    jcxz SkipLabel
    dec  cx
SkipLabel:
    ENDM
         .
         .
         .
```

If **LOCAL** is used in a macro, it must be used immediately following the **MACRO** directive. Multiple labels can be declared local with a single **LOCAL** directive, and multiple **LOCAL** directives can be used:

```
         .
         .
         .
TEST_MACRO      MACRO
    LOCAL       LoopTop,LoopEnd,SkipInc
    LOCAL       NoEvent,MacroDone
         .
         .
         .
    ENDM
         .
         .
         .
```

The names actually assigned to local labels are of the form

   ??XXXX

where *XXXX* is a hexadecimal number between 0 and 0FFFFh. Consequently, you should not assign your own labels names that start with ??, since these might conflict with the local labels Turbo Assembler generates.

Forward references to macros are not allowed; macros must be defined before they're invoked. This makes good sense, in light of our earlier discussion of forward references, since Turbo Assembler has no idea how many bytes it would have to reserve for a forward-referenced macro. Otherwise, though, macros can be defined anywhere in a source module.

Any valid assembler line can appear in a macro. This includes data definition directives, as well as code, and even includes segment directives, labels of all sorts, and listing control directives.

There are several conditional assembly directives that are designed specifically for use in macros; these include **IFDIF**, **IFIDN**, **IFDIFI**, **IFIDNI**, **IFB**, and **IFNB**. There are also several conditional error directives for use in macros, including **ERRDIF**, **ERRIDN**, **ERRDIFI**, **ERRIDNI**, **ERRB**, and **ERRNB**. Refer to Chapter 5 in this manual and Chapter 3 in the *Reference Guide* for information about these directives.

There are a number of special operators that you can use within macros:

&	Substitute operator
<>	Literal text string operator
!	Quoted character operator
%	Expression evaluate operator
;;	Suppressed comment

The & substitution operator has been discussed in the previous section on macros. This and the other special operators are all defined more fully in Chapter 2 of the *Reference Guide*.

Fancy Data Structures

Turbo Assembler provides three directives to ease the task of managing complex data structures: **STRUC**, **RECORD**, and **UNION**. You've probably noticed that the directive names are similar to those used by high-level languages, and, indeed, there are some similarities between Turbo Assembler's data structure directives and those of high-level languages.

Don't be misled, however; as you will see, assembly language data structure directives, while helpful, are less sophisticated than those of high-level languages. For example, assembly language doesn't limit the scope of the name of a structure element to that structure, so every structure element name must be unique in its source module.

Also, unlike C and Pascal, assembly language data structure directives are conveniences, not necessities; there are ways to handle data structures, records, and unions in assembler without using the data structure directives. Nonetheless, the data structure directives *are* convenient and well worth knowing about.

The following discussion applies to Turbo Assembler operating in MASM mode. In Ideal mode, Turbo Assembler supports considerably more powerful forms of the data structure directives. Consult Chapter 12 to learn more about the enhanced features of Ideal mode.

One point about Turbo Assembler's fancy data structures before we begin: Structures, records, and unions can appear anywhere in a source module, as long as they are never forward-referenced by instructions or directives.

The STRUC Directive

The **STRUC** directive, which lets you define a data structure, is useful whenever you have to deal with data that's partitioned into logical groups. For those of you who are familiar with C, **STRUC** is similar to C's **struct** statement.

For example, suppose you want to define a data structure containing a name, age, and income for one client. Here's such a structure:

```
CLIENT     STRUC
NAME       DB    'Name goes here ....'
AGE        DW    ?
INCOME     DD    ?
CLIENT     ENDS
```

The *CLIENT* structure contains three fields: The *NAME* field, which contains a name up to 20 characters in length; the *AGE* field, which contains an age stored as a 16-bit value; and the *INCOME* field, which contains an income stored as a 32-bit value.

You could use the *CLIENT* structure as follows:

```
           .
           .
           .
CLIENT     STRUC
NAME       DB    'Name goes here ....'
AGE        DW    ?
INCOME     DD    ?
CLIENT     ENDS
           .
           .
           .
       .DATA
MisterBark     CLIENT     <'John Q. Bark',32,10000>
           .
           .
           .
       .CODE
           .
           .
           .
       mov  ax,[MisterBark.Age]
```

```
        mov  bx,OFFSET MisterBark
        mov  ax,WORD PTR [bx.INCOME]
        mov  dx,WORD PTR [bx.INCOME+2]
         .
         .
         .
```

There's much to examine in this example. First, notice that structure definitions end with the **ENDS** directive. This is the same directive that ends segment definitions. It's all right to nest structure definitions inside segment definitions. For example, the following defines a structure inside a data segment:

```
         .
         .
         .

_Data   SEGMENT   WORD PUBLIC 'DATA'
         .
         .
         .

Test    STRUC
         .
         .
         .

Test    ENDS
         .
         .
         .

_Data   ENDS
         .
         .
         .
```

Second, note that the variable *MisterBark* of structure type *CLIENT* is created as if there were a new data type named *CLIENT*, and in fact that's exactly what you've done by defining the *CLIENT* structure. In fact, if you use the **SIZE** operator on a *CLIENT* structure, you'll get the value 26, which is the size of the structure.

When *MisterBark* is created, three parameters to the declaration are provided within angle brackets. These parameters become the initial values for the corresponding fields of *MisterBark*; the string 'John Q. Bark' is the initial value of the *NAME* field, 32 is the initial value of the *AGE* field, and 10,000 is the initial value of the *INCOME* field.

You need not specify the initial value of any or all of the fields of a structured variable when you create it. For example,

```
    MisterBark   CLIENT   <>
```

doesn't initialize any of the fields of *MisterBark*, and

```
MisterBark    CLIENT    <,,19757>
```

initializes only the *INCOME* field. However, the angle brackets are required even if no fields are initialized.

If you don't specify an initial value when you create a memory variable, there are two possible ways in which the initial value of each field can be set. If you specified a value for a given field when you defined the structure type, that's the default value assigned to that field. If you specified a question mark for a given field when you defined the structure type, the default value for that field is 0.

For example, in the following code, an initial value is specified for only one field of *MisterBark*—the *NAME* field—when *MisterBark* is created. However, an initial value is specified for the *AGE* field when the *CLIENT* structure is defined, so that's the value assigned to the *AGE* field of *MisterBark*. No value is specified in either place for the *INCOME* field, so the *INCOME* field is initialized to 0. Here's the example:

```
       .
       .
       .
CLIENT    STRUC
NAME      DB    'Name goes here ....'
AGE       DW    21
INCOME    DD    ?
CLIENT    ENDS
       .
       .
       .
       .DATA
MisterBark    CLIENT    <'John Q. Bark'>
       .
       .
       .
```

The result of this code is that the *NAME* field is initialized to 'John Q. Bark', the *AGE* field is initialized to 21, and the *INCOME* field is initialized to 0. Note that the initial value for the *NAME* field specified when *MisterBark* is created overrides the initial value specified when the *CLIENT* structure was defined.

You can initialize arrays of structures with the **DUP** operator. For example,

```
Clients    CLIENT    52 DUP (<>)
```

creates the array *Clients*, consisting of 52 structures of type *CLIENT*, each initialized to the default values.

If you look back to the original structure example, you'll see a new operator there—the period (.) operator. The period operator is actually just another form of the plus operator for memory-addressing; that is, all the following lines do exactly the same thing:

```
        .
        .
        .
mov   ax,[bx.AGE]
mov   ax,[bx].AGE
mov   ax,[bx+AGE]
mov   ax,[bx]+AGE
        .
        .
        .
```

The period operator is often used with structure references for consistency with C notation, which also uses the period operator, and to make it clear that a structure field is being accessed; you can use whichever operator you prefer—period or plus.

The structure fields defined with the **STRUC** directive are actually labels equated to the offset of the field in the structure. Given the earlier definition for *CLIENT* and *MisterBark*, the following two lines are equivalent:

```
        .
        .
        .
mov   [MisterBark.AGE],ax
mov   [MisterBark+20],ax
        .
        .
        .
```

and this would work as well:

```
        .
        .
        .
AGE_FIELD EQU   20
        .
        .
        .
      mov   [MisterBark+AGE_FIELD],ax
        .
        .
        .
```

Advantages and Disadvantages of Using STRUC

Why use **STRUC**, then? For one thing, structure fields provide data-typing; Turbo Assembler knows *MisterBark.AGE* in the first example is a word-sized variable, since there *AGE* is a structure element, but *MisterBark+AGE* in the second example has no inherent size.

For another, it's much easier to change a structure definition than to change constant offsets, or even a set of equates. For example, if you decided that the *NAME* field should be 30 characters long, all you'd have to do is change the entry for *NAME* in the *CLIENT* definition. If you were using equates, you'd have to manually calculate and change the offsets of both the *AGE* and *INCOME* fields; in a larger structure, you'd have quite a bit of work to do.

Finally, **STRUC** makes it easy to create and initialize data structures.

In short, **STRUC** is a convenient and maintainable way to create and access data structures. On the other hand, assembler data structures are by no means as error-proof as C data structures. For example, when you use a register to point to a data structure, there's no way for Turbo Assembler to tell whether the register contains a pointer to a valid data structure of that type. In the following code, BX is loaded with 0, but there's no way for Turbo Assembler to know whether or not there's a valid *CLIENT* data structure at offset 0:

```
       .
       .
       .
    mov  bx,0
    mov  dx,[bx.AGE]
       .
       .
       .
```

This is not a problem with assembly language; rather, it reflects the nature of assembly language. When there's a choice between letting you have complete freedom in programming and protecting you from yourself, assembly language gives you the freedom. The important thing to keep in mind is that Turbo Assembler can perform only limited error-checking on your structure references; it's up to you to make sure you've got the right pointers loaded.

Unique Structure Field Names

One somewhat annoying result of the fact that structure field names are actually just labels is that structure field names must be unique in their source module. For example, if you defined the *CLIENT* structure in a given source module, you couldn't have a label named *INCOME* anywhere else in that module, not even in another structure. *INCOME* is just a label with the value 22, and of course, you can't have two labels with the same name in a single source module. The following will produce an error, due to the attempted redefinition of *AGE*:

```
        .
        .
        .
CLIENT   STRUC
NAME     DB   'Name goes here ....'
AGE      DW   ?
INCOME   DD   ?
CLIENT   ENDS
        .
        .
        .
AGE  EQU  21
        .
        .
        .
```

Nesting Structures

Structures can be nested; for example,

```
        .
        .
        .
        .DATA
        .
        .
        .
AGE_STRUC STRUC
YEARS     DW   ?
MONTHS    DW   ?
AGE_STRUC ENDS
        .
        .
        .
CLIENT   STRUC
NAME     DB   'Name goes here ....'
AGE      AGE_STRUC <>
INCOME   DW        ?
CLIENT   ENDS
        .
        .
```

```
          .
MisterBark      CLIENT      <>
          .
          .

          .
     .CODE
          .
          .

          .
     mov  dx,[MisterBark.AGE.MONTHS]
     mov  si,OFFSET MisterBark
     mov  cx,[si.AGE.YEARS]
          .
          .
          .
```

nests an *AGE_STRUC* structure named *AGE* in the *CLIENT* structure, then references the *MONTHS* and *YEARS* fields of *AGE* in the *CLIENT* structure *MisterBark*.

Initializing Structures

There are a few cautions regarding the initialization of structures. First, if you attempt to initialize a string field of a structure with a string that is longer than the field, an assembly error will be generated.

Second, the only kind of field that can be initialized with a string value is a string field. The following would not assemble:

```
          .
          .
          .
TEST STRUC
TEXT DB    30 DUP (' ')
TEST ENDS
          .
          .
          .
TStruc    TEST <'Test string'>
          .
          .
          .
```

even though *TEXT* was initialized to spaces, because Turbo Assembler considers *TEXT* to be an array of 30 spaces, not a string of 30 characters. The following would assemble:

```
            .
            .
            .
TEST STRUC
TEXT DB   'String goes here ............'
TEST ENDS
            .
            .
            .

TStruc    TEST <'Test string'>
            .
            .
            .
```

Third, while you can define more than one data element as belonging to a single structure field, you can only initialize, at most, one element per field when you create an instance of that structure. For example, in the following code, when *TestStruc* is created, the first byte of field *A* is initialized to 1, and the first byte of field *B* is initialized to 2, while the second byte of each field is initialized to 20h (a space):

```
            .
            .
            .
T     STRUC
A     DB    0ffh,0ffh
B     DB    0ffh,0ffh
T     ENDS
            .
            .
            .
TestStruc T    <1,2>
            .
            .
            .
```

In this section, we've discussed the MASM mode version of the **STRUC** directive. In Ideal mode, the **STRUC** directive is considerably more powerful, providing more of the features available when using structures in high-level languages; refer to Chapter 12 for information about Ideal mode.

The RECORD Directive

The **RECORD** directive provides you with a means to define bit fields within a byte or word. The bit field definitions can then be used to generate masks to isolate one or more of the bit fields, as well as shift counts to right-justify any bit field. The **RECORD** directive bears no relation to the Pascal **record** statement.

Suppose you want to define a data structure that contains three 1-bit flags and a 12-bit value. You could do this with the **RECORD** directive as follows:

```
TEST_REC  RECORD    FLAG1:1,FLAG2:1,FLAG3:1,TVAL:12
```

This example defines three flags, named *FLAG1*, *FLAG2*, and *FLAG3*, and a data field named *TVAL*. The value after the colon for each field specifies that field's size in bits; each of the flags is one bit in size, and *TVAL* is 12 bits in size.

How are the fields stored within the record? That's a bit complex. The first field, *FLAG1*, is the leftmost (most significant) bit of the record. The second field, *FLAG2*, is the next most significant bit of the record, and so on, until you reach *TVAL*, which ends at the least significant bit of the record. However, the record is only 15 bits in size, leaving one bit in the word unaccounted for. (Records are always exactly 8 or 16 bits long.) The rule is that records as a whole are always right-justified in a byte or word.

As we said, it's a bit complex. Here's an example to clarify things. A record of type *TEST_REC* is defined with a line like

```
TRec TEST_REC  <1,0,0,52h>
```

Here we've created the variable *TRec* of record type *TEST_REC*. The values in the angle brackets are made the initial values of the corresponding fields, so the *FLAG1* field of *TRec* is initialized to 1, the *FLAG2* and *FLAG3* fields are initialized to 0, and the *TVAL* field is initialized to 52h. Figure 10.1 shows the locations and initial values of the four fields of *TRec*.

Figure 10.1: Locations and Initial Values of the Fields in TRec

If the overall size of a record (the sum total of all the fields) is 8 bits or less, the record is stored in a byte; otherwise, the record is stored in a word. Records longer than 16 bits are not supported except when 80386 assembly is enabled; in which case, records up to 32 bits in size are allowed.

Initializing a record variable is much like initializing a structure variable. If you specify an initial value for a given record field when you create the record variable, the field is initialized to that value, as illustrated by the last example.

If you don't specify an initial value for a given record field when you create a record variable, there are two possible default values. When you create a record type, you can optionally specify a default value for any or all fields. For example,

```
TEST_REC   RECORD    FLAG1:1=1,FLAG2:1=0,FLAG3:1,TVAL:12=0fffh
```

specifies default values of 1 for *FLAG1*, 0 for *FLAG2*, and 0FFFh for *TVAL*, with no explicit default value for *FLAG3*. The default value for any field lacking an explicit default value is 0, so the default value for *FLAG3* is 0.

So, given the following definition of *TEST_REC* and creation of *TRec*

```
        .
        .
        .
    .DATA
        .
        .
        .
TEST_REC   RECORD    FLAG1:1=1,FLAG2:1=0,FLAG3:1,TVAL:12=0fffh
        .
        .
        .
TRec TEST_REC   <,1,,2>
        .
        .
        .
```

the fields are initialized as follows:

- *FLAG1* initialized to 1
- *FLAG2* initialized to 1
- *FLAG3* initialized to 0
- *TVAL* initialized to 2

The overall value of the record variable *TRec* is 6002h. Note that initial values specified when a record variable is *created* override initial values specified when the record type is *defined*.

Once defined, a record type is much like any other data type. You can, for example, use a record type with the **SIZE** operator, and you can define arrays of records with the **DUP** operator. For example, the following declares an array of 90 records of type *TEST_REC*:

```
TRecArray TEST_REC  90 DUP (<1,1,1,0>)
```

As with **STRUC** field names, record field names are labels. Since labels can only be defined once in a source module, this means that all record field names must be unique within their source module.

Accessing Records

Now that you know how to create a record and how the various fields in a record are stored, you're ready to learn how to access records. You might reasonably think that you could access record fields the way you access structure fields, as in

```
mov  al,[TRec.FLAG2]    ;this doesn't work!!!
```

but that's not the case. The 8086 can only work with 8- or 16-bit wide memory operands, so there's no way to load a 1-bit field, for instance, into a register. What you *can* do with record fields is determine their size in bytes, determine how many bits they need to be shifted to be right-justified, and generate masks to isolate them. In other words, even though the 8086 doesn't let you work directly with record fields, Turbo Assembler supports manipulating record fields with instructions such as **AND** and **SHR**.

The value of a given record field is the number of bits by which you'd have to shift the record in order to right-justify that field (that is, place bit 0 of the field at bit 0 of the record). For instance,

```
        .
        .
        .
mov  al,FLAG1
mov  ah,TVAL
        .
        .
        .
```

loads AL with 14 and AH with 0, so

```
        .
        .
        .
mov  ax,[TRec]
mov  cl,FLAG1
shr  ax,cl
        .
        .
        .
```

right-justifies the *FLAG1* field of *TRec* in AX.

The value of a given record type itself is the byte or word value that would be generated by creating a record with given initial values. For example,

```
mov  ax,TEST_REC <1,1,1,0fffh>
```

loads AX with 7FFFh, the value you'd get if you created a *TEST_REC* type record with the initial values <1,1,1,0FFFh>. Bear in mind the distinction between loading AX with the record type *TEST_REC*, as in the last example, and loading AX with the record variable *TRec*, as in

```
            .
            .
            .
TEST_REC  RECORD    FLAG1:1=1,FLAG2:1=0,FLAG3:1,TVAL:12=0fffh
            .
            .
            .
TRec TEST_REC  <,1,,2>
            .
            .
            .
          .CODE
            .
            .
            .
          mov  ax,[TRec]
            .
            .
            .
```

which loads AX with 6002h, the value of the variable *TRec*.

The WIDTH Operator

The **WIDTH** operator returns the size of a record or record field in bits. For example, the following line stores 15, the number of bits in a *TEST_REC* record, in AL:

```
mov  al,WIDTH TEST_REC   ;size of a TEST_REC record in bits
```

and the following stores 1, the width of each of the flag fields, in AL, AH, and BL, and 12, the width of the *TVAL* field, in BH:

```
    .
    .
    .
mov  al,WIDTH FLAG1
mov  ah,WIDTH FLAG2
```

```
mov  bl,WIDTH FLAG3
mov  bh,WIDTH TVAL
.
.
.
```

The MASK Operator

Finally, the **MASK** operator returns a mask suitable for isolating a record or record field with the **AND** instruction. For example,

```
mov  ax,MASK TEST_REC
```

stores 7FFFh in AX, and

```
.
.
.
mov  ax,MASK TEST_REC
mov  dx,[TRec]
and  dx,ax
.
.
.
```

stores the value of the record *TRec* in DX, masking off bit 15, which isn't part of the *TEST_REC* record.

MASK is more useful when used to isolate an individual record field. The following detects whether the *FLAG3* field of *TRec* is set:

```
.
.
.
mov  ax,[TRec]
and  ax,MASK FLAG3
jz   Flag3NotSet
.
.
.
```

Note that the **TEST** instruction can be used non-destructively in place of **AND**; the following performs the same test as the previous example without modifying any registers or memory locations:

```
    .
    .
    .
jz      Flag3NotSet
    .
    .
    .
```

The **MASK** operator is also useful for manipulating record fields in conjunction with the shift instructions, as you'll see shortly.

Why Use Records

Now you've seen what records are and how they're used. When would you really want to use records? Well, records aren't used all that often, but they are handy when you've got multiple data fields encoded in a single byte or word. Some variables used by the BIOS are structured as records. For example, the low byte of the BIOS equipment flag variable, which stores equipment-related information (such as what video adapter is active and the number of floppy drives present) is a record of the structure

```
EQ_FLAG RECORD NUMDISKS:2,VIDEO:2,RSRVD:2,MATHCHIP:1,AREDISKS:1
```

where

- *NUMDISKS* is the number of floppy disk drives installed minus 1.
- *VIDEO* indicates what sort of display adapter is currently active.
- *RSRVD* is a field reserved for different uses in different IBM microcomputers.
- *MATHCHIP* is 1 if a numeric coprocessor such as an 8087 is installed.
- *AREDISKS* is 1 if any floppy disk drives are installed.

Here's a function that uses the *EQ_FLAG* record and the record operators to return the setting of the display adapter field of the BIOS equipment flag variable:

```
;
; Returns current setting of the display adapter field of
; the BIOS equipment flag variable.
;
; Input: None
;
; Output:
;    AL = 0 if no display adapter is currently selected
;         1 if 40x25 color display is currently selected
;         2 if 80x25 color display is currently selected
;         3 if 80x25 monochrome display is currently selected
```

```
;
; Registers destroyed: AX,CL,ES
;
EQ_FLAG RECORD NUMDISKS:2,VIDEO:2,RSRVD:2,MATHCHIP:1,AREDISKS:1
;

GetBIOSEquipmentFlag        PROC
     mov  ax,40h
     mov  es,ax                ;point ES to the BIOS data segment
     mov  al,es:[10h]          ;get the low bit of the equipment flag
     and  al,MASK VIDEO        ;isolate the display adapter field
     mov  cl,VIDEO             ;get the number of bits to shift
                               ; the display adapter field right to
                               ; right-justify it
     shr  al,cl                ;right-justify the display adapter field
     ret
GetBIOSEquipmentFlag        ENDP
```

Here's a complementary function that sets the display adapter field of the BIOS equipment flag to a specified value:

```
;
; Sets the display adapter field of the BIOS equipment flag
; variable.
;
; Input:
;    AL = 0 if no display adapter is currently selected
;         1 if 40x25 color display is currently selected
;         2 if 80x25 color display is currently selected
;         3 if 80x25 monochrome display is currently selected
;
; Output: None
;
; Registers destroyed: AX,CX,ES
;
EQ_FLAG RECORD NUMDISKS:2,VIDEO:2,RSRVD:2,MATHCHIP:1,AREDISKS:1
;

SetBIOSEquipmentFlag        PROC
     mov  cx,40h
     mov  es,cx                ;point ES to the BIOS data segment
     mov  cl,VIDEO             ;get the number of bits to shift
                               ; the passed value left to align it
                               ; with the display adapter field
     shl  al,cl                ;align the value
     mov  ah,es:[10h]          ;get the low bit of the equipment flag
     and  ah,NOT MASK VIDEO
                               ;clear the display adapter field
     and  al,MASK VIDEO        ;make sure the new display adapter
                               ; field setting is valid
```

```
        or    al,ah              ;insert the new display adapter
                                 ; field setting in the equipment flag value
        mov   es:[10h],al        ;set the new equipment flag
        ret
SetBIOSEquipmentFlag    ENDP
```

In this section, we've discussed the MASM mode version of the **RECORD** directive. The Ideal mode version of the **RECORD** directive differs slightly from the MASM mode version; see Chapter 12 for information about Ideal mode.

The UNION Directive

The **UNION** directive provides a way to reference a given memory location as more than one data type. **UNION** is similar to C's **union** statement.

Suppose you have a counter that you use sometimes as an 8-bit counter and sometimes as a 16-bit counter. You could declare it to be a union of the two with

```
        .
        .
        .
FLEX_COUNT      UNION
COUNT8          DB    ?
COUNT16         DW    ?
FLEX_COUNT      ENDS
        .
        .
        .
```

Note that, as with **STRUC, UNION** definitions must end with **ENDS**.

Given the previous definition of the *FLEX_COUNT* union, you could create and use a dual-purpose counter as follows:

```
        .
        .
        .
        .DATA
Counter    FLEX_COUNT     <?,?>
        .
        .
        .
        .CODE
        .
        .
        .
        mov  [Counter.COUNT16],0ffffh
```

```
LoopTop:
        .
        .
        .
        dec  [Counter.COUNT16]
        jnz  ShortLoopTop
        .
        .
        .
        mov  [Counter.COUNT8],255
ShortLoopTop:
        .
        .
        .
        dec  [Counter.COUNT8]
        jnz  ShortLoopTop
        .
        .
        .
```

As with **STRUC,** the period operator is used to reference union fields; the plus operator could be used as well. Referencing a variable by way of its union fields is equivalent to using type overrides. The preceding example is equivalent to

```
        .
        .
        .
        .DATA
Counter  DW   ?
        .
        .
        .
        .CODE
        .
        .
        .
        mov  WORD PTR [Counter],0ffffh
LoopTop:
        .
        .
        .
        dec  WORD PTR [Counter]
        jnz  LoopTop
        .
        .
        .
        mov  BYTE PTR [Counter],255
ShortLoopTop:
```

```
        .
        .
        .
dec  BYTE PTR [Counter]
jnz  ShortLoopTop
        .
        .
        .
```

The advantage of using a union over using type overrides is that you're much more likely to use the correct union element name than you are to remember the type override in every instance. Also, the multiple-mode operation of a union variable is instantly apparent when you look at the variable's definition, so code containing unions is easier to understand and maintain.

You can nest both unions and structures within unions. For example, the following union allows a 4-byte memory variable to be accessed as either a doubleword-sized segment:offset pointer or as a word-sized offset variable and a word-sized segment variable:

```
        .
        .
        .
SEG_OFF    STRUC
POFF       DW    ?
PSEG       DW    ?
SEG_OFF    ENDS
        .
        .
        .
PUNION     UNION
DPTR       DD        ?
XPTR       SEG_OFF   <>
PUNION     ENDS
        .
        .
        .
.CODE
        .
        .
        .
mov  [bx.XPTR.POFF],si
mov  [bx.XPTR.PSEG],ds
        .
        .
        .
```

```
les  di,[bx.DPTR]
   .
   .
   .
```

As with **STRUC** and **RECORD**, the field names defined with **UNION** are normal labels, with no scope limitations. Consequently, union field names must be unique in their source module.

In this section, we've discussed the MASM mode version of the **UNION** directive. In Ideal mode, the **UNION** directive is considerably more powerful, providing more of the features available when using structures in high-level languages; refer to Chapter 12 for information about Ideal mode.

Segment Directives

In Chapter 4, you learned how to use the simplified segment directives, and you learned enough about the standard segment directives to be able to make a working program. Now we're going to discuss each of the standard segment directives in detail, and provide you with more information about what the simplified segment directives do. We're also going to show you a sample program that uses several code and data segments, to give you a feel for how multisegment programs operate.

Recall that the simplified segment directives are easier to use but less powerful than the standard segment directives. The standard segment directives we cover in the next sections are **SEGMENT, GROUP,** and **ASSUME.**

The SEGMENT Directive

The **SEGMENT** directive is used to start a segment. Each **SEGMENT** directive must have a matching **ENDS** to terminate that segment. Unlike the simplified segment directives, **SEGMENT** gives you complete control over the attributes of each segment.

The complete form of the **SEGMENT** directive is

```
name SEGMENT align combine use 'class'
```

where *align, combine, use,* and *class* are all optional. We'll discuss each of these fields in turn.

The name and align Fields

name is the name of the segment. Segment names are labels, so they must be unique in their source modules. The same name must be used with **ENDS** when the segment is ended.

align specifies the memory boundary on which the segment should start. The following are valid alignments:

- **BYTE** uses the next available byte address.
- **DWORD** uses the next doubleword-aligned address.
- **PAGE** uses the next page address (256-byte aligned).
- **PARA** uses the next paragraph address (16-byte aligned).
- **WORD** uses the next word-aligned address.

If no alignment is explicitly specified, paragraph-alignment is used.

Byte-alignment makes for the most compact programs. Word-alignment is preferable on 16-bit computers such as the AT, since 16-bit processors operate more efficiently on word-aligned data; doubleword-alignment is preferable on 32-bit computers for much the same reason. Paragraph-alignment is necessary for segments that will be a full 64K long.

The combine Field

combine controls the manner in which segments of the same name in other modules will be combined with this segment when the modules that make up the program are linked together. *combine* can be any one of the following types:

AT	**PRIVATE**
COMMON	**PUBLIC**
MEMORY	**STACK**

You might find it useful to refer to the later section (on page 465), "The Simplified Segment Directives," which shows the combine types used by high-level languages.

A combine type of **AT** causes the start of the segment to be placed at a specific address in memory. No code is actually generated; instead, **AT** segments are used as templates for accessing memory areas such as the ROM BIOS data segment and display memory. For example,

```
              .
              .
              .
VGA_GRAPHICS_MEMORY SEGMENT AT 0A000h
BitMapStart    LABEL       BYTE
VGA_GRAPHICS_MEMORY ENDS
              .
              .
              .
        mov  ax,VGA_GRAPHICS_MEMORY
        mov  es,ax
        ASSUME      es:VGA_GRAPHICS_MEMORY
        mov  di,OFFSET BitMapStart
        mov  cx,08000h
        sub  ax,ax
        cld
        rep  stosw
              .
              .
              .
```

clears the VGA graphics screen.

A combine type of **COMMON** specifies that the beginning of this segment and the beginning of all other segments of the same name should be aligned, so that the segments overlay each other. The total segment size is only the size of the largest segment of this name. One way in which the **COMMON** combine type can be used is by including a file that defines a **COMMON** segment in each module referencing that segment, so that all modules effectively share exactly the same segment.

A combine type of **PUBLIC** instructs the linker to concatenate this segment with other segments of the same name, so the segments are effectively pieced together to make a larger segment. The total size of the segment is the sum of the size of all segments of this name. As with all segments, the total size of **PUBLIC** segments can't exceed 64 Kb. **PUBLIC** is used when multiple modules share the same segment, but each defines its own variables. Variables in **PUBLIC** segments are often shared between modules by way of **GLOBAL** directives.

The **MEMORY** combine type is the same as **PUBLIC**.

A combine type of **STACK** instructs the linker to concatenate all segments of this name into one segment, and to build the EXE file so that SS:SP is set to point to the end of this segment when the program is run. This is a specialized combine type to be used for the stack and nothing else.

Finally, a combine type of **PRIVATE** instructs the linker not to combine this segment with any other segments. This allows you to define segments that are local to a given module, without having to worry about possible conflicts if segments of the same name are used in other modules. Segments default to combine type **PRIVATE** if no combine type is specified.

The use and class Fields

The *use* field of the **SEGMENT** directive is for 80386 assembly only; Chapter 11 offers more information on the *use* field.

The *class* field is used to control the order in which the linker places segments. All segments of a given class are placed in a contiguous block of memory, no matter what their order is in the source code. The section "The Simplified Segment Directives" shows the classes used by high-level languages; for simplicity, you might want to follow these conventions. (The next section has more information about segment ordering.)

Segment Size, Type, Name, and Nesting

The cumulative size of the segments in a class is limited only by the availability of memory at run-time; however, no individual segment can exceed 64K.

Note that the class type, if present, must be enclosed in quotes. Also, class types must be unique in their source modules; that is, no label used in a given module may have the same name as a class type used in that module.

You can define the same segment name multiple times in the same source module; all instances are considered to refer to a single segment. However, you must make sure that all definitions of a given segment in a source module have the same attributes; otherwise, Turbo Assembler will generate an error.

One handy way to avoid such errors is to specify attributes only the first time you define a segment in a given source module. When a redefined segment with no attributes is encountered, Turbo Assembler automatically uses the attributes specified when the segment was first defined.

Finally, segments can be nested, which means you can define a segment before you end an earlier segment, as follows:

```
        .
        .
        .
DataSeg   SEGMENT PARA PUBLIC 'DATA'
        .
        .
        .
```

```
        ·
DataSeg2   SEGMENT PARA PRIVATE 'FAR_DATA'
        ·
        ·
        ·
DataSeg2   ENDS
        ·
        ·
        ·
DataSeg    ENDS
        ·
        ·
        ·
```

Nesting is not generally useful, but there is at least one case where it's handy, and that's in a macro. In order to define a segment in a macro, you'd normally have to end and then restart the current segment, and to do that you'd need to know the current segment's name, which is not necessarily obvious in the context of a macro. By contrast, segment-nesting allows you to define a segment without ever knowing what the name of the current segment is, as follows:

```
        ·
        ·
        ·
TEST MACRO
        ·
        ·
        ·
TestSeg    SEGMENT WORD PRIVATE 'FAR_DATA'
        ·
        ·
        ·
TestSeg    ENDS
        ·
        ·
        ·
        ENDM
        ·
        ·
        ·
```

After a nested segment ends, Turbo Assembler simply resumes assembling into the segment that was active when the nested segment began.

Segment-Ordering

By and large, you don't need to worry about the order in which the segments end up in the .EXE files you create. First of all, the order in which segments appear in .EXE files doesn't often matter. Second, most of the cases in which you might care about segment order are easily handled by a high-level language compiler or the **DOSSEG** directive. If you're linking to a high-level language, that language's compiler will usually control the segment order. If you're writing a pure assembler program and have specified the **DOSSEG** directive, your segments will end up in Microsoft-standard segment order, as follows:

- Segments of class **CODE**
- Segments of class other than **CODE** that are not part of **DGROUP**
- Segments that are part of **DGROUP**, in the following order:
  - Segments of classes other than **STACK** and **BSS**
  - Segments of class **BSS**
  - Segments of class **STACK**

If you're curious about the order in which the linker is placing your segments, just use the /s command-line switch to instruct TLINK to generate a detailed segment map file and take a look at the map file.

A question remains: How are segments ordered if you aren't linking to a high-level language and you don't use the **DOSSEG** directive? Most of the time, you'll have no need to know the answer to that question, but in case it does matter to you, here's the answer. (It's a bit more complex than you might think.)

When no explicit segment-ordering, such as that forced by **DOSSEG**, is in effect, the linker groups all segments of a given class together, where the class of a segment is specified by the class field of the **SEGMENT** directive. The groups of segments themselves are placed in the .EXE file simply in the order in which the linker encounters them; the first segment class the linker encounters in loading the .OBJ files is placed first in the .EXE file, the second segment class encountered comes next, and so on. This means that the order in which .OBJ files are linked affects the final order of the segments in the .EXE file.

Now you've got the segments loosely ordered by class. How, then, are the segments within each class ordered? Once again, they're placed in the .EXE file in the order in which the linker encountered them. One factor here is the order in which the .OBJ files are linked; another factor is the order in which the segments are placed in each .OBJ file. Turbo Assembler gives you two choices regarding the order in which segments appear in .OBJ files.

The **.SEQ** directive instructs Turbo Assembler to place segments in the .OBJ file in the order in which they appear in the source file. With sequential-ordering, the order of the segments in a given source module can affect the order of the segments in the .EXE file. This is the default mode of operation of Turbo Assembler, so sequential segment-ordering will occur even if you omit the **.SEQ** directive, as long as the **.ALPHA** directive is not used.

The **.ALPHA** directive instructs Turbo Assembler to place segments in the .OBJ file in alphabetic order. With alphabetic-ordering, the order of the segments in a given source module does not affect the order of the segments in the .EXE file. This is the default mode of operation of some older assemblers, so you may, on occasion, have to use **.ALPHA** in order to get assembler programs to run properly.

So, now you've got segments loosely ordered by class, and ordered within the class by the order of appearance of the segments. You can control the order of appearance of segments within the class both by the order in which .OBJ files are linked and by the **.SEQ** and **.ALPHA** directives. If **.SEQ** is selected, the order of appearance of segments in a given source module can affect the order of the segments in the .EXE file.

You can see that segment-ordering is no simple matter. Odds are, though, that you'll never have to worry about segment order; it doesn't usually make any difference anyway, and when it does, a high-level compiler or the **DOSSEG** directive generally takes care of segment-ordering for you.

The GROUP Directive

The **GROUP** directive is used to combine two or more segments into one logical entity, so that all the segments can be addressed relative to a single segment register.

Suppose you have a program that accesses data in two segments. Normally, you'd have to load a segment register and perform a new **ASSUME** each time you wanted to access first one segment and then the other; that's both time-consuming and a nuisance. It's far easier to combine the segments into a single group named *DataGroup*, load DS with the start of *DataGroup*, **ASSUME** DS to *DataGroup*, and then access either segment at any time. Here's the code:

```
            .
            .
            .
DataGroup GROUP       DataSeg1,DataSeg2
            .
            .
            .
DataSeg1  SEGMENT    PARA PUBLIC 'DATA'
MemVar1   DW   0
DataSeg1  ENDS
            .
            .
            .
DataSeg2  SEGMENT    PARA PUBLIC 'DATA'
MemVar2   DW   0
DataSeg2  ENDS
            .
            .
            .
      mov  ax,DataGroup
      mov  ds,ax
      ASSUME      ds:DataGroup
            .
            .
            .
      mov  ax,[MemVar1]
      mov  [MemVar2],ax
            .
            .
            .
```

Why would you want to use groups when using a single segment name and the combine type **PUBLIC** produces the same result more easily? Actually, in pure assembler programs, there's not that much need for groups, although you can certainly use them if you want. Groups are primarily used when interfacing assembler code to high-level languages. In particular, the group **DGROUP** is used by high-level languages to allow the stack, initialized near data, uninitialized near data, and constant segments to be accessed relative to a single segment register.

The one *key* rule with groups is that all the segments in a group must lie within a single 64 Kb segment, since they must all be accessed relative to a single segment register. Bear in mind that segment-ordering is dependent on many factors, as discussed in the last section, so segments might lie some distance apart if you're not careful. The safest approach is to declare all segments in a group to be of the same class, and to define them one after the other at the start of all modules they're defined in.

However, when you are either linking to a high-level language or have used the **DOSSEG** directive anywhere in your program, there's no need to worry about making sure that the segments in **DGROUP** are kept together; in both these cases, the linker automatically makes all segments in **DGROUP** adjacent.

While the segments in a group must fit within a 64 Kb segment, they do not have to be contiguous when linked. Non-grouped segments can lie between the segments that make up a group.

Note: If you do use a group, you must be careful to always use the group name with **ASSUME** whenever you load a segment to point to the group. Otherwise, Turbo Assembler will generate offsets relative to the segment start, not the group start, even though the segment register is pointing to the group start. For example, the following would cause errors given the previous definition of **DGROUP**:

```
       .
       .
       .
mov   ax,DGROUP
mov   ds,ax
ASSUME      ds:Stack      ;will produce incorrect offsets!
       .
       .
       .
```

Instead, use

```
       .
       .
       .
mov   ax,DGROUP
mov   ds,ax
ASSUME      ds:DGROUP
       .
       .
       .
```

In short, if you load a segment register to point to a group, be sure to **ASSUME** to that group, not to any of its component segments.

MASM, the Microsoft Macro Assembler, has a bug regarding using the **OFFSET** operator with groups. This bug also surfaces when initializing data to the address of labels in a group. In the interests of compatibility, Turbo Assembler reproduces this bug. The workaround for this bug is to always place group override prefixes on labels when you use them with the **OFFSET** operator or use them to initialize data. (See "Forgetting Group

Overrides in Operands and Data Tables," on page 271 in Chapter 5 for more information.)

The ASSUME Directive

The **ASSUME** directive lets you tell Turbo Assembler what segment or group a given segment register is pointing to. Note that this is not the same as actually loading a segment register to point to that segment; you must do that separately with the **MOV** instruction. The purpose of **ASSUME** is to allow Turbo Assembler to check the validity of your memory references and to automatically insert segment override prefixes on your memory accesses as needed.

An **ASSUME** for CS must appear before any code in each source module, so that Turbo Assembler knows what segment to assume the instructions are in for purposes of jumps, calls, and setting the starting address of the program.

Other **ASSUME** directives for the various segment registers can be inserted as often as needed in any source module. The assumed segment for any segment register can be changed whenever you wish. Any or all segment assumptions can be changed with a single **ASSUME** directive.

You can specify an assumption for a segment register with either a segment name, a group name, or a segment extracted from a label with the **SEG** operator. Additionally, you can use the **NOTHING** keyword to instruct Turbo Assembler to assume that any or all segment registers aren't pointing to any segment.

Here's an example of using **ASSUME**:

```
Stack     SEGMENT   PARA STACK 'STACK'
    DB    512 DUP (0)
Stack     ENDS
TGROUP    GROUP     DataSeg1,DataSeg2
DataSeg1  SEGMENT   PARA PUBLIC 'DATA'
    .
    .
    .
DataSeg1  ENDS
DataSeg2  SEGMENT   PARA PUBLIC 'DATA'
    .
    .
    .
DataSeg2  ENDS
    .
    .
    .
```

```
            .
DataSeg3   SEGMENT    PARA PUBLIC 'DATA'
MemVar     DW    0
            .
            .
            .
DataSeg3   ENDS
            .
            .
            .
CodeSeg    SEGMENT    PARA PUBLIC 'CODE'
       ASSUME    cs:CodeSeg,ds:TGROUP,ss:Stack,es:NOTHING
ProgramStart:
       mov   ax,TGROUP
       mov   ds,ax
       ASSUME    ds:TGROUP
            .
            .
            .
       mov   ax,SEG MemVar              ;same as DataSeg3
       mov   es,ax
       ASSUME    es:SEG MemVar
            .
            .
            .
       push ds
       pop  es
       mov  ax,CodeSeg
       mov  ds,ax
       ASSUME    ds:CodeSeg,es:TGROUP
            .
            .
            .
CodeSeg    ENDS
       END ProgramStart
```

If an **ASSUME** directive refers to a group, the specified segment register is assumed to point to the start of that group. However, if an **ASSUME** directive refers to a segment that's part of a group, the segment register is assumed to point to the start of the segment, not the group. This can cause problems, since segment registers are generally set to point to the start of groups, not segments that make groups. For example, the following would load AX from the wrong memory location, since DS points to the start of **TGROUP**, but the **ASSUME** statement incorrectly indicates that DS points to the start of *DataSeg2*:

```
          .
          .
          .
TGROUP    GROUP      DataSeg1,DataSeg2
DataSeg1  SEGMENT    PARA PUBLIC 'DATA'
          .
          .
          .
DataSeg1  ENDS
DataSeg2  SEGMENT    PARA PUBLIC 'DATA'
MemVar    DW    0
DataSeg2  ENDS
          .
          .
          .
CodeSeg   SEGMENT    PARA PUBLIC 'CODE'
      ASSUME     cs:CodeSeg
          .
          .
          .
      mov  ax,TGROUP
      mov  ds,ax
      ASSUME     ds:DataSeg2          ;not correct!!! (should be TGROUP)
      mov  ax,[MemVar]                ;will load from the wrong offset,
                                      ; relative to DataSeg2 rather than TGROUP
          .
          .
          .
```

When you use the simplified segment directives, it's generally not necessary to use **ASSUME**, since Turbo Assembler automatically generates the appropriate segment assumptions. However, if you change any segment registers while using the simplified segment directives, you will have to perform the appropriate **ASSUME** directives. For example, the following sets DS to point to the **.DATA** segment, the **.CODE** segment, the **.FARDATA** segment, and finally back to the **.DATA** segment:

```
          .
          .
          .
.DATA
          .
          .
          .
.FARDATA
          .
          .
          .
.CODE
```

```
        mov  ax,@data
        mov  ds,ax
        ASSUME    ds:@data
        .
        .

        .
        mov  ax,@code
        mov  ds,ax
        ASSUME    ds:@code

        .
        .

        .
        mov  ax,@fardata
        mov  ds,ax
        ASSUME    ds:@fardata
        .

        .
        mov  ax,@data
        mov  ds,ax
        ASSUME    ds:@data
        .
        .
```

As we've pointed out before, the **ASSUME** directive can cause Turbo
Assembler to insert segment override prefixes on memory accesses
whenever Turbo Assembler (operating on the basis of the **ASSUME**
directives you've issued) thinks that's necessary to access a given memory
variable. For example, Turbo Assembler will put an ES: override on the
instruction that accesses *MemVar* in the following code, since the **ASSUME**
directive incorrectly indicates that DS can't reach the segment where
MemVar resides:

```
        .
        .
        .
DataSeg   SEGMENT    PARA PUBLIC 'DATA'
MemVar    DB   ?
        .
        .
        .
DataSeg   ENDS
        .
        .
        .
CodeSeg   SEGMENT    PARA PUBLIC 'CODE'
        ASSUME    cs:CodeSeg,ds:NOTHING,es:DataSeg
        .
```

```
        .
        .
        .
    mov   ax,DataSeg
    mov   ds,ax
    mov   es,ax
    mov   [MemVar],1
        .
        .
        .
```

Consequently, you should exercise care in making sure that your **ASSUME** directives correspond to the actual settings of the segment registers at all times.

The Simplified Segment Directives

We discussed the simplified segment directives in some detail in Chapter 4. However, the main aspect of simplified segment directives that we haven't covered yet is exactly what segments the various simplified segment directives create. That's not something you'll normally need to know, but if you're mixing simplified and standard segment directives, you might need that information.

The segments and segment groups created by the **.CODE, .DATA, .DATA?, .STACK, .CONST, .FARDATA,** and **.FARDATA?** directives depend on the memory model selected by the **.MODEL** directive. (Recall that we discussed memory models in Chapter 4.) The following tables show the correspondence of memory models and the segments created by the simplified segment directives:

Table 10.1: Default Segments and Types for Tiny Memory Model

Directive	Name	Align	Combine	Class	Group
.CODE	_TEXT	WORD	PUBLIC	'CODE'	DGROUP
.FARDATA	FAR_DATA	PARA	private	'FAR_DATA'	
.FARDATA?	FAR_BSS	PARA	private	'FAR_BSS'	
.DATA	_DATA	WORD	PUBLIC	'DATA'	DGROUP
.CONST	CONST	WORD	PUBLIC	'CONST'	DGROUP
.DATA?	_BSS	WORD	PUBLIC	'BSS'	DGROUP
.STACK	STACK	PARA	STACK	'STACK'	DGROUP

Table 10.2: Default Segments and Types for Small Memory Model

Directive	Name	Align	Combine	Class	Group
.CODE	_TEXT	WORD	PUBLIC	'CODE'	
.FARDATA	FAR_DATA	PARA	private	'FAR_DATA'	
.FARDATA?	FAR_BSS	PARA	private	'FAR_BSS'	
.DATA	_DATA	WORD	PUBLIC	'DATA'	DGROUP
.CONST	CONST	WORD	PUBLIC	'CONST'	DGROUP
.DATA?	_BSS	WORD	PUBLIC	'BSS'	DGROUP
.STACK	STACK	PARA	STACK	'STACK'	DGROUP

Table 10.3: Default Segments and Types for Medium Memory Model

Directive	Name	Align	Combine	Class	Group
.CODE	name_TEXT	WORD	PUBLIC	'CODE'	
.FARDATA	FAR_DATA	PARA	private	'FAR_DATA'	
.FARDATA?	FAR_BSS	PARA	private	'FAR_BSS'	
.DATA	_DATA	WORD	PUBLIC	'DATA'	DGROUP
.CONST	CONST	WORD	PUBLIC	'CONST'	DGROUP
.DATA?	_BSS	WORD	PUBLIC	'BSS'	DGROUP
.STACK	STACK	PARA	STACK	'STACK'	DGROUP

Table 10.4: Default Segments and Types for Compact Memory Model

Directive	Name	Align	Combine	Class	Group
.CODE	_TEXT	WORD	PUBLIC	'CODE'	
.FARDATA	FAR_DATA	PARA	private	'FAR_DATA'	
.FARDATA?	FAR_BSS	PARA	private	'FAR_BSS'	
.DATA	_DATA	WORD	PUBLIC	'DATA'	DGROUP
.CONST	CONST	WORD	PUBLIC	'CONST'	DGROUP
.DATA?	_BSS	WORD	PUBLIC	'BSS'	DGROUP
.STACK	STACK	PARA	STACK	'STACK'	DGROUP

Table 10.5: Default Segments and Types for Large or Huge Memory Model

Directive	Name	Align	Combine	Class	Group
.CODE	name_TEXT	WORD	PUBLIC	'CODE'	
.FARDATA	FAR_DATA	PARA	private	'FAR_DATA'	
.FARDATA?	FAR_BSS	PARA	private	'FAR_BSS'	
.DATA	_DATA	WORD	PUBLIC	'DATA'	DGROUP
.CONST	CONST	WORD	PUBLIC	'CONST'	DGROUP
.DATA?	_BSS	WORD	PUBLIC	'BSS'	DGROUP
.STACK	STACK	PARA	STACK	'STACK'	DGROUP

Table 10.6: Default Segments and Types for Turbo Pascal (TPASCAL) Memory Model

Directive	Name	Align	Combine
.CODE	CODE	BYTE	PUBLIC
.DATA	DATA	WORD	PUBLIC

In past chapters, you've probably noticed that programs using the simplified segment directives don't need **ASSUME**, **GROUP**, or **ENDS** directives. The **.MODEL** directive automatically performs the appropriate **ASSUME** directives for the selected memory mode, assuming the segments shown in the preceding tables. **.MODEL** also performs the group definition for **DGROUP**, as shown in the previous tables.

As for **ENDS**, the start of a new segment with a simplified segment directive—for example, **.CODE** or **.DATA**—automatically ends the current segment, if there is one.

Take a look now at the more esoteric simplified segment directives: **.DATA?**, **.CONST**, **.FARDATA**, and **.FARDATA?**. **.FARDATA** is really the only one of these you'll ever use in a pure assembler program; the others are strictly for matching the segment usage of high-level languages.

.DATA? starts the segment that is to contain uninitialized near data in **DGROUP**. Since both the **.DATA** and **.DATA?** segments are in the same group, there's really no reason not to simply skip using **.DATA?** altogether and use question marks to define uninitialized data in the **.DATA** segment, except when you're following the conventions of a high-level language.

.CONST, which starts the segment that is to contain constant near data in **DGROUP**, falls into the same category as **.DATA?**. You might as well put your constant data in **.DATA** and skip **.CONST**, except when you're following the conventions of a high-level language.

.FARDATA is used to create a far data segment unique to a given source module; that is, a segment that's not shared with any other module. That segment is named **FAR_DATA** but is of combine type **PRIVATE**, so it's not combined with any other segment. **.FARDATA** allows you to define up to 64K of local data storage in each module. Of course, if you use **.FARDATA**, you must set a segment register to point to that segment, as follows:

```
      .MODEL    small
      .DATA
InitValue DW    0
      .FARDATA
MemArray  DW    100 DUP (?)
      .CODE
      .
      .
```

```
    .
mov  ax,@data
mov  ds,ax
mov  ax,@fardata
mov  es,ax
mov  ax,[InitValue]
ASSUME    es:@fardata;
mov  di,OFFSET MemArray
mov  cx,100
cld
rep  stosw
    .
    .
    .
```

Note that the predefined label **@fardata** contains the name of the segment defined with the **.FARDATA** directive.

While a segment defined with **.FARDATA** isn't shared with any other module (as, for example, the segment defined with **.DATA** is), you can use **GLOBAL** to share specific variables in the **.FARDATA** segment with other modules. For example, the following makes *MemVar* available to other modules:

```
     .MODEL    small
     .FARDATA
     GLOBAL    MemVar:WORD
MemVar   DW   0
     .
     .
     .
```

Another module could then reference *MemVar* as follows:

```
.MODEL    small
GLOBAL    MemVar:WORD
.DATA
  .
  .
  .
.CODE
  .
  .
  .
mov  ax,SEG MemVar
mov  ds,ax
ASSUME    ds:SEG MemVar
```

```
mov  ax,[MemVar]
     .
     .
     .
```

Note that the declaration of *MemVar* as **GLOBAL** comes before any segment is declared. This is necessary because a global declaration of a given variable must be performed either inside the variable's segment or outside all segments. Since, by definition, no module can share another module's **.FARDATA** segment, the declaration of *MemVar* must be performed outside all segments.

.FARDATA? is much like **.FARDATA**, except that it creates a private segment named **FAR_BSS**. **FAR_BSS** segments are used by high-level languages for uninitialized far data. If you're not interfacing to a high-level language, there's no reason you shouldn't define your uninitialized far data in the segment defined with **.FARDATA** and forget about **.FARDATA?**. True, the **.FARDATA** segment gives you an additional 64 Kb of far storage, but if you really need more than 64 Kb of far storage that's unique to a given module, you should probably be using the standard segment directives anyway.

If you do use **.FARDATA?**, the predefined label **@fardata?** contains the name of the segment defined by **.FARDATA**, suitable for use in **ASSUME** directives and in loading segment registers.

A Sample Multisegment Program

The next program has two code segments and two data segments. This is hardly a comprehensive example of multisegment programming, but we don't have the space for a program running to hundreds or thousands of lines; this one will serve to give you a feel for switching data segments, loading full segment:offset pointers, and calling code in other segments.

Here's the example:

```
;
; Program to demonstrate use of multiple code and data segments.
;
; Reads a string from the console, stores it in one data
; segment, copies the string to another data segment, converting
; it to lowercase in the process, then prints the string to the
; console. Uses functions in another code segment to read,
; print, and copy the string.
;
Stack   SEGMENT   PARA STACK 'STACK'
    DB   512 DUP (?)
```

```
Stack      ENDS

MAX_STRING_LENGTH    EQU  1000

SourceDataSeg  SEGMENT   PARA PRIVATE 'DATA'
InputBuffer    DB    MAX_STRING_LENGTH DUP (?)
SourceDataSeg  ENDS

DestDataSeg    SEGMENT   PARA PRIVATE 'DATA'
OutputBuffer   DB    MAX_STRING_LENGTH DUP (?)
DestDataSeg    ENDS

SubCode   SEGMENT   PARA PRIVATE 'CODE'
     ASSUME    cs:SubCode
;
; Subroutine to read a string from the console. String end is
; marked by a carriage-return, which is converted to a
; carriage-return/linefeed pair so it will advance to the next
; line when printed. A 0 is added to terminate the string.
;
; Input:
;    ES:DI - location to store string at
;
; Output: None
;
; Registers destroyed: AX,DI
;
GetString PROC FAR
GetStringLoop:
     mov  ah,1
     int  21h                           ;get the next character
     stosb                              ;save it
     cmp  al,13                         ;is it a carriage-return?
     jnz  GetStringLoop ;no-not done yet
     mov  BYTE PTR es:[di],10
     mov  BYTE PTR es:[di+1],0          ;end the string with a linefeed
                                        ; and a 0

     ret
GetString ENDP
;
; Subroutine to copy a string, converting it to lowercase.
;
; Input:
;    DS:SI - string to copy
;    ES:DI - place to put string
;
; Output: None
;
; Registers destroyed: AL, SI, DI
;
```

```
CopyLowercase   PROC FAR
CopyLoop:
    lodsb
    cmp  al,'A'
    jb   NotUpper
    cmp  al,'Z'
    ja   NotUpper
    add  al,20h                     ;convert to lowercase if it's uppercase
NotUpper:
    stosb
    and  al,al                      ;was that the 0 that ends the string?
    jnz  CopyLoop                   ;no, copy another character
    ret
CopyLowercase   ENDP
;
; Subroutine to display a string to the console.
;
; Input:
;    DS:SI - string to display
;
; Output: None
;
; Registers destroyed: AH,DL,SI
;
DisplayString   PROC FAR
DisplayStringLoop:
    mov  dl,[si]                    ;get the next character
    and  dl,dl                      ;is this the 0 that ends the string?
    jz   DisplayStringDone          ;yes, we're done
    inc  si                         ;point to the following character
    mov  ah,2
    int  21h                        ;display the character
    jmp  DisplayStringLoop
DisplayStringDone:
    ret
DisplayString   ENDP
SubCode    ENDS

Code SEGMENT    PARA PRIVATE 'CODE'
    ASSUME      cs:Code,ds:NOTHING,es:NOTHING,ss:Stack
ProgramStart:
    cld                             ;make string instructions increment
                                    ; their pointer registers
;
; Read a string from the console into InputBuffer.
;
    mov  ax,SourceDataSeg
    mov  es,ax
    ASSUME      es:SourceDataSeg
```

```
        mov  di,OFFSET InputBuffer
        call GetString                      ;read string from the console and
                                            ; store it at ES:DI
;
; Print a linefeed to advance to the next line.
;
        mov  ah,2
        mov  dl,10
        int  21h
;
; Copy the string from InputBuffer to OutputBuffer, converting
; it to lowercase in the process.
;
        push es
        pop  ds
        ASSUME      ds:SourceDataSeg
        mov  ax,DestDataSeg
        mov  es,ax
        ASSUME      es:DestDataSeg
        mov  si,OFFSET InputBuffer          ;copy from DS:SI...
        mov  di,OFFSET OutputBuffer         ;...to ES:DI...
        call CopyLowercase                  ;...making it lowercase
;
; Display the lowercase string.
;
        push es
        pop  ds
        ASSUME      ds:DestDataSeg
        mov  si,OFFSET OutputBuffer
        call DisplayString                  ;display string at DS:SI to the console
;
; Done.
;
        mov  ah,4ch
        int  21h
Code ENDS
        END  ProgramStart
```

Note that, in this example, the subroutines come before the main program. This is done in order to avoid forward references, since the subroutines and the main program reside in different code segments. If the main program came first, you'd have to put **FAR PTR** overrides on each subroutine call because Turbo Assembler can't automatically assemble far forward-referenced jumps. Given the way the program is organized, however, all the subroutine calls are backward references, so Turbo Assembler can automatically generate far calls to the subroutines.

Otherwise, the program is quite straightforward. The subroutines use full segment:offset pointers to data, and the main program sets DS and ES to different data segments as needed. Note the use of the string instructions when copying the string and converting it to lowercase; since **LODS** defaults to using DS and **STOS** uses ES, these instructions are ideally suited for use in code that must access two segments at once.

11

The 80386 and Other Processors

So far, we've focused on assembly language programming for the 8086 processor. (We've also implicitly covered the 8088, which is used in the IBM PC and XT, since the 8088 is basically an 8086 with an 8-bit external data bus.) The 8086 is not the only processor Turbo Assembler supports, however; there is a whole family of 8086-superset processors, known as the iAPx86 family, and a family of math coprocessors that are supersets of the 8087, as well.

The most exciting member of the iAPx86 family is, without a doubt, the 80386, which brings minicomputer power to personal computers. Nonetheless, each of the members of the iAPx86 family has interesting enhancements over the basic 8086. Let's look at the issues involved in programming the various iAPx86-family processors.

First, we'll look at the ways in which the 80186 and 80286 processors extend the capabilities of the 8086. Next, we'll look at 80386 programming: see how to enable Turbo Assembler's 80386 features, examine the new segment types used in 80386 programming, and look at the new registers, addressing modes, and instructions of the 80386. After that, we'll examine Turbo Assembler's powerful ability to mix 16- and 32-bit instructions and segments, and we'll look at some sample 80386 code. Finally, we'll take a brief look at the ways in which the 80287 and 80387 math coprocessors extend the capabilities of the 8087.

Switching Processor Types in Assembler Code

Turbo Assembler defaults to supporting the assembly of 8086 code only. In order for Turbo Assembler to support another iAPx86-family processor or coprocessor, you must issue the appropriate directive. The following directives tell Turbo Assembler what type of processor to support when assembling code:

.186	.286C	.287	.386C	.387	.8087
.286	.286P	.386	.386P	.8086	

These directives can be inserted anywhere in assembler source files, and take effect immediately. Multiple processor-type directives can be placed in a single source file; at any given point in a source file, the last processor type specified is the processor type currently selected.

The **.8086** directive can be used anytime to instruct Turbo Assembler to return to supporting 8086 assembly only. (For the remainder of this chapter, all references made to the 8086 apply to the 8088 as well.)

For example, the following function adds two 32-bit values by using 8086 code, then 80386 code, and finally 8086 code again:

```
        .MODEL    small
        .CODE
Add32       PROC
        mov  ax,[bp+4]      ;get low half of source 1
        mov  dx,[bp+6]      ;get high half of source 1
        mov  bx,[bp+8]      ;get low half of source 2
        mov  cx,[bp+10]     ;get high half of source 2
        .386               ;use 80386 registers for actual addition
        shl  eax,16
        mov  ax,dx
        rol  eax,16        ;put 32 bits of source 1 in EAX
        mov  dx,cx
        shl  edx,16        ;put 32 bits of source 2 in EDX
        mov  dx,bx
        add  eax,edx       ;add source 1 and source 2
        rol  eax,16
        mov  dx,ax         ;put high half of result in DX
        shr  eax,16        ;low half of result is in AX
        .8086
        ret
Add32       ENDP
        END
```

The 80186 and 80188

The 80186 is the iAPx86-family processor most like the 8086. The 80186 supports all the instructions of the 8086 and adds a few new instructions, along with extended forms of some 8086 instructions. In addition, the 80186 is considerably faster than the 8086 at many operations, especially memory address calculations, so the 80186 runs code written for the 8086 at a significantly higher speed than does the 8086.

The 80188 is program-compatible with the 80186; the only difference between the two is that the 80186 has a 16-bit external data bus, and the 80188 has an 8-bit external data bus.

Enabling 80186 Assembly

Turbo Assembler support for assembly of 80186 code is enabled with the .186 directive.

Next, we'll take a look at the new and extended instructions of the 80186. For detailed information about 80186 instructions, see Chapter 3 of the *Reference Guide*.

Before we begin, take note that the 8086 does not recognize any of the instructions we're about to discuss. Consequently, any program that uses even one of the new or extended instructions of the 80186 won't run on an 8086.

New Instructions

Here are the new 80186 instructions:

BOUND	**INS**	**OUTS**	**PUSHA**
ENTER	**LEAVE**	**POPA**	

PUSHA and POPA

PUSHA and **POPA** provide an efficient means by which to push and pop all eight general-purpose registers. **PUSHA** pushes the eight general-purpose registers onto the stack in the order AX, CX, DX, BX, SP, BP, SI, DI. **POPA** pops DI, SI, BP, BX, DX, CX, and AX from the stack, reversing the action of **PUSHA**. SP is not popped by **POPA**; instead, SP is incremented by 16, the length of the block of registers pushed on the stack by **PUSHA**, and the value of SP pushed by **PUSHA** is cleared from the stack by **POPA** and thrown away. The segment registers, the flags, and the instruction pointer are not affected by **PUSHA** or **POPA**.

For example, the code

```
     .186
       .
       .
       .
SampleFunction PROC
     pusha
       .
       .
       .
     popa
     ret
SampleFunction ENDP
       .
       .
       .
```

preserves all 8 general-purpose registers with just two instructions, rather than the 16 instructions required to push and pop each register separately. (Don't forget to use the **.186** directive to enable 80186 assembly before using 80186-specific instructions such as **PUSHA** and **POPA**.)

Be aware that while **PUSHA** is faster than eight separate **PUSH** instructions, it is slower than three or four pushes; if you only need to preserve a few registers, it's best to save just those registers with **PUSH**. The same is true of **POPA** and **POP**.

ENTER and LEAVE

ENTER and **LEAVE** are used to set up and discard stack frames, in which passed parameters and local (automatic) variables can be accessed relative to BP. **ENTER** and **LEAVE** are particularly useful when interfacing assembler functions to stack-oriented languages such as C. (See Chapter 6 for information on interfacing assembler functions to Turbo C, Chapter 9 for interfacing to Turbo Prolog, Chapter 7 for interfacing to Turbo Pascal, and Chapter 8 for interfacing to Turbo Basic.)

ENTER preserves the calling routine's BP, sets BP to point to the start of the passed parameters (if any) in a new stack frame, adjusts SP as needed to allocate room for local variables, and even copies a block of pointers to higher-level stack frames into the new stack frame if necessary.

LEAVE undoes everything **ENTER** does, restoring both BP and SP to the state they were in before the corresponding **ENTER** was executed.

For example, the following function uses **ENTER** to set up a C-compatible stack frame with 20 bytes reserved for local variables, and uses **LEAVE** to discard that stack frame and restore the calling code's stack frame:

```
         .
         .
         .
SampleFunction PROC
     enter 20,0
         .
         .
         .
     leave
     ret
SampleFunction ENDP
         .
         .
         .
```

The first operand to **ENTER** is a 16-bit immediate value specifying the number of bytes to reserve for local variables in the new stack frame. The second operand to **ENTER** is an 8-bit immediate value specifying the nesting level of the function for which the new stack frame is being created; basically, this operand specifies the number of stack frame pointers to be copied from the calling code's stack frame into the new stack frame.

Note that a **RET** instruction is required after **LEAVE** in order to return to the calling code; **LEAVE** discards the current stack frame, but does not perform a return.

ENTER and **LEAVE** do not preserve any of the calling code's registers; **PUSH** and **POP** or **PUSHA** and **POPA** should be used for this purpose.

BOUND

BOUND checks that a 16-bit value is within a signed range specified by two adjacent words of memory, with the upper bound stored at the address immediately above the lower bound. Both bounds are treated as signed values, so a maximum range of $-32,768$ to $+32,767$, inclusive, can be specified. Values matching the upper and lower bounds are considered to fall within the specified range.

BOUND is generally used to guard against attempts to access before the beginning or past the end of an array. For example, this code checks whether BX is in the range 0 to 99, inclusive, before using it as an index into the 100-byte array *TestArray*.

```
        .
        .
        .
    .DATA
TestArrayBounds  LABEL   DWORD
    DW    0                       ;lower array bound (inclusive)
    DW    99                      ;upper array bound (inclusive)
TestArray  DB    100 DUP (?)
    .
    .
    .
    .CODE
    .
    .
    .
    mov   ax,@data
    mov   ds,ax
    .
    .
    .
    bound bx,[TestArrayBounds]
    mov   al,[TestArray+bx]
    .
    .
    .
```

If BX is not in the range, an **INT 5** is generated. An interrupt-handler for **INT 5** must, of course, be set up before **BOUND** can be used.

The first operand to **BOUND** is the 16-bit general-purpose register containing the value to be range-checked. The second operand to **BOUND** is the doubleword containing the range. This doubleword contains the signed 16-bit lower bound as its lower word and the signed 16-bit upper bound as its upper word.

One tricky point about **BOUND** is that the instruction pointer pushed when **INT 5** is generated by a failed bounds test points to the **BOUND** instruction that caused the **INT 5**, not the following instruction. If the failing condition is not corrected by the **INT 5** handler before it executes an **IRET**, the same **BOUND** instruction will generate another **INT 5**, and so on, indefinitely. Consequently, **INT 5** handlers for **BOUND** instructions should either issue a message and terminate the program without executing an **IRET** or correct the out-of-range condition before executing an **IRET** to continue.

INS and OUTS

INS and **OUTS** support efficient data transfer between I/O ports and memory.

INS moves one or more bytes (or words) from an I/O port pointed to by DX to a memory array pointed to by ES:DI, incrementing DI by 1 (or 2) after each byte (or word) is transferred (or decrementing SI if the direction flag is set). DX is not affected by **INS**. As with all string instructions that write to memory, the use of ES as the destination segment cannot be overridden.

OUTS moves one or more bytes (or words) from a memory array pointed to by DS:SI to an I/O port pointed to by DX, incrementing SI by 1 (or 2) after each byte (or word) is transferred (or decrementing SI if the direction flag is set). DX is not affected by **OUTS**. A segment register other than DS can be selected with a segment override prefix. The following code uses **INSB** to copy a block of 300h bytes to memory from I/O port 3000h, then uses **OUTSB** to copy that block of bytes to I/O port 3001h:

```
        .
        .
        .
    cld
    mov   ax,@data
    mov   ds,ax
    mov   es,ax
    mov   dx,3000h
    mov   di,OFFSET Buffer
    mov   cx,300h
    rep   insb                  ;copy 300h bytes to buffer from port
    mov   dx,3001h
    mov   si,OFFSET Buffer
    mov   cx,300h
    rep   outsb                 ;copy 300h bytes from buffer to port
        .
        .
        .
```

Extended Versions of 8086 Instructions

The 80186 offers extended versions of several 8086 instructions as well:

IMUL	**ROL**	**SAR**
PUSH	**ROR**	**SHL**
RCL	**SAL**	**SHR**
RCR		

Pushing Immediate Values

While the 8086 can push register or memory operands only, the 80186 can push an immediate value as well:

```
push    19
```

Pushing an immediate value is useful for passing constant parameters to functions on the stack. For example, the 8086 code for this C call,

```
Average(5, 2);
```

is this:

```
mov     ax,2
push    ax
mov     ax,5
push    ax
call    _Average
add     sp,4
```

and can be reduced to this on the 80186:

```
push    2
push    5
call    _Average
add     sp,4
```

Shifting and Rotating by Immediate Values

While the 8086 can only rotate or shift by either 1 bit or the number of bits specified by the contents of CL, the 80186 can rotate or shift by a constant value:

```
    .
    .
    .
ror     ax,3
shl     dl,7
    .
    .
    .
```

This is convenient for performing multi-bit shifts without having to load CL with the shift count. For example, the following 8086 code to multiply AX by 256,

```
        .
        .
        .
mov    cl,8
shl    ax,cl
        .
        .
        .
```

becomes this on the 80186:

```
shl    ax,8
```

Multiplying by an Immediate Value

The 8086 can only multiply an 8- or 16-bit register or memory operand by AL or AX, placing the result in AX or DX:AX. The 80186 provides two new forms of multiplication for use when the product of a 16-bit multiplication will fit in 16 bits.

One new form of multiplication multiplies a 16-bit register by a 16-bit immediate value and stores the result back in the 16-bit register. For example, this code multiplies DX by 4 and places the product in DX:

```
imul   dx,4
```

The first operand, which can be any 16-bit general-purpose register, is both the source of one of the factors and the destination for the product. The second operand, which must be a 16-bit immediate value, is the other factor.

The other new form of multiplication multiplies a 16-bit register or memory location by a 16-bit immediate value and stores the result in a specified 16-bit register. For example, this code multiplies DX by 600h and places the product in CX:

```
imul   cx,dx,600h
```

Similarly, this code multiplies the 16-bit value at [BX+SI+1] by 3 and places the product in AX.

```
imul   ax,[bx+si+1],3
```

The first operand to this form of **IMUL** is the destination for the product. This operand can be any 16-bit general-purpose register. The second operand, which can be any 16-bit general-purpose register or memory location, is the source of one of the factors. The third operand, which must be a 16-bit immediate value, is the other factor.

A bit of thought will show that the first of the new forms of multiplication is actually just a subset of the second new form. For example, this following code,

```
imul  si,10
```

is just a shorthand form of

```
imul  si,si,10
```

The underlying hex code is the same for both new forms of the **IMUL** instruction. Nonetheless, it's convenient to be able to use the simpler two-operand **IMUL** when the same register serves as both source and destination.

With either of the new forms of multiplication, any portion of the result that does not fit in 16 bits is lost; if significant bits are lost, considering the result to be a signed value, the carry and overflow flags are set. The new forms of multiplication make no distinction between signed and unsigned multiplication, since the result is only 16 bits long, and the lower 16 bits of the product of both signed and unsigned 16-bit by 16-bit multiplies are always the same. Consequently, only the **IMUL** instruction may be used to denote the new forms of multiplication.

The 80286

The 80286 was the first iAPx86-family processor to eliminate the 1 Mb memory limitation and the first to support memory protection and virtual memory. The 80286 provides all the instructions of the 8086 and 80186, and adds a number of instructions that support management of a sophisticated memory architecture.

The 80286 has two modes of operation: real mode and protected mode. An 80286 operating in real mode is very similar to an 80186, providing exactly the same instruction set and nothing more. This is the mode in which 80286-based computers such as the IBM AT run PC-DOS and applications such as Quattro and Turbo Pascal.

The memory management features of the 80286 are only available in protected mode. And it's only in this mode that multiple programs can be run at once without interfering with each other, and more than 1 Mb of memory can be addressed. This is the mode in which 80286-based computers run OS/2.

The protected-mode instructions of the 80286 follow:

CLTS	**LIDT**	**LMSW**
LGDT	**LLDT**	**LTR**

These 80286 instructions are intended for operating system usage only; applications should never need to (or be able to) use protected-mode instructions. The use of these instructions, and the protected mode of the 80286 in general, are specialized and complex topics that we won't go into in this manual.

The 80286 adds two new status states to the flags register: the nested task bit and the I/O privilege-level field. Like the protected-mode instructions, both bits are intended for use by systems software only and are of no concern to the applications programmer. The 80286 also contains several new registers that can be manipulated only with protected-mode instructions, such as the Task register, the Machine Status Word register, and the Global Descriptor Table register; again, these registers are not used by applications, so we will not cover them in this manual.

Enabling 80286 Assembly

Turbo Assembler support for assembly of nonprotected-mode 80286 code is enabled with the **.286** directive. (The **.286C** directive also enables Turbo Assembler support for 80286 instructions, for compatibility with earlier assemblers.)

Note that the **.286** directive implicitly enables support for all 8086 and 80186 instructions, since the 80286 supports the full instruction set of earlier iAPx86-family processors.

Support for protected-mode 80286 instructions is enabled with the **.286P** directive. Nonprotected-mode 80286 instructions are enabled by the **.286P** directive as well, just as if a **.286** directive had been executed.

For detailed information about 80286 instructions, refer to Chapter 3 of the *Reference Guide*.

One important point about protected-mode 80286 instructions is that the 8086 and 80186 do not recognize any of these instructions. Consequently, any program that uses protected-mode instructions won't run on an 8086 or 80186. However, the 80386 does support both the protected-mode and nonprotected-mode instructions of the 80286.

The 80386

The 80386 processor is a landmark in the evolution of the microcomputer, providing new and extended instructions, an expanded set of 32-bit registers, linear segments up to 4 gigabytes long, the ability to emulate multiple 8086 processors simultaneously, a barrel shifter for fast shifts and rotates, paged memory, higher clock speeds than any previous iAPx86-family processor (resulting in faster execution), and more. As you might expect, extensions to 8086/80186/80286 assembly language are needed to support the full power of the 80386. Turbo Assembler provides a full set of 80386 extensions, supporting all modes and features of the 80386.

The 80386 is a remarkably sophisticated processor—orders of magnitude more complex than the 8086—so we can't cover the many aspects of programming the 80386. We can, however, take a look at the 80386 support built into Turbo Assembler.

Selecting 80386 Assembly Mode

As with the 80286, there are two sorts of 80386 instructions, privileged and non-privileged. Any program can execute non-privileged instructions, while only programs executing at a current privilege level of 0 (the most-privileged level) can execute privileged instructions. The privileged instructions of the 80386 are a superset of the 80286's privileged instructions and, like 80286 privileged instructions, are intended for operating system use only.

Support for non-privileged 80386 instructions is enabled with the **.386** directive. (The **.386C** directive enables Turbo Assembler support for 80386 instructions for compatibility with earlier assemblers.)

Note that the **.386** directive implicitly enables support for all 8086 and 80186 instructions and all 80286 non-privileged instructions, since the 80386 supports the full instruction set of earlier iAPx86-family processors.

Support for privileged 80386 instructions is enabled with the **.386P** directive. Non-privileged 80386 instructions are enabled by the **.386P** directive as well, just as if a **.386** directive had been executed. Since the 80386 supports all privileged instructions of the 80286, the **.386P** directive implicitly enables support for all 80286 privileged instructions.

New Segment Types

The ability of the 80386 to support either 80286-style 64 Kb segments or linear segments up to 4 Gb (gigabytes) in length requires two new segment types, **USE16** and **USE32**.

A 16-bit offset, either stored in a base or index register (BX, SI, DI, or BP) or used as a direct addressing offset, is all that's needed in order to point to any location in a 64K segment. This is the mode of operation of the 80286 (and the 8086). 80386 segments that have a maximum length of 64K are given a use type of **USE16**, as follows:

```
    .386
    .
    .
    .
DataSeg    SEGMENT    USE16
Var1 DW    ?
Ptr1 DW    Var1
DataSeg    ENDS
    .
    .
    .
CodeSeg    SEGMENT    USE16
    ASSUME     cs:CodeSeg
    mov   ax,DataSeg
    mov   fs,ax
    ASSUME     fs:DataSeg
    mov   [Var1],0              ;set Var1 to zero
    mov   bx,[Ptr1]            ;load a 16-bit pointer to Var1
    inc   WORD PTR fs:[bx]     ;increment Var1
    .
    .
    .
CodeSeg    ENDS
    .
    .
    .
```

Note the use of FS, one of the two new extra segments (along with GS) available on the 80386.

Note also that an offset stored in any of the 80386's eight general-purpose 32-bit registers can be used to address a **USE16** segment, as long as the magnitude of the offset doesn't exceed 0FFFFh (65535).

A 32-bit offset, stored in any of the eight general-purpose 32- bit registers or used as a direct addressing offset, is needed to point to any given location in a 4 Gb segment. 80386 segments that have a maximum length of 4 Gb are given a use type of **USE32**, as follows:

```
        .386
        .
        .
        .
BigDataSeg      SEGMENT    USE32
Var1 DW    ?
Ptr1 DD    Var1
BigDataSeg      ENDS
        .
        .
        .
CodeSeg    SEGMENT USE16
    ASSUME    cs:CodeSeg
    mov  ax,BigDataSeg
    mov  fs,ax
    ASSUME    fs:BigDataSeg
    mov  [Var1],0               ;set Var1 to zero
    mov  eax,[Ptr1]             ;load 32-bit pointer to Var1
    inc  WORD PTR fs:[eax]      ;increment Var1
        .
        .
        .
CodeSeg    ENDS
        .
        .
        .
```

Note the use of EAX as a pointer register; the 80386 allows all eight general-purpose 32-bit registers (EAX, EBX, ECX, EDX, ESI, EDI, EBP, and ESP) to be used as either base or index registers, as discussed in "New Addressing Modes" on page 499.

The **SMALL** and **LARGE** operators can be used to override the default offset size of a given operand. **SMALL** forces the use of a 16-bit offset, and **LARGE** forces the use of a 32-bit offset. For example,

```
        .386
        .
        .
        .
CodeSeg    SEGMENT USE16
    ASSUME    cs:CodeSeg
    mov  ax,DataSeg
    mov  ds,ax
    ASSUME    ds:DataSeg
    mov  ax,[LARGE TestLoc]
        .
```

```
          .
          .
          .
CodeSeg   ENDS
          .
          .
          .

DataSeg   SEGMENT   USE32
TestLoc   DW    0
DataSeg   ENDS
          .
          .
          .
```

successfully makes a forward reference to *TestLoc* (even though *TestLoc* is in a **USE32** segment) by using **LARGE** to force the reference to **TestLoc** to be performed with a 32-bit offset. Without the **LARGE** override, an error would be generated, since the assembler assumes 16-bit offsets for forward references made within the **USE16** segment *CodeSeg*.

The action of **SMALL** and **LARGE** is actually a bit more subtle than a simple selection between 16- and 32-bit offset size. **SMALL** instructs Turbo Assembler to assemble a given instruction for use with the 8086's 16-bit addressing modes, which are inherently capable of addressing only 64 Kb of memory. **LARGE**, on the other hand, instructs Turbo Assembler to assemble a given instruction to use the 80386's new 32-bit addressing modes (see "New Addressing Modes" on page 499), which are capable of addressing 4 Gb of memory.

For example, the code

```
          .
          .
          .
          .386
          .
          .
          .
CodeSeg   SEGMENT   USE16
          .
          .
          .
          mov   ax,[SMALL ebx+esi+1]
          .
          .
          .
CodeSeg   ENDS
          .
          .
          .
```

assembles to

```
mov    ax,[bx+si+1]
```

Here, **SMALL** told Turbo Assembler to use an 8086-style 16-bit addressing mode, so instead of EBX and ESI, the assembled code uses BX and SI. However, the code

```
        .
        .
        .
        .386
        .
        .
        .
CodeSeg    SEGMENT    USE16
        .
        .
        .
        mov  ax,[SMALL eax+ecx+1]
        .
        .
        .
CodeSeg    ENDS
        .
        .
        .
```

will not assemble, since EAX+ECX+1 is not a valid 16-bit memory addressing mode. (On the other hand, EAX+ECX+1 *is* a valid 32-bit memory addressing mode, as you will see in the section "New Addressing Modes.")

Take a look at the section, "Mixing 16-Bit and 32-Bit Instructions and Segments," on page 517 for more information about **SMALL** and **LARGE** and for information regarding the interaction of small and large operators with **USE16** and **USE32** segments. The issue of selection between **USE32** and **USE16** segments is also covered in that section.

One important implication of the selection of **USE16** or **USE32** segments concerns the size of indirect jumps. We'll look at this area in the section entitled "The 32-Bit Instruction Pointer" (page 496).

If neither **USE32** nor **USE16** is specified in a segment definition, **USE32** is always assumed when assembling for the 80386.

Simplified Segment Directives and 80386 Segment Types

If you use both **.386** and the simplified segment directives, segments default to **DWORD** alignment. This makes sense, given that 80386-based computers run fastest with doubleword-aligned data.

When you use the simplified segment directives, Turbo Assembler generates **USE32** segments if **.386** is given before the **.MODEL** directive, and **USE16** segments if **.386** is given after the **.MODEL** directive. For example, this code creates 32-bit code and data segments:

```
.386
.MODEL    large
.DATA
.
.
.
.CODE
.
.
.
```

while this code creates 16-bit code and segments:

```
.MODEL    large
.386
.DATA
.
.
.
.CODE
.
.
.
```

The FWORD 48-Bit Data Type

An interesting point about **USE32** segments is that the size of a far pointer (that is, a full segment:offset pointer) to a location in a **USE32** segment is 6 bytes rather than the customary 4 bytes because offsets in **USE32** segments are 32 bits in size. For example, with a **USE16** segment, a far pointer to an 8000h-byte buffer *Buffer* is stored in 4 bytes and loaded as follows:

```
        .386
         .
         .
         .
DataSeg        SEGMENT    USE16
Buffer         DB    8000h DUP (?)
BufferPtr LABEL      DWORD
          DW   OFFSET Buffer
          DW   SEG Buffer
DataSeg        ENDS
         .
         .
         .
CodeSeg        SEGMENT    USE16
    ASSUME     cs:CodeSeg
    mov  ax,DataSeg
    mov  ds,ax
    ASSUME     ds:DataSeg
    les  bx,[BufferPtr]          ;load ES:BX with 16-bit segment
                                 ; and 16-bit offset of Buffer
         .
         .
         .
CodeSeg        ENDS
         .
         .
         .
```

With a **USE32** segment, on the other hand, a far pointer to *Buffer* is stored in 6 bytes and loaded as follows:

```
        .386
         .
         .
         .
DataSeg        SEGMENT    USE32
Buffer         DB    8000h DUP (?)
BufferPtr LABEL      FWORD
          DD   OFFSET Buffer
          DW   SEG Buffer
DataSeg        ENDS
         .
         .
         .
CodeSeg        SEGMENT    USE32
    ASSUME     cs:CodeSeg
    mov  ax,DataSeg
    mov  ds,ax
    ASSUME     ds:DataSeg
        les  ebx,[BufferPtr]     ;load ES:EBX with 16-bit segment
```

```
                      ; and 32-bit offset of Buffer
        .
        .
        .
CodeSeg        ENDS
        .
        .
        .
```

Note the use of the new **FWORD** data type. **FWORD** values are 6 bytes long. **FWORD PTR** operators may be used just like **BYTE PTR, WORD PTR,** and **DWORD PTR** operators.

```
    lgs   esi,FWORD PTR [BufferPtr]
```

There is also a new directive, **DF,** for defining 6-byte variables:

```
        .386
        .
        .
        .
DataSeg    SEGMENT USE32
FPtr DF    ?
DataSeg    ENDS
        .
        .
        .
CodeSeg    SEGMENT USE32
    ASSUME     cs:CodeSeg
    mov   ax,DataSeg
    mov   ds,ax
    ASSUME     ds:DataSeg
    mov   eax,OFFSET DestinationFunction
    mov   DWORD PTR [FPtr],eax
    mov   ax,SEG DestinationFunction
    mov   WORD PTR [FPtr+4],ax
    jmp   [FPtr]
        .
        .
        .
CodeSeg    ENDS
        .
        .
        .
```

New Registers

The 80386 extends the general-purpose registers, flags register, and instruction pointer of the 8086 to 32 bits in size, and adds two new segment registers. Figure 11.1 shows the register set of the 80386, with 80386 extensions to the basic 8086 register set shaded.

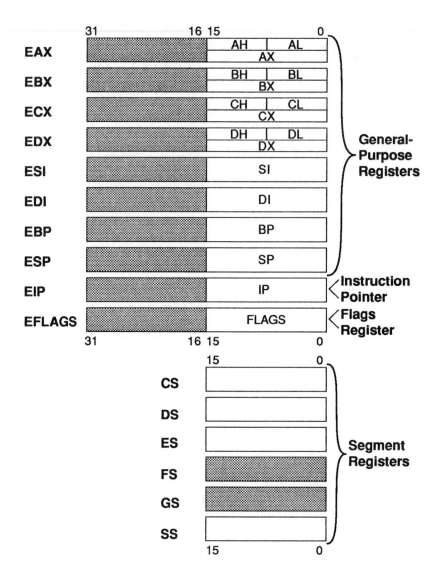

Figure 11.1: The Registers of the 80386

In addition, the 80386 contains several special registers, some new and some compatible with the 80286, that can be manipulated only with privileged instructions. As with the 80286, these registers are used only by systems software, so we won't cover them in this manual.

Let's examine the new registers of the 80386.

The 32-Bit General-Purpose Registers

The 32-bit versions of the general-purpose registers are called EAX, EBX, ECX, EDX, ESI, EDI, EBP, and ESP. The lower 16 bits of these registers form the 8086's set of 16-bit registers we've come to know so well; for example, the lower 16 bits of EAX are register AX. Similarly, the lower 8 bits of EAX are register AL. Consequently, portions of register EAX may now be referred to by four different names: the 32-bit EAX register, the 16-bit AX register, and the 8-bit AH and AL registers. The same is true of EBX, ECX, and EDX.

The 32-bit general-purpose registers of the 80386 are used in the same way as are the 16- and 8-bit registers. For example, this code stores 1 in EAX, sets EBX to 0, and adds EAX to EBX:

```
.
.
.
mov  eax,1
sub  ebx,ebx
add  ebx,eax
.
.
.
```

The 32-bit general-purpose registers can be used wherever the familiar 16-bit registers can be used.

There is one slight shortcoming in accessing 32-bit registers: There's no way to directly use the upper 16 bits of a 32-bit register as a 16-bit register. If you want to use the upper 8 bits of AX as a register, you can just refer to AH; and if you want to use the lower 16 bits of ESI as a register, you can just refer to SI. But there's no equivalent way to refer to the upper 16 bits of, say, EAX. This can be a nuisance when working with a mixture of word- and doubleword-sized values, but there is a reasonable workaround.

To access the upper 16 bits of a 32-bit register, just rotate the register 16 bits in either direction, access the lower 16 bits of the register, and rotate the register 16 bits again. For instance, the following code loads a 16-bit value into AX, rotates EDX 16 bits to swap the high and low words of EDX, moves AX into DX, and swaps the high and low words of EDX again.

```
      .
      .
      .
mov   ax,[Sample16BitValue]
ror   edx,16
mov   dx,ax
ror   edx,16
      .
      .
      .
```

The net effect: The value initially loaded into AX is ultimately moved into the high word of EDX. While this procedure is awkward, it is not as slow as it might seem; thanks to the 80386's barrel shifter, each **ROR** instruction takes only three cycles to execute.

The 32-Bit Flags Register

The lower word of the 80386's flags register is identical to the 80286's flags register. The upper 16 bits of the 80386's flags register contains two new flags. One of the new flags indicates whether the 80386 is currently executing as a virtual 8086, and the other new flag is intended for use in writing debugging tools. These flags are generally not used by applications software.

The 32-Bit Instruction Pointer

The 80386's instruction pointer is 32 bits in size, in contrast to the 8086's 16-bit instruction pointer. This extended instruction pointer supports code segments up to 4 Gb in length.

The 80386's extended instruction pointer creates some complications in specifying indirect jumps via memory. For example, the following code clearly specifies a far indirect jump with a 16-bit segment and a 32-bit offset:

```
jmp   [FWORD PTR JumpVector]
```

Consider the following, however:

```
jmp   [DWORD PTR JumpVector]
```

Is this a near 32-bit indirect jump or a far indirect jump with a 16-bit segment and a 16-bit offset? Either type of jump may legitimately be specified with a **DWORD** operand.

Here's where the **LARGE** and **SMALL** operators come in handy. The construct

```
jmp    SMALL [DWORD PTR JumpVector]
```

assembles as a far indirect jump to the address specified by the 16-bit segment and 16-bit offset stored at *JumpVector*, and

```
jmp    LARGE [DWORD PTR JumpVector]
```

assembles as a near indirect jump to the address specified by the current CS and the 32-bit offset stored at *JumpVector*. In the first case, the **SMALL** operator instructs Turbo Assembler to treat the jump as if it were occurring from a **USE16** segment; in **USE16** segments, 32-bit indirect jump operands consist of a 16-bit segment and a 16-bit offset. In the second case, the **LARGE** operator instructs Turbo Assembler to treat the jump as if it were occurring in a **USE32** segment; in **USE32** segments, 32-bit indirect jump operands consist of 32-bit offsets only.

Note that **SMALL** and **LARGE** appear outside the brackets in the preceding examples; the positioning of **SMALL** and **LARGE** is significant. When **SMALL** and **LARGE** appear outside the brackets, they affect the operand size, in this case, the size of the jump. When **SMALL** and **LARGE** appear inside the brackets, they affect the address size. For example, this code instructs Turbo Assembler to use a near 32-bit offset to point to *JumpVector*, but does not tell Turbo Assembler whether to treat the value stored at *JumpVector* as a near 32-bit offset or a far 16-bit segment and 16-bit offset combination:

```
jmp    [LARGE DWORD PTR JumpVector]
```

So this does not resolve the original problem of determining the type of the jump.

LARGE and **SMALL** can be used both inside and outside the brackets in a single expression. For instance, this code specifies a far indirect jump to the 16-bit segment and 16-bit offset address stored at the doubleword variable *JumpVector*, which is itself addressed with a near 32-bit offset:

```
jmp    SMALL [LARGE DWORD PTR JumpVector]
```

New Segment Registers

The 80386 adds two new segment registers, FS and GS to the four segment registers supported by the 8086. The two new segment registers are not dedicated to any particular function, and no instructions or addressing modes access FS or GS by default. Consequently, the use of FS or GS is never required, but they can be handy for code that accesses data in several segments at once.

FS and GS are used just as ES is used for nonstring instructions, by means of a segment override prefix. The override prefix may be explicit:

```
      .386
      .
      .
      .
TestSeg   SEGMENT   USE16
SCRATCH_LEN EQU       1000h
Scratch   DB    SCRATCH_LEN DUP (?)
TestSeg   ENDS
      .
      .
      .
CodeSeg   SEGMENT USE16
      ASSUME    cs:CodeSeg
      mov  ax,TestSeg
      mov  fs,ax
      mov  bx,OFFSET Scratch
      mov  cx,SCRATCH_LEN
      mov  al,0
ClearScratch:
      mov  fs:[bx],al
      inc  bx
      loop ClearScratch
      .
      .
      .
CodeSeg   ENDS
      .
      .
      .
```

or implicit, by way of an **ASSUME** directive:

```
      .386
      .
      .
      .
TestSeg   SEGMENT   USE16
```

```
SCRATCH_LEN EQU     1000h
Scratch   DB    SCRATCH_LEN DUP (?)
TestSeg   ENDS
    .
    .
    .

CodeSeg   SEGMENT   USE16
    ASSUME     cs:CodeSeg
    mov   ax,TestSeg
    mov   gs,ax
    ASSUME   gs:TestSeg
    sub   bx,bx
    mov   cx,SCRATCH_LEN
    mov   al,0
ClearScratch:
    mov   [Scratch+bx],al
    inc   bx
    loop ClearScratch
    .
    .
    .

CodeSeg   ENDS
    .
    .
    .
```

In the last example, the directive **ASSUME GS:TestSeg** told Turbo Assembler to automatically insert an override prefix on each access by name (as opposed to access by pointer register) to variables in *TestSeg*, so you didn't have to explicitly type the override prefix. The override prefix is, however, still there in the executable code, adding an extra byte to the size of each instruction that accesses memory by way of the FS or GS register. Consequently, whenever possible, it's preferable to use the DS register (or the ES register as the destination of a string instruction) instead of the FS or GS register.

New Addressing Modes

The 80386 supports all the memory addressing modes of the 8086, 80186, and 80286, and adds a set of powerful new addressing modes as well. *Any* of the eight 32-bit, general-purpose registers of the 80386 may be used as a base register, and *any* 32-bit, general-purpose register other than SP may be used as an index register. By contrast, the 8086 allows only BX and BP to be used as base registers, and only SI and DI to be used as index registers.

For example, suppose that EDI contains 10000h and EAX contains 4. Then the following code is a perfectly legal instruction on the 80386, incrementing the byte at offset 10006h (10000h + 4 + 2) in the segment pointed to by DS:

```
inc   BYTE PTR [edi+eax+2]
```

Here's another example of the 80386's new addressing capabilities:

```
      .
      .
      .
mov   ecx,[esp+4]
mov   ebx,[esp+8]
mov   WORD PTR [ecx+ebx],0
      .
      .
      .
```

The 80386 can do still more in the new addressing modes, however. The index register can be multiplied by 2, 4, or 8 as part of the calculation of the memory address, simply by placing *2, *4, or *8 after the index register, a feature known as *index scaling*. For instance, the ninth doubleword-sized entry in the table *DwordTable* can be loaded into EAX with this code:

```
      .
      .
      .
mov   ebx,8
mov   eax,[DwordTable+ebx*4]
      .
      .
      .
```

which is equivalent to

```
      .
      .
      .
mov   ebx,8
shl   ebx,2
mov   eax,[DwordTable+ebx]
shr   ebx,2
      .
      .
      .
```

Index scaling can be extremely useful for accessing elements in word, doubleword, and quadword arrays. For example, consider the following code, which sorts the elements in a word array in ascending order:

```
      .386
      .
```

```
            .
            .
            .
    CodeSeg    SEGMENT    USE32
        ASSUME     cs:CodeSeg
            .
            .
            .
;
; Sorts a word array in ascending order.
;
; Input:
;    DS:EBX - pointer to start of word array to sort
;    EDX - length of array in word elements
;
; Registers destroyed:
;    AX, ECX, EDX, ESI, EDI
;
SortWordArray  PROC
        and  edx,edx
        jz   EndSortWordArray
        mov  esi,0                          ;compare element 0 to all other
                                            ; elements first

SortOnNextWord:
        dec  edx                            ;count down number to compare
        jz   EndSortWordArray
        mov  ecx,edx                        ;number of elements to compare this
                                            ; element against

        mov  edi,esi                        ;compare this element to all remaining
                                            ; elements

CompareToAllRemainingWords:
        inc  edi                            ;index of next element to compare
        mov  ax,[ebx+esi*2]
        cmp  ax,[ebx+edi*2]                 ;is the current element less
                                            ; than the compared element?

        jbe  NoSwap                         ;yes, no need to swap them
        xchg ax,[ebx+edi*2]                 ;swap the current and
        mov  [ebx+esi*2],ax                 ; compared elements
NoSwap:
        loop CompareToAllRemainingWords
        inc  esi                            ;point to next element to compare to
                                            ; all remaining elements

        jmp  SortOnNextWord
EndSortWordArray:
        ret
SortWordArray  ENDP
            .
            .
            .
```

```
CodeSeg   ENDS
     .
     .
     .
```

SortWordArray keeps the element numbers, or indexes, of the current and compared elements in ESI and EDI. These values are not pointers, or counts by two, even though the array is a word array; rather, they are simple scalar array indexes, just as *n* is an array index in the C statement

```
i = Array[n];
```

The key in *SortWordArray* is that the index scaling feature of the 80386 allows you to multiply the indexes by two as part of the memory addressing field, thereby converting the indexes to offsets into a word array.

If only one register is used to address memory, that register is always considered to be the base register. If two registers are used to address memory, the leftmost register inside the brackets is considered the base register, and the rightmost register is considered the index register. If, however, scaling is used with one of two registers inside the brackets, the scaled register is always considered to be the index register.

The question of which register is the base register is important because by default the base register controls the segment to which a given memory access refers. Memory accesses made with EBP or ESP as the base register refer to the segment pointed to by SS, while memory accesses made with EAX, EBX, ECX, EDX, ESI, or EDI as the base register refer to the segment pointed to by DS. For example, the following instructions refer to DS:

```
mov   al,[eax]
xchg  edx,[ebx+ebp]
shr   BYTE PTR [esi+esp+2],1
mov   [ebp*2+edx],ah
sub   cx,[esi+esi*2]
```

and the following instructions refer to SS:

```
rol   WORD PTR [ebp],1
dec   DWORD PTR [esp+4]
add   ax,[eax*2+esp]
mov   [ebp*2],edi
```

The default segment selected by the base register can be overridden with either an explicit segment override prefix or as the result of an **ASSUME** directive. For example,

```
        .386
          .
          .
          .
TestSeg    SEGMENT    USE32
Array1     DW     100h DUP (0)
TestSeg    ENDS
          .
          .
          .

CodeSeg    SEGMENT    USE16
    ASSUME     cs:CodeSeg
    mov  ax,TestSeg
    mov  fs,ax
    ASSUME     fs:TestSeg
    mov  dx,[ebx+Array1]       ;implicit override as a result of ASSUME
    mov  esi,OFFSET Array1
    mov  cx,100h
IncLoop:
    inc  WORD PTR fs:[esi]     ;explicit override
    inc  esi
    inc  esi
    loop IncLoop
          .
          .
          .

CodeSeg    ENDS
          .
          .
          .
```

The new addressing modes of the 80386 work with 32-bit memory-addressing registers only; 16-bit registers can only be used for memory addressing in the same limited way that they are on the 8086. For example, the following **MOV** instruction is illegal, even on an 80386:

```
mov    ax,[cx+dx+10h]
```

Index scaling of 16-bit registers is also not allowed. And 16- and 32-bit registers can't be combined for memory-addressing purposes; so, for example, this code cannot be used:

```
add  dx,[bx+eax]
```

New Instructions

Next, we're going to take a look at the new and extended instructions of the 80386. For detailed information about 80386 instructions, see Chapter 3 in the *Reference Guide*.

Note: Keep in mind that the 8086, 80186, and 80286 do not recognize any of the new and extended instructions we're about to discuss. Consequently, any program that uses the new or extended instructions of the 80386 won't run on earlier processors.

Here are the new instructions of the 80386:

BSF	**BTR**	**LFS**	**MOVZX**
BSR	**BTS**	**LGS**	**SET***xx*
BT	**CDQ**	**LSS**	**SHLD**
BTC	**CWDE**	**MOVSX**	**SHRD**

Testing Bits

The bit-test instructions of the 80386 are **BT, BTC, BTR,** and **BTS. BT** is the basic bit-test operation, copying the value of a specified bit into the carry flag. For example, the following code jumps to *Bit3Is1* only if bit 3 of EAX is nonzero:

```
        .
        .
        .
        bt   eax,3
        jc   Bit3Is1
        .
        .
        .
Bit3Is1:
        .
        .
        .
```

If EAX contains 00000008h, this code will jump to *Bit3Is1*; if EAX contains 0FFFFFFF7h, the preceding code will not jump. The first operand to **BT** is the 16- or 32-bit, general-purpose register or memory location containing the bit to test. The second operand is the bit number to test, specified by either an 8-bit immediate value or the contents of a 16- or 32-bit, general-purpose register. If a register is used as the second operand, its size must match the size of the first operand.

Note that the number of the bit to test can be specified by a register as well as an immediate value, and the field to be bit-tested can be in memory as well as in a register. Here's a valid way to set the carry flag to the state of bit 5 of the word at the address *Table+ebx+esi * 2*:

```
     .
     .
     .
mov  ax,5
bt   WORD PTR [Table+ebx+esi*2],ax
     .
     .
     .
```

Remember that bit numbers are counted from zero at the least-significant bit up to the most-significant bit. If AL contains 80h, then bit 7 of AL is set.

BTC is exactly like **BT** except that the value copied to the carry flag is the complement of the specified bit. That is, the carry flag is 1 if the specified bit is 0, and the carry flag is 0 if the specified bit is 1. **BTC** saves the need for a **CMC** instruction whenever a carry status that is the inverse of the bit under test is required.

BTR is also just like **BT** except that the specified bit is set to 0 after its value is copied to the carry flag. Similarly, **BTS** sets the specified bit to 1 after its value is copied to the carry flag. These bit-test instructions are useful for both testing and setting the status of a flag in a single indivisible instruction. (By *indivisible*, we mean that it is impossible for an interrupt to occur between the testing of the flag and the setting of the flag to the new value.)

Scanning Bits

The **BSF** and **BSR** instructions of the 80386 are useful for finding the first or last bit that is nonzero in a word or dword operand. **BSF** scans the source operand, starting with bit 0 (the least-significant bit), for the first bit that is nonzero. If all bits in the source operand are zero, the zero flag is cleared; otherwise, the zero flag is set and the bit number of the first nonzero bit found is loaded into the destination register.

As an example, this code uses **BSF** to locate the first (least-significant) nonzero bit in DX; since the first nonzero bit in DX is located at bit 2, a 2 is loaded into CX.

```
     .
     .
     .
mov  dx,0001101010101100b
```

```
        bsf  cx,dx
        jnz  AllBitsAreZero
        shr  dx,cl
        .
        .
        .

AllBitsAreZero:
        .
        .
        .
```

CL is then used as the value to shift DX by, with the result that DX is shifted to the right by exactly the amount needed to move the least-significant nonzero bit to bit 0.

The second operand to **BSF** is the 16- or 32-bit, general-purpose register or memory location to scan, and the first operand is the 16- or 32-bit, general-purpose register in which to store the number of the first nonzero bit in the scanned data. Both operands must be the same size.

BSR is similar to **BSF** except that **BSR** scans from the most-significant bit of the source operand toward the least-significant bit. In this example, the index of the most-significant nonzero bit in *TestVar*, 27, is placed into EAX:

```
        .
        .
        .
TestVar   DD    0FFFFF00h
        .
        .
        .
        bsr  eax,[TestVar]
        .
        .
        .
```

Moving Data with Sign- or Zero-Extension

MOVZX and **MOVSX** allow you to copy an 8- or 16-bit value into a 16- or 32-bit, general-purpose register without wasting instructions on extending the value to the destination size. **MOVZX** pads out the most-significant bits of the destination with zeros, while **MOVSX** sign-extends the value to the destination's size. Both instructions are used just like a standard **MOV**.

For example, with 8086 instructions, the following is required to copy an unsigned value in DL to BX:

```
        .
        .
        .
    mov  bl,dl
    sub  bh,bh
        .
        .
        .
```

while on the 80386, the single instruction

```
    movzx    bx,dl
```

does the job. Sign-extension is even tougher with 8086 instructions. To copy the signed byte-memory variable *TestByte* to DX without **MOVSX**, the following is required:

```
        .
        .
        .
    mov  al,[TestByte]
    cbw
    mov  dx,ax
        .
        .
        .
```

but **MOVSX** does the job with just one instruction:

```
    movsx    dx,[TestByte]
```

MOVZX and **MOVSX** can also move 8-bit values to 32-bit registers:

```
    movsx    eax,al
```

Converting to DWORD or QWORD Data

The 8086 provides the **CBW** and **CWD** instructions for converting signed byte values in AL to signed words, and signed word values in AX to signed doublewords, respectively. The 80386 adds two more signed conversion instructions, **CWDE** and **CDQ**, which make good use of the 80386's 32-bit registers.

CWDE converts a signed word value stored in AX into a signed doubleword value, just as **CWD** does. The difference between the two is that while **CWD** places the 32-bit result in DX:AX, **CWDE** places the 32-bit result in EAX, where it can readily be manipulated by the 80386's 32-bit instructions.

For example, the end result of

```
    .
    .
    .
mov  ax,-1
cwde
    .
    .
    .
```

is the 32-bit value –1 in EAX.

CDQ converts a signed doubleword value in EAX into a signed quadword (8-byte) value in EDX:EAX. The code

```
    .
    .
    .
mov  eax,-7
cdq
    .
    .
    .
```

stores the value –7 in the 64-bit register pair EDX:EAX, with the high doubleword of the result, 0FFFFFFFFh, stored in EDX, and the low doubleword of the result, 0FFFFFFF9h (-7), stored in EAX.

Shifting Across Multiple Words

Multiple-word shifts—for example, shifting a 32-bit value 4 bits to the left—are a nuisance on the 8086, since each word must be shifted one bit at a time, with bits flowing one by one from one register to the next through the carry flag. The **SHRD** and **SHLD** instructions of the 80386 remedy this situation by supporting multiple-bit shifts across two registers, or between a register and a memory location.

For example, suppose a 32-bit value is stored in DX:AX on an 8086. The following is required to shift that 32-bit value left (toward the most-significant bit) by four bit positions:

```
    .
    .
    .
shl  ax,1
rcl  dx,1
shl  ax,1
```

```
rcl  dx,1
shl  ax,1
rcl  dx,1
shl  ax,1
rcl  dx,1
     .
     .
     .
```

On an 80386, the same result can be accomplished with just two instructions:

```
     .
     .
     .
shld dx,ax,4
shl  ax,4
     .
     .
     .
```

(Of course, the whole 32-bit value could simply have been stored in EAX and shifted with

```
shl  eax,4
```

but the example code was intended to illustrate the advantage of using **SHLD** rather than 8086 instructions.)

The first operand to **SHLD** is the 16- or 32-bit, general-purpose register or memory location to shift; the second operand is the 16- or 32-bit, general-purpose register to shift bits in from; and the third operand is the number of bits to shift by. The sizes of the first and second operands must match. The third operand may be either an immediate value or CL; in the latter case, the destination is shifted the number of bits specified by CL.

SHRD is much like **SHLD**, but shifts from the most-significant bit toward the least-significant bit. In this example, the 64-bit value stored in *TestQWord* is shifted right by 7 bits:

```
     .
     .
     .
mov  cl,7
mov  eax,DWORD PTR [TestQword+4]
shrd DWORD PTR [TestQword],eax,cl
shr  eax,cl
mov  DWORD PTR [TestQword+4],eax
     .
     .
     .
```

Setting Bytes Conditionally

A common application for conditional tests and jumps is to set a memory location to reflect a certain status. For instance, you may want to set flags to indicate whether two variables are equal, whether a pointer is null, or whether the carry flag was set by a previous operation. The 8086 is less than ideal for such operations, since multiple instructions (including time-wasting jumps) are required to set a flag to reflect the results of a conditional test. The 80386 provides the powerful group of **SET** instructions to speed such test-and-set cases.

For example, imagine that you want to set the memory variable *TestFlag* only if the most-significant bit of AX is set. On the 8086, you would have to do the following:

```
          .
          .
          .
          mov  [TestFlag],0    ;assume the MSB isn't set
          test ah,80h
          jz   MSBNotSet
          mov  [TestFlag],1
MSBNotSet:
          .
          .
          .
```

On the 80386, all you need do is this:

```
          .
          .
          .
          test  ah,80h
          setnz [TestFlag]
          .
          .
          .
```

and *TestFlag* will be set to 1 if bit 7 of AH is 1, and to 0 if bit 7 of AH is 0.

You can test any of the familiar jump conditions with a **SET** instruction: **SETNC** sets the destination to 1 if the carry flag is 0 and resets the destination to 0 if the carry flag is 1; **SETS** sets the destination if the sign flag is 1 and resets it if the sign flag is 0; and so on. The operand to a **SET** instruction may be an 8-bit, general-purpose register or an 8-bit memory variable; 16- and 32-bit operands are not permitted.

Loading SS, FS, and GS

The 8086 instruction **LDS** allows you to load both DS and one of the general-purpose registers from memory with a single instruction, thereby setting up a far pointer very efficiently. **LES** provides a similar capability, but loads ES instead of DS. The 80386 adds three new instructions for loading far pointers: **LSS**, **LFS**, and **LGS**, which load far pointers based on the SS, FS, and GS segment registers, respectively.

For example, this loads a far pointer to the video bit map at A000:0000 into GS:BX:

```
        .
        .
        .
DataSeg       SEGMENT   USE16
ScreenPointer LABEL     DWORD
    dw    0
    dw    0A000h
DataSeg       ENDS
        .
        .
        .
CodeSeg       SEGMENT   USE16
    ASSUME    cs:CodeSeg, ds:DataSeg
    mov   ax,DataSeg
    mov   ds,ax
        .
        .
        .
    lgs   bx,[ScreenPointer]
        .
        .
        .
CodeSeg       ENDS
        .
        .
        .
```

As with **LDS** and **LES**, either small or large far pointers may be loaded with **LSS**, **LFS**, and **LGS**; see the section entitled "The FWORD 48-Bit Data Type" on page 491 for information about small and large far pointers.

Extended Instructions

The 80386 not only adds a number of powerful new instructions to the 8086/80186/80286 instruction set, but extends a number of existing instructions as well. The extended instructions follow:

CMPS	JC	JNAE	JNLE	JPO	OUTS
IMUL	JCXZ	JNB	JNO	JS	POPA
INS	JE	JNBE	JNP	JZ	POPF
IRET	JG	JNC	JNS	LODS	PUSHA
JA	JGE	JNE	JNZ	LOOP	PUSHF
JAE	JL	JNG	JO	MOV	SCAS
JB	JLE	JNGE	JP	MOVS	STOS
JBE	JNA	JNL	JPE		

In addition, many instructions can handle 32-bit operands on the 80386, even though their mnemonics haven't explicitly changed.

Special Versions of MOV

The 80386 supports special forms of the **MOV** instruction that allow code running at privilege level 0 (the most-privileged level) to move data between the 32-bit, general-purpose registers and special 80386 registers. Here are the 80386 registers that can be accessed in this way:

CR0	DR0	DR3	TR6
CR2	DR1	DR6	TR7
CR3	DR2	DR7	

For example, debug register DR0 could be loaded with a linear address to be trapped on with

```
    .
    .
    .
.386P
    .
    .
    .
mov  eax,OFFSET FunctionEntry
mov  dr0,eax
    .
    .
    .
```

and the system control flags could be loaded from control register CR0 into EDX with

```
        .
        .
        .
.386P
        .
        .
        .
mov  edx,cr0
        .
        .
        .
```

Note that the **.386P** directive must be in effect in order for Turbo Assembler to assemble the special forms of **MOV**, since they are privileged instructions.

In general, the special 80386 registers that can be accessed by the new forms of the **MOV** instruction are used by systems software only, and are not used by applications.

32-Bit Versions of 8086 Instructions

Many 8086 instructions are extended to take on new 32-bit addressing and operand capabilities on the 80386. The following code performs a 32-bit subtraction of the 32-bit EBX register from the 32-bit variable at address *EBP+EAX * 8+10h*, with 32-bit registers used to point to the destination memory location:

```
sub  DWORD PTR [ebp+eax*8+10h],ebx
```

The 32-bit capabilities added to most 8086 instructions don't require a new instruction mnemonic; the 32-bit nature of the operation is generally indicated by the operands or by the segment type the operation occurs in. Several 8086 instructions do, however, require new mnemonics in order to support their extended 32-bit, 80386 capabilities. We'll look at these instructions next.

New Versions of LOOP and JCXZ

The **LOOP, LOOPE, LOOPNE,** and **JCXZ** instructions normally operate on the 16-bit CX register. The 80386 provides both 16-bit and 32-bit versions of these instructions; the 32-bit versions operate on ECX rather than CX.

The **LOOP, LOOPE,** and **LOOPNE** instructions use either CX or ECX as the loop counter, depending on whether the segment they are a 16-bit or a 32-bit segment. If you want to make sure that CX is always used as the loop control register, even in a 32-bit segment, use the word form of these instructions: **LOOPW, LOOPWE,** and **LOOPWNE.** Likewise, if you want to make sure that ECX is always used as the loop control register, use the double-word form of these instructions: **LOOPD, LOOPDE,** and **LOOPDNE.**

LOOPD decrements ECX and jumps to the destination offset if the resulting value is not zero. For example, the following loop is executed 80000000h times:

```
        .
        .
        .
        mov    ecx,80000000h
LoopTop:
        loopd LoopTop
        .
        .
        .
```

LOOPDE decrements ECX and jumps to the destination offset while the zero flag is 1 and ECX is not zero. (**LOOPDZ** is another form of the same instruction.) Similarly, **LOOPDNE** decrements ECX and jumps to the destination offset while the zero flag is 0 and ECX is not zero. (**LOOPDNZ** is equivalent.) For instance, the following loop repeats until either the value read from the I/O port at DX becomes 09h or the port has been checked 10000000h times, whichever comes first:

```
        .
        .
        .
        mov      ecx,10000000h
LoopTop:
        in       al,dx
        cmp      al,09h
        loopdne  LoopTop
        jnz      TimedOut
        .
        .
        .

TimedOut:
        .
        .
        .
```

Note that the action of **JNZ** in this example reflects the result of the comparison, not of **LOOPDNE,** since loop instructions don't affect the status flags. The 80386 also provides a version of **JCXZ** suited to 32-bit operations. Where **JCXZ** jumps if CX is zero, **JECXZ** jumps if ECX is zero. For example, the following loop is capable of handling 32-bit counts:

```
        .
        .
        .
LoopTop:
     jecxz LoopEnd
        .
        .
        .
     jmp    LoopTop
LoopEnd:
        .
        .
        .
```

New Versions of the String Instructions

On the 80386, all string instructions may operate on byte, word, or doubleword values. The doubleword versions of the string instructions simply end with *d* rather than the usual *w* or *b*. The new instructions follow:

CMPSD	**MOVSD**	**SCASD**
INSD	**OUTSD**	**STOSD**
LODSD		

Each of these instructions works with 32 bits of data at a time, and increments or decrements its associated pointer registers by four on each repetition. For example, the following code fragment uses **MOVSD** to copy the two doublewords starting at the offset *DwordTable* to the two doublewords starting at the offset *Buffer*:

```
        .
        .
        .
cld
mov  si,OFFSET DwordTable
mov  di,OFFSET Buffer
mov  cx,2
rep  movsd
        .
        .
        .
```

This produces the same result as the following code, which uses **MOVSB**:

```
     .
     .
     .
cld
mov  si,OFFSET DwordTable
mov  di,OFFSET Buffer
mov  cx,8
rep  movsb
     .
     .
     .
```

One way to think of the doubleword string instructions is that their relationship to the word string instructions is similar to that of the word string instructions to the byte string instructions.

IRETD

IRETD is similar to **IRET**. It pops EIP, then CS as a doubleword (discarding the higher word), then EFLAGS as a doubleword.

PUSHFD and POPFD

PUSHFD pushes the full 32-bit flags register of the 80386 onto the stack. **POPFD** pops the full 32-bit flags register from the stack.

By contrast, **PUSHF** and **POPF** push and pop only the lower 16 bits of the flags register.

PUSHAD and POPAD

PUSHAD pushes the eight 32-bit, general-purpose registers onto the stack in the following order: EAX, ECX, EDX, EBX, ESP, EBP, ESI, EDI. The value pushed for ESP is the value of ESP at the start of the **PUSHAD** instruction. **POPAD** pops seven of the eight 32-bit, general-purpose registers from the stack, reversing the order of **PUSHAD** so that EDI, ESI, EBP, EBX, EDX, ECX, and EAX can be saved with **PUSHAD** and then restored with **POPAD**. ESP is not restored by **POPAD**, but instead is incremented by 32 to discard the block of the eight 32-bit, general-purpose registers previously pushed by **PUSHAD** from the stack. The previously pushed value of ESP is ignored.

By contrast, **PUSHA** and **POPA** push and pop only the lower 16 bits of the eight general-purpose registers.

New Versions of IMUL

In addition to the 8086/80186/80286 forms of **IMUL**, the 80386 provides what is perhaps the most convenient form of **IMUL** yet: Any general-purpose register or memory location can be multiplied by any general-purpose register with the result stored back in one of the source registers. Gone is the need to have one of the operands be a constant, or for the accumulator to be the destination. For example,

```
imul  ebx,[edi*4+4]
```

multiplies EBX by the doubleword value stored at memory address `edi*4+4`, and stores the result back into EBX.

As you can see, the first operand to this form of **IMUL** is the destination register; this operand may be any 16- or 32-bit, general-purpose register. The second operand may be any 16- or 32-bit, general-purpose register or memory location. The sizes of the two operands must match. The overflow and carry flags are set to 1 if the result, considered a signed value, is too large for the destination.

As you might expect, the 80386 also extends the 8086/80186/80286 forms of **IMUL** to support 32-bit operands. For example, this code multiplies ECX times 10000000h and stores the result in EBP:

```
imul  ebp,ecx,10000000h
```

and this multiplies EAX times EBX and stores the result in EDX:EAX:

```
imul  ebx
```

Mixing 16-Bit and 32-Bit Instructions and Segments

Normally, you'll want to have only 16-bit (**USE16**) segments. Even in this case, you can still use the 32-bit registers for arithmetic and logical operations.

You can also use any combination of 16-bit and 32-bit data and code segments. Unless you are writing operating system software and know exactly what you are doing, there is absolutely no reason for you to use 32-bit code segments. Unless you take special measures to switch the processor into a mode suitable for executing 32-bit code segments, there is no way they'll work under DOS. Future operating systems may give you ways to meaningfully use 32-bit code segments, but for now, you shouldn't use them.

However, there is no reason why you can't use 32-bit data segments in your programs and take advantage of the "flat" addressing provided by the 32-bit registers of the 80386.

Let's review the key aspects of **USE16** and **USE32** segments. **USE16** segments can be a maximum of 64 Kb in length, so any location in a **USE16** segment can be pointed to with a 16-bit address. **USE32** segments, on the other hand, can be as long as 4 Gb in length, so a 32-bit address is required to point to an arbitrary location in a **USE32** segment. (**Note:** **USE32** codee segments *only* work in protected mode.)

Clearly, if you need segments longer than 64 Kb, you must use **USE32**. By contrast, there's no case in which you *must* use **USE16** segments. This may well lead you to wonder why we don't just simplify things and use 32-bit segments all the time. The answer lies in the way in which the 80386 supports word and doubleword operands and 16- and 32-bit offsets.

The 80386 evolved from the 8086, which uses a single bit to distinguish between its only two operand sizes, 8- and 16-bits. The 8086 has a single set of memory-addressing modes—the familiar modes involving BX, SI, DI, and BP—supporting 16-bit offsets only. This code fragment has an 8-bit operand size and uses an 8086-style 16-bit addressing mode to address memory:

```
mov   al,[bx+1000h]
```

In **USE16** code segments, the 80386 normally still uses the same bit as does the 8086 to select between 8- and 16-bit operands and still uses 16-bit offsets. However, any given instruction in a **USE16** segment may be converted to support 32-bit operands by placing an operand-size prefix (066h) before the instruction; in this case, the size bit of the instruction selects between 8- and 32-bit operands instead of 8- and 16-bit operands.

Similarly, any given instruction in a **USE16** segment may be converted to use the 80386's 32-bit addressing modes (a large address, as described in the earlier section "New Addressing Modes" on page 499) by placing an address-size prefix (067h) before the instruction.

For example, the code assembled from

```
        .
        .
        .
        .386
        .
        .
        .
DataSeg   SEGMENT   USE16
TestLoc   DD    ?
```

```
DataSeg   ENDS
   .
   .
   .
CodeSeg   SEGMENT   USE16
    mov  ax,DataSeg
    mov  ds,ax
    ASSUME   ds:DataSeg
    db   66h
    mov  ax,WORD PTR [TestLoc]
   .
   .
   .
CodeSeg   ENDS
   .
   .
   .
```

loads the 4 bytes at *TestLoc* into EAX, rather than the 2 bytes at *TestLoc* into AX because the operand-size prefix transforms the operand size of the instruction to 32 bits.

Along the same lines, instructions in **USE32** code segments normally access 8- or 32-bit operands and normally use the 32-bit addressing modes of the 80386; however, operand-size and address-size prefixes can be used to cause individual instructions to operate in 16-bit mode (that is, 8086 mode, with word operands and/or small addresses), just as if they were in a **USE16** segment.

In short, the operand-size and address-size prefixes can cause an instruction executing in a **USE16** code segment to act as if it were in a **USE32** segment, and can cause an instruction executing in a **USE32** code segment to act as if it were in a **USE16** segment.

Don't worry about learning to use operand-size and address-size prefixes in your 80386 code; the generation of the prefixes necessary to use 16-bit features in **USE32** segments or 32-bit features in **USE16** segments is handled by Turbo Assembler transparently to the programmer. For example, if you use the following instruction in a **USE32** code segment,

```
mov   [bx],ax
```

Turbo Assembler automatically prefixes the instruction with an operand-size prefix and an address-size prefix. We've explained the workings of the size prefixes here only so you'll understand the key element in selecting between 16- and 32-bit segment sizes: the need to minimize the number of size prefixes generated.

Suppose, for example, that you selected a **USE16** segment and then only referred to doubleword-sized operands, addressed with 32-bit addressing modes, such as

```
mov    eax,[edx+ecx*2+1]
```

Turbo Assembler would have to generate operand-size and/or address-size prefixes for virtually every instruction in your code causing the size of your code to balloon and performance to suffer. Given a **USE32** segment, however, the same code would require no size prefixes at all.

You can now see that the segment-size selection process is a bit more complex than it seemed. If you need a segment larger than 64 Kb, you must select a **USE32** segment. If you need a segment smaller than 64 Kb, you should select a **USE32** segment if you use more 32- than 16-bit operands and addressing modes. And you should select a **USE16** segment if the reverse is true. It's not always easy to tell which segment type would be more efficient, but you can always assemble your code both ways and see which is more compact.

Now you can also see why the **LARGE** and **SMALL** operators are sometimes necessary to allow forward references to assemble. Since the **USE** type of the code segment determines the default size of address references, forward references are assumed to be of the same size as the code segment **USE** type. **LARGE** must be used for forward references from **USE16** code segments to **USE32** data segments, and you may want to use **SMALL** in order to force use of 16-bit addressing for forward references from **USE32** code segments to **USE16** data segments.

An Example 80386 Function

Let's look at some sample 80386 code. Desirable as it would be to examine a complete 80386 program, that's just not possible right now, since there's no widely used 80386-based operating system, and therefore no standard way to request memory, accept keystrokes, display output, or even terminate a program. Instead, let's look at a complete function written in 80386 assembler.

Our sample function, named *CalcPrimes*, takes advantage of the tremendous length of a **USE32** segment to calculate all primes in a given range in a very straightforward way; the function simply calculates all multiples of all numbers in the range 2 to the maximum prime desired, marking every multiple in a single huge table as being non-prime. On an 8086, this approach would work well only for arrays shorter than 64 Kb, the maximum segment size, and would break down entirely at 1 Mb, the maximum amount of memory the 8086 processor can address.

By contrast, **USE32** segments and 32-bit registers make it possible for the 80386 to easily handle a table up to nearly 4 Gb in length; in fact, the 80386 can, with help from paged memory, even handle memory requirements in the terabyte (1000 Gb) range! Of course, the calculation times for checking such enormous primes would be unacceptably long, but that's the point; unlike the 8086 and 80286, the 80386's memory-addressing architecture is not a limiting factor for programs requiring tremendous amounts of memory.

Here's *CalcPrimes*:

```
;
; Sample 80386 code to calculate all primes between
; 0 and MAX_PRIME (inclusive).
;
; Input: None
;
; Output:
;    ES:EAX - a pointer to PrimeFlags, which contains a 1 at
;    the offset of each number that is a prime and a 0 at
;    the offset of each number that is not a prime.
;
; Registers destroyed:
;    EAX, EBX
;
; Based on an algorithm presented in "Environments,"
; by Charles Petzold, PC Magazine, Vol. 7, No. 2.
;
      .386

MAX_PRIME EQU  1000000                   ;highest # to check for being prime

DataSeg        SEGMENT   USE32
PrimeFlags     DB    (MAX_PRIME + 1) DUP (?)
DataSeg        ENDS

CodeSeg   SEGMENT   USE32
     ASSUME    cs:CodeSeg
CalcPrimes     PROC
     push ds                             ;save caller's DS
     mov  ax,DataSeg
     mov  ds,ax
     ASSUME     ds:DataSeg
     mov  es,ax
     ASSUME     es:DataSeg
```

```
;
; Assume all numbers in the specified range are primes.
;
      mov   al,1
      mov   edi,OFFSET PrimeFlags
      mov   ecx,MAX_PRIME+1
      cld
      rep   stosb
;
; Now eliminate all numbers that aren't primes by calculating all
; multiples (other than times 1) less than or equal to MAX_PRIMES
; of all numbers up to MAX_PRIME.
;
      mov   eax,2                    ;start with 2, since 0 & 1 are primes,
                                     ; and can't be used for elimination
                                     ; of multiples
PrimeLoop:
      mov   ebx,eax                  ;base value to calculate
                                     ; all multiples of
MultipleLoop:
      add   ebx,eax                  ;calculate next multiple
      cmp   ebx,MAX_PRIME            ;have we checked all
                                     ; multiples of this number?
      ja    CheckNextBaseValue       ;yes, go to next number
      mov   [PrimeFlags+ebx],0       ;this number is not prime, since
                                     ; it's a multiple of something
      jmp   MultipleLoop             ;eliminate the next multiple
CheckNextBaseValue:
      inc   eax                      ;point to next base value (the
                                     ; next value to calculate all
                                     ; multiples of)
      cmp   eax,MAX_PRIME            ;have we eliminated all multiples?
      jb    PrimeLoop                ;no, check the next set of multiples
;
; Return a pointer to the table of prime and non-prime statuses
; in ES:EAX.
;
      mov   eax,OFFSET PrimeFlags
      pop   ds                       ;restore caller's DS
      ret
CalcPrimes    ENDP
CodeSeg       ENDS
          END
```

Notice how easily the 80386 allows you to handle 32-bit integers and an array 1,000,000 bytes in length; in fact, the whole function is, remarkably, only 20 bytes in length. *CalcPrimes* returns, as its result, a large far pointer to the table *PrimeFlags*, in which the offset corresponding to each number contains a 1 if that number is prime and a 0 if that number is not prime. For example, *PrimeFlags+3* would be 1, since 3 is a prime number, and *PrimeFlags+4* would be 0, since 4 is not.

The length of *PrimeFlags*, and the largest number to be checked as to whether it is a prime, are defined by the equated symbol *MAX_PRIME*. It would actually be more practical to have the calling routine pass the address of a table of arbitrary size to *CalcPrimes*, along with the largest number to be checked (which would presumably also be the length of the table minus 1). *CalcPrimes* could then meet the prime-calculation needs of any calling code on the fly, rather than having to be reassembled to handle new table sizes. The preceding example uses a local *PrimeFlags* primarily to illustrate the use of **USE32**.

A version of *CalcPrimes* that works with passed table and table length parameters follows:

```
;
; Sample 80386 code to calculate all primes between
; 0 and a specified value (inclusive).
;
; Input (assumes a large far call, with 6 bytes of return address
; pushed on the stack):
;
;    ESP+06h on entry (last parameter pushed) - the
;    doubleword value of the maximum number to be checked as
;    to whether it is a prime.
;
;    ESP+0Ah on entry (first parameter pushed) - a large far
;    (6 byte offset) pointer to the table in which to store a
;    1 at the offset of each number that is a prime and a 0 at
;    the offset of each number that is not a prime. The table
;    must be at least [ESP+06h]+1 bytes in length, where
;    [ESP+06h] is the other parameter.
;
; Output: None
;
; Registers destroyed:
;    EAX, EBX, EDX, EDI
;
; Based on an algorithm presented in "Environments,"
; by Charles Petzold, PC Magazine, Vol. 7, No. 2.
;
        .386

CodeSeg  SEGMENT  USE32
        ASSUME   cs:CodeSeg
CalcPrimes      PROC FAR
        push es                         ;save caller's ES
        push fs                         ;save caller's FS
```

```
;
; Get parameters.
;
     mov   ecx,[esp+4+06h]
     lfs   edx,[esp+4+0ah]
;
; Assume all numbers in the specified range are primes.
;
     push  fs
     pop   es                       ;point ES to table's segment
     mov   al,1
     mov   edi,edx
     cld
     push  ecx                      ;save maximum number to check
     inc   ecx                      ;set up to maximum number, inclusive
     rep   stosb
     pop   ecx                      ;get back maximum number to check
;
; Now eliminate all numbers that aren't primes by calculating all
; multiples (other than times 1) less than or equal to the
; maximum number to check of all numbers up to the maximum number
; to check
;
     mov   eax,2                    ;start with 2, since 0 & 1 are primes,
                                    ; and can't be used for elimination of
                                    ; multiples
PrimeLoop:
     mov   ebx,eax                  ;base value to calculate
                                    ; all multiples of
MultipleLoop:
     add   ebx,eax                  ;calculate next multiple
     cmp   ebx,ecx                  ;have we checked all multiples of this
                                    ; number?
     ja    CheckNextBaseValue       ;yes, go to next number
     mov   BYTE PTR fs:[edx+ebx],0  ;this number is not prime, since
                                    ; it's a multiple of something
     jmp MultipleLoop               ;eliminate the next multiple
CheckNextBaseValue:
     inc eax                        ;point to next base value (the
                                    ; next value to calculate all
                                    ; multiples of)

     cmp eax,ecx                    ;have we eliminated all multiples?
     jb  PrimeLoop                  ;no, check the next set of multiples
     pop fs                         ;restore caller's FS
     pop es                         ;restore caller's ES
     ret
CalcPrimes    ENDP
CodeSeg       ENDS
        END
```

The 80287

The instruction set of the 80287 math coprocessor is exactly the same as the instruction set of the 8087, with one exception. The exception is the **FSETPM** instruction of the 80287, which places the 80287 in protected mode. 80287 protected mode corresponds to the protected mode of the 80286 processor, with which the 80287 is normally coupled (although the 80287 is sometimes used with the 80386 as well). Of course, any program that uses **FSETPM** will not run on an 8087, since the 8087 doesn't support that instruction.

Turbo Assembler support for 80287 assembly is enabled with the **.287** directive. For detailed information about 80287 instructions, see Chapter 3 in the *Reference Guide*.

The 80387

The instruction set of the 80387 math coprocessor is a superset of the 8087/80287 instruction set. The new instructions of the 80387 follow:

FCOS	**FSINCOS**	**FUCOMP**
FPREM1	**FUCOM**	**FUCOMPP**
FSIN		

FUCOM performs an unordered compare between ST(0) and another 80387 register. This instruction is just like **FCOM** except that the result status is set to unordered if one of the operands is a NAN, rather than generating an invalid-operation exception as **FCOM** does in that case. **FUCOMP** performs an unordered compare and pops the 80387's stack, and **FUCOMPP** performs an unordered compare and pops the stack twice.

FCOS calculates the cosine of the ST(0) register, **FSIN** calculates the sine of the ST(0) register, and **FSINCOS** calculates the sine and cosine of the ST(0) register.

FPREM1 calculates an IEEE-compatible remainder of ST(0) divided by ST(1).

Don't forget that any program that uses any of these instructions will not run on an 8087 or 80287. Also, because the 80387 handles real-mode and protected-mode operations in the same way, it ignores the **FSETPM** instruction on the 80287.

Turbo Assembler support for 80387 assembly is enabled with the **.387** directive. For detailed information about 80387 instructions, see Chapter 3 of the *Reference Guide*.

12

Turbo Assembler Ideal Mode

For those of you who are struggling to make MASM do your bidding, this may be the most important chapter in the manual. In addition to near-perfect compatibility with MASM syntax, Turbo Assembler smooths the bumps and grinds of assembly language programming with a MASM derivative we call Ideal mode.

Among other things, Ideal mode lets you know solely by looking at the source text exactly how an expression or instruction operand will behave. There's no need to memorize a storehouse of knowledge for all of MASM's many quirks and tricks. Instead, with Ideal mode, you write clear, concise expressions that do exactly what you want.

Ideal mode uses nearly all of MASM's same keywords, operators, and statement constructions. This means you can explore Ideal mode's features one at a time without having to learn a large number of new rules or keywords. All Ideal mode features are extensions or reorganizations of existing MASM capabilities.

This chapter describes the features of Ideal mode and explains how using Ideal mode's new syntax rules can save you time and effort. We'll also discuss in detail all the new capabilities of Ideal mode and explain the differences between Ideal and MASM syntaxes.

What is Ideal Mode?

Turbo Assembler's Ideal mode introduces a new syntax for expressions and instruction operands. The new syntax isn't radically different from existing

MASM syntax; rather, Ideal mode is a simpler and cleaner implementation of MASM operators and keywords, using forms that make better sense, both to you and to Turbo Assembler.

Ideal mode adds strict type-checking to expressions. Strict type-checking helps reduce errors caused by assigning values of the wrong types to registers and variables, and by using constructions that appear correct in the source text but are assembled differently than you expect. Instead of playing guessing games with values and expressions, as Ideal mode lets you write code that makes logical and aesthetic sense.

Because of strict type-checking, Ideal mode expressions are both easier to understand and less prone to producing unexpected results. And, as a result, many of the MASM problems we warn you about in other chapters disappear under Ideal mode's watchful eye.

Ideal mode also has a number of features that make programming easier for novices and experts alike. Some of these features include the following:

- duplicate member names among multiple structures
- complex HIGH and LOW expressions
- predictable **EQU** processing
- correct handling of grouped data segments
- improved consistency among directives
- sensible bracketed expressions

Why Use Ideal Mode?

There are many good reasons why you should use Turbo Assembler's Ideal mode. If you are just learning assembly language, you can easily construct Ideal mode expressions and statements that have the effects you desire. You don't have to fiddle around trying different things until you get an instruction that does what you want. If you are an experienced assembly language programmer, you can use Ideal mode features to write complex programs using language extensions such as nestable structures and unions.

As a direct benefit of a cleaner syntax, Ideal mode assembles files 30% faster than MASM mode. The larger your projects and files, the more savings in assembly time you'll gain by switching to Ideal mode.

Strong type-checking rules, enforced by Ideal mode, let Turbo Assembler catch errors that you would otherwise have to find at run-time or by debugging your code. This is similar to the way high-level language compilers assist you by pointing out questionable constructions and mismatched data sizes.

Although Ideal mode uses a different syntax for some expressions, you can still write programs that assemble equally well in both MASM and Ideal modes. You can also switch between MASM and Ideal modes as often as necessary within the same source file. This is especially helpful when experimenting with Ideal mode features, or when converting existing programs written in the MASM syntax. You can switch to Ideal mode for new code that you add to your source files while maintaining full MASM compatibility for other portions of your program.

Entering and Leaving Ideal Mode

Use the **IDEAL** and **MASM** directives to switch between Ideal and MASM modes. Turbo Assembler always starts assembling a source file in MASM mode. To switch to Ideal mode, include the **IDEAL** directive in your source file before using any Ideal mode capabilities. From then on, or until the next **MASM** directive, all statements behave as described in this chapter. You can switch back and forth between MASM and Ideal modes in a source file as many times as you wish and at any place. Here's a sample:

```
DATA SEGMENT          ;start in MASM mode
abc  LABEL BYTE       ;abc addresses xyz as a byte
xyz  DW   0           ;define a word at label xyz
DATA ENDS             ;end of data segment

     IDEAL            ;switch to Ideal mode

SEGMENT CODE          ;segment keyword now comes first
PROC MyProc           ;proc keyword comes first, too
     .
     .                ;Ideal mode programming goes here
     .
ENDP MyProc           ;repeating MyProc label is optional
ENDS                  ;repeating segment name not required

     MASM             ;switch back to MASM mode

CODE SEGMENT          ;name now required before segment keyword
Func2 PROC            ;name now comes before proc keyword, too
     .
     .                ;MASM-mode programming goes here
     .
     IDEAL            ;switch to Ideal mode again!
     .
     .                ;do some programming in Ideal mode
     .
     MASM             ;back to MASM mode. Getting dizzy?
```

```
Func2 ENDP          ;name again required before keyword
CODE ENDS           ;name again required here
```

As you can see, in Ideal mode, directive keywords such as **PROC** and **SEGMENT** appear before the identifying symbol names, the reverse of MASM's order. Also, you have the option of repeating a segment or procedure name after the **ENDP** and **ENDS** directives. Adding the name can help clarify the program by identifying the segment or procedure that is ending. This is a good idea, especially in programs that nest multiple segments and procedures. You don't have to include the symbol name after **ENDP** and **ENDS**, however.

MASM and Ideal Mode Differences

This section describes the main differences between Ideal and MASM modes. If you know MASM, you may want to experiment with individual features by converting small sections of your existing programs to Ideal mode. Just remember to surround the new code with the **IDEAL** and **MASM** keywords. By following this scheme, a kind of learn-as-you-go approach to Ideal mode proficiency, you can assemble your current programs without having to revise every instruction to use Ideal mode's special features. Eventually, of course, you may decide to program exclusively in Ideal mode. Or you may choose to mix and match MASM and Ideal mode modules. The choice is yours to make.

Ideal-Mode Tokens

Turbo Assembler reads and understands your program by dividing the text into individual words or symbols called tokens. Examples of tokens include labels such as *VALUE*, *NAME*, or *AGE*, plus other symbols, numbers, parts of expressions, and arithmetic operators such as +, –, * and /.

Two types of tokens, symbols and floating-point numbers, have slightly different forms in Ideal mode. As described next, these changes clarify several ambiguities in the MASM syntax.

Symbol Tokens

In the case of Ideal mode symbols, a period (.) is not permitted as part of a symbol name. You can use a period only as a structure member operator or in a floating-point number.

Structure and union members (some people call them fields) are not defined as global symbols, in other words, as being accessible from every place in your program. Structure and union members exist only within the structure to which they belong. This lets you have multiple structures that contain members with the same names. You can also duplicate member names outside of a structure for other purposes, as in this sample:

```
Pennies  DW 0
STRUC Heaven
Dimes    DW ?
Nickels  DW ?
Pennies  DW ?        ;no conflict
ENDS
Take  Heaven <>
```

They say you can't take it with you but, just in case they're wrong, this example shows how to create a variable with three fields, storing your net worth in dimes, nickels, and pennies in a structure named *Heaven*. The fields *Dimes* and *Nickels* are unique to the structure. *Pennies*, though, occurs twice. First, there's *Pennies* outside the structure's pearly gates, and then there's *Pennies* from *Heaven*.

Seriously, this example demonstrates that the same name, *Pennies*, can occur both inside and outside of a structure with no conflict, something that you can't do in MASM to save your soul.

The variable *Pennies* outside of *Heaven* is distinct from the member *Pennies* used inside the structure. Consequently, to reference a duplicated name inside of a structure requires three elements: the structure name, a period, and the member name. In this example, *Take.Pennies* equals the offset of the *Pennies* field inside *Heaven*. *Pennies* alone, however, equals the offset to the variable outside of the structure.

Duplicate Member Names

Ideal mode also lets you duplicate member names in different structures. The members can be of the same or of different types, as in the following two structures, both of which have *Size* fields of the same type and in the same postion, plus *Amount* fields of different types in different positions:

```
STRUC SomeStuff
Size     DW  ?
Flag     DB  ?
Amount   DW  ?
ENDS

STRUC OtherStuff
```

```
Size      DW    ?        ;no conflict here
Amount    DB    ?        ;nor here
ENDS
```

Floating-Point Tokens

In Ideal mode, floating-point decimal numbers must always include a period (.):

```
FP    DT    1.0e7  ;Ideal mode floating-point value
```

This defines a 10-byte floating-point value, named FP, equal to 1.0e7. In MASM mode, you can use the acceptable, though less clear, form:

```
FP    DT    1E7    ;MASM mode floating-point value
```

This may not seem so bad until you consider what happens if, in an earlier section of the program, you issue a **.RADIX 16** command that changes the default number base from decimal to hexadecimal. In this case, disaster strikes as MASM now assembles your floating-point value as the hexadecimal number 01E7! By requiring you to use a decimal point, Ideal mode never accidentally confuses floating-point and hexadecimal numbers this way.

Text and Numeric Equates (EQU and = Directives)

EQU definitions, also called equates, are always treated as text in Ideal mode. In MASM mode, equates are sometimes treated as text and, at other times, as numbers. Consider these examples:

```
;Declare a few equates
A    =     4
B    =     5
C    EQU   B + A
B    =     6

;Declare a variable
V    DW    C              ;9 in MASM mode, 10 in Ideal mode
```

MASM evaluates $B + A$ when processing the **EQU** expression. At this time, A equals 4 and B equals 5; therefore, C equals 9. Ideal mode processes the same expression differently, storing in string form everything that follows **EQU**, in this case, $B + A$. Later, Ideal mode substitutes this string where C appears. In this example, because the expression evaluation is delayed until the declaration of variable V and because B was previously redefined to 6, variable V equals 10 (6+4) in Ideal mode.

In Ideal mode, **EQU** always defines a string. An equal sign (=) always defines a calculated expression. It might help you to remember this rule if you visualize an equal sign (=) evaluating expressions immediately and **EQU** delaying expression evaluation until the place where the constant name appears. By the way, some people refer to this as "early" and "late" binding.

Expressions and Operands

The biggest difference between Ideal and MASM mode expressions is the way square brackets function. In Ideal mode, square brackets always refer to the contents of the enclosed quantity. Brackets never cause implied additions to occur. Many standard MASM constructions, therefore, are not permitted by Ideal mode.

Square Brackets [ ] Operator

In Ideal mode, square brackets must be used in order to get the contents of an item. For example,

```
mov  ax,wordptr
```

displays a warning message. You are are trying to load a pointer (*wordptr*) into a register (AX). The correct form is

```
mov  ax,[wordptr]
```

Plainly, you are loading the contents of the location addressed by *wordptr* (in the current data segment at DS) into AX.

If you wish to refer to the offset of a symbol within a segment, you must explicitly use the **OFFSET** operator, as in this example:

```
mov  ax,OFFSET wordptr
```

Example Operands

Let's examine a few confusing, though typical, bracketed operands that MASM mode accepts, and then compare the examples with the correct and easier-to-understand forms that Ideal mode requires. As you'll see, Ideal mode's unambiguous use of brackets helps make your intentions perfectly clear:

```
mov  ax,[bx][si]      ;MASM mode
```

This causes a syntax error in Ideal mode. If brackets specify the contents of memory, then this instruction appears to be loading both the value addressed by BX plus the value addressed by SI into AX at the same time. Of course, you can do no such thing. What you probably mean, and what Ideal mode requires, is this:

```
mov   ax,[bx+si]        ;Ideal mode
```

Now, the instruction is clear. The contents of the memory location at the **OFFSET BX+SI**, relative to the current data segment addressed by DS, is loaded into AX. (The size of the memory location is a 16-bit word because AX is a 16-bit register. If you replace AX with AL, or another 8-bit register, then the size of the memory location is a byte.) Here's a similar example:

```
mov   ax,es:[bx][si]    ;MASM mode
```

This also causes an Ideal mode error. The instruction seems to be saying, "apply an ES: segment override to the value addressed by BX, and add the whole shebang to the contents of the memory location addressed by SI, loading the result (whatever that is) into AX." This is senseless, of course, and you probably mean this:

```
mov   ax,[es:bx+si]     ;Ideal mode
```

Good! This adds the BX and SI registers together, giving an offset value relative to segment register ES, overridden from the default data segment DS. The 16-bit contents of this location is loaded into AX. Here's another MASM example that you'll often see:

```
mov   ax,6[bx]          ;MASM mode
```

A mathematician might think you are multiplying 6 times the value of the location addressed by BX. Or, is this some kind of undocumented array indexing technique, or just a typing error? Actually, it's none of the above, as the Ideal mode form shows

```
mov   ax,[bx+6]         ;Ideal mode
```

Of course! You want to load into AX the contents of the location in the current data segment 6 bytes away from the offset specified by BX. More clear than that, you cannot get. Expressions in MASM mode, though, are not always so understandable:

```
mov   ax,es:[bp+8][si+6]    ;MASM mode
```

Let's see, you take the value 8 bytes away from BP, apply a segment override ES:, and...no, the override must go with the value 6 bytes from SI. But no, that's not right, maybe you take the value at BP+8, add to the contents of [SI+6], apply an override and... Oh, forget it! Ideal mode makes this and other complex operands easy to read and easy to write:

```
mov    ax,[es:bp+si+14]     ;Ideal mode
```

Obviously, the value located at offset BP+SI+14 in segment ES is loaded into AX, plain and simple. Believe it or not, there's more:

```
mov    al,BYTE PTR [bx]     ;MASM mode
```

MASM apparently allows you to specify the contents of memory locations as byte pointers, at least that's what this instruction appears to be doing. You can, of course, point to bytes or words only with pointers (registers and labels) as Ideal mode makes perfectly evident:

```
mov    al,[BYTE PTR bx]     ;Ideal mode
```

Obviously, you are telling Turbo Assembler that BX is a byte pointer, loading into register AL the byte located BX bytes from the start of the current data segment. One more example and then we're done:

```
rep    movs BYTE PTR [di],[si]          ;MASM mode
```

MASM appears to allow you to convert characters addressed by DI (and maybe SI?) into byte pointers. Of course, you can't do that. What you no doubt mean, and what Ideal mode wants to see, is this:

```
rep    movs [BYTE PTR di], [BYTE PTR si]     ;Ideal mode
```

Although this is longer, registers DI and SI are clearly byte pointers for the **MOVS** instruction.

These examples are by no means complete, and you probably will encounter many other confusing MASM operands with brackets. When this happens, try switching to Ideal mode, even if just for that one instruction. Then, use the foregoing samples as guides to rewriting the instruction in a form that you can understand. By doing this, you can use Ideal mode not only to help you write better and more readable programs, but also to help you understand bracketed constructions that, in MASM, are frequently about as clear as mud on a foggy day.

Operators

The changes made to the expression operators in Ideal mode increase the power and flexibility of some operators while leaving unchanged the overall behavior of expressions. The precedence levels of some operators have been changed to facilitate common operator combinations. (Refer to Chapter 2 in the reference manual for a list of operator precedence and a complete description of all the operators in MASM and Ideal modes.)

Periods In Structure Members

To accurately specify the structure members to which you are referring, the period (.) structure member operator is far more strict in Ideal mode. The expression to the left of a period must be a structure pointer. The expression to the right must be a member name in that structure. Using the earlier *SomeStuff* and *OtherStuff* structure examples, here's how to load registers with the values of specific structure members:

```
;Declare variables using the structure types
S_Stuff SomeStuff <>
O_Stuff OtherStuff <>
mov  ax,[S_Stuff.Amount]     ;load word value
mov  bl,[O_Stuff.Amount]     ;load byte value
```

Pointers to Structures

Often, you'll want to use a register containing the address of a structure, in other words, the offset to the first byte of a structure stored in memory. Or, you might have a memory variable that addresses a structure. In these cases, to reference a specific structure member by name, you must tell Turbo Assembler which structure you are referring to:

```
mov cx,[(SomeStuff PTR bx).Amount]
```

This lets Turbo Assembler know that BX is a pointer to a *SomeStuff* structure and that you want to load the contents of the *Amount* field from that structure into register CX. The parentheses are required because the period (.) operator has higher precedence than **PTR**. Without parentheses, Ideal mode tries to bind *Amount* to BX, which is impossible, of course, because registers do have field names. Only structures have field names and, therefore, you must convert pointers to structures before referring to fields in structures that the registers address.

The SYMTYPE Operator

Because an Ideal mode symbol cannot start with a period, the **.TYPE** operator in MASM mode is named **SYMTYPE** in Ideal mode (see Chapter 1 in the *Reference Guide*). Despite the name change, the directive works identically in both modes with one exception: **SYMTYPE** will not return a value for an undefined identifier. Otherwise, this operator returns the types of various symbols.

```
Abyte    DB   0
Aword    DW   0
Array    DD   20 DUP (8)
Btype    =    SYMTYPE Abyte      ;1
Wtype    =    SYMTYPE Aword      ;2
Atype    =    SYMTYPE Array      ;4
```

The HIGH and LOW Operators

In Ideal mode, the **HIGH** and **LOW** operators have two meanings. Usually, **HIGH** specifies the high (most-significant) byte of a constant and **LOW** specifies the **LOW** (least-significant) byte as in

```
MaxVal   =    1234h
         mov ah, HIGH MaxVal   ;loads 12h into AH
         mov al, LOW MaxVal    ;loads 34h into AL
```

In Ideal mode, **HIGH** and **LOW** can be used also to select the high or low part of a memory-referencing expression:

```
WordVal  DW   0
DblVal   DD   0
QVal     DQ   0
     mov  bl, [BYTE LOW WordVal]
     mov  ax, [WORD HIGH DblVal]
     mov  ax, [WORD LOW QVal]
```

The first **MOV** instruction loads BL with the low byte of the 2-byte word labeled by *WordVal*. The second **MOV** loads AX with the high word of the 4-byte value stored at *DblVal*. The third **MOV** loads AX with the lowest word of the 8-byte (quadword) value at *QVal*. Notice that the syntax is the same as for the **PTR** operator, with **BYTE** or **WORD** keywords before the **LOW** or **HIGH** operators, plus a memory-referencing expression.

You can also use **HIGH** and **LOW** together to extract just the information you need from a multiple-byte value:

```
DVal DD   12345678h
     mov  al,[BYTE LOW WORD HIGH DVal]   ;loads 34h into AL
```

In combination with **BYTE** and **WORD**, the **LOW** and **HIGH** keywords extract bytes and words from any position in a variable. Here, *DVal* is a doubleword, 4-byte quantity. To better understand complex combinations such as this, read the expression from left to right. In this case, the move instruction loads AL with "the low byte (**BYTE LOW**) of the high word (**WORD HIGH**) of *Dval*."

The Optional PTR Operator

You can use shorthand pointer overrides in expressions. To do this, omit the **PTR** operator. For example,

```
[BYTE PTR OverTheRainbow]
```

in Ideal mode shorthand is the same as

```
[BYTE OverTheRainbow]
```

The SIZE Operator

The **SIZE** operator in Ideal mode reports the actual number of bytes occupied by a data item. This makes it easy to determine the lengths of strings:

```
theTitle     DB    "The Sun Also Rises"
theAuthor    DB    "Ernest Hemingway", 0
titleSize    =     SIZE theTitle          ; Ideal--18, MASM--1
authorSize   =     SIZE theAuthor         ; Ideal--16, MASM--1
```

In this example, *theTitle* and *theAuthor* are strings. In MASM mode, the **SIZE** operator equals the **LENGTH** of a name multiplied by its **TYPE**. The **LENGTH** equals the number of items allocated, in this case 1. (Even though a string has multiple characters, **LENGTH** considers strings to be single-byte items by virtue of the **DB** directive.) The **TYPE** value for **DB** is also 1. Consequently, in MASM mode, both *titleSize* and *authorSize* equal 1, which is not much help in trying to calculate the string lengths.

In Ideal mode, **SIZE** returns the number of bytes occupied by the first item after storage-allocation directives like **DB** or **DW**. Because of this, *titleSize* equals the number of characters in *theTitle*. Likewise, *authorSize* equals the number of characters in the string, *theAuthor*. Notice, however, that *theAuthor* ends in a 0 byte, marking the string end. **SIZE** does not take this byte into account, returning only the number of characters in the preceding string. In fact, **SIZE** returns the length of only the first item in any list of multiple values. For example,

```
CountDown    DB    9,8,7,6,5,4,3,2,1,"Blast off"
TwoLines     DB    "First line", 13, 10, "Second line"
CDsize       =     SIZE CountDown                     ;1
TLsize       =     SIZE TwoLines                      ;10
```

Here, *CountDown* addresses 9-byte values followed by the string, "Blast off." Even so, **SIZE** of *CountDown* (*CDSize*) in both Ideal and MASM modes equals 1, the size of the first element in the list. The same is not true of the second example, *TwoLines*, which is a typical way to store two strings separated with an ASCII carriage return (13) and linefeed (10). But the two strings are labeled in the program under one name, *TwoLines*. **SIZE** again returns the size of the first item in this series, in this case, the string "First line." In Ideal mode, *TLSize* equals 10, the number of characters in the string. In MASM mode, *TLSize* equals 1, the size of the first **DB** element, a single byte (character).

Directives

Directives in Ideal mode function identically and, in most cases, have the same names as their MASM-mode equivalents. However, there are a few important differences among similar directives in both modes, as this section explains.

Listing Controls

Because a symbol cannot start with a period (.) in Ideal mode, all MASM mode listing controls begin with percent signs (%). Also, several names have been changed to more accurately describe the operations controlled by the directives. The following table shows the listing control directives in both modes:

MASM Mode	Ideal Mode
.CREF	%CREF
.LALL	%MACS
.LFCOND	%CONDS
.LIST	%LIST
.SFCOND	%NOCONDS
.XALL	%NOMACS
.XCREF	%NOCREF
.XLIST	%NOLIST

Because the percent sign (%) starts all listing control directives in Ideal mode, the **%OUT** directive in MASM mode becomes **DISPLAY** in Ideal mode:

```
DISPLAY "Starting to Assemble I/O Driver"
```

Directives Starting with a Period (.)

Other MASM directives that start with periods (.) are renamed for clarity. For instance, all processor control directives such as .286, which look more like a number than a directive, now start with *P*, as in **P286N**. All forced error directives of the form **.ERR***xxx* have been renamed **ERRIF***xxx*. Several other directives have the same names minus the leading periods.

The following table lists the directives that start with a period in MASM mode and the Ideal mode equivalents:

MASM Mode	Ideal Mode	MASM Mode	Ideal Mode
.186	P186	.ERR2	ERRIF2
.286	P286N	.ERRB	ERRIFB
.286C	P286N	.ERRDEF	ERRIFDEF
.286P	P286	.ERRDIF	ERRIFDIF
.287	P287	.ERRDIFI	ERRIFDIFI
.386	P386N	.ERRE	ERRIFE
.386C	P386N	.ERRIDN	ERRIFIDN
.386P	P386	.ERRIDNI	ERRIFIDNI
.387	P387	.ERRNB	ERRIFNB
.8086	P8086	.ERRNDEF	ERRIFNDEF
.8087	P8087	.ERRNZ	ERRIF
.CODE	CODESEG	.FARDATA	FARDATA
.CONST	CONST	.FARDATA?	UFARDATA
.DATA	DATASEG	.MODEL	MODEL
.DATA?	UDATASEG	.RADIX	RADIX
.ERR	ERR	.STACK	STACK
.ERR1	ERRIF1		

Reversed Directive and Symbol Name

Ideal mode's parsing order is simpler than MASM's. If the first token is a keyword, it determines the operation to be performed by the directive. If the first token is not a keyword, then the second token determines the operation.

Because of this change, some operations have reversed directive and symbol name orders, as the next table details:

MASM Mode	Ideal Mode
name **ENDP**	**ENDP** [name]
name **ENDS**	**ENDS** [name]
name **GROUP** *segs*	**GROUP** name segs
name **LABEL** *type*	**LABEL** name type
name **MACRO** *args*	**MACRO** name args
name **PROC** *type*	**PROC** name type
name **RECORD** *args*	**RECORD** name args
name **SEGMENT** *args*	**SEGMENT** name args
name **STRUC**	**STRUC** *name*
name **UNION**	**UNION** *name*

Notice that **ENDS** and **ENDP** do not require matching names to close the definitions. If you include a name, spell it the same as in the preceding **SEGMENT** or **PROC** directive. Some programmers always include the name to add extra readability to their programs. This is especially useful when using nested procedures or segments, but is not required.

Some directives are identical in both MASM and Ideal modes. For example, the following directives define symbols as part of the language syntax and, therefore, are the same in both modes:

=	**DD**	**DQ**
:	**DF**	**DT**
DB	**DP**	**DW**
		EQU

Quoted Strings as Arguments to Directives

The **INCLUDE** directive takes a quoted file name in Ideal mode:

```
INCLUDE "MYDEFS.INC"
```

In MASM mode you don't have to use quotes:

```
INCLUDE MYDEFS.INC
```

%TITLE and **%SUBTTL** also require their title strings to be surrounded by quotes:

```
%TITLE    "Macro Definitions"          ;comment ignored
%SUBTTL   "Block Structuring Macros"   ;comment ignored
```

As these two examples demonstrate, requiring quotes around titles and subtitles lets you add comments at the ends of these lines. The comments are not included in the listing file. In MASM mode, everything after **.TITLE** and **.SUBTTL** becomes part of the title string, including any comments.

Segments and Groups

The way that Turbo Assembler handles segments and groups in Ideal mode can make a large difference in getting a program up and running. If you're like most people, you probably shudder at the thought of dealing with a bug that has anything to do with the interaction of segments and groups.

Much of the difficulty in this process stems from the arbitrary way that MASM and, therefore, Turbo Assembler's MASM mode, make assumptions about references to data or code within a group. Fortunately, Ideal mode alleviates some of the more nagging problems caused by MASM segment and group directives as you'll see in the information that follows.

Accessing Data in a Segment Belonging to a Group

In Ideal mode, any data item in a segment that is part of a group is considered to be principally a member of the group, not the segment. An explicit segment override must be used for Turbo Assembler to recognize the data item as a member of the segment.

MASM mode handles this differently: Sometimes a symbol is considered to be part of the segment instead of the group. In particular, MASM mode treats a symbol as part of a segment when the symbol is used with the **OFFSET** operator but as part of a group when the symbol is used as a pointer in a data allocation. This can be confusing because, when you directly access the data without **OFFSET**, MASM incorrectly generates the reference relative to the segment instead of the group.

An example will help explain how you can easily get into trouble with MASM's addressing quirks. Consider the following incomplete MASM program, which declares three data segments:

```
dseg1    SEGMENT PARA PUBLIC 'data'
v1       DB      0
dseg1    ENDS

dseg2    SEGMENT PARA PUBLIC 'data'
v2       DB      0
dseg2    ENDS

dseg3    SEGMENT PARA PUBLIC 'data'
v3       DB      0
dseg3    ENDS

DGROUP   GROUP   dseg1,dseg2,dseg3
cseg     SEGMENT PARA PUBLIC 'code'

         ASSUME  cs:cseg,ds:DGROUP

start:
         mov     ax,OFFSET v1
         mov     bx,OFFSET v2
         mov     cx,OFFSET v3
cseg     ENDS
         END     start
```

The three segments, *dseg1*, *dseg2*, and *dseg3*, are grouped under one name, **DGROUP**. As a result, all the variables in the individual segments are stored together in memory. In the program source text, each of the individual segments declares a byte variable, labeled *v1*, *v2*, and *v3*.

In the code portion of this MASM program, the offset addresses of the three variables are loaded into registers AX, BX, and CX. Because of the earlier **ASSUME** directive and because the data segments were grouped together, you might think that MASM would calculate the offets to the variables relative to the entire group in which the variables are eventually stored in memory.

But this is not what happens! Despite your intentions, MASM calculates the offsets of the variables relative to the individual segments, *dseg1*, *dseg2*, and *dseg3*. It does this even though, the three segments are combined into one data segment in memory, addressed here by register DS. It makes no sense to take the offsets of variables relative to individual segments in the program text when those segments are combined into a single segment in memory. The only way to address such variables is to refer to their offsets relative to the entire group.

To fix the problem in MASM requires you to specify the group name along with the **OFFSET** keyword:

```
mov    ax,OFFSET DGROUP:v1
mov    bx,OFFSET DGROUP:v2
mov    cx,OFFSET DGROUP:v3
```

Although this now assembles correctly and loads the offsets of *v1*, *v2*, and *v3* relative to **DGROUP** (which collects the individual segments), you might easily forget to specify the **DGROUP** qualifier. If you make this mistake, the offset values will not correctly locate the variables in memory and you'll receive no indication from MASM that anything is amiss. In Ideal mode, there's no need to go to all this trouble:

```
        IDEAL
SEGMENT dseg1   PARA PUBLIC 'data'
v1      DB      0
ENDS

SEGMENT dseg2   PARA PUBLIC 'data'
v2      DB      0
ENDS

SEGMENT dseg3   PARA PUBLIC 'data'
v3      DB      0
ENDS

GROUP   DGROUP  dseg1,dseg2,dseg3
SEGMENT cseg    PARA PUBLIC 'code'

        ASSUME  cs:cseg, ds:DGROUP

start:
        mov     ax,OFFSET v1
        mov     ax,OFFSET v2
        mov     ax,OFFSET v3

ENDS
        END     start
```

The offsets to *v1*, *v2*, and *v3* are correctly calculated relative to the group that collects the individual segments to which the variables belong. Ideal mode does not require the **DGROUP** qualifier to refer to variables in grouped segments. MASM mode does require the qualifier and, even worse, gives no warning of a serious problem should you forget to specify the group name in every single reference.

Defining Near or Far Code Labels

When defining near and far **LABEL** or **PROC** symbols, references to a symbol are relative to the group containing the segment. If a symbol's segment is not part of a group, the symbol is relative to the segment. This means you do not have to **ASSUME CS** to a segment in order to define near or far symbols. In MASM mode,

```
CODE SEGMENT
     ASSUME    cs:CODE
```

```
XYZ   PROC FAR
      .
      .                           ;MASM procedure code
      .
XYZ   ENDP
CODE ENDS
```

becomes the following in Ideal mode:

```
SEGMENT CODE
PROC XYZ FAR
      .
      .                           ;Ideal mode procedure code
      .
ENDP
ENDS
```

This change doesn't add any new capabilities to MASM mode. But it does relieve you of telling the assembler something Ideal mode can usually figure out by itself.

External, Public, and Global Symbols

Wherever you must supply a type (**BYTE**, **WORD**, and so on), for example, with the **EXTRN** or **GLOBAL** directives, you can use a structure name:

```
STRUC   MoreStuff
HisStuff DB   0
HerStuff DW   0
ItsStuff DB   0
ENDS
EXTRN   SNAME:MoreStuff
```

This capability, combined with the enhancements to the period (.) operator described earlier, lets you refer to structure members that are external to your source module. This is exactly as if you had declared the members inside both modules. The **SIZE** operator also correctly reports the size of external data structures. Every **PUBLIC** symbol emitted in Ideal mode occurs where **PUBLIC** is specified. This is also useful for redefining variables. MASM mode emits all the public symbols at the end of the program, limiting the ways in which you can redefine public symbols. For example,

```
Perfect = 8
    PUBLIC   Perfect      ;declare Perfect public
Perfect = 10              ;redefine Perfect's value
```

In Ideal mode, the **PUBLIC** *Perfect* equals 8, even though the module redefines *Perfect* after the **PUBLIC** declaration. In MASM mode, because the **PUBLIC** symbols are emitted at the end of the module, another module that imports this symbol via an **EXTRN** declaration receives a *Perfect 10*.

Miscellaneous Differences

This section describes a few additional differences between MASM and Ideal modes.

Suppressed Fixups

Turbo Assembler in Ideal mode does not generate segment-relative fixups for private segments that are page- or paragraph-aligned. Because the linker does not require such fixups, assembling programs in Ideal mode can result in smaller object files that also link more quickly than object files generated by MASM mode. The following demonstrates how superfluous fixups occur in MASM but not in Ideal mode:

```
SEGMENT DATA PRIVATE PARA
VAR1 DB    0
VAR2 DW    0
ENDS
SEGMENT CODE
    ASSUME ds:DATA
    mov  ax,VAR2              ;no fixup needed
ENDS
```

This difference has no effect on code that you write. The documentation here is simply for your information.

Operand for BOUND Instruction

The **BOUND** instruction expects a **WORD** operand, not a **DWORD**. This lets you define the lower and upper bounds as two constant words, eliminating the need to convert the operand to a **DWORD** with an explicit **DWORD PTR**. In MASM mode, you must write

```
BOUNDS    DW   1,4             ;lower and upper bounds
BOUND     DWORD PTR BOUNDS     ;required for MASM mode
```

but, in Ideal mode, you need only write

```
BOUNDS   DW   1,4             ;lower and upper bounds
    BOUND   [BOUNDS]          ;legal in Ideal mode
```

Comments Inside Macros

In Ideal mode, comments within macros are treated as strings. To substitute a dummy parameter within a macro comment, you must precede the parameter with an ampersand (&):

```
MACRO DOUBLE ARG
    shl  ARG,1      ;multiply &ARG by two
ENDM
```

When using this macro in Ideal mode with **DOUBLE BX**, the listing file shows

```
shl bx,1           ;multiply BX by two
```

On the other hand, if the macro is defined as

```
MACRO DOUBLE ARG
    shl  ARG,1      ;multiply ARG by two
ENDM
```

the listing file does not replace ARG:

```
shl bx,1           ;multiply ARG by two
```

Local Symbols

Turbo Assembler's local symbol capability is automatically enabled when you switch to Ideal mode, exactly as if you had entered the **LOCALS** directive.

A Comparison of MASM and Ideal Mode Programming

To wrap up this chapter and give you a feeling for the differences between Ideal and MASM modes, here is the same program in both Ideal and MASM mode. By reading through these examples and by examining the numbered comments after the listings, you'll be able to appreciate the advantages offered by Ideal mode syntax.

Please understand that these programs are not intended as examples of good programming style: The instructions merely demonstrate the Ideal mode concepts discussed in this chapter, and show only a sampling of the most common Ideal mode capabilities and differences from MASM.

The example programs read a single line from the console, convert the text to uppercase, and then display the result before returning to DOS. To mark where the program code differs in the MASM and Ideal mode programs, we've added a comment (beginning with a semicolon) and a number. For example, ;#4 directs you to read the corresponding description number 4 following the listings in the section "An Analysis of MASM And Ideal Modes" on page 551. Also, to make the Ideal mode differences stand out, we've stripped most of the comments from its example. Read the first program to understand how the code operates. Read the second program to compare the Ideal-mode enhancements.

MASM Mode Sample Program

```
; File <masexmpl.asm>
; MASM mode example program to uppercase a line
        TITLE  Example MASM Program      ;this comment is in the title!
        .286

bufsize  =  128                          ;size of input and output buffers

dosint MACRO intnum
        mov  ah,intnum                   ;assign FN number to AH
        int  21h                         ;call DOS function &INTNUM
ENDM

STK SEGMENT STACK
        DB   100h DUP (?)                ;reserve stack space
STK ENDS

DATA SEGMENT WORD
inbuf    DB    bufsize DUP (?)           ;input buffer
outbuf   DB    bufsize DUP (?)           ;output buffer
DATA ENDS

DGROUP GROUP STK,DATA                    ;group stack and data segs

CODE SEGMENT WORD
        ASSUME   cs:CODE                 ;assume CS is code seg
start:
        mov  ax,DGROUP                   ;assign address of DGROUP
        mov  ds,ax                       ;segment to DS
        ASSUME   ds:DGROUP               ;default data segment is DS
        mov  dx,OFFSET DGROUP:inbuf      ;load into DX inbuf offset
        xor  bx,bx                       ;standard input
        call readline                    ;read one line
        mov  bx,ax                       ;assign length to BX
```

```
        mov  inbuf[bx],0            ;add null terminator
        push ax                     ;save AX on stack
        call mungline              ;convert line to uppercase
        pop  cx                     ;restore count
        mov  dx,OFFSET DGROUP:outbuf ;load into DX outbuf offset
        mov  bx,1                   ;standard output
        dosint    40h               ;write file function
        dosint    4ch               ;exit to DOS

;Read a line, called with dx => buffer, returns count in AX
readline PROC NEAR
        mov  cx,bufsize             ;specify buffer size
        dosint    3fh               ;read file function
        and  ax,ax                  ;set zero flag on count
        ret                         ;return to caller
readline ENDP

;Convert line to uppercase
mungline PROC NEAR
        mov  si,OFFSET DGROUP:inbuf ;address inbuf with SI
        mov  di,0                   ;initialize DI
@@uloop:
        cmp  BYTE PTR[si],0         ;end of text?
        je   @@done                 ;if yes, jump to @@done
        mov  al,[si]                ;else get next character
        and  al,not 'a' - 'A'       ;convert to uppercase
        mov  outbuf[di],al          ;store in output buffer
        inc  si                     ;better to use lodsb,stosb
        inc  di                     ;...this is just an example!
        jmp  @@uloop                ;continue converting text
@@done:  ret
mungline ENDP                       ;end of procedure
CODE ENDS                           ;end of code segment
        END  start                  ;end of text and DOS entry point
```

Ideal Mode Sample Program

```
; File <idlexmpl.asm>
; Ideal mode example program to uppercase a line
        IDEAL                                       ;#1
        %TITLE    "Example Ideal-Mode Program"      ;#2
        P286N                                       ;#3

BufSize  =    128

MACRO dosint intnum                                 ;#4
        mov  ah,intnum
        int  21h
ENDM
```

```
        SEGMENT STK STACK                                ;#5
            DB    100h DUP (?)
        ENDS                                             ;#6

        SEGMENT DATA WORD                                ;#7
        inbuf    DB    Bufsize DUP (?)
        outbuf   DB    bufSize DUP (?)
        ENDS DATA                                        ;#8

        GROUP DGROUP STK,DATA                            ;#9

        SEGMENT CODE WORD                                ;#10
            ASSUME    cs:CODE
        start:
            mov   ax,DGROUP
            mov   ds,ax
            ASSUME    ds:DGROUP
            mov   dx,OFFSET inbuf                         ;#11
            xor   bx,bx
            call  readline
            mov   bx,ax
            mov   [inbuf + bx],0                          ;#12
            push  ax
            call  mungline
            pop   cx
            mov   dx,OFFSET outbuf                        ;#13
            mov   bx,1
            dosint   40h
            dosint   4ch

        ;Read a line, called with dx => buffer, returns count in AX
        PROC readline NEAR                               ;#14
            mov   cx,BufSize
            dosint   3fh
            and   ax,ax
            ret
        ENDP                                             ;#15

        ;Convert line to uppercase
        PROC mungline NEAR                               ;#16
            mov   si,OFFSET inbuf                         ;#17
            mov   di,0
        @@uloop:
            cmp   [BYTE si],0                             ;#18
            je    @@done
            mov   al,[si]
            and   al,not 'a' - 'A'
            mov   [outbuf + di],al                        ;#19
            inc   si
            inc   di
```

```
LODSB/STOSB
     jmp  @@uloop
@@done:  ret
ENDP mungline                                        ;#20
ENDS                                                 ;#21
     END  start
```

An Analysis of MASM And Ideal Modes

The following paragraphs detail the differences between MASM and Ideal mode constructions, directives, and operands in the two previous programs. The numbers refer to the comments in the Ideal mode example. Compare these lines with the MASM example.

1. Use the **IDEAL** directive to switch into Ideal mode. By default, Turbo Assembler always starts assembling your source file in MASM mode. You need to use the **MASM** directive only when you want to switch back into MASM mode after having earlier switched to Ideal mode.

2. The percent sign in front of **%TITLE** reminds you that this directive affects the listing file (if you decide to create one by specifying a listing file name or by using the /L command-line option when you assemble the program). Ideal mode uses **%TITLE** instead of **TITLE** (without the percent sign) and also requires you to surround the title string with quotes (" "). This lets you put a comment on the line that, in MASM mode, becomes part of the title—probably not what you intended.

3. The **.286** directive in MASM mode is **P286N** in Ideal mode. Because symbols cannot start with a period (.) in Ideal mode, all MASM processor and other directives that start with periods are changed. The statement in the listing does not serve any useful purpose in this program other than to show the difference between the two modes. The program does not use any 80286 instructions.

4. In Ideal mode, the name of the macro comes after the **MACRO** directive, not before as in MASM mode.

5. The name of the segment in a **SEGMENT** directive comes after the directive in Ideal mode.

6. When using **ENDS** to close a segment in Ideal mode, you don't need to supply the matching segment name as you do in MASM mode. (You may add the name after the **ENDS** directive, however, if you prefer.)

7. Same as 5. Again, the **SEGMENT** keyword comes before the name.

8. If you supply a matching segment name for the **ENDS** directive, the name comes after the directive and not before as in MASM mode. You can delete the name (DATA) if you wish.

9. In Ideal mode, the **GROUP** directive precedes the name of the data segment group (which is **DGROUP**). After this comes the list of data segments you are grouping under this name. In MASM, **GROUP** and the name are reversed.

10. Same as 5. The **SEGMENT** keyword precedes the name.

11. You don't have to use a group qualifier here with the **OFFSET** operator. Ideal mode presumes that **INBUF** is relative to the start of **DGROUP** because **INBUF** is inside one of the individual segments collected under this group name. In MASM, you have to remember to specify *DGROUP : inbuf* to correctly locate offsets to variables in grouped segments.

12. The [**INBUF**+BX] operand is valid in both Ideal and MASM modes, but the same line in the MASM mode version, **INBUF**[BX], is not valid in Ideal mode. In Ideal mode, all memory-referencing operands must be surrounded by square brackets.

13. Same as 11. Here again, you do not need to specify the group name to reference a variable in a grouped segment. In MASM, to obtain the correct offset to **OUTBUF**, you have to write **DGROUP:outbuf**. Forget the **DGROUP** qualifier and, in this example, you'd store your output in the stack, with no warning from MASM that something is seriously wrong!

14. The name of a procedure in a **PROC** directive comes after the directive, not before as required by MASM mode.

15. When you use **ENDP** to close a procedure in Ideal mode, you don't have to supply the matching procedure name as you do in MASM mode.

16. Same as 14. The **PROC** directive proceeds the procedure name.

17. Same as 11. Again, you don't need to write **DGROUP:inbuf**, as you do in MASM.

18. In Ideal mode, you can optionally omit the **PTR** operator when you set the size of an expression. The MASM mode expression **BYTE PTR ABC** is identical to **BYTE ABC** in Ideal mode.

19. Same as 12. In Ideal mode, when referring to the contents of memory, always put the memory-referencing expression inside brackets.

20. Optionally place a matching procedure name after the **ENDP** directive, not before as in MASM mode.

21. Same as 6. **ENDS** does not require a matching segment name, although you can add the name if you prefer.

References

Crawford, John H., and Patrick P.Gelsinger. *Programming the 80386*. Alameda: Sybex, Inc., 1987.

Duncan, Ray. *Advanced MS-DOS*. Redmond: Microsoft Press, 1986.

Lafore, Robert. *Assembly Language Primer for the IBM PC & XT*. New York: The Waite Group, 1984.

Murray, William H., and Chris Pappas. *80386/80286 Assembly Language Programming*. Berkeley: Osborne/McGraw-Hill, 1986.

Norton, Peter, and John Socha. *Peter Norton's Assembly Language Book for the IBM PC*. New York: Brady Communications, 1986.

Rector, Russell, and George Alexy. *The 8086 Book*. Berkeley: Osborne/McGraw-Hill, 1980.

Sargent III, Murray, and Richard L. Shoemaker. *The IBM PC from the Inside Out*. Reading: Addison-Wesley, 1986.

Skinner, Thomas P. *An Introduction to Assembly Language Programming for the 8086 Family*. New York: John Wiley & Sons, Inc., 1985.

Turley, James L. *Advanced 80386 Programming Techniques*. Berkeley: Osborne/McGraw-Hill, 1988.

Wilton, Richard. *Programmer's Guide to PC and PS/2 Video Systems*. Redmond: Microsoft Press, 1987.

Index

E

/e option 64
EAX register 495
EBP register 495
EBX register 495
ECX register 495
EDI register 495
EDX register 495
ELSE directive 234
ELSEIF directives 239
EMUL directive 65
END directive 81, 88
    start address and 88
ENDIF directive 234
ENDM directive 419
ENDP directive
    Ideal mode 541
    subroutines and 177
ENDS directive 115, 452, 467
    Ideal mode 541
ENTER instruction (80186) 478
EQU directive 188
    angle brackets and 192
    Ideal vs. MASM mode 528, 532
equal (=) directive 64
equate substitutions 188
.ERR1 directive 240
.ERR2 directive 240
.ERR directive 240
.ERRB directive 241
.ERRDEF directive 241
.ERRE directive 241
.ERRNB directive 241
.ERRNDEF directive 241
.ERRNZ directive 241
error messages 14
    conditional 240
    source file line display 75
errors, programming 242-275, *See
    also* pitfalls
ES register 45
    ASSUME directive and 116
    .DATA directive and 110
    LES instruction and 511
    string instructions and 257, 402
ESI register 495
ESP register 495

exclamation mark operator
    within macros 433
.EXE files 1, 11
execution, END directive and 88
EXITM directive 431
expressions 93
    Ideal mode 533
    initializing variables 133
    operators in 93
external symbols *See* symbols,
    external
extra segment 45
    segment overrides and 404
EXTRN directive 210
    Ideal vs. MASM mode 545
    Turbo C and 315
    Turbo Pascal and 343

F

far data 112, 113
    Ideal mode 544
FAR PTR operator 141
    forward jumps and 417
far subroutines 177
FAR type 136
    FAR PTR operator and 141
.FARDATA? directive 113, 469
@fardata? symbol 113
.FARDATA directive 113, 467
@fardata symbol 113
FCOS instruction 525
@FileName symbol 114
??Filename variable 194
files
    .ASM 61
    configuration 77
    include 214
    indirect 77
    listing 61, 216, *See also* listing files
flags register 29
    80286 485
    80386 496
    problems 265
    string instructions 203
floating-point
    emulation 64
    Ideal vs. MASM mode 532

X

/x option 75
.XRF files 61
XCHG instruction 147
XLAT instruction
    operands to 262
XOR instruction 158

Z

/z option 75
/zd option 76
zero CX value
    string instructions and 255
zero flag 30
    conditional jumps and 168
    loops and 172
/zi option 76